Lecture Notes in Computer Science 11601

Commenced Publication in 1973
Founding and Former Series Editors:
Gerhard Goos, Juris Hartmanis, and Jan van Leeuwen

More information about this series at http://www.springer.com/series/7407

Michal Hospodár · Galina Jirásková (Eds.)

Implementation and Application of Automata

24th International Conference, CIAA 2019
Košice, Slovakia, July 22–25, 2019
Proceedings

Springer

Editors
Michal Hospodár
Slovak Academy of Sciences
Košice, Slovakia

Galina Jirásková
Slovak Academy of Sciences
Košice, Slovakia

ISSN 0302-9743 ISSN 1611-3349 (electronic)
Lecture Notes in Computer Science
ISBN 978-3-030-23678-6 ISBN 978-3-030-23679-3 (eBook)
https://doi.org/10.1007/978-3-030-23679-3

LNCS Sublibrary: SL1 – Theoretical Computer Science and General Issues

This Springer imprint is published by the registered company Springer Nature Switzerland AG
The registered company address is: Gewerbestrasse 11, 6330 Cham, Switzerland

Preface

This volume contains the papers presented at the 24th International Conference on Implementation and Application of Automata (CIAA 2019) organized by the Košice branch of the Mathematical Institute of the Slovak Academy of Sciences and the Slovak Artificial Intelligence Society (SAIS) in Košice, Slovakia, during July 22–25, 2019.

The CIAA conference series is a major international venue for the dissemination of new results in the implementation, application, and theory of automata. The previous 23 conferences were held in various locations all around the globe: Charlottetown (2018), Marne-la-Vallée (2017), Seoul (2016), Umeå (2015), Giessen (2014), Halifax (2013), Porto (2012), Blois (2011), Winnipeg (2010), Sydney (2009), San Francisco (2008), Prague (2007), Taipei (2006), Nice (2005), Kingston (2004), Santa Barbara (2003), Tours (2002), Pretoria (2001), London Ontario (2000), Potsdam (WIA 1999), Rouen (WIA 1998), and London Ontario (WIA 1997 and WIA 1996).

The topics of this volume include: complexity of languages and language operations, regular expressions, picture languages, jumping automata, input-driven and two-dimensional automata, tree languages and tree transducers, architecture of oritatami systems, intruder deduction problem, context-sensitive flash codes, rational relations, and algorithms for manipulating sequence binary decision diagrams.

There were 29 submissions from 20 different countries: Belgium, Canada, China, Croatia, Czech Republic, France, Germany, Hungary, India, Israel, Italy, Japan, Poland, Portugal, Russia, Slovakia, South Korea, Spain, Sweden, and the USA.

The submission, single-blind peer-review process, and the collating of the proceedings were supported by the EasyChair conference system. Each submission was reviewed by at least three Program Committee members, except for five that received two reviews.

The committee selected 17 papers for presentation at the conference and publication in this volume. The program also included five invited talks by Marián Dvorský, Christos Kapoutsis, Sebastian Maneth, Alexander Okhotin, and Helmut Seidl.

We would like to thank the Program Committee members and the external reviewers for their help in selecting the papers. We are also very grateful to all invited speakers, contributing authors, session chairs, and all the participants who made CIAA 2019 possible.

We also thank the editorial staff at Springer, in particular, Alfred Hofmann, Anna Kramer, and Christine Reiss, for their guidance and help during the publication process of this volume, and for supporting the event through publication in the LNCS series.

Last but not least, we would like to thank the conference sponsors for their financial support, and the Organizing Committee members, Peter Gurský, Ivana Krajňáková, Peter Mlynárčik, Viktor Olejár, Matúš Palmovský, and Juraj Šebej, for their help with organizing the social program, preparing conference materials, and for taking care of the IT support as well as the financial issues of the conference. All of this was always carefully checked and slightly criticized by Jozef Jirásek to whom our sincere gratitude goes as well.

We all are looking forward to the next CIAA in Loughborough, UK.

May 2019

Michal Hospodár
Galina Jirásková

Organization

Steering Committee

Jean-Marc Champarnaud	Université de Rouen, Rouen, France
Markus Holzer (Chair)	Justus Liebig University, Giessen, Germany
Oscar Ibarra	University of California, Santa Barbara, USA
Kai T. Salomaa (Co-chair)	Queen's University, Kingston, Ontario, Canada
Hsu-Chun Yen	National Taiwan University, Taipei, Taiwan

Program Committee

Francine Blanchet-Sadri	University of North Carolina, USA
Marie-Pierre Béal	Université Paris-Est Marne-la-Vallée, France
Cezar Câmpeanu (Co-chair)	University of Prince Edward Island, Canada
Jan Daciuk	Gdańsk University of Technology, Poland
Jürgen Dassow	University of Magdeburg, Germany
Mike Domaratzki	University of Manitoba, Canada
Dora Giammarresi	University of Rome Tor Vergata, Italy
Yo-Sub Han	Yonsei University, Seoul, South Korea
Markus Holzer	Justus Liebig University, Giessen, Germany
Artur Jeż	University of Wrocław, Poland
Galina Jirásková (Chair)	Slovak Academy of Sciences, Košice, Slovakia
Jarkko Kari	University of Turku, Finland
Stavros Konstantinidis	Saint Mary's University, Halifax, Canada
Michal Kunc	Masaryk University, Brno, Czech Republic
Sylvain Lombardy	Bordeaux Institute of Technology, France
Andreas Malcher	Justus Liebig University, Giessen, Germany
Andreas Maletti	Universität Leipzig, Germany
František Mráz	Charles University, Prague, Czech Republic
Cyril Nicaud	Université Paris-Est Marne-la-Vallée, France
Giovanni Pighizzini	University of Milan, Italy
Bala Ravikumar	Sonoma State University, USA
Daniel Reidenbach	Loughborough University, UK
Rogério Reis	University of Porto, Portugal
Kai Salomaa	Queen's University, Kingston, Canada
Shinnosuke Seki	The University of Electro-Communications, Japan
Brink van der Merwe	Stellenbosch University, South Africa
György Vaszil	University of Debrecen, Hungary
Mikhail Volkov	Ural Federal University, Ekaterinburg, Russia
Bruce Watson	Stellenbosch University, South Africa
Abuzer Yakaryılmaz	University of Latvia, Riga, Lativa
Hsu-Chun Yen	National Taiwan University, Taipei, Taiwan

Additional Reviewers

Anselmo, Marcella
Blair, Dakota
Caron, Pascal
Dando, Louis-Marie
Demaille, Akim
Gebhardt, Kilian
Gusev, Vladimir
Hashimoto, Kenji
Horváth, Géza
Ko, Sang-Ki
Kufleitner, Manfred
Landwehr, Patrick
Madonia, Maria
Mereghetti, Carlo
Miklarz, Clément
Montoya, Juan Andrés
Smith, Taylor J.
Villagra, Marcos
Wendlandt, Matthias

Invited Speakers

Marián Dvorský	CEAi Slovakia s.r.o., Košice, Slovakia
Christos A. Kapoutsis	Carnegie Mellon University, Doha, Qatar
Sebastian Maneth	Universität Bremen, Germany
Alexander Okhotin	St. Petersburg State University, Russia
Helmut Seidl	Technische Universität München, Germany

Sponsors

City of Košice
Slovak Society for Computer Science
CEAi Slovakia s.r.o., Košice, Slovakia
VSL Software, a.s., Košice, Slovakia

Abstracts of Invited Talks

Large Scale Sorting in Distributed Data Processing Systems

Marián Dvorský

CEAi Slovakia s.r.o., Košice, Slovakia
marian.dvorsky@gmail.com

Specialized distributed systems, such as MapReduce [3] or Spark [4] are being used to process large amounts of data. At the core of these systems is a *shuffle* operation which reorganizes the data represented as (*key, value*) pairs according to keys, to implement basic data transforms such as aggregations or joins. The shuffle operation can be viewed as large distributed sorting.

Fundamental research has been focused on figuring out bounds on the amount of data that needs to be shuffled, see for example [1]. This talk will focus instead on the problem of efficient shuffling itself.

For the most challenging applications the amount of data sorted exceeds the total amount of memory available in these systems, so sorting is *external*. Lower bounds on external sorting have been well studied, see for example [2]. However, less is known about optimal algorithms for large scale sorting in distributed, fault-tolerant environments.

We will discuss the problem of large scale sorting, its role in data processing systems, recent advances in implementation of sorting algorithms in real-world cloud systems, and open problems.

References

1. Afrati, F.N., Sarma, A.D., Salihoglu, S., Ullman, J.D.: Upper and lower bounds on the cost of a map-reduce computation. Proc. VLDB **6**(4), 277–288 (2013). https://doi.org/10.14778/2535570.2488334
2. Aggarwal, A., Vitter, J.S.: The input/output complexity of sorting and related problems. Commun. ACM **31**(9), 1116–1127 (1988). https://doi.org/10.1145/48529.48535
3. Dean, J., Ghemawat, S.: Mapreduce: simplified data processing on large clusters. In: OSDI 2004: Sixth Symposium on Operating System Design and Implementation, vol. 6, pp. 137–150. San Francisco, CA (2004). https://doi.org/10.1145/1327452.1327492
4. Zaharia, M., et al.: Resilient distributed datasets: a fault-tolerant abstraction for in-memory cluster computing. In: Gribble, S.D., Katabi, D. (eds.) In: Proceedings of 9th USENIX Symposium on Networked Systems Design and Implementation, NSDI 2012, pp. 15–28. USENIX Association (2012). https://www.usenix.org/conference/nsdi12/technical-sessions/presentation/zaharia

Alternation in Two-Way Finite Automata

Christos A. Kapoutsis

Carnegie Mellon University in Qatar, Doha, Qatar
cak@cmu.edu

Abstract. In this talk we will overview two-way alternating finite automata (2AFAs). We will first list and reconcile the various definitions of what a 2AFA is, as they have appeared in the literature; as well as the various corresponding definitions of what it means for a 2AFA to accept its input. We will then study the computability and size complexity of 2AFAs. A large part of the latter study will involve the polynomial-size alternating hierarchy and its relation to its natural variants in terms of predicates and oracles. We will conclude with a list of open questions.

Deciding Equivalence of Tree Transducers by Means of Precise Abstract Interpretation

Helmut Seidl

Fakultät für Informatik, TU München, Germany
seidl@in.tum.de

Abstract. This presentation reviews the construction of the earliest normal form for top-down tree transducers. It will indicate how this construction allows to decide equivalence of deterministic top-down tree transducers and how it can be used to decide whether a top-down tree transducer is functional. The earliest normal form also opens up the way for decidability of equivalence for functional sequential tree-to-string transducers, as well as for deterministic macro tree transducers, at least when they are basic and separated. Interestingly, both the construction of the earliest normal form as well as it application to equivalence for the given class of macro tree transducers rely on techniques borrowed from precise abstract interpretation.

Contents

Invited Talks

Static Garbage Collection

Sebastian Maneth(✉)

FB3 - Informatik, Universität Bremen, Bremen, Germany
maneth@uni-bremen.de

Abstract. We present a method that allows to bound the sizes of intermediate trees in a composition of macro tree transducers. Macro tree transducers are a powerful model of tree translation which, for instance, includes all attribute grammars (seen as tree-to-tree translators). The idea of the method is to change a transducer in the composition so that it does not produce output nodes that will be removed (and ignored) by a subsequent transducer in the composition. This can be considered as a form of static garbage collection, where garbage is never produced by any transducer. We then give three applications of this result and show that (1) compositions of macro tree transducers can be computed in linear time with respect to the sum of sizes of input and output trees, (2) finiteness of ranges of compositions of macro tree transducers is decidable, and (3) the macro tree transducer composition hierarchy collapses when restricted to functions of linear size increase.

Let $f_1, \ldots, f_n$ be functions and let s be an element in the domain of f_1. Consider the sequential composition

$$f_1 \circ f_2 \circ \cdots f_{n-1} \circ f_n(s).$$

For us, this means the value $f_n(f_{n-1}(\cdots f_2(f_1(s))\cdots))$, which is in contrast to common mathematical notation. In our setting, each function f_i computes a *tree-to-tree transformation*, where "tree" means "finite, ordered, ranked, rooted, and node-labeled tree". In this talk we present a technique which allows to restrict the sizes of all intermediate results $f_1(s), f_2(f_1(s)), \ldots, f_{n-1}(f_{n-2}(\cdots f_1(s)\cdots))$ of the composition. The idea is that if a function f_i (with $i \in \{2, \ldots, n\}$) deletes certain input nodes or input subtrees, then the previous function that produces the input for f_i should be altered in such a way that these nodes and subtrees are never produced. Thus, if we consider as "garbage" the nodes in intermediate trees that are deleted (and ignored) later, then our method can be considered as a form of "garbage collection".

Each f_i in our setting is defined by a finite-state transducer of a certain type, called macro tree transducer. We can statically alter these transducers into a new sequence of transducers so that every transducer (except the first one) produces at least one output node for each input leaf and for each monadic input node, thus arriving at a technique of "static garbage collection".

This idea of static garbage collection was first presented at FSTTCS 2002 [8] and was used at FSTTCS 2003 [9] to prove that the macro tree transducer hierarchy collapses when restricted to functions of linear size increase. Recently a new

M. Hospodár and G. Jirásková (Eds.): CIAA 2019, LNCS 11601, pp. 3–9, 2019.
https://doi.org/10.1007/978-3-030-23679-3_1

presentation of these results was given [2]; this version formalizes all techniques and technical contributions in terms of tree-walking tree transducers (which are similar to attribute grammars). Here we stick to the original formalization using macro tree transducers.

1 Macro Tree Transducers

Macro tree transducers [5,6] (for short, MTTs) were invented in the 1980s as formal model for syntax-directed translation. They can be seen as functional programs that take trees as input, produce trees as output, and perform pattern matching on the input tree in order to produce output trees via concatenating output nodes on top of recursively produced output trees. MTTs can also be seen as generalization of top-down tree transducers and context-free tree grammars. Top-down tree transducers themselves are a natural generalization from strings to trees of the finite-state string transducers (often called "generalized sequential machines"). Note that MTTs are strictly more powerful than attribute grammars [7] (seen as tree-to-tree transducers by not interpreting their output expressions). Here is an example of an MTT that proves this strictness.

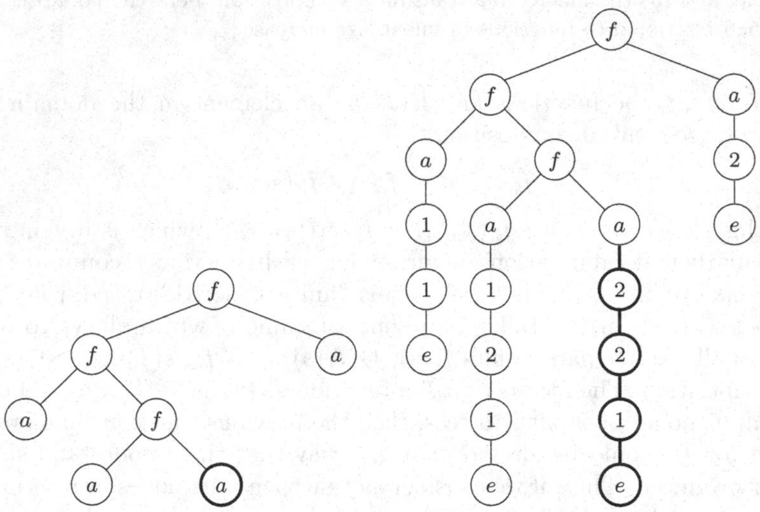

Fig. 1. An input tree and the corresponding output tree for the transducer of Example 1.

Example 1. We define the MTT M which takes as input trees over the ranked alphabet $\Sigma = \{f^{(2)}, a^{(0)}\}$ meaning that each f-labeled node has exactly two children, and each a-labeled node has zero children. The transducer outputs trees over the ranked alphabet $\Delta = \{f^{(2)}, a^{(1)}, 1^{(1)}, 2^{(1)}, e^{(0)}\}$. Intuitively, the transducer adds under each leaf u of the input tree a monadic tree over $\{1, 2, e\}$ that corresponds to the reverse Dewey-path of u. For instance, the marked node u on the left of Fig. 1 has Dewey path 1.2.2 (because u can be reached from the root node by navigating to its first child, and from that node to its second child, and from that node again to the second child). The reverse of this string, seen as a monadic tree over $\{1, 2, e\}$ is the tree $2(2(1(e)))$ which is marked in the tree in the right of Fig. 1. The MTT M for this translation has the following rules:

$$\begin{array}{ll} q_0(f(x_1, x_2)) & \to f(q(x_1, 1(e)), q(x_2, 2(e))) \\ q_0(a) & \to a(e) \\ q(f(x_1, x_2), y) & \to f(q(x_1, 1(y)), q(x_2, 2(y))) \\ q(a, y) & \to a(y) \end{array}$$

The state q of the MTT M uses an *accumulating parameter* denoted y (such parameters are of type output tree) in which it computes the reverse Dewey path of the current input node. Note that if a state occurs in the right-hand side of a rule of an MTT, then its first argument must be one of the input variables x_i. The rules are used as rewrite rules in the usual way. Thus, the initial tree $q_0(f(f(a, f(a, a)), a))$ rewrites via the first rule to

$$f(q(f(a, f(a, a)), 1(e), q(a, 2(e)))).$$

Via the last rule the latter tree rewrites to $f(q(f(a, f(a, a)), 1(e), a(2(e))))$.

The reason why the translation τ from the example cannot be realized by any attribute grammar (seen as tree transducer) is, that for such attributes transducers, the relationship of number of distinct output subtrees to the size of the input subtree is bounded by a constant (see Lemma 5.43 of [6]). This should be intuitively clear, because an attribute grammar associates to each node of the input tree a fixed number of attributes, in which certain output trees will be computed. To see that τ does not have this property, consider an input tree that is a full binary tree of size 2^n and height n; it is translated into an output tree that contains $O(n \cdot 2^n)$-many distinct output subtrees.

Note that all MTTs and all other transducers considered in this note are **total and deterministic**. This means that for every state q and input symbol f the transducer has exactly one rule with left-hand side $q(f(\dots), \dots)$. A *top-down tree transducer* is an MTT which does not use any accumulating parameters in its rules.

2 Productive Macro Tree Transducers

A macro tree transducer is productive if for each input node that is either a leaf or a monadic node, it produces at least one output node. An MTT can be made productive by restricting the way in which it deletes input nodes. There are four ways in which an MTT can delete nodes:

1. *Deletion of Parameters.* Consider the rule

$$q(h(x_1), y_1, y_2) \to g(q'(x_1, y_2), a).$$

This rule deletes the first parameter y_1. We will want to remove all such rules and guarantee that every parameter from the left-hand side of a rule also appears in the right-hand side of the rule. An MTT with this property is call *parameter non-deleting.*
2. *Erasure due to Parameters.* Consider the following rule of a parameter non-deleting MTT:

$$q(a, y_1) \to y_1$$

Since this rule "consumes" an input leaf labeled a but does not produce any new output nodes, it is called "erasing". An MTT which contains no rule with right-hand size equal to the tree y_1 is called "non-erasing".
3. *Input Tree Deletion.* Consider the rule

$$q(f(x_1, x_2), y_1, y_2) \to g(q(x_2, y_2, y_1), a).$$

Here, the input subtree x_1 does not occur in the right-hand side and is thus deleted (and ignored). However, we must be careful: many different states may be processing the current f-labeled input node. The first subtree of that node is only deleted, if *all* these states q' have a (q', f)-rule in which x_1 does not appear. Accordingly, an MTT is "non-deleting" if there is no reachable state set $\overline{Q}$, input symbol f, and number i such that for all states in $q' \in \overline{Q}$, the (q', f) rule does not contain the input variable x_i. The *state set* of node u of an input tree s consists of all states that appear in the tree $M_{q_0}(s')$, where s' is obtained from s be replacing the subtree at node u by a new symbol for which the transducer has no rules.
4. *Skipping of Monadic Input Nodes.* A rule of the form

$$q(h(x_1), y_1, \ldots, y_m) \to q'(x_1, y_{j_1}, \ldots, y_{j_m})$$

such that $\{y_1, \ldots, y_m\} = \{1, 2, \ldots, m\}$ is called a skipping-rule. An MTT is non-skipping if there is no reachable state set $\overline{Q}$ and unary input symbol h such that for every $q' \in \overline{Q}$ the (q', h)-rule is a skipping-rule.

It was already shown in [3] that for every MTT M one can construct an equivalent MTT with regular look-ahead such that M' is parameter non-deleting and non-erasing. Note that for a state q of M which has m parameters and an input tree s, the tree $M_q(s)$ obtained by rewriting the tree $q(s, y_1, \ldots, y_m)$ using the rules of M, is a tree over output symbols plus leaves labeled by parameters from $Y_m = \{y_1, \ldots, y_m\}$. For any strict subset Y of Y_m, the set $T_\Delta[Y]$ of all trees over Δ in which each $y \in Y$ occurs at least once is a regular tree language. Since inverses of macro tree translations M_q effectively preserve the regular tree languages (see [5]), we can determine via regular look-ahead which particular subset Y of parameters of any state will occur in the corresponding output tree. According to this information, we change the state calls in a right-hand side to only contain the arguments which will not be deleted. Similarly, we can determine via look-ahead if $M_q(s)$ is equal to y_1 and if so, remove from a right-hand side every call to q by selecting its first parameter argument.

In order to remove the deletion of input subtrees, we can transform a given MTT M into the composition of a linear top-down tree transducer T, followed by an MTT which is nondeleting. The idea of the transducer T is to simulate the state behavior of M, i.e., to compute in its state the current state set of M. If no input tree is deleted for input symbol f, then T produces f as output and proceeds. If for all states in the current state set the rules of M delete input variables $x_{i_1}, \ldots, x_{i_k}$ (with $i_1 < \cdots < i_k$), then T outputs a new symbol $f_{i_1,\ldots,i_k}$ of lower rank (according to k) and proceeds.

To remove skipping of monadic input nodes we proceed similarly and construction a composition of a linear top-down tree transducer T and a non-skipping MTT M. As before, T computes the current state set of M in its state, and uses this information in order to remove the skipped monadic nodes.

Since the look-ahead can be transferred to the first transducer, and linear top-down tree transducers (with look-ahead) are closed under composition we obtain

$$\text{MTT} \subseteq \text{LT}^{\text{R}} \circ \text{MTT}_{\text{prod}}$$

where LT^{R} denotes the class of linear top-down tree transformations with regular look-ahead, and MTT_{prod} denotes the class of macro tree transformations that are *productive*. Productive means all the four forms of deletion are not present, i.e., the translation is realized by an MTT that is parameter non-deleting, non-erasing, non-deleting, and non-skipping. Since any MTT can be realized by the composition of a top-down tree transducer and a linear (with respect to the input variables) MTT, we also have that $\text{MTT} \subseteq \text{T}^{\text{R}} \circ \text{LMTT}_{\text{prod}}$. Since MTTs are closed under right-composition with T^{R} we obtain by induction that for every k,

$$\text{MTT}^k \subseteq \text{LT}^{\text{R}} \circ T_{\text{prod}} \circ \text{LMTT}^k_{\text{prod}} \qquad (*)$$

where T_{prod} denotes the class of translations realized by productive top-down tree transducers. Each τ translation in the $(k+1)$-fold composition on the right side of the inclusion, except the first one, has *linear bounded input*, i.e., there exists a constant c such that for every $(s,t) \in \tau$, the size of s is smaller than $c \cdot |t|$. The reason for this is that for every input leaf and for every input monadic node τ produces at least one output node (thus, c can be chosen as $c = 2$).

3 Applications

We now mention a few applications of our static garbage collection result $(*)$. It is well known that attribute grammars can be evaluated in linear time (with respect to the sum of sizes of input and output tree), assuming that the evaluation of each semantic rule takes constant time (see [1]). Since every linear macro tree transducer can be simulated by an attribute grammar, we obtain that each transduction in $(*)$ can be evaluated in time linear in the sum of sizes of input and output tree. Since all translations except the first one have linear bounded input, the size of every intermediate tree in $(*)$ is smaller than $c \cdot |t|$ for some constant c (where t is the output tree of the composition). Hence, given an input tree s, the entire composition $t = \tau(s)$ can be computed in time $O(|s| + |t|)$.

Next, let us show that $(*)$ can be used to decide the finiteness of ranges of compositions of MTTs, i.e., of languages L in $\cup_{k\geq 1}\mathrm{MTT}^k(\mathrm{REGT})$, where REGT denotes the class of regular tree languages. Since REGT is closed under linear top-down tree transducers (with regular look-ahead), $(*)$ implies that $L = \tau(R)$ can be obtained by a composition τ of only productive transducers applied to a regular tree language R. Since all input trees that generate a certain output tree are bounded in size, according to the linear bounded input property, L is finite if an only if $\tau^{-1}(R)$ is finite. The letter set is effectively a regular tree language (Theorem 6.4 of [5]), and finiteness is easily decided for a regular tree language.

Last, let us show that $(*)$ implies that the macro tree transducer hierarchy collapses for functions of linear size increase. It is easy to see that if $f \circ g$ is of linear size increase and g is of linear bounded input, then also f is of linear size increase. This implies that each translation in the composition on the right-hand side of $(*)$ is of linear size increase (note that every linear top-down tree transduction is of linear size increase). Since macro tree transductions of linear size increase are closed under composition (this follows, e.g., from the fact that they can be characterized by MSO definable tree transductions [4]), we obtain that every composition of MTTs that is of linear size increase, can be realized by just one single MTT.

References

1. Deransart, P., Jourdan, M. (eds.): Attribute Grammars and their Applications. LNCS, vol. 461. Springer, Heidelberg (1990). https://doi.org/10.1007/3-540-53101-7
2. Engelfriet, J., Inaba, K., Maneth, S.: Linear bounded composition of tree-walking tree transducers: linear size increase and complexity. CoRR abs/1904.09203 (2019). http://arxiv.org/abs/1904.09203
3. Engelfriet, J., Maneth, S.: Macro tree transducers, attribute grammars, and MSO definable tree translations. Inf. Comput. **154**(1), 34–91 (1999). https://doi.org/10.1006/inco.1999.2807
4. Engelfriet, J., Maneth, S.: Macro tree translations of linear size increase are MSO definable. SIAM J. Comput. **32**(4), 950–1006 (2003). https://doi.org/10.1137/S0097539701394511
5. Engelfriet, J., Vogler, H.: Macro tree transducers. J. Comput. System Sci. **31**(1), 71–146 (1985). https://doi.org/10.1016/0022-0000(85)90066-2
6. Fülöp, Z., Vogler, H.: Syntax-Directed Semantics - Formal Models Based on Tree Transducers. Monographs in Theoretical Computer Science. An EATCS Series. Springer, Heidelberg (1998). https://doi.org/10.1007/978-3-642-72248-6
7. Knuth, D.E.: Semantics of context-free languages. Math. Syst. Theory **2**(2), 127–145 (1968). https://doi.org/10.1007/BF01692511

8. Maneth, S.: The complexity of compositions of deterministic tree transducers. In: Agrawal, M., Seth, A. (eds.) FSTTCS 2002. LNCS, vol. 2556, pp. 265–276. Springer, Heidelberg (2002). https://doi.org/10.1007/3-540-36206-1_24
9. Maneth, S.: The macro tree transducer hierarchy collapses for functions of linear size increase. In: Pandya, P.K., Radhakrishnan, J. (eds.) FSTTCS 2003. LNCS, vol. 2914, pp. 326–337. Springer, Heidelberg (2003). https://doi.org/10.1007/978-3-540-24597-1_28

Graph-Walking Automata: From Whence They Come, and Whither They are Bound

Alexander Okhotin(✉)

St. Petersburg State University,
7/9 Universitetskaya nab., Saint Petersburg 199034, Russia
alexander.okhotin@spbu.ru

Abstract. Graph-walking automata are finite automata walking on graphs given as an input; tree-walking automata and two-way finite automata are their well-known special cases. Graph-walking automata can be regarded both as a model of navigation in an unknown environment, and as a generic computing device, with the graph as the model of its memory. This paper presents the known results on these automata, ranging from their limitations in traversing graphs, studied already in the 1970s, to the recent work on the logical reversibility of their computations.

1 Introduction

A graph-walking automaton (GWA) walks over a given graph by moving from one node to another along the edges. It is equipped with finite memory, and at each step it uses its current state and the label of the current node to determine its action, that is, which edge to follow and which new state to enter.

A natural prototype for a graph-walking automaton is a robot exploring an unknown environment using limited internal memory and leaving no marks in the environment. A typical task is to traverse the entire graph, for instance, in search for a specially marked node. The most famous example of this task is found in the classical Greek myth about Theseus traversing the Labyrinth and slaying the Minotaur therein.

To be exact, Theseus is faced with three consecutive tasks: first, *finding the Minotaur in the Labyrinth;* second, *slaying him;* and third, *finding the way out.* As the myth is usually told, the main difficulty was to find the way out of the Labyrinth, once the Minotaur is slain. However, as illustrated in Fig. 1, Theseus was fortunate to be helped by Ariadne, whose thread allowed him to return to the gate of the Labyrinth in time $O(n)$. Even though the myth does not explain how Theseus found the Minotaur, it is not difficult to see that even Ariadne's thread alone is sufficient to traverse the entire graph by using an inefficient form of depth-first search.

Supported by the Russian Science Foundation, project 18-11-00100.

M. Hospodár and G. Jirásková (Eds.): CIAA 2019, LNCS 11601, pp. 10–29, 2019.
https://doi.org/10.1007/978-3-030-23679-3_2

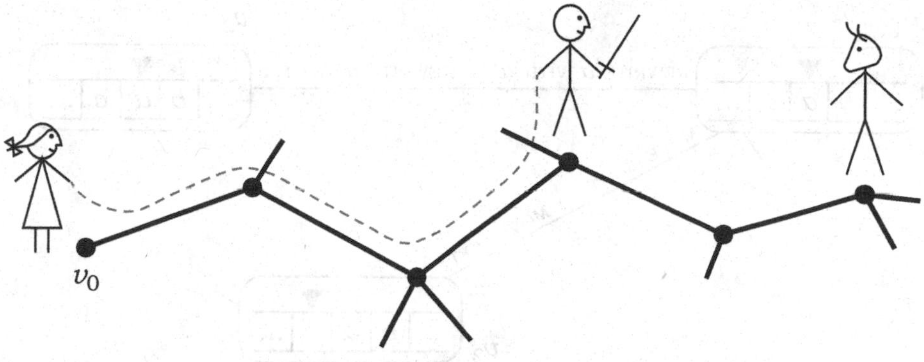

Fig. 1. Theseus searching for the Minotaur in a graph with the help of Ariadne's thread.

If Theseus were to accomplish his task with no Ariadne to guide him, he would act as a graph-walking automaton. In this case, already the problem of *finding* the Minotaur would present a substantial difficulty. This problem, in general, amounts to traversing the entire graph. The question of whether there exists a finite automaton that can traverse any given undirected graph by following its edges was reportedly first proposed by Michael Rabin: in his 1967 public lecture, he conjectured that this is impossible [12]. The conjecture was confirmed by Budach [9], who proved that for every graph-walking automaton there is a planar graph that it cannot fully traverse. In other words, there is a maze, in which Theseus, without Ariadne, would not even find the Minotaur.

This result by no means contradicts the assumptions made by the Ancient Greeks. Indeed, Theseus had to traverse one particular maze—the Cretan Labyrinth—which was apparently constructed in the way that reaching the Minotaur from the gate was easy, whereas finding the way back was hard. This suggests the following formal representation of the task faced by Theseus if Ariadne turns her back on him: on his own, he begins at the gate to the Labyrinth (the initial node v_0) and, acting as a graph-walking automaton, presumably finds the Minotaur; then, can he return to v_0 while still acting as a graph-walking automaton? Unexpectedly, there is a positive solution to this problem: if there exists a graph-walking automaton that leads Theseus from the Labyrinth gate to the Minotaur, then there is also a graph-walking automaton that leads him back to the gate; this was established by Kunc and Okhotin [19], based on a general idea discovered of Sipser [28]. Roughly speaking, the resulting graph-walking automaton *backtracks all possible paths that lead to the Minotaur according to the method employed by Theseus.*

Besides the direct interpretation of graph traversal as motion in a discrete environment, graph-walking automata also serve as a model of computation. Two simple cases of graph-walking automata are well-known in the literature. First, there are the *two-way deterministic finite automata* (2DFA), which traverse a given input string as a graph that consists of a single path; they are

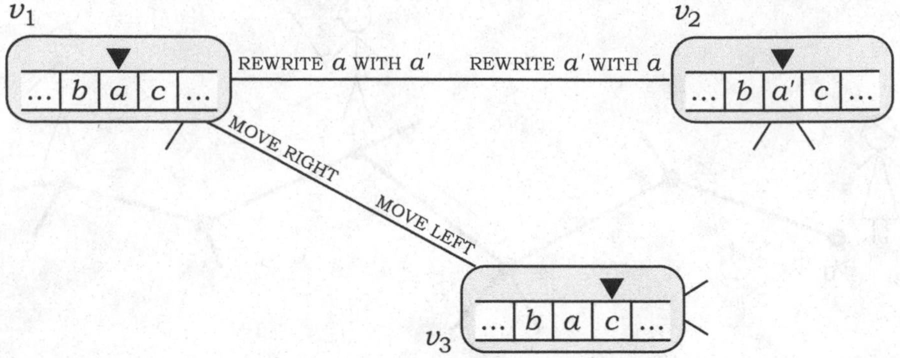

Fig. 2. Memory configurations of a Turing machine modelled by a graph.

notable for being equivalent to one-way finite automata [15,26], as well as for having a nondeterministic variant that can be determinized, with important complexity issues surrounding the complexity of determinization [16]. The other model are the *tree-walking automata* (TWA), which traverse trees in the same sense as do the graph-walking automata: in contrast to the case of 2DFA, these automata are weaker in power than the "one-way" (bottom-up or top-down) tree automata [8], and their nondeterministic variant is strictly more powerful than the deterministic case [7].

Many other models of computation can be represented as graph-walking automata. The graph represents the memory of a machine: nodes are memory configurations, and edges are elementary operations on the memory. This graph is implicitly constructed for every input object, and then the computation of the machine is interpreted as a walk over this graph. For example, for a Turing machine, nodes correspond to different head positions and tape contents, as illustrated in Fig. 2. If a Turing machine has *bac* on the tape, with the head at a in a state q, and if it executes a stationary transition that rewrites a with a' and enters a state q', this corresponds to a GWA at v_1 in the state q, moving to v_2 in the state q'.

This way, many general ideas on computation, such as nondeterminism, reversibility, halting, probabilistic computation, etc., which are defined for various models of computation, admit a unified representation in terms of graph-walking automata. Many standard research problems, such as the complexity of testing membership and emptiness, closure properties and state complexity, can also be represented and studied for graph-walking automata. The particular models of computation can then be regarded as *families of input graphs*, potentially reducing the difference between the models to graph-theoretic properties. This view of graph-walking automata as a powerful general model in automata theory further motivates their study.

This paper gives a brief overview of the graph-walking automaton model. The overview begins with the basic definitions: *graphs* traversed by automata are

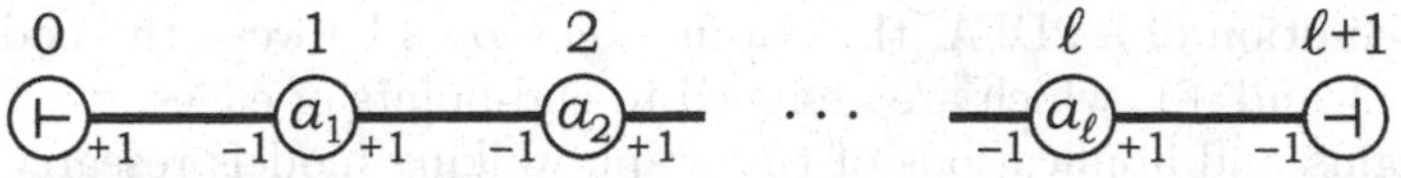

Fig. 3. A string $w = a_1 a_2 \dots a_\ell$ with end-markers, represented as a graph with $V = \{0, 1, 2, \dots, \ell, \ell+1\}$.

defined in Sect. 2, followed by a definition of graph-walking automata in Sect. 3; justifications for various details of the definitions are provided. Section 4 presents the most well-known result in the area, that there is no graph-walking automaton that can traverse every graph—that is, that Theseus, without Ariadne's thread, would not find the Minotaur in the Labyrinth. The fundamental construction of a graph-walking automaton that simulates the computations of another graph-walking automaton *backwards* is explained in Sect. 5; by this result, if Theseus finds the Minotaur, then he can find his way back by tracing back his footsteps. The next Sect. 6 describes the applications of this construction to reversible computing: every graph-walking automaton can be transformed to a reversible graph-walking automaton that accepts the same set of finite graphs. Using this result, the closure of graph-walking automata under Boolean operations is established in Sect. 7. Section 8 defines the basic decision problems for graph-walking automata. Possible variants of the graph-walking automaton model are discussed in Sect. 9, whereas algorithms for graph exploration based on other models are briefly mentioned in Sect. 10. The last Sect. 11 suggests some directions for the future study of graph-walking automata.

2 Graphs

A definition of graph-walking automata naturally begins with the form of the graphs on which they walk. There are quite a few details to be fixed: are graphs directed or undirected? finite or infinite? is the initial node specifically marked or not? is the degree of nodes bounded or unbounded? what kind of labels are there to guide the automaton?

Different choices lead to different models, and perhaps, once the theory of graph-walking automata reaches maturity, the difference between the resulting models shall be formally investigated. In the definitions given in the literature, the details were chosen to fit the motivating applications, such as exploring an unknown environment, and representing models of computations in a unified setting.

The relation to other models of computations begins with the simplest case of graph-walking automata: the deterministic two-way finite automata (2DFA), A string, as it is processed by a 2DFA, is the simplest case of a graph. This is a finite connected undirected graph, with its nodes corresponding to positions in the string, and accordingly labelled with input symbols and end-markers (⊢, ⊣). The nodes are connected into a chain, as illustrated in Fig. 3. As per the standard definition of a 2DFA, the automaton moves between the nodes in the directions -1 and $+1$, which are assigned to end-points of edges.

The origins and applications of the graph-walking models researched so far lead to the following choices in the basic definitions.

Graphs are undirected, and every edge can be traversed in both directions. This is a natural assumption under the maze-walking interpretation, where one can always retract the last step. If a graph is taken as a model of a memory, this means that every modification of the memory carried out in a single operation can always be reversed by applying another single operation. In particular, there cannot be a "global reset" operator that erases an unbounded amount of information.

Graphs may, in theory, be infinite, although an accepting computation of a graph-walking automaton still must be a *finite* walk over the input graph. This corresponds to the intuition of traversing a maze, which may be infinite, yet Theseus has to slay only one Minotaur and get back within a finite time. This also fits the definition of classical computation: for instance, even though a Turing machine is equipped with unbounded memory, it must terminate in finitely many steps in order to accept.

However, dealing with infinite graphs in graph-walking automata is usually difficult, and, in particular, all results presented in this paper hold only for finite graphs.

The initial node is specifically marked, that is, upon entering a node, the automaton knows whether it is initial or not. Over this point, there is a certain discrepancy between different applications. On the one hand, the initial node is the gate to the Labyrinth, where Theseus begins his journey, and where to he expects to get back after slaying the Minotaur: of course, upon visiting a node, it should be immediately visible whether it is the gate.

On the other hand, a marked initial node in a computing device means that the machine always knows whether its memory is in the initial configuration. This holds for simpler kinds of automata, such as 2DFA, which can see whether their heads are in the initial position. However, for a Turing machine, this means that at any moment it should know whether its entire work-tape is clear; in practice, this would require re-scanning the tape.

Some of the existing results on graph-walking automata assume graphs with a marked initial node, and some results refer to the case of an unmarked initial node.

The degree of nodes is bounded by a constant. Furthermore, the end-points of edges meeting at each node are labelled with different *directions* from a fixed finite set D. This is necessary for an automaton to distinguish between these edges, and to be able to proceed in each available direction.

In a maze, this means that a bounded number of corridors meet at every junction, and that each outgoing corridor has a unique label. For a computing device, directions are elementary operations on the memory, and following an edge means applying that operation.

In order to handle graphs of unbounded degree, nodes of higher degrees can be split into subgraphs, and so this restiction is actually inessential.

Nodes are labelled, and so are the end-points of edges. Node labels are analogous to symbols in a string, and the set of possible labels is accordingly denoted by Σ. At every moment of its computation, a graph-walking automaton can observe only the label of the current node v, denoted by $a = \lambda(v)$. Furthermore, the label of a node determines the set of directions available in that node, denoted by D_a, with $D_a \subseteq D$, Knowing this label and using its internal state, the automaton decides, in which direction from D_a to proceed, and which state to enter.

In a string, there are two directions: to the previous symbol (-1) and to the next symbol $(+1)$, with $D = \{-1, +1\}$. It is essential that moving to the direction $+1$ and then to the direction -1 always leads back to the same symbol: that is, $+1$ and -1 are *opposite directions.* In the general case of graphs, every direction d in D must have an opposite direction $-d \in D$, defined by a bijective operator $-\colon D \to D$.

With the above details fixed, graphs processed by a graph-walking automaton are defined over a ***signature****,* which includes a set of directions, a set of node labels, and a set of available directions for each node label, as well as identifies the labels for the initial node. A signature is generalization of an alphabet for the case of graphs.

Definition 1 (Kunc and Okhotin [19]**).** *A* signature *is a quintuple* $\mathcal{S} = (D, -, \Sigma, \Sigma_0, \langle D_a \rangle_{a \in \Sigma})$, *where*

- D *is a finite set of* directions, *that is, labels at the end-points of edges;*
- $-\colon D \to D$ *is a bijective operator that defines the opposite direction, it satisfies* $-(-d) = d$ *for all* $d \in D$;
- Σ *is a finite set of* node labels;
- $\Sigma_0 \subseteq \Sigma$ *is a non-empty subset of labels allowed in the initial node, whereas all other nodes have to be labelled with elements of* $\Sigma \setminus \Sigma_0$;
- *each* $D_a \subseteq D$, *with* $a \in \Sigma$, *is the set of directions avaliable in all nodes labelled with* a, *so that every such node must have degree* $|D_a|$, *with the incident edges corresponding to the elements of* D_a.

Graphs over a signature $\mathcal{S}$ are undirected labelled graphs defined as follows.

Definition 2 (Kunc and Okhotin [19]**).** *A* graph *over a signature* $\mathcal{S} = (D, -, \Sigma, \Sigma_0, \langle D_a \rangle_{a \in \Sigma})$ *is a quadruple* $(V, v_0, +, \lambda)$, *where*

- V *is a set of* nodes;
- $v_0 \in V$ *is the* initial node;
- $\lambda\colon V \to \Sigma$ *is a function assigning a label to each node* $v \in V$, *so that the label* $\lambda(v)$ *is in* Σ_0 *if and only if* $v = v_0$;

- $+\colon V \times D \to V$ *is a function representing the edges of the graph: it is defined in each node* $v \in V$ *and for each direction* $d \in D_{\lambda(v)}$ *applicable in that node, so that the neighbour of* v *in the direction* d *is denoted by* $v + d$.
  The neighbour of v *in the direction* $-d$ *is accordingly defined by* $v - d$. *The graph must satisfy the condition* $(v+d)-d = v$, *for all* $v \in V$ *and* $d \in D_{\lambda(v)}$. *In particular,* $D_{\lambda(v+d)}$ *must have the direction* $-d$.

A graph with an unmarked initial node *is defined in the same way, but with no special label for* v_0: *every node* $v \in V$ *must have* $\lambda(v) \notin \Sigma_0$.

Example 1. Strings over an alphabet Γ delimited by left and right end-markers ($\vdash$, $\dashv$) are represented as graphs over a signature $\mathcal{S} = (D, -, \Sigma, \Sigma_0, \langle D_a \rangle_{a \in \Sigma})$ with directions $D = \{+1, -1\}$, where $-(+1) = -1$, and with node labels $\Sigma = \Gamma \cup \{\vdash, \dashv\}$. The only initial label is the left end-marker: $\Sigma_0 = \{\vdash\}$. The set of directions at each input symbol $a \in \Gamma$ is $D_a = \{+1, -1\}$. Only one direction available at each end-marker: $D_\vdash = \{+1\}$, $D_\dashv = \{-1\}$.

Every connected graph over the signature $\mathcal{S}$ is a labelled path graph of the form depicted in Fig. 3. It corresponds to a string over Γ.

3 Automata

Definition 3 (Kunc and Okhotin [19]). *A* deterministic graph-walking automaton *over a signature* $\mathcal{S} = (D, -, \Sigma, \Sigma_0, \langle D_a \rangle_{a \in \Sigma})$ *is a quadruple* $\mathcal{A} = (\mathcal{S}, Q, q_0, \delta, F)$, *in which*

- Q *is a finite set of states;*
- $q_0 \in Q$ *is the initial state;*
- $F \subseteq Q \times \Sigma$ *is a set of acceptance conditions;*
- $\delta\colon (Q \times \Sigma) \setminus F \to Q \times D$ *is a partial transition function, with* $\delta(q, a) \in Q \times D_a$ *for all* a *and* q *where it is defined.*

The automaton gets a graph $(V, v_0, +, \lambda)$ over the signature $\mathcal{S}$ as an input. At each point of its computation, the automaton is at a node $v \in V$ in a state $q \in Q$; the pair (q, v) is known as the automaton's *configuration*. The initial configuration is (q_0, v_0), that is, the automaton begins at the initial node in its initial state. At each step of the computation, while in a configuration (q, v), the automaton observes the symbol $\lambda(v)$ and evaluates its transition function on $\delta(q, \lambda(v))$. There are three possibilities.

- If this value is defined, let $\delta(q, \lambda(v)) = (q', d)$. Then the automaton moves in the direction d and enters the state q', so that the next configuration is $(q', v + d)$.
- If δ is undefined on $(q, \lambda(v))$, then the automaton halts. If $(q, \lambda(v)) \in F$, it accepts the input graph, and if $(q, \lambda(v)) \notin F$, it rejects.

The computation on a given graph is uniquely defined, and it can either be infinite, or accepting, or rejecting. The set of graphs recognized by the automaton $\mathcal{A}$ consists of all graphs over the signature $\mathcal{S}$ on which it halts and accepts.

Example 2. Let $\mathcal{S} = (D, -, \Sigma, \Sigma_0, \langle D_a \rangle_{a \in \Sigma})$ be a signature for strings over an alphabet Γ represented as graphs, as defined in Example 1. A graph-walking automaton over this signature is a deterministic two-way finite automaton (2DFA).

Another well-known special case of graph-walking automata are the *tree-walking automata* operating on trees of a bounded degree. This model was first defined by Aho and Ullman [1, Sect. VI], and later Bojańczyk and Colcombet [7, 8] showed that these automata are weaker than bottom-up and top-down tree automata, and that their nondeterministic variant cannot be determinized. Since a string is a special case of a tree with out-degree 1, the signature for trees processed by these automata generalizes the one from Example 1 by providing additional directions.

Example 3. Trees of degree k with nodes labelled by symbols from a set Γ are defined over a signature $\mathcal{S} = (D, -, \Sigma, \Sigma_0, \langle D_a \rangle_{a \in \Sigma})$, with the set of directions $D = \{+1, \ldots, +k, -1, \ldots, -k\}$, where each direction $+i$ means going down to the i-th successor, whereas $-i$ points from the i-th successor to its predecessor. The directions $+i$ and $-i$ are opposite: $-(+i) = -i$.

Nodes are labelled with the symbols from a set $\Sigma = \{\top, \bot_1, \ldots, \bot_k\} \cup (\Gamma \times \{1, \ldots, k\})$. The root node v_0 is labelled by the top marker ($\top$), with $D_\top = \{+1\}$ and $\Sigma_0 = \{\top\}$. Each i-th bottom marker ($\bot_i$) has $D_{\bot_i} = \{-i\}$, and serves as a label for leaves. Internal nodes are labelled with elements of $\Gamma \times \{1, \ldots, k\}$, so that a label (a, i), with $a \in \Gamma$ and $i \in \{1, \ldots, k\}$, indicates a node containing a symbol a, which is the i-th successor of its predecessor; the set of available directions is $D_{(a,i)} = \{-i, +1, \ldots, +k\}$.

Connected graphs over this signature are exactly the k-ary trees augmented with a top marker and with bottom markers.

4 To Find the Minotaur

In terms of graph-walking automata, the problem of maze exploration is represented as follows. In the signature, the alphabet Σ contains two special labels, one marking the initial node, and the other marking the location of the Minotaur. A graph-walking automaton has to test whether the given Labyrinth contains at least one Minotaur, as illustrated in Fig. 4.

This problem is often stated for graphs with an unmarked initial node: in other words, Theseus appears in the middle of the Labyrinth and has to test whether there is at least one Minotaur in the Labyrinth. In this setting, there is the following well-known result.

Theorem 1 (Budach [9]**).** *There exists a signature $\mathcal{S}$, such that for every graph-walking automaton $\mathcal{A}$ over $\mathcal{S}$ there is a planar graph G over $\mathcal{S}$, with an unmarked initial node, such that the computation of $\mathcal{A}$ of G does not visit one of its nodes.*

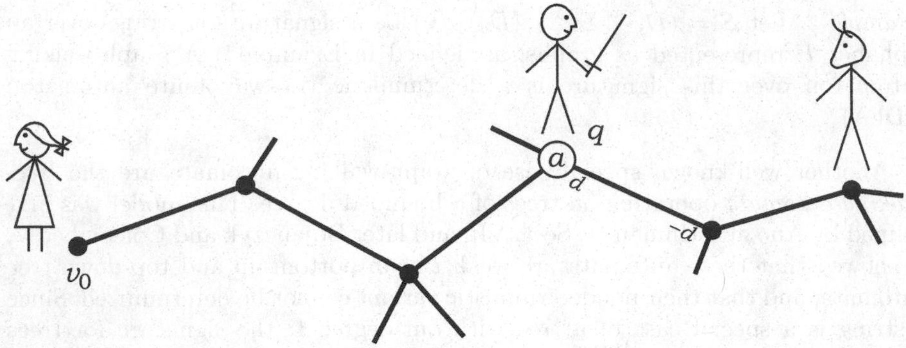

Fig. 4. Theseus using finite memory and node and edge labels to search for the Minotaur without Ariadne's thread.

The original proof of this result was very sophisticated. Later, the following short and clear proof was discovered.

Lemma 1 (Fraigniaud et al. [12]**).** *For every $d \geqslant 3$, let the signature $\mathcal{S}_d = (D, -, \Sigma, \Sigma_0, \langle D_a \rangle_{a \in \Sigma})$ have $D = \{1, \ldots, d\}$, with $-i = i$ for all $i \in D$, $\Sigma = \{a\}$, $\Sigma_0 = \varnothing$ and $D_a = D$. Then, for every n-state graph-walking automaton $\mathcal{A}$ over $\mathcal{S}$ there is a planar connected graph $G = (V, v_0, +, \lambda)$ over $\mathcal{S}$ with unmarked initial node and with $|V| \leqslant n + d + 3$, on which $\mathcal{A}$ does not visit all nodes.*

Proof (a sketch). Since $\Sigma = \{a\}$, all nodes of the graph appear identical, and the automaton's transitions by a induce a sequence of states $q_0, q_1, \ldots$, and a sequence of directions $d_1, d_2, \ldots$, with $\delta(q_i, a) = (q_{i+1}, d_{i+1})$. The sequence of states is periodic with some period p, with $p \in \{1, \ldots, n\}$, so that $q_{i+p} = q_i$ for all $i \geqslant n - 1$. Therefore, the sequence of directions has the same period.

At first, it is convenient to assume that the automaton operates on an infinite tree. Then, the periodic part of the sequence of directions can either drive the automaton into a cycle, or set it into periodic motion leading away from the initial node. In the former case, the automaton actually visits only finitely many nodes of the tree; it is sufficient to take the resulting subtree with one extra node, and to reconnect the unused edges between these nodes.

In case the automaton moves away along a periodic sequence of directions, the general idea is to *merge two nodes* of the infinite tree that are visited in the same state, thus effectively replacing this tree with a finite "trap", on which the automaton follows the same periodic trajectory. Consider the example in Fig. 5(top), where the sequence of directions is $a(bccabacab)^\omega$, with the same state q visited after each prefix in $a(bccabacab)^*$. The periodic part contains a detour cc, and with this detour omitted, it takes the form $babacab$. Let periodic part of the sequence, with all detours removed, be of the form $\alpha\beta\alpha^R$, where $\alpha, \beta \in D^*$ and α^R denotes the reversal of α: in Fig. 5(top), $\alpha = ba$ and $\beta = bac$. The plan is to join the nodes on the border of β, so that the periodic part visits α twice. The resulting trap is given in Fig. 5(bottom left).

It remains to add one extra node and fill in the missing nodes, as done in Fig. 5(bottom right).

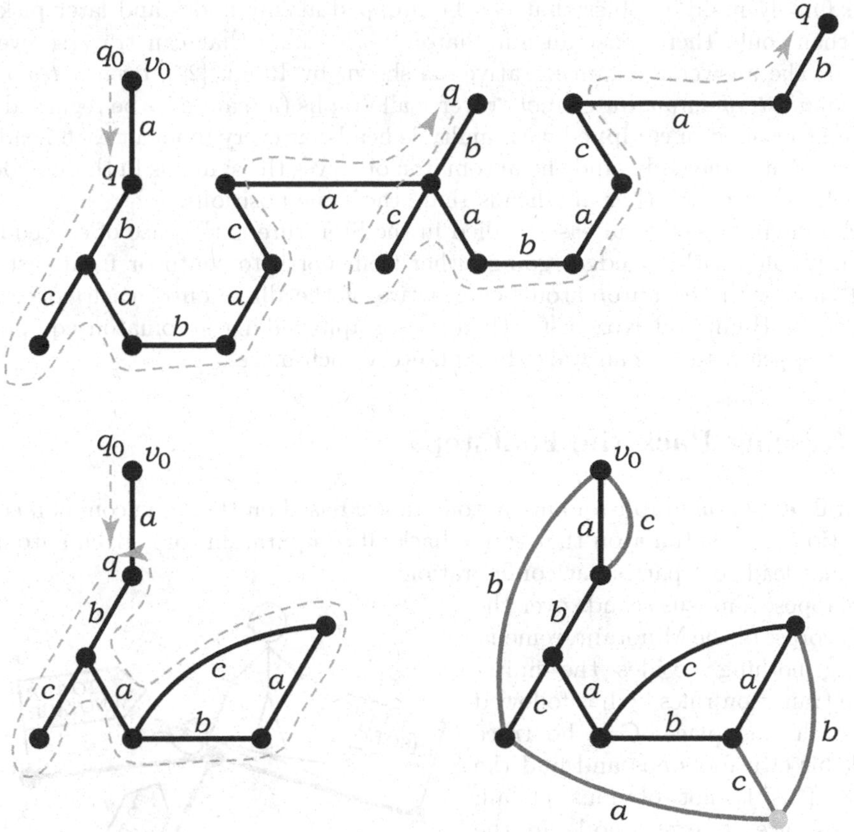

Fig. 5. Construction of a trap in the proof of Lemma 1: (top) A periodic sequence on an infinite tree; (bottom left) A trap constructed by merging two nodes in the periodic part; (bottom right) The trap with an unreachable node and all missing transitions added.

The full proof has several complicated cases, such as the case when the periodic part with detours removed is an odd palindrome. However, all cases are handled by a similar, yet more sophisticated construction, with the periodic computation condensed into looping in a finite trap. □

The above proof does not directly apply to the case of graph-walking automata with a marked initial node, because every appearance of v_0 in various places of the sequence disrupts the argument. One can likely work around these issues by an extensive case analysis. A concise new proof of this result for the marked case has been found by Martynova [22], and shall be published in due time.

Since the problem of graph exploration is an important algorithmic problem, if graph-walking automata cannot handle it in general, then the question is, which models can? For instance, if graph-walking automata were equipped with finitely many pebbles that can be dropped at any nodes and later picked up, then could there exist an automaton of this kind that can traverse every maze? The answer is again negative; as shown by Rollik [27], even a *team of communicating automata* cannot traverse all graphs (a team may be regarded as a single automaton equipped with multiple heads: at every moment each head is stationed at some node, and the automaton observes the symbols in those nodes, as well as senses whether any heads share the same position).

An interesting special case studied in the literature is the case of embedded plane graphs, with all edges going either from north to south or from east to west, and with the automaton being aware of the direction of each edge. As proved by Blum and Kozen [6], there is a graph-walking automaton equipped with *two pebbles* that can walk through every such maze.

5 Tracing Back the Footsteps

Several results on graph-walking automata are based on the same common construction of an automaton that traces back all computations of a given automaton that lead to a particular configuration.

Suppose Theseus stands over the fresh corpse of the Minotaur, remembering nothing besides the finite-state transition rules he has followed to reach this place. Can he trace back his own footsteps and find the exit? This is not obvious at all: for instance, if every node in the Labyrinth is equipped with a plaque "to the Minotaur" pointing to the most suitable edge, then the Minotaur can be found using a one-state transition table. However, such plaques would not help getting back: as illustrated in the picture, Theseus would not even know the penultimate node on his path to the Minotaur.

Nevertheless, the answer to the question is positive, and Theseus can always find the way back by tracing back all the paths that would lead him to the Minotaur according to his own transition rules. This is done using the general idea of *backtracking the tree of accepting computations*, discovered by Sipser [28] in his study of halting space-bounded computations. This idea has been reused many times: for instance, Lange et al. [21] applied it in their proof of the equivalence of deterministic space $O(s(\ell))$ to reversible space $O(s(\ell))$. Kondacs and Watrous [17] have improved the details of Sipser's construction, leading to a simulation of an n-state 1DFA by a reversible 2DFA with as few as $2n$ states. Geffert et al. [14], Muscholl et al. [24] and Morita [23] used the same idea to produce similar constructions for various automaton models, with various degree of efficiency.

Actually, this construction applies to particular automaton models so easily, for the reason that it is *correct in the general case of graph-walking automata*—and therefore it holds true for their particular cases, such as all automaton models to which it was previously applied.

In order to define the construction for tracing back the footsteps of a graph-walking automaton, the following property of automata turns out to be useful. A GWA is said to be *direction-determinate*, if it always remembers the direction, in which it came to the current node.

Definition 4. *A graph-walking automaton* $\mathcal{A} = (\mathcal{S}, Q, q_0, \delta, F)$ *over a signature* $\mathcal{S} = (D, -, \Sigma, \Sigma_0, \langle D_a \rangle_{a \in \Sigma})$, *is* direction-determinate, *if, for some partial function* $d \colon Q \to D$, *whenever a transition* $\delta(p, a)$ *leads the automaton to a state* q, *it must move in the direction* $d(q)$.

Then, for each $a \in \Sigma$, *the transitions by* a *are defined by a partial function* $\delta_a \colon Q \to Q$, *with* $\delta(p, a) = (q, d(q))$, *where* $q = \delta_a(p)$.

Every graph-walking automaton with a set of states Q can be transformed to a direction-determinate automaton with the set of states $Q \times D$, which simply remembers the last direction it has taken in the second component of its state, without ever using this information.

Lemma 2 (Kunc and Okhotin [19]**).** *For every direction-determinate graph-walking automaton* $\mathcal{A} = (\mathcal{S}, Q, q_0, \delta, F)$, *there exists an automaton over the same signature* $\mathcal{S}$ *and with the set of states* $\overrightarrow{Q} \cup [Q]$, *where* $\overrightarrow{Q} = \{ \overrightarrow{q} \mid q \in Q \}$ *and* $[Q] = \{ [q] \mid q \in Q \}$, *which, on any finite graph, backtracks all computations of* $\mathcal{A}$ *leading to any accepting configuration* $(\widehat{q}, \widehat{v})$, *with* $(\widehat{q}, \lambda(\widehat{v})) \in F$, *in the following sense: if* $\mathcal{B}$ *begins its computation in the configuration* $([\widehat{q}], \widehat{v} - d(\widehat{q}))$, *then it passes through all such configurations* $([q], v)$, *that the computation of* $\mathcal{A}$ *beginning in* $(q, v + d(q))$ *accepts in the configuration* $(\widehat{q}, \widehat{v})$.

Proof (a sketch). The automaton $\mathcal{B}$ traverses the tree of all computations of $\mathcal{A}$ that terminate in the configuration $(\widehat{q}, \widehat{v})$. The construction is based on ordering the states in Q, which implies an ordering on the branches of the computation tree. Then, whenever $\mathcal{B}$ finds a configuration of $\mathcal{A}$ that has some predecessors, it proceeds with tracing back the *least* of the computation paths leading to the current configuration. Once $\mathcal{B}$ reaches a configuration of $\mathcal{A}$ without predecessors, it switches to forward simulation, which is carried out in the states $\overrightarrow{Q}$. In these "forward states", for every configuration of $\mathcal{A}$ visited by $\mathcal{B}$, it tries to trace back the *next* computation path according to the chosen ordering. If the path being traced forward is already greater than the other paths meeting at the present point, then the forward simulation continues. This way, the entire tree of computations converting in the chosen configuration is eventually traversed. □

Sipser's [28] paper actually contains two methods for implementing this kind of computation tree traversal: his first method involves *remembering two states*

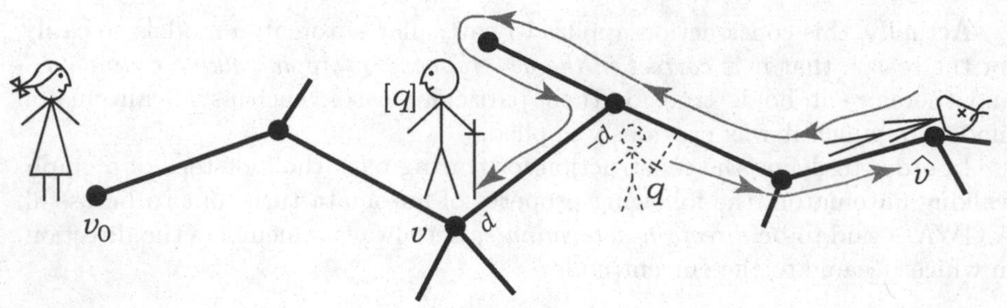

Fig. 6. Theseus tracing back his path from the gate to the Minotaur: on the way back, he is in the configuration $([q], v)$ if, on his way forward, he would reach the Minotaur from the configuration $(q, v + d(q))$.

of the original automaton, that is, produces the set of states $Q \times Q$; the second method sketched by Sipser [28] requires *remembering a state and a symbol*, that is, uses the states $Q \times \Sigma$. The improvement contributed by Kondacs and Watrous [17] was to *remember a state and one bit*, using states $Q \times \{0, 1\}$. The construction in Lemma 2 implements the method of Kondacs and Watrous [17] for graph-walking automata, which seem to be the natural limit of the applicability of this method.

Lemma 2 directly implies the promised result that if Theseus can find the Minotaur using finite-state transition rules, then he can get back, as illustrated in Fig. 6. In terms of graph-walking automata, this is formalized as follows.

Definition 5. *A graph-walking automaton* $\mathcal{A} = (\mathcal{S}, Q, q_0, \delta, F)$ *is called* returning, *if it can accept only at the initial node, that is,* $F \subseteq Q \times \Sigma_0$.

Theorem 2 (Kunc and Okhotin [19]**).** *For every n-state graph-walking automaton $\mathcal{A}$ over some signature $\mathcal{S} = (D, -, \Sigma, \Sigma_0, \langle D_a \rangle_{a \in \Sigma})$, with $|D| = d$, there exists a direction-determinate returning graph-walking automaton with $3dn$ states that accepts the same set of finite graphs.*

Proof (a sketch). The given GWA $\mathcal{A}$ is first transformed to a dn-state direction-determinate GWA $\mathcal{B}$. By Lemma 2, there is a $2dn$-state direction-determinate automaton $\mathcal{C}$ that traces back all accepting computations of $\mathcal{B}$. The promised returning automaton operates as follows: first, it behaves as $\mathcal{B}$ until it reaches an accepting configuration; then, it behaves as $\mathcal{C}$, accepting if it ever encounters the initial configuration of $\mathcal{B}$, and rejecting if it ever returns to its accepting configuration.

Remark 1 (Martynova [22]*).* If the resulting returning graph-walking automaton is not required to be direction-determinate, then it is sufficient to use only $(2d + 1)n$ states. The new automaton first behaves as $\mathcal{A}$ until acceptance, and then proceeds with simulating $\mathcal{C}$.

The property of being returning is crucial for Theseus, and it can also be useful in other exploration problems. On the other hand, as a property of computing devices, it is not always relevant: for instance, if a Turing machine is represented as a graph-walking automaton, then being returning only means that it always restores the original contents of its tapes before acceptance.

As it shall now be demonstrated, the construction for tracing back the accepting computations can ensure several important general properties of abstract machines.

6 Reversible Computation

Reversibility is a stronger form of determinism: a deterministic machine is reversible, if its computations are also backward deterministic, that is, given its current configuration, its configuration at the previous step can always be uniquely determined. This is an interesting theoretical notion.

Furthermore, reversibility of computations is important from the point of view of the physics of computation [5]: according to *Landauer's principle* [20], a logically irreversible erasing of one bit of information incurs dissipation of $kT \ln 2$ joules of energy, where k is the Boltzmann constant and T is the temperature. Reversible computing, in theory, can avoid this effect. Furthermore, since the laws of quantum mechanics are reversible, reversible computing is the basic case of quantum computing. These applications further motivate theoretical studies on reversible computation.

In automata theory, Kondacs and Watrous [17] showed that reversible 2DFA can recognize every regular language, whereas reversible 1DFA, as well as one-way quantum automata (1QFA) recognize a proper subset of regular languages. Every Turing machine can be simulated by a reversible Turing machine [5]. Lange et al. [21] proved that the class of sets recognized by reversible Turing machines in space $O(s(n))$, denoted by RSPACE$(s(n))$, is equal to DSPACE$(s(n))$. This was done by applying Sipser's [28] method for tracing back accepting computations. The same method was used a few times for different automaton models, showing that their reversible subclass is as powerful as the full deterministic class. This general argument again works for graph-walking automata, and can be established in a clearer form for this model.

Definition 6 (Kunc and Okhotin [19]**).** *A graph-walking automaton* $\mathcal{A} = (\mathcal{S}, Q, q_0, \delta, F)$ *is called* reversible, *if it is direction-determinate and returning, every partial transformation* δ_a *is injective, and for each initial label* $a_0 \in \Sigma_0$, *there is at most one state* q *with* $(q, a_0) \in F$.

To put it simple, reversibility means that every computation can equally be executed backwards. In particular, given a finite graph with $\lambda(v_0) = a_0$, which can only be accepted in the configuration (q, v_0), one can proceed with backtracking a potential accepting computation beginning in this configuration. Since all partial transformations are injective, the predecessor configuration shall always be uniquely defined, until one of the following two outcomes: either the simulation backtracks to the initial configuration (q_0, v_0), or an unreachable configuration is reached. In the latter case, the automaton rejects this graph.

The automaton constructed in Lemma 2 is actually reversible.

There is also a notion of a *strongly reversible* graph-walking automaton, satisfying some further requirements: in particular, if a graph is rejected, then it can be rejected only in the initial node, in a particular configuration (q_{rej}, v_0); furthermore, all transformations δ_a with $a \notin \Sigma_0$ must be bijective. As long as the input graph is finite, this forces the automaton to halt on every input in one of the two predetermined configurations at the initial node.

Theorem 3 (Kunc and Okhotin [19]). *For every n-state direction-determinate returning graph-walking automaton, there exists a strongly reversible graph-walking automaton with $2n+1$ states recognizing the same set of finite graphs.*

Proof (a sketch). First, Lemma 2 is applied to the given returning automaton $\mathcal{A}$. The resulting automaton is augmented with a new initial state, in which it initiates tracing back the computations of $\mathcal{A}$ leading to its accepting configuration (owing to the fact that all accepting configurations of $\mathcal{A}$ are at the initial node). □

Corollary 1. *For every n-state graph-walking automaton over a signature with d directions, there is a strongly reversible automaton with $6dn+1$ states that recognizes the same set of finite graphs.*

The notion of a reversible automaton applies to infinite graphs as well. Unfortunately, the above construction of a reversible automaton is apparently useless in that case. Indeed, on an infinite graph, the constructed reversible GWA may, and typically will, immediately rush away from the initial node along an infinite path, perfectly reversibly and perfectly uselessly.

7 Closure Properties and State Complexity

In the case of string languages, a plenty of regularity-preserving operations are known. The study of how they affect the number of states in finite automata is known as the *state complexity*. The state complexity of all reasonable operations on 1DFA and 1NFA is known perfectly well. For unambiguous automata (1UFA) and for two-way automata (2DFA, 2NFA), there are only partial results, and many interesting problems are still open.

Closure properties of graph-walking automata are a new subject, and, at the moment, there are hardly any operations to be studied besides the Boolean operations. The existing results on graph-walking automata easily imply their closure under all Boolean operations.

Theorem 4. *Let $\mathcal{A}$ and $\mathcal{B}$ be two graph-walking automata, with m and n states, respectively, defined over the same signature $\mathcal{S} = (D, -, \Sigma, \Sigma_0, \langle D_a \rangle_{a \in \Sigma})$ with $|D| = d$. Then, there exist:*

1. *a graph-walking automaton $\mathcal{C}$ with $6dm + n + 1$ states that accepts a finite graph if and only if it is in the union $L(\mathcal{A}) \cup L(\mathcal{B})$;*

2. *a graph-walking automaton* $\mathcal{D}$ *with* $(2d+1)m+n$ *states that accepts a finite graph if and only if it is in the intersection* $L(\mathcal{A}) \cap L(\mathcal{B})$*;*
3. *a graph-walking automaton* $\mathcal{E}$ *with* $6dm+1$ *states that accepts a finite graph if and only if it is in the complement* $\overline{L(\mathcal{A})}$.

Proof (a sketch). (Union) To begin with, the first automaton $\mathcal{A}$ is made strongly reversible, so that it halts on every input at the initial node. Then the automaton $\mathcal{C}$ for the union simulates the $\mathcal{A}$, and accepts if it accepts, or proceeds with simulating $\mathcal{B}$ if it rejects.

(Intersection) By Theorem 2 and Remark 1, the first automaton is made returning. The automaton $\mathcal{D}$ first simulates it until it returns and is about to accept; if this happens, then it turns to simulating $\mathcal{B}$.

(Complementation) It is sufficient to make the automaton strongly reversible, and then exchange the acceptance and rejection decisions. □

8 Decision Problems

The most commonly studied decision problems on automata include the membership problem (whether a given automaton accepts a given input); the emptiness problem (whether a given automaton accepts any input); the universality problem (whether a given automaton accepts every input); the equivalence problem (whether two given automata accept exactly the same inputs); and the inclusion problem (whether every input accepted by the first of the two given automata is accepted by the other). In each case, the "input" is taken to be any graph over the same signature as the automaton.

The membership problem for graph-walking automata is obviously decidable in time $O(mn)$, where n is the size of the automaton and m is the size of the input. One simply has to run the automaton until it accepts or rejects, or until mn steps have been made, after which it can be pronounced looped.

The rest of the problems (emptiness, universality, equivalence, inclusion) are reducible to each other in view of the closure under all Boolean operations. Whether these problems are decidable, remains unknown. If "emptiness" is interpreted as the existence of a graph accepted by the automaton that belongs to a certain family, then, for certain families of graphs, such as for all grids, the problem becomes undecidable [29]. However, since a graph-walking automaton cannot ensure that a given graph is a grid, this undecidability is hardly relevant to the properties of automata. For the emptiness problem in the form "does there exist any graph over the signature that is accepted by the automaton?", it is unknown whether it is decidable or not.

In the special cases of 2DFA and TWA, the same problems are well-known to be decidable, One way of showing this for 2DFA is to define the *behaviour function* of the given automaton on substrings, which specifies the outcome of a computation entering a substring from the left or from the right in every possible state. Since there are finitely many such functions, one can determine the set of functions that are actually implemented on some substring. This is sufficient to decide whether any string is accepted. For TWA over k-ary trees, the algorithm is the same, using subtrees instead of substrings, and dealing with computations enterable from $k+1$ different sides. Here the number of behaviour functions is still finite, leading to the same enumeration of functions implemented on some trees.

The problem with graphs is that, for graphs of an unrestricted form, it seems impossible to have an upper bound on the number of entry points to subgraphs. Then, a full enumeration of implementable behaviour functions cannot be done, and the argument breaks down.

9 Variants of Graph-Walking Automata

This paper concentrates on one particular kind of graph-walking automata, as explained and justified in Sects. 2 and 3. What kind of other related models could be considered?

First, one can consider different definitions of graphs. Graphs may be *directed*, in the sense that some edges can be passed only in one direction. An example of a GWA operating on a directed graph is a 1DFA, in which the graph is a directed chain. Could any interesting results be obtained along these lines?

The case of infinite graphs is definitely interesting, yet all the constructions presented in this paper are valid only for finite graphs. Some new ideas are needed to handle the infinite case.

The case of an unmarked initial node does not look much different from the marked case. However, all results related to reversibility rely on the initial node's being marked. It remains to investigate whether this is really essential or not.

Leaving the form of the graphs alone, it is interesting to consider the standard modes of computation for graph-walking automata. Most models of computations, from one-way finite automata to Turing machines, have all kinds of variants: reversible, deterministic, nondeterministic, unambiguous, probabilistic, alternating, etc. These definitions apply to graph-walking automata as well. What kind of results could one expect?

As proved by Bojańczyk and Colcombet [7], nondeterministic tree-walking automata cannot be determinized, and so this holds for graph-walking automata in general. However, graph-walking automata over some signatures *can* be determinized, and, for instance, it would be interesting to characterize those signatures. The unambiguous mode of computation is yet to be investigated even for the tree-walking automata.

A kind of one-way model for graphs, the *tilings on a graph*, was considered by Thomas [29]. A tiling assigns labels to all nodes of the graph, so that the labellings of all small subgraphs satisfy certain given conditions. A deterministic graph-walking automaton, and even a nondeterministic one, can be simulated by a tiling. In the case of trees, tilings are bottom-up tree automata, and, by the result of Bojańczyk and Colcombet [7], tree-walking automata are weaker than tilings. This extends to graph-walking automata, yet some special cases are worth being considered.

10 Graph Exploration Algorithms

Since there is no GWA that can traverse any graph, this means that searching in the graph requires devices or algorithms that either use internal memory of more than constant size, or store any information in the nodes of the graph, or do both. In these terms, Ariadne's thread can be regarded as information stored in the nodes. The standard depth-first search includes both Ariadne's thread (as the stack) and marks left in the visited nodes.

Many new algorithms for graph exploration are being developed. For instance, Disser et al. [10] presented a solution using $O(\log \log n)$ pebbles and $O(\log n)$ internal states; this is one of the several algorithms obtained by derandomizing randomized algorithms for graph exploration, which were first investigated by Aleliunas et al. [3]. Algorithms by Albers and Henzinger [2], and by Panaite and Pelc [25] are aimed to minimize the number of edge traversals. Algorithms for searching in a graph with an unbounded degree of nodes have recently been presented by Asano et al. [4] and by Elmasry et al. [11].

From the point of view of automata theory, the question is: can the graph-walking automata be somehow extended to contribute to the more practical methods of graph exploration?

11 Conclusion

The study of graph-walking automata looks like a promising direction in automata theory, yet, at the moment, it is still in its infancy. There are only a few isolated results, which are useful for representing the general form of known generic ideas, but insufficient to form a theory. On the other hand, there are plenty of uninvestigated basic properties, and some of them may turn out relatively easy to determine.

A suggested possible starting point for research is finding a new special case of graphs, along with a motivation for considering it, and then investigate its basic properties. It would be particularly fortunate to find an intrinsically interesting simple case: for instance, for 2DFA, their simple case is the case of a unary alphabet [13,14,18], for which much more is known than for 2DFA over multiple-symbol alphabets. Is there such a non-trivial class of non-path graphs that could similarly drive the early research on graph-walking automata?

References

1. Aho, A.V., Ullman, J.D.: Translations on a context free grammar. Inf. Control **19**(5), 439–475 (1971)
2. Albers, S., Henzinger, M.R.: Exploring unknown environments. SIAM J. Comput. **29**(4), 1164–1188 (2000). https://doi.org/10.1137/S009753979732428X
3. Aleliunas, R., Karp, R.M., Lipton, R.J., Lovász, L., Rackoff, C.: Random walks, universal traversal sequences, and the complexity of maze problems. In: Proceedings of 20th Annual Symposium on Foundations of Computer Science, FOCS 1979, pp. 218–223. IEEE Computer Society (1979). https://doi.org/10.1109/SFCS.1979.34

4. Asano, T., et al.: Depth-first search using $O(n)$ bits. In: Ahn, H.-K., Shin, C.-S. (eds.) ISAAC 2014. LNCS, vol. 8889, pp. 553–564. Springer, Cham (2014). https://doi.org/10.1007/978-3-319-13075-0_44
5. Bennett, C.H.: The thermodynamics of computation–a review. Int. J. Theor. Phys. **21**(12), 905–940 (1982). https://doi.org/10.1007/BF02084158
6. Blum, M., Kozen, D.: On the power of the compass (or, why mazes are easier to search than graphs). In: Proceedings of 19th Annual Symposium on Foundations of Computer Science, FOCS 1978, pp. 132–142. IEEE Computer Society (1978). https://doi.org/10.1109/SFCS.1978.30
7. Bojańczyk, M., Colcombet, T.: Tree-walking automata cannot be determinized. Theor. Comput. Sci. **350**(2–3), 164–173 (2006). https://doi.org/10.1016/j.tcs.2005.10.031
8. Bojańczyk, M., Colcombet, T.: Tree-walking automata do not recognize all regular languages. SIAM J. Comput. **38**(2), 658–701 (2008). https://doi.org/10.1137/050645427
9. Budach, L.: Automata and labyrinths. Math. Nachr. **86**(1), 195–282 (1978). https://doi.org/10.1002/mana.19780860120
10. Disser, Y., Hackfeld, J., Klimm, M.: Undirected graph exploration with $O(\log \log n)$ pebbles. In: Krauthgamer, R. (ed.) Proceedings of 27th Annual ACM-SIAM Symposium on Discrete Algorithms, SODA 2016, pp. 25–39. SIAM (2016). https://doi.org/10.1137/1.9781611974331.ch3
11. Elmasry, A., Hagerup, T., Kammer, F.: Space-efficient basic graph algorithms. In: Mayr, E.W., Ollinger, N. (eds.) Proceedings of 32nd International Symposium on Theoretical Aspects of Computer Science, STACS 2015. LIPIcs, vol. 30, pp. 288–301. Schloss Dagstuhl - Leibniz-Zentrum fuer Informatik (2015). https://doi.org/10.4230/LIPIcs.STACS.2015.288
12. Fraigniaud, P., Ilcinkas, D., Peer, G., Pelc, A., Peleg, D.: Graph exploration by a finite automaton. Theoret. Comput. Sci. **345**(2–3), 331–344 (2005). https://doi.org/10.1016/j.tcs.2005.07.014
13. Geffert, V., Mereghetti, C., Pighizzini, G.: Converting two-way nondeterministic unary automata into simpler automata. Theoret. Comput. Sci. **295**, 189–203 (2003). https://doi.org/10.1016/S0304-3975(02)00403-6
14. Geffert, V., Mereghetti, C., Pighizzini, G.: Complementing two-way finite automata. Inf. Comput. **205**(8), 1173–1187 (2007). https://doi.org/10.1016/j.ic.2007.01.008
15. Kapoutsis, C.: Removing bidirectionality from nondeterministic finite automata. In: Jędrzejowicz, J., Szepietowski, A. (eds.) MFCS 2005. LNCS, vol. 3618, pp. 544–555. Springer, Heidelberg (2005). https://doi.org/10.1007/11549345_47
16. Kapoutsis, C.A.: Two-way automata versus logarithmic space. Theory Comput. Syst. **55**(2), 421–447 (2014). https://doi.org/10.1007/s00224-013-9465-0
17. Kondacs, A., Watrous, J.: On the power of quantum finite state automata. In: Proceedings of 38th Annual Symposium on Foundations of Computer Science, FOCS 1997, pp. 66–75. IEEE Computer Society (1997). https://doi.org/10.1109/SFCS.1997.646094
18. Kunc, M., Okhotin, A.: Describing periodicity in two-way deterministic finite automata using transformation semigroups. In: Mauri, G., Leporati, A. (eds.) DLT 2011. LNCS, vol. 6795, pp. 324–336. Springer, Heidelberg (2011). https://doi.org/10.1007/978-3-642-22321-1_28
19. Kunc, M., Okhotin, A.: Reversibility of computations in graph-walking automata. In: Chatterjee, K., Sgall, J. (eds.) MFCS 2013. LNCS, vol. 8087, pp. 595–606. Springer, Heidelberg (2013). https://doi.org/10.1007/978-3-642-40313-2_53

20. Landauer, R.: Irreversibility and heat generation in the computing process. IBM J. Res. Dev. **5**(3), 183–191 (1961). https://doi.org/10.1147/rd.53.0183
21. Lange, K., McKenzie, P., Tapp, A.: Reversible space equals deterministic space. J. Comput. Syst. Sci. **60**(2), 354–367 (2000). https://doi.org/10.1006/jcss.1999.1672
22. Martynova, O.: Personal Communication, April 2019
23. Morita, K.: A deterministic two-way multi-head finite automaton can be converted into a reversible one with the same number of heads. In: Glück, R., Yokoyama, T. (eds.) RC 2012. LNCS, vol. 7581, pp. 29–43. Springer, Heidelberg (2013). https://doi.org/10.1007/978-3-642-36315-3_3
24. Muscholl, A., Samuelides, M., Segoufin, L.: Complementing deterministic tree-walking automata. Inf. Process. Lett. **99**(1), 33–39 (2006). https://doi.org/10.1016/j.ipl.2005.09.017
25. Panaite, P., Pelc, A.: Exploring unknown undirected graphs. J. Algorithms **33**(2), 281–295 (1999). https://doi.org/10.1006/jagm.1999.1043
26. Rabin, M.O., Scott, D.S.: Finite automata and their decision problems. IBM J. Res. Dev. **3**(2), 114–125 (1959). https://doi.org/10.1147/rd.32.0114
27. Rollik, H.: Automaten in planaren graphen. Acta Inform. **13**, 287–298 (1980). https://doi.org/10.1007/BF00288647
28. Sipser, M.: Halting space-bounded computations. Theoret. Comput. Sci. **10**, 335–338 (1980). https://doi.org/10.1016/0304-3975(80)90053-5
29. Thomas, W.: On logics, tilings, and automata. In: Albert, J.L., Monien, B., Artalejo, M.R. (eds.) ICALP 1991. LNCS, vol. 510, pp. 441–454. Springer, Heidelberg (1991). https://doi.org/10.1007/3-540-54233-7_154

Contributed Papers

Enumerated Automata Implementation of String Dictionaries

Robert Bakarić, Damir Korenčić, and Strahil Ristov(✉)

Department of Electronics, Ruđer Bošković Institute,
Bijenička 54, 10000 Zagreb, Croatia
{robert.bakaric,damir.korencic,ristov}@irb.hr

Abstract. Over the last decade a considerable effort was invested into research on implementing string dictionaries. String dictionary is a data structure that bijectively maps a set of strings to a set of integers, and that is used in various index-based applications. A recent paper [18] can be regarded as a reference work on the subject of string dictionary implementations. Although very comprehensive, [18] does not cover the implementation of a string dictionary with the enumerated deterministic finite automaton, a data structure naturally suited for this purpose. We compare the results for the state-of-the-art compressed enumerated automaton with those presented in [18] on the same collection of data sets, and on the collection of natural language word lists. We show that our string dictionary implementation is a competitive variant for different types of data, especially when dealing with large sets of strings, and when strings have more similarity between them. In particular, our method presents as a prominent solution for storing DNA motifs and words of inflected natural languages. We provide the code used for the experiments.

Keywords: String dictionary · Enumerated DFA · Recursive automaton · LZ trie · DNA indexing

1 Introduction

A string dictionary is an abstract data structure that stores a set of strings from a corpus and maps them to a set of unique integer identifiers in a bijective manner. Conceptually, a string dictionary can be regarded as an invertible minimal perfect hashing. String dictionaries are used widely, and while the most obvious application is the indexing of a corpus, there exist a variety of diverse areas of usage that include natural language processing, information retrieval, database management, web graphs, internet routing and bioinformatics. In general, string dictionaries are used wherever it is beneficiary to replace a complex string with a single number. A very comprehensive list of applications can be found in [18].

Supported in part by Croatian Science Foundation grant No. IP-2018-01-7317 and European Regional Development Fund [KK.01.1.1.01.0009 - DATACROSS].

M. Hospodár and G. Jirásková (Eds.): CIAA 2019, LNCS 11601, pp. 33–44, 2019.
https://doi.org/10.1007/978-3-030-23679-3_3

The relevant parameters of a string dictionary implementation are the size, the look-up time, and the construction time. In order of importance, string dictionaries should be compact, allow for a fast look-up, and shouldn't take too long to construct. Recently, there has been an increased interest in research on implementation of string dictionaries [2,4,15,18]. The most comprehensive and up-to-date paper is [18], where the performances of various methods and data structures have been analyzed. In particular, hashing, front coding, FM-index and compressed tries are combined with Huffman statistical codes, Re-Pair grammar compression and/or bit-level data compression methods. However, although impressively wide in coverage, [18] does not include considerations of one data structure, the *enumerated deterministic finite automaton* (EDFA), that appears to be a natural embodiment of a string dictionary.

Deterministic finite automata (DFA) are the best representations of simple lexicons [9], and the enumeration is a simple modification that produces the full functionality of a string dictionary. Consequently, compressed enumerated DFA is a straightforward candidate for implementation of string dictionaries.

In this paper we present the analysis of the *LZ trie* implementation of a compressed automaton as a string dictionary. LZ trie is the state-of-the-art in DFA compression, and we show experimentally that *enumerated LZ trie* (ELZT) is a viable alternative to other string dictionary implementation methods. In particular, ELZT emerges as the best choice for the sets of strings with a high similarity between the strings. The examples of such string sets are natural language lexicons and collections of DNA segments.

The paper is organized as follows. In the next section we present the relevant work on string dictionaries, in Sect. 3 we describe the enumerated automaton, in Sect. 4 we give a short overview of the LZ trie automata compression, in Sect. 5 we describe the experiments, present the results, and provide a link to the code, in Sect. 6 we give some final remarks on possible usage of compressed automaton as a string dictionary, and we conclude in Sect. 7.

2 String Dictionary

String dictionary is defined as a data structure on a set S of n strings $string_i$ for $i = 1, \ldots, n$ that bijectively maps $string_i$ to i, and, inversely, i to $string_i$. Using the terminology of [18], we call the mapping operations *locate* and *extract*.

- $locate(string_i)$ returns unique i if $string_i$ is in S, and 0 otherwise
- $extract(i)$ returns $string_i$ if $1 \leq i \leq n$

It follows that $locate(extract(i)) = i$ and $extract(locate(string_i)) = string_i$. String dictionaries can be implemented in several different ways. The most obvious are arrays - combined with binary search or hash addressing, tries, and lists organized in buckets. Various less specialized data structures exist that have *locate* and *extract* as a part of their functionality. In fact, any data structure that can support rank and select operations is regarded as a string dictionary

[1,3,11,13,20]. Different tree implementations, in particular, can support *locate* and *extract* among other functionalities [1,3,20].

Such, more universal, data structures, where rank and select are only part of the functionality, are, as a rule, larger and slower than necessary. On the other hand, specialized approaches focus on the size and the look-up speed of a string dictionary, and a fast construction is advantageous. Several papers deal exclusively with the optimal implementation of a static string dictionary [2,4, 15,18]. We focus on the static string dictionaries since they can be optimized for space, and in most of the applications the set of stored strings does not change very often.

Martínez-Prieto et.al. in [18] provide a very comprehensive survey of possible string dictionary implementations, together with some novel solutions. They describe the details of various combinations of data structures and data compression methods, and provide extensive experimental results on eight different data sets. Fundamental data structures that are used are hash tables, lists, and compressed tries, combined with statistical compression, front coding, grammar compression, succinct data structures, and bit-sequence compression. Different methods are shown to be best suited for different parameters of the string dictionary usage. In particular, compressed tries are, in general, the most efficient method regarding the compression factor, but are slower to search than compressed hashing dictionaries. Some of the implementations can support prefix, suffix and substring search, but they may not be optimal concerning the size and/or the speed. With regard to this, the authors of [18] have, for each type of the experimental data, chosen one implementation as the preferred one. In all cases that is a front coded dictionary with bucket headers compressed with Hu-Tucker codes, and the rest of the buckets compressed with either Re-Pair grammar compression [16] or with Huffman coding. We refer the reader to [18] for many details of these implementations. Front coded dictionaries are regarded as the favorite method because they achieve among the best compression ratios, while the speed of the look-up is also among the best of the tested implementations. The compressed trie implementation, that in most cases produced the best compression ratio, has the disadvantage of being much slower to search.

In [18], when using tries, the associations between strings and their ID numbers are achieved by storing the ID numbers in leaves. In this way each path in the trie leads to a unique label. We will present the results obtained with compressed EDFA, where a different approach of path annotation is employed, that often leads to a better compression while still allowing for a competitive look-up speed.

3 Enumerated Deterministic Finite Automaton

A deterministic finite automaton is defined as a quintuple $A = (Q, \Sigma, \delta, q_0, F)$, where Q is a finite set of states, Σ is a finite alphabet, $q_0 \in Q$ is a start state, $F \subseteq Q$ is a set of accepting states, and $\delta : Q \times \Sigma \Rightarrow Q$ is a transition function. A DFA stores, or recognizes, a finite set of words, and is easy to implement in a compact manner while supporting a fast look-up. It is a data structure of choice for storing word lists in various applications.

We define the enumerated automaton as an acyclic deterministic finite automaton with the property that an integer N_i is associated with each state q_j, where N_i is the number of accepting states that can be reached by traversing the state q_j. Besides with the states, depending on the implementation, N_i can also be associated with the transitions δ_j in the automaton. In that case, N_i is the number of different paths that extend the current transition and lead to an accepting state. A very basic example of the enumerated DFA with numbers associated with transitions is presented in Fig. 1. This layout is in accordance with the linked list implementation of automata transitions. That is the method we use in our compressed EDFA data structure, described in the following section. During construction, every transition δ_j is assigned a counter C_j that counts the number of words, accepted by the automaton, that use δ_j. For example, in the automaton in Fig. 1 three words use transition $\delta(q_0, a)$, two words use transition $\delta(q_1, b)$, and transitions $\delta(q_2, c)$ and $\delta(q_1, c)$ are both used by a single word. When storing a set of words in a finite state recognizer, the alphabetical ordering of the input is customary and often implied when dealing with static string dictionaries.

The locate and extract functions are executed by using a counter Cnt when traversing the automaton. To perform $locate(string_i)$, Cnt is initialized to 1 and incremented while traversing the path that accepts $string_i$. When passing through an accepting state Cnt is incremented by 1, and on each branching in the automaton Cnt is incremented by the values C_j stored in the transitions that are skipped. In that manner, at the point when $string_i$ is accepted Cnt has the value i, which is the ordinal number of $string_i$ in the sorted input string set. In the example on Fig. 1, when string abc is accepted the value of Cnt is 2 since Cnt was incremented by 1 when traversing q_2, and when ac is accepted $Cnt = 3$ because it was incremented by 2 when skipping a transition out of q_1. Of course, Cnt can be initialized to 0 and then the final accepting states would also have to be counted in.

To perform $extract(i)$, Cnt is set to i, and then decremented as the automaton is traversed from the start state. In each state outgoing transitions are visited sequentially. In each transition δ_i, the value of the associated integer C_i is compared with the current value of Cnt. Depending on the result, the traversal of states and transitions continues in the following manner:

- If $C_j > Cnt$, δ_j is followed to the next state. If the next state is accepting, Cnt is decremented by 1;
- If $C_j < Cnt$, δ_j is skipped and Cnt is decremented by C_j;
- If $C_j == Cnt$, δ_j is followed to the next state. If the next state is accepting, Cnt is decremented by 1. If at that point $Cnt == 0$, the concatenation of labels on the path from start state to the current state produces $string_i$.

Using the example of the automaton in Fig. 1, the first case would apply with $Cnt = 2$ (abc) and transition $\delta(q_0, a)$. The second case would apply with

$Cnt = 3$ (ac) and transition $\delta(q_1, b)$. Finally, with the initial $Cnt = 3$, after skipping transition $\delta(q_1, b)$, Cnt is decremented by 2 and the third case is applied with $Cnt = 1$ and transition $\delta(q_1, c)$, i.e., b is skipped and ac is accepted.

Enumerated automaton is a well known concept. It has been introduced in [21] as a *hashing transducer*, and again in [17] where it was called a *numbered automaton*. Subsequently, it has often been proposed as an integrated part in more complex applications [5,6,22,25]. A detailed description of the method, with the examples, can be found in [9], in the section on perfect hashing. Bearing in mind its relative triviality, it is somewhat surprising that EDFA hasn't yet been mentioned in the context of string dictionary. Enumerated automaton is practically synonymous with string dictionary, apart from substring search facility supported by some implementations addressed in [18]. It would appear that enumerated automaton is not well known outside the field of automata research.

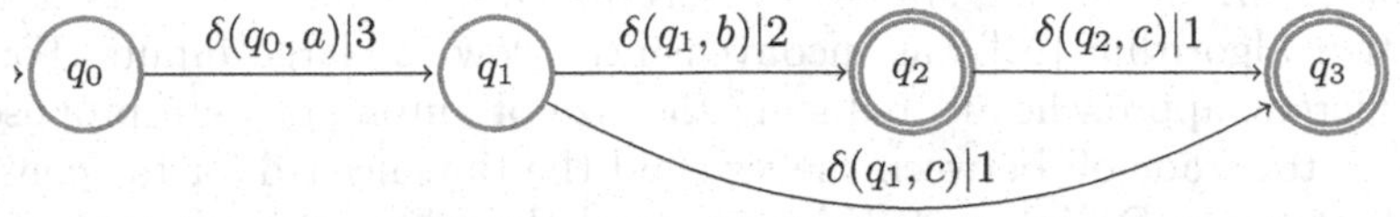

Fig. 1. A very simple enumerated automaton with numbers in transitions, recognizing language (ab, abc, ac).

EDFA has the functionality of the minimal perfect hashing function and, at the same time, its inverse. This property can be conserved both in the minimized automaton and in the compressed versions. Deterministic automata are, in general, amenable to implementations with efficient data structures that enable fast look-up and good compression. Although compressing the automaton naturally slows the look-up, this effect does not have to be very pronounced. In the next chapter we will describe the state-of-the-art method for compressing DFAs that we have used for our implementation of the string dictionary.

4 LZ Trie Implementation of EDFA

Minimization of DFA is a well researched procedure that leads to a very compact recognizer of a finite language, as the minimal automaton has no redundant states [9]. A few authors have explored the possibility of further automata compression by merging not only the states but also any repeated substructure in the automaton [8,14,24,26]. This approach has been named a *recursive automaton* in [14]. A recursive deterministic finite automaton (RDFA) is defined as $A = (Q, \Sigma, \delta, r, q_0, F)$, where Q is a finite set of states, Σ is a finite alphabet of symbols , $q_0 \in Q$ is a start state, $F \subseteq Q$ is a set of accepting states, and $\delta : Q \times \Sigma \Rightarrow Q$ and $r : Q \Rightarrow Q$ are partial transition functions. The difference from ordinary DFA is the function $r : Q \Rightarrow Q$ that denotes "recursive" transitions in the automaton. These transitions are called recursive because they act as the calls to the part of the structure itself, i.e., they are directed to a previous path in the automaton. After traversing the defined length of the addressed path, the recursive procedure returns to the point of the original recursive transition. A recursive transition can address a well formed subautomaton, or it can be used to "recycle" only a part of a state [9].

The best RDFA implementation regarding the compression factor is LZ trie[1] described in [22]. LZ trie method compresses the initial trie automaton using a general LZ paradigm of replacing the repeated parts of the structure with (shorter) pointers. The states are implemented with linked lists, as a result, the original trie and the derived compressed format can be regarded as a Mealy recognizer, an automaton that has accepting transitions instead of states. LZ trie is a succinct data structure where the compression is extended to the level of using the optimal number of bits for each component, and that supports look-up without decompression.

Although LZ trie is the state-of-the-art in DFA compression, the original construction algorithm [22] was inconveniently slow for large inputs. For this reason different approaches to reducing the size of automata were proposed in [10] as a better trade-off between the size and the time needed for the construction. In that paper Daciuk and Weis presented the work on space optimization of automata implementations from Jan Daciuk's *fsa* package [7]. Incidentally, they have also included the experiments with the enumerated versions of the automata. The increase in the size of the enumerated automaton, compared to the ordinary compressed automaton, is reported to be 23% on the average. For LZ trie, the average increase in the size of the enumerated automaton is 11% for the data sets from [18], and 38% for natural language word lists, as presented in Tables 1 and 2, respectively. Five data sets from Table 2 are the same as in [10], and, although the differences in the sizes of the enumerated and ordinary compressed automata are larger with LZ trie, the actual sizes of the enumerated automata are smaller. In this work we focus on the compression factor, for this reason, and for the lack of space, we have not included analysis of the data structures from [10] in our experiments. Nonetheless, when all parameters of string dictionary usage are considered, some of the automata methods in [10] might have a potential to be competitive to those suggested in [18].

Finally, a new algorithm for LZ trie construction, that works faster even than the solutions presented in [10], was published in [23], along with the open source code. We have augmented that software to include enumeration, and this was used in the experiments to produce *enumerated LZ trie* (ELZT).

---

[1] There exists a certain ambiguity in the literature regarding usage of the term LZ trie. As employed in [22], and in this paper, the term denotes a specific data structure (and the corresponding method of construction) - a trie compressed with a variant of the LZ method; while in [19] LZTrie denotes a trie of phrases used in LZ compression procedure. This inconsistency is due to the simultaneous publication process of the two papers.

5 Experiments and Results

We have compared ELZT with the methods highlighted in [18] on the same data sets and on the same computer. These results are shown in Table 1. Additionally, in Table 2 we present the results of the experiments on a collection of natural language word lists. Such data sets are frequent in natural language processing, but haven't been included in the test data in [18]. The hardware configuration we have used for the experiments is 3.6 GHz Intel Xeon Gold 5122 processor with 256 GB RAM. The `LZT` software we have used for the construction of LZ trie and ELZT can be found at https://github.com/dkorenci/lzt. To obtain the results for methods proposed in [18], we have used their `libCSD` software published at https://github.com/migumar2/libCSD. Incidentally, this software does not produce a compressed file as the output of the XBW implementation. We have obtained the sizes reported in Tables 1 and 2 by printing out the values returned by `XBW::size()`. Compressed sizes are given as the percentage of the original size. Look-up time is calculated as the average between the time needed for the *locate* and *extract* operations. In the case of front coding and ELZT both operations are of approximately equal speed, and in the case of XBW *extract* is, on the average, about 50% slower than *locate*. Times for the *extract* and *locate* operations were measured on a randomized inputs of 10000 words/IDs using the published software from [18] and this paper. We have emphasized in bold the best results regarding compression.

5.1 Datasets from [18]

Table 1 summarizes results for the eight datasets that were used as test data in [18]. The detailed description of the datasets can be found in [18], we give here a short overview:

Geo. names consists of 5.5 M geographic terms; *Words* is a 25.6 M words dictionary of web pages; *Word seqs.*, English (36.7 M) and Spanish (39.2 M), are two sides of the phrase table of a parallel English-Spanish corpus; *URIs* consists of 26.9 M different URIs; *URLs* consists of 18.5 M different URLs; *Literals* consists of 27.6 M different literals from a DBpedia dataset; *DNA* consists of 9.2 M DNA segments, each twelve nucleotides long.

The results in Table 1 are given as follows. The authors of [18] have singled out Hu-Tucker front coding implementation as the best compromise between the size and the look-up speed. Furthermore, following the same criterion, they suggest the bucket size in the range from 2 to 32. Smaller values yield faster look-up, while larger bucket sizes lead to a better compression. We report the results with the largest recommended value since we are predominantly interested in compression. The results for this implementation are presented in the "front coding" section of Table 1. The best compression results for different datasets were obtained with different methods for coding of the buckets: *rp* denotes Re-Pair compression, and *huff* denotes Huffman coding. The smaller bucket size would lead to a faster look-up speed (in some cases doubling it) and a faster construction, but the increase in the dictionary size would be large. For example, with the bucket size of 2, the increase in dictionary size is ×2 for *geonames* and ×6 for *URIs* datasets.

We also give the results for XBW, a compressed trie representation [12], that in all cases produces the most compact string dictionaries of all methods in [18]. In particular, the results are presented for the *XBW-rrr* variant proposed in [18] as the best for compression. (And, as it appears, this is the only variant available in `libCSD` software.) XBW method produces smaller dictionaries but it has much worse look-up time than the front coding implementations, in one case up to hundred times slower. Front coding is a good overall compromise between size and speed. In the cases where Huffman coding of the bucket strings leads to better compression than Re-Pair, the front coding method excels in the speed of construction.

Results for the enumerated and ordinary LZ trie are obtained using the compression algorithm from [23]. We give the sizes for the plain compressed LZ trie (i.e., without enumeration) as they are relevant for the approach described in Sect. 6.1. ELZT produces smallest dictionaries in half of the cases, and it appears that this method works better with larger inputs. It should be mentioned that, same as reported in [18], we haven't been able to produce XBW variant for Literals dataset with `libCSD` software. Enumerated LZ trie has the advantage of a faster lookup than XBW. On the other hand, the look-up speed is up to twenty times slower than with front coding. On the average, construction time is considerably lower than with other implementations, except for Huffman coded variant of front coding. The one exception, Literals dataset, indicate that the datasets proposed in [18] indeed cover a wide variety of data types.

5.2 Natural Language Word Lists

Table 2 presents results for six files that store lists of natural language word forms. SOWPODS is the scrabble tournament word list - it is the largest list of English words that we have been able to find. The rest of the files are a selection of natural language word lists used in [10]. They are available at https://github.com/dweiss/paper-fsa-compression.

The best front coding method for all datasets, regarding the compressed dictionary size, is the plain front coding (without Hu-Tucker) with Re-Pair compressed strings in buckets. The results for this implementation, with the bucket size set to 32, are given in Table 2. Interestingly, the compression with the rest of the front coding implementations is much worse. Obviously, coding of the bucket headers is more efficient with longer strings.

Again, for all datasets, the XBW variant produces the smallest dictionaries of all the methods from [1]. Overall, the ELZT is the most compact implementation for all word lists except for English. This is probably due to the fact that English word forms have less inflection than the rest of the included languages. It is noteworthy that with English the performance of ELZT again improves with a larger dataset.

Table 1. Comparison of the results for datasets from [18] obtained with the best overall method from [18] (front coding), the best method regarding the compression factor from [18] (XBW), and with ELZT. LZT is the compressed automaton without enumeration. Construction time is given in seconds.

		Geo. names	Words	Word seq.(en)	Word seq.(sp)	URIs	URLs	Literals	DNA
Size (MB)		81.6	257.1	983.3	1127.9	1311.9	1372.1	1590.6	114.1
Front coding	Compressed size	28.5%	31.3%	13.1%	13.1%	6.4%	10.2%	10.8%	12.6%
	Bucket coding	rp	huff	rp	rp	huff	rp	rp	huff
	Construction time	101	4	3598	7031	4	9567	974	1
	Look-up time (μs)	5	3	5	5	3	9	12	2
XBW	Compressed size	**22.2%**	**21.7%**	**9.7%**	**9.4%**	2.7%	8.2%	–	9.8%
	Construction time	200	456	2246	2686	290	2963	–	100
	Look-up time (μs)	49	36	94	104	297	151	–	25
ELZT	Compressed size	30.9%	31.7%	12%	11.4%	**1.4%**	**6.9%**	**8.4%**	**4.6%**
	Construction time	49	168	397	445	63	312	1814	14
	Look-up time (μs)	59	51	76	75	60	113	87	14
LZT size		*27.9%*	*28.0%*	*10.9%*	*10.3%*	*1.2%*	*6.0%*	*7.6%*	*4.0%*

5.3 Discussion

Compared to front coding, the sizes of ELZT implemented dictionaries vary from approximately the same to several times smaller. The look-up speed is an order of magnitude slower, and the construction time is better in most cases, except when blindingly fast Huffman codes are used. The Huffman variant is not very efficient regarding compression, except in one of the tested cases. Compared to XBW, ELZT compression is from 50% worse to 100% better, the average look-up speed is slightly better, and the construction process is much faster.

It can be observed that the relative compression efficiency of ELZT improves with the increased size of the input. Presumably, strings in larger sets are more similar to each other, and it is known that LZ trie is very efficient with similar strings [22].

The main shortcoming of ELZT is a lower look-up speed than with the front coding method. However, both implementations allow for a fast look-up and the difference may not be observable in practice. Furthermore, in real life scenarios most of the queries are performed on skewed distributions of entries - often only a small fraction of the corpus is queried for most of the time. In such cases, a cached list of queries could lead to a reduced number of searches in the dictionary and the differences in look-up speed may become unnoticeable. As a result, we believe that in the majority of applications the compression factor may be the most important parameter of string dictionary implementation.

Several implementations from [18] support prefix and suffix search, and FM index and XBW support substring search, too. With ELZT the prefix search is implied, and the suffix search is trivially solved by building the automaton from inverted strings. In principle, substring search can be implemented with rotated strings, but the size of ELZT in that case probably wouldn't be competitive.

Table 2. Results for natural language word lists. FC denotes plain front coding with additional Re-Pair coding of the buckets. XBW is the best compression method from [18]. LZT is the compressed automaton without enumeration. Construction time is given in seconds.

		SOWPODS	English	French	Polish	German	Russian
Size (MB)		2.71	0.70	2.48	17.05	2.73	9.13
Word count		267751	74317	221376	1365467	219862	808310
FC	Compressed size	24%	26.6%	19.4%	18.1%	20.3%	19.7%
	Construction time	0.2	0.1	0.1	0.7	0.1	0.4
	Look-up time (μs)	1	1	3	3	2	2
XBW	Compressed size	**15.1%**	**19.9%**	11.1%	8.7%	10.5%	9.6%
	Construction time	2	0.5	1.5	11.5	1.4	5.2
	Look-up time (μs)	22	20	27	35	29	32
ELZT	Compressed size	19.1%	26.5%	**6.8%**	**3.2%**	**9.8%**	**4.5%**
	Construction time	0.4	0.1	0.2	1.5	0.3	0.8
	Look-up time (μs)	16	20	27	33	27	22
LZT size		*14.9%*	*21.1%*	*5.0%*	*2.1%*	*7.1%*	*3.0%*

6 Additional Considerations

6.1 Run-Time Enumeration

If the storage space is critical, instead of the enumerated version, a plain compressed LZ trie can be used to emulate string dictionary. The enumeration can be performed in the run-time by traversing all paths of the automaton, counting the traversals for each transition, and storing the results in a separate table. LZT uses constant size coding, therefore only a table of size $O(T)$ is needed, where T is the number of transitions in the automaton.

This can be done at the expense of the run-time memory, and the time needed for the initialization. The time overhead approximately equals the time required for listing of all the words in the memory, which is much faster than the look-up. For large datasets, a few extra minutes should be enough for the initialization. The sizes of LZ tries are given in Tables 1 and 2.

With the variable size coding, as used in some automata implementations in [10], the additional processing would be necessary for mapping the positions of states to the counter values in the table.

6.2 Compressing a Two-Part Dictionary

A dictionary in the everyday sense consists of two parts, an entry and an "explanation". A typical example is the natural language translation table. The two sides of such a dictionary can be stored in respective string dictionaries, while ID-to-ID mappings connecting both sides are stored separately. If there is a relation between the ordering of the data in both sides, as is often the case in natural language processing, the ID-to-ID table can be efficiently compressed.

The advantages and the details of such a system are described in [22] on the example of a French phonetic lexicon. This is a compelling case of string dictionary usage, and we have implemented and published the code for this method as a separate part of the LZT software package.

7 Conclusion

Efficient implementations of string dictionaries have received an increased attention recently. However, none of the involved researchers has so far considered the enumerated automaton implementation that has been known for almost three decades. We amend this quirky omission and show how EDFA compares with other implementations. Based on the performed experiments we can conclude that ELZT, our variant of a compressed EDFA, is a competitive data structure for universal string dictionary usage, and particularly for storing DNA segments and word forms of inflected natural languages.

Acknowledgment. We are grateful to Miguel Martínez-Prieto for kindly providing data sets used in [18].

References

1. Arroyuelo, D., Cánovas, R., Navarro, G., Sadakane, K.: Succinct trees in practice. In: Blelloch, G.E., Halperin, D. (eds.) ALENEX 2010, pp. 84–97. SIAM, Philadelphia (2010). https://doi.org/10.1137/1.9781611972900.9
2. Arz, J., Fischer, J.: LZ-compressed string dictionaries. In: DCC 2014, pp. 322–331. IEEE (2014). https://doi.org/10.1109/DCC.2014.36
3. Benoit, D., Demaine, E.D., Munro, J.I., Raman, R., Raman, V., Rao, S.S.: Representing trees of higher degree. Algorithmica **43**(4), 275–292 (2005)
4. Brisaboa, N.R., Cánovas, R., Claude, F., Martínez-Prieto, M.A., Navarro, G.: Compressed string dictionaries. In: Pardalos, P.M., Rebennack, S. (eds.) SEA 2011. LNCS, vol. 6630, pp. 136–147. Springer, Heidelberg (2011). https://doi.org/10.1007/978-3-642-20662-7_12
5. Daciuk, J., van Noord, G.: Finite automata for compact representation of language models in NLP. In: Watson, B.W., Wood, D. (eds.) CIAA 2001. LNCS, vol. 2494, pp. 65–73. Springer, Heidelberg (2002). https://doi.org/10.1007/3-540-36390-4_6
6. Daciuk, J., van Noord, G.: Finite automata for compact representation of tuple dictionaries. Theor. Comput. Sci. **313**(1), 45–56 (2004)
7. Daciuk, J.: Experiments with automata compression. In: Yu, S., Păun, A. (eds.) CIAA 2000. LNCS, vol. 2088, pp. 105–112. Springer, Heidelberg (2001). https://doi.org/10.1007/3-540-44674-5_8
8. Daciuk, J., Piskorski, J.: Gazetteer compression technique based on substructure recognition. In: Kłopotek, M.A., Wierzchoń, S.T., Trojanowski, K. (eds.) IIPWM 2006. AINSC, vol. 35, pp. 87–95. Springer, Heidelberg (2006). https://doi.org/10.1007/3-540-33521-8_9
9. Daciuk, J., Piskorski, J., Ristov, S.: Natural language dictionaries implemented as finite automata. In: Martín-Vide, C. (ed.) Mathematics, Computing, Language, and Life: Frontiers in Mathematical Linguistics and Language Theory, vol. 2, pp. 133–204. World Scientific & Imperial College Press, London (2010)

10. Daciuk, J., Weiss, D.: Smaller representation of finite state automata. In: Bouchou-Markhoff, B., Caron, P., Champarnaud, J.-M., Maurel, D. (eds.) CIAA 2011. LNCS, vol. 6807, pp. 118–129. Springer, Heidelberg (2011). https://doi.org/10.1007/978-3-642-22256-6_12
11. Ferragina, P., Grossi, R., Gupta, A., Shah, R., Vitter, J.S.: On searching compressed string collections cache-obliviously. In: PODS 2008, pp. 181–190. ACM, New York (2008). https://doi.org/10.1145/1376916.1376943
12. Ferragina, P., Luccio, F., Manzini, G., Muthukrishnan, S.: Structuring labeled trees for optimal succinctness, and beyond. In: FOCS 2005, pp. 184–196. IEEE Computer Society (2005). https://doi.org/10.1109/SFCS.2005.69
13. Ferragina, P., Venturini, R.: The compressed permuterm index. ACM Trans. Algorithms **7**(1), 10:1–10:21 (2010). https://doi.org/10.1145/1868237.1868248
14. Georgiev, K.: Compression of minimal acyclic deterministic FSAs preserving the linear accepting complexity. In: Mihov, S., Schulz, K.U. (eds.) Proceedings Workshop on Finite-State Techniques and Approximate Search 2007, pp. 7–13 (2007)
15. Grossi, R., Ottaviano, G.: Fast compressed tries through path decompositions. ACM J. Exp. Algorithmics **19**(1), 3.4:1.1–3.4:1.20 (2014)
16. Larsson, N.J., Moffat, A.: Off-line dictionary-based compression. Proc. IEEE **88**(11), 1722–1732 (2000). https://doi.org/10.1109/5.892708
17. Lucchesi, C.L., Kowaltowski, T.: Applications of finite automata representing large vocabularies. Softw. Pract. Exp. **23**(1), 15–30 (1993)
18. Martínez-Prieto, M.A., Brisaboa, N., Cánovas, R., Claude, F., Navarro, G.: Practical compressed string dictionaries. Inf. Syst. **56**(C), 73–108 (2016)
19. Navarro, G.: Indexing text using the Ziv-Lempel trie. J. Discret. Algorithms **2**(1), 87–114 (2004). https://doi.org/10.1016/S1570-8667(03)00066-2
20. Raman, R., Raman, V., Rao, S.S.: Succinct indexable dictionaries with applications to encoding k-ary trees and multisets. In: Eppstein, D. (ed.) Proceedings of SODA 2002, pp. 233–242. ACM/SIAM, Philadelphia (2002)
21. Revuz, D.: Dictionnaires et lexiques: méthodes et algorithmes. Ph.D. thesis, Institut Blaise Pascal, Paris, France (1991)
22. Ristov, S.: LZ trie and dictionary compression. Softw. Pract. Exp. **35**(5), 445–465 (2005). https://doi.org/10.1002/spe.643
23. Ristov, S., Korenčić, D.: Fast construction of space-optimized recursive automaton. Softw. Pract. Exp. **45**(6), 783–799 (2014). https://doi.org/10.1002/spe.2261
24. Ristov, Strahil, Laporte, Eric: Ziv Lempel compression of huge natural language data tries using suffix arrays. In: Crochemore, Maxime, Paterson, Mike (eds.) CPM 1999. LNCS, vol. 1645, pp. 196–211. Springer, Heidelberg (1999). https://doi.org/10.1007/3-540-48452-3_15
25. Skibiński, P., Grabowski, S., Deorowicz, S.: Revisiting dictionary-based compression. Softw. Pract. Exp. **35**(15), 1455–1476 (2005). https://doi.org/10.1002/spe.678
26. Tounsi, L., Bouchou, B., Maurel, D.: A compression method for natural language automata. In: FSMNLP 2008, pp. 146–157. IOS Press, Amsterdam (2009)

New Approaches for Context Sensitive Flash Codes

Gilad Baruch[1], Shmuel T. Klein[1], and Dana Shapira[2(✉)]

[1] Department of Computer Science, Bar Ilan University, 52900 Ramat Gan, Israel
gilad.baruch@biu.ac.il, tomi@cs.biu.ac.il

[2] Deparment of Computer Science, Ariel University, 40700 Ariel, Israel
shapird@g.ariel.ac.il

Abstract. Rewriting codes for flash memory enable the multiple usage of the same storage space, under the constraint that 0-bits can be changed into 1-bits, but not vice versa. Context sensitive rewriting codes extend this idea by incorporating also information gathered from surrounding bits. Several new and better context sensitive rewriting codes based on automata are presented and analyzed. Empirical simulations show a good match with the theoretical results.

1 Introduction

One of the most popular storage media today is flash memory [1,2], and they are ubiquitous in our computers, cell phones and many other devices we use on a daily basis. Flash memory has many distinctive features that differ from those of the magnetic memory used so far, in particular, writing zeros or ones is not symmetrical: changing a 0 into a 1 is cheap and can be performed for each individual bit, whereas the switch from 1 to 0 is only possible by erasing entire blocks (of size 0.5 MB or more), and is considered as being so expensive that one tries to avoid it, or at least, delay it as much as possible.

This technical difficulty gave rise to the development of so-called *rewriting codes*, see, for example, [3,8], which try to reuse the *same* storage space, after a block of bits has already been used to encode some data in what we shall call a *first round* of encoding. When new data should be encoded in a *second round*, the question is how to use the same bits again, without having to erase the entire block before rewriting. The problem can be generalized to three or more writing rounds, all with the same constraint of changing only 0s to 1s.

In fact, Rivest and Shamir [9] suggested a simple way to use 3 bits of memory to encode two rounds of the four possible values of 2 bits long before flash memory became popular. They called these special codes *Write-Once Memory* (WOM), and we shall refer to the Rivest-Shamir code below as RS-WOM.

To measure the efficiency of a given rewriting code, we define a compression ratio, referred to as *sum-rate* in the rewriting codes literature, as the number of provided *information bits* divided by the number of actually used *storage bits*. The number of information bits is in fact the information content of the data,

M. Hospodár and G. Jirásková (Eds.): CIAA 2019, LNCS 11601, pp. 45–57, 2019.
https://doi.org/10.1007/978-3-030-23679-3_4

whereas the number of storage bits depends on the way the data is encoded. For a standard binary encoding, information and storage bits are equivalent, giving a baseline of 1. For rewriting codes, we use the combined number of storage bits of all (two or more) writing rounds, thus the above mentioned RS-WOM-code yields a ratio of $\frac{4}{3} = 1.333$. For two rounds, the theoretical best possible ratio is $\log 3 = 1.585$, see [10], and the best ratio achieved so far is 1.493 [11].

Many rewriting codes, and RS-WOM in particular, treat each encoded element independently of those preceding it. A new paradigm of *context sensitive* rewriting codes was introduced in [6] and extended and analyzed in [7], suggesting to use a Fibonacci encoding in the first round. Such a binary encoding has the property that it contains no adjacent 1-bits [5], which means that every 1-bit must be followed by a zero. This can then be exploited in a second round to store new information in these 0-bits, which can be located using their context. The resulting compression ratio, though, was only 1.19 in the best case and 1.145 at average, which is inferior even to the simple RS-WOM.

The present work introduces several new context sensitive rewriting codes and shows their performance either analytically or by means of empirical tests. They improve the previously known codes but still do not always outperform RS-WOM. The main contribution is the development of the new methods themselves, showing several techniques how the Fibonacci based rewriting codes can be extended. We did, so far, not succeed in improving the best state-of-the-art compression ratio, but other researchers might find some new variants that do, following similar ideas as those to be presented below.

The next section recalls some details of the Fibonacci WOM codes. Section 3 presents enhanced context sensitive flash codes. Experimental results are presented in Sect. 4, and Sect. 5 concludes.

2 Fibonacci WOM Codes

Any integer can be represented as a binary string in many different ways. The standard representation uses the powers of 2 as basis elements, whereas Fibonacci codes are based on the famous Fibonacci sequence, defined by $F_i = F_{i-1} + F_{i-2}$ for $i \geq 1$, and the boundary conditions $F_0 = 1$ and $F_{-1} = 0$.

Any integer x can be decomposed into a sum of distinct Fibonacci numbers, and can therefore be represented by a binary string $c_r c_{r-1} \cdots c_2 c_1$ of length r, called its Fibonacci or Zeckendorf representation [12], such that $x = \sum_{i=1}^{r} c_i F_i$. The representation of x will be unique if one starts with the *largest* Fibonacci number F_r smaller or equal to x and then continues recursively with $x - F_r$. For example, $77 = 55 + 21 + 1 = F_9 + F_7 + F_1$ so its binary Fibonacci representation would be 101000001. As a result of this encoding procedure, there are never consecutive Fibonacci numbers in any of these sums, or, equivalently, the corresponding binary representation does not contain adjacent 1s.

Fibonacci WOM codes are constructed in three stages. In the first step, the n bits of the block are transformed into a block of size $r = 1.44n$ by considering the n bits as the standard binary representation of some integer and recoding this integer into its Fibonacci representation. The resulting block will be longer, since more bits are needed, but generally also sparser, because of the property of prohibiting adjacent 1s. When the data is not needed anymore and can be overwritten, the next essential step is to fill in a maximal number of 1-bits without violating the non-adjacency property of the Fibonacci encoding. This means that in a run of zeros of odd length $2i + 1$, every second zero is turned on, and this is true also for a run of zeros of even length $2i$, except that for the even length, the last bit is left as zero, since it is followed by a 1. As a result of this filling strategy, the data block still does not have any adjacent 1s, but the lengths of the 1-limited zero-runs are now either 1 or 2, and the length of the leading run is either 0 or 1.

Finally, in the third step new data is encoded in the bits immediately to the right of every 1-bit. Since it is known that these positions contained only zeros at the end of step 2, they can be used at this stage to record new data, and their location can be identified. It has been shown that the compression efficiency of the Fibonacci WOM code is 1.194, 1.028, and 1.145, in the best, worst and average cases. In the following sections we show how the compression performance can be improved by extending the above idea.

3 Enhanced Context Sensitive Flash Codes

3.1 Fibonacci + 2 ⟶ 1

The storage penalty incurred by passing from the standard binary representation to the Fibonacci representation is a factor of $\log_\phi 2 = 1.44$, for any block size n, where $\phi = 1.618$ is the golden ratio obtained by taking the ratio of two consecutive Fibonacci numbers F_{k+1}/F_k and letting $k \rightarrow \infty$. Thus each of the n bits in the first round represents only $\frac{1}{1.44}$ of a data bit of the original data.

The best case of the WOM code suggested in [7] occurs when every second bit in the Fibonacci representation is a 1, in which case $\frac{n}{2}$ data bits can be written in the second round, giving a total compression ratio of

$$\frac{1}{n}\left(\frac{1}{1.44}n + \frac{1}{2}n\right) = 1.194. \tag{1}$$

The following simple method achieves the same ratio, but not only on a single best case input, but for *all* possible outcomes of the first writing round, which, as before, is based on writing the data in its Fibonacci representation. The second step, however, treats every non-overlapping pair of successive bits separately. There are only three kinds of possible pairs: `00`, `01` and `10`. If one wishes to write `0`, the pair is left unchanged, that is, `00`, `01` and `10` all represent the value `0` in the second round. In case one wishes to output a `1`, the pair is overwritten by the pair `11`.

Each bit in the second round is thus encoded using 2 of the n bits, which again yields the same compression ratio as in (1).

3.2 Ternary + 2 $\longrightarrow$ 1

A further improvement may be based on the awareness that the above method does not take advantage of the fact that the pair 01 is never followed by 10, suggesting to relax the requirements of the Fibonacci representation used in the first round. Instead of prohibiting the appearance of the substring 11 altogether, which is equivalent to using a Fibonacci encoding, we forbid the occurrence of the pattern 11 only at odd indices in the string (indices are numbered starting with 0), but allow 11 to appear at even indices. In other words, if we parse the string in pairs and therefore consider only pairs starting at even indices, 01 may be followed by 10, since in this case the 11 formed by the concatenation of 01 and 10 occurs at an odd index and is therefore permitted. In fact, using this encoding, every number is now represented in a ternary code using the symbols 00, 01 and 10.

In the second round, the bit stream is parsed into pairs of bits just as in the second round of the Fibonacci + 2 $\rightarrow$ 1 method of the previous subsection, so that the second round again adds $\frac{1}{2}$ to the compression ratio. To calculate the improved contribution of the first round, note that a string of k trits (ternary digits) can be used to store numbers between 0 and $3^k - 1$ in ternary representation. If each trit is encoded by two bits, an n-bit number in binary representation uses $\log(3^{\frac{n}{2}}) = \frac{n}{2}\log_2 3 = \frac{1.58n}{2} = 0.792n$ bits in the first round. The total compression ratio is thus

$$\frac{1}{n}\left(0.792n + \frac{1}{2}n\right) = 1.292. \tag{2}$$

3.3 Fibonacci + Lookahead

We revert back to the Fibonacci encoding for the first round, and suggest a different way to exploit our knowledge that 01 is not followed by 10. The idea is to consider a lookahead technique to the currently processed bit, and act according to both its value and the value of the new bits we wish to write. Denote the value of the currently processed bit by C.

As above, if it is a 1-bit that needs to be written in the second round, the following pair of bits, whose value is either 00, 01 or 10, is turned into 11. If, on the other hand, we wish to write a 0-bit, then if $C = 0$, this single bit suffices for the encoding. If $C = 1$, it must be followed by a zero, so the pair 10 can be used to encode the 0 value. Decoding of the second round is according to the automaton of Fig. 1.

As example, assume that in the first round we are interested in storing the value 112. The corresponding Fibonacci representation, 1001000010, appears on the top line of Fig. 2. Suppose the new data to be stored is the number 38 in its standard binary form, that is 100110, presented on the second line. The third line of Fig. 2 are the bits that are actually stored in the second round.

As a decoding example, consider the binary stream output of the second writing round, 1101011110, of Fig. 2. Following the decoding automaton of Fig. 1,

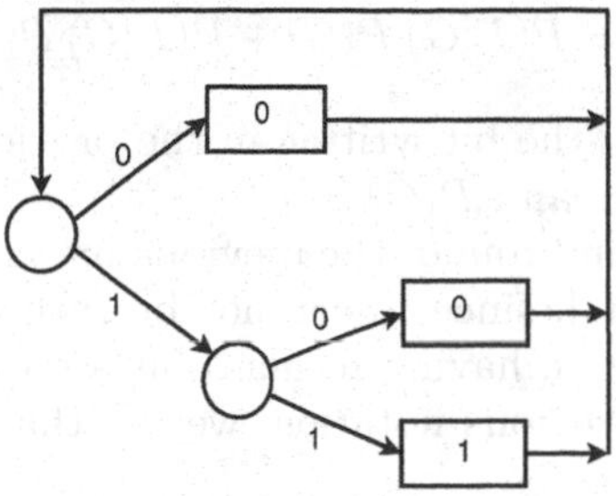

Fig. 1. Fibonacci + lookahead decoding automaton.

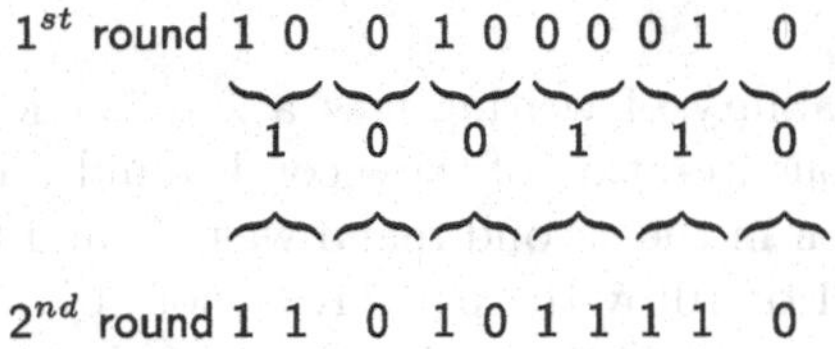

Fig. 2. Fibonacci + lookahead encoding example.

the input is parsed as 11 0 10 11 11 0, in which spaces are inserted for clarity, and the decoded output is 1 0 0 1 1 0, as expected.

In the worst case, every bit to be written in the second round will require two bits, either because a 1 is to be written, or because the currently seen pair is 10, so we get a ratio of 1.19 as already shown.

For the average case, we need to know the distribution of the pairs 00, 01 and 10 in a Fibonacci encoded strings. Denote them by p_{00}, p_{01} and p_{10}, respectively. Consider the parsing into pairs of an infinite stream of bits that has been generated under the Fibonacci constraint that no adjacent 1's appear. If we shift the parsing by a single bit, all 10 pairs turn into 01 pairs and vice versa. On the other hand, such a shift should not affect the overall probabilities of the occurrences of the different pairs, so we may conclude that $p_{01} = p_{10}$. However, since every 1-bit is followed by 0, p_{10} is equal to p_1, the probability of a single 1, which has been shown in [4] to be $p_1 = \frac{1}{2}\left(1 - \frac{1}{\sqrt{5}}\right) = 0.2764$. We can thus also derive $p_{00} = 1 - 2p_1 = 0.447$.

To evaluate the average compression ratio, we assume that the data we wish to write has a 1-bit density of q, with $0 < q \leq \frac{1}{2}$. For random data, $q = \frac{1}{2}$, which is not unrealistic, as this will be the case for most compressed or encrypted files. If $q > \frac{1}{2}$, we may just encode the 1's complement of the data.

The decoding of the second round is done by iterations processing either a single or a pair of bits. We first need to know the probability of the event F, that the first bit of a given decoding iteration is a 0-bit. This will be evaluated by conditioning on the bits written in the preceding iteration. Let G stand for the event that the last bit written in the previous iteration of the second round was a 0. We have that

$$P(F) = P(F|G)\,P(G) + P(F|\overline{G})\,P(\overline{G}).$$

But G occurs if and only if the bit written in the previous iteration was a 0, so we know that $P(G) = 1 - q$ and $P(\overline{G}) = q$.

If at the end of the second round, the previous bit was a 0, this was also true at the end of the first round, since 1s can not be turned into zeros. Therefore, the event $F|G$ is equivalent to having seen a 0-bit after a 0-bit in the Fibonacci encoding, and using our previous notation, we get that the probability $p_{\text{0-0}}$ of this event is

$$p_{\text{0-0}} = P(F|G) = \frac{p_{00}}{p_{00} + p_{01}} = \frac{1 - 2p_1}{1 - p_1} = \frac{1}{\sqrt{5}\,\frac{1}{2}\left(1 + \frac{1}{\sqrt{5}}\right)} = \frac{1}{\frac{\sqrt{5}+1}{2}} = \frac{1}{\phi} = 0.618.$$

$P(F|\overline{G})$ is the probability of writing now a zero bit knowing that the last bit written in the previous iteration of the second round was a 1. We thus know that the bit value written in the second round was a 1 and has been encoded by overwriting either 00, 01 or 10 by the pair 11. Denote by R the value of the bit pair which has been overwritten. If $R = 01$, the following bit must be a zero, so the probability $P(F|\overline{G} \wedge (R = 01)) = 1$. In the other cases, $R = 00$ and $R = 10$, and the last bit written was a 0, we thus get $P(F|\overline{G} \wedge (R = 00 \vee R = 10)) = p_{\text{0-0}}$, the probability of writing a 0 after a 0. Putting it together, we derive

$$P(F) = p_{\text{0-0}}(1 - q) + \left(p_{01} \cdot 1 + (p_{10} + p_{00})p_{\text{0-0}}\right) q \;=\; 0.618 + 0.105\,q.$$

To calculate the expected number of bits $E(N)$ to be written in the second round, note that we write a single bit only if the current bit was a 0 at the end of the first round, and we wish to write a 0-bit. Denote this event as Y, then we have $P(Y) = P(F)(1 - q)$. In fact, F has been defined relative to the second round, but as mentioned, a zero in some bit position at the end of the second round implies that this bit was also a 0 at the end of the first round. If Y does not occur, two bits will be written, so the expected number of bits is $P(Y) + 2(1 - P(Y)) = 2 - P(Y)$, and substituting the values above, we get

$$E(N) = 2 - (0.618 + 0.105\,q)(1 - q) = 0.105\,q^2 + 0.513\,q + 1.382.$$

This yields as average compression ratio $1/(\log_\phi 2) + 1/E(N)$, and in particular, for $q = \frac{1}{2}$, we get 1.295, and for $q \to 0$, the ratio approaches 1.418, which is better than RS-WOM.

3.4 Fibonacci + 3 $\longrightarrow$ 2

We now extend the methods by treating larger blocks. Instead of encoding single bits by pairs, we aim at encoding bit-pairs by triplets, as done in the RS-WOM code. Each such triplet is interpreted as one of the four possible bit pairs: 00, 01, 10 or 11, and is transformed into another bit triplet representing the following bit pair to be written in the second round.

The first round of RS-WOM encodes the four possible pair values by either 000, 001, 010 or 100. We use again the standard Fibonacci encoding, which yields one more possible triplet: 101. For the second round, the data is parsed into packages of three consecutive bits, and the translation from the given to the newly generated triplet is done according to graph given in Fig. 3. We use a color code to help the reader, where red, blue, yellow and green nodes represent the pairs 00, 01, 10 and 11. To enable viewing the differences on non-colored output, we also label the nodes with the initials R, B, Y and G of their colors. Any permutation could be used to match colors and pairs, as long as it is fixed throughout.

The nodes on the left hand side of Fig. 3 represent the possible triplets resulting from the Fibonacci encoding of the first round. A transformation from triplet x to triplet y is indicated by a directed edge (x, y), and all these transformations are according to the flash memory constraint that a 0 can be turned into a 1, but not a 1 into a 0. The white node, representing 000, has four outgoing edges, one to each color. The yellow node, representing 100, has only three outgoing edges, to the three colors which differ from yellow. Thus if we want to represent the yellow pair, the corresponding triplet is left unchanged, which is similar to the second round encoding of RS-WOM. Similarly, the green and blue nodes, representing 010 and 001, have also only three outgoing edges, to their complementing colors.

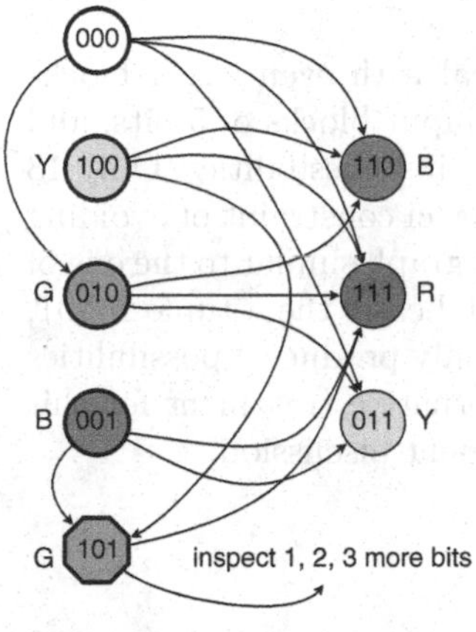

Fig. 3. Transitions for $3 \rightarrow 2$ encoding. (Color figure online)

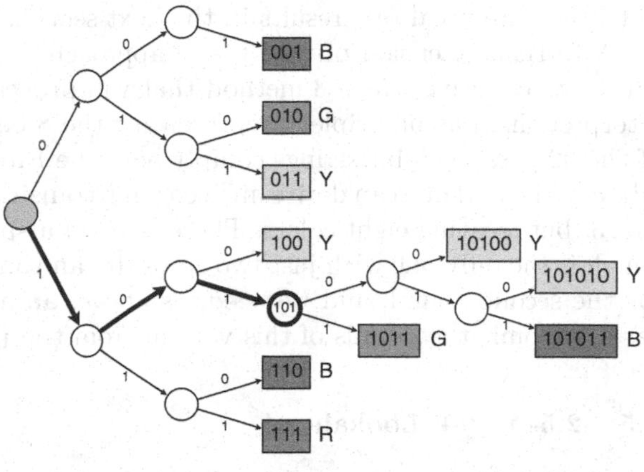

Fig. 4. Decoding automaton for the second round of Fibonacci + $3 \rightarrow 2$ encoding. (Color figure online)

If the input triplet is 101, it needs a special treatment, which is why the corresponding node appears as an octagon in Fig. 3 rather than as a circle. The problem is that it is the sole possible triplet having only a single 0-bit, so there are only two options for encoding in the second round: either leave the triplet as 101, or transform it into 111. To overcome this difficulty, since we need 4 options to be encoded, we inspect and use some of the consecutive bits. Consider the following cases:

1. If the color we wish to encode is **red**, 101 is turned into 111;
2. otherwise (green, yellow or blue), denote the three bits immediately following the triplet 101 as b_1, b_2 and b_3. Since 101 ends with a 1-bit, we have $b_1 = 0$.
   (a) If the color we wish to encode is **green**, set $b_1 \leftarrow 1$;
   (b) otherwise (yellow or blue), leave b_1 as zero. If the color we wish to encode is yellow, inspect the following bit b_2, which can be either 0 or 1. If $b_2 = 0$, leave it and use this to indicate that yellow has been chosen. If $b_2 = 1$, then we know that $b_3 = 0$. Therefore
      i. If the color we wish to encode is **yellow**, leave $b_3 = 0$;
      ii. otherwise (**blue**), turn $b_3 \leftarrow 1$.

Note that if we see 101 at the end of the second round, its origin is either (1) a 101 triplet already at the end of the first round, or (2) it may have been obtained from a transformation of 100 or 001 to encode the color green. In both cases, we need to inspect the following bits. For case (2), only one more bit is necessary, for case (1), we need one, two or three additional bits.

The decoding automaton corresponding to this encoding can be seen in Fig. 4. The initial state is the gray node at the root of the tree, and the back edges from the leaves to the initial state have been omitted. The special node 101 and the path leading to it are emphasized. We omit here the analysis of this method, but bring empirical test results in the next section.

A further extension of this $3 \rightarrow 2$ approach to deal with even larger blocks can be to conceive a $5 \rightarrow 3$ method that will process input blocks of 5 bits, and interpret them as bit triplets, representing the 8 encoding possibilities. Only 13 of the 32 possible 5-bit strings comply with the Fibonacci constraint of avoiding adjacent 1s, and one can derive an according transition graph similar to the one of Fig. 3, but treating eight colors. There is again a special case, the 5-tuple 10101, which is the only one with just two zeros. It can thus only produce 4 possibilities for the second round, and we need, as above, an alternative treatment for this case. We omit the details of this variant from the present discussion.

3.5 2.5-Ary + Lookahead

The following variant generalizes the Fibonacci approach for the first round and can then be combined with any of the suggested encodings for the second round, $2 \rightarrow 1$, $3 \rightarrow 2$ or *lookahead*. The idea is to enforce the non-adjacency property of 1-bits by simply inserting a 0-bit after each 1-bit. In other words, we encode, in the first round, a `0` by itself, but a `1` by the pair `10`. The output is then a bit sequence with the same property as the Fibonacci encoding, but we gain the additional property that there is no need to handle entire blocks, and the data can be processed as a stream, similar to the RS-WOM code.

This first round can then be combined with any of the above mentioned schemes for the second round, and we present the best combination, using the *lookahead* method described in Sect. 3.3 in the second round. That is, if a 1 bit is to be written in the second round, the following pair of bits is turned into 11, and if a 0 bit is to be written, it is encoded as 0 if the following bit is already a 0 and as 10 if the following bit is a 1.

Since the ternary approach processes 2 bits to get 3 values and a binary approach processes one bit to get 2 values, the current method which processes one or two bits to get 2 values is some compromise, so we call it 2.5-ary. At first sight, this 2.5-ary approach seems to be disadvantageous, because the storage overhead incurred by passing from the standard binary representation to this variant is a factor of 1.5 for an evenly distributed bit-stream, instead of only 1.44 for the Fibonacci encoding. However, the probability of a 1 bit may vary, and it is not necessarily equal to $\frac{1}{2}$ as for random, compressed or encrypted data. A case in point would be the MNIST database[1] of handwritten digits that is commonly used in the Machine Learning and Computer Vision communities; the average 1-bit probability in MNIST is about 0.11.

For evenly distributed inputs the worst case is, again, when every bit to be written in the second round requires two bits and the ratio is $\frac{1}{n}\left(\frac{1}{1.5}n + \frac{1}{2}n\right) = 1.167$. However, the situation is much better for the average case.

The compression ratio is evaluated as a function of two parameters: the probabilities of a 1-bit in the input stream of the first round, p_{f}, and in the input stream of the second round, p_{s}. We need, however, also the probability $p_{\mathsf{f}}^{\mathsf{out}}$ at the *output* of the first round. The number of 1s at the output of the first round remains the same as for its input, but the expected length of the encoding has changed: by substituting a 1 by two bits and a 0 by a single bit, the expected expansion was by a factor of $1(1-p_{\mathsf{f}})+2p_{\mathsf{f}} = 1+p_{\mathsf{f}}$, so we conclude that $p_{\mathsf{f}}^{\mathsf{out}} = \frac{p_{\mathsf{f}}}{1+p_{\mathsf{f}}}$, and the contribution of the first round to the compression ratio of the 2.5-ary method is $\frac{1}{1+p_{\mathsf{f}}}$.

As to the second round, two bits are overwritten for writing a 1-bit, and when writing a 0-bit in the second round, two bits are overwritten only in case 10 is encountered, and just a single bit otherwise. This sums up to an expected number of bits N_s written in the second round of

$$E(N_s) = 2\,p_{\mathsf{s}} + (1-p_{\mathsf{s}})\big(2p_{\mathsf{f}}^{\mathsf{out}} + 1\,(1-p_{\mathsf{f}}^{\mathsf{out}})\big) = 2\,p_{\mathsf{s}} + (1-p_{\mathsf{s}})\left(\frac{1+2p_{\mathsf{f}}}{1+p_{\mathsf{f}}}\right).$$

The compression ratio of the 2.5-ary+*lookahead* method is thus $\frac{1}{1+p_{\mathsf{f}}} + \frac{1}{E(N_s)}$. For example, if we assume random data with $p_{\mathsf{f}} = p_{\mathsf{s}} = \frac{1}{2}$, we get $\frac{2}{3} + \frac{3}{5} = 1.267$. However, if the data of both rounds is taken from the MNIST dataset with $p_{\mathsf{f}} = p_{\mathsf{s}} = 0.11$, the achieved compression ratio is 1.735.

4 Experimental Results

We have run the following simulation tests to check our theory. For each value i, $1 \le i \le 50$, we have randomly generated 100 independent bitvectors with

[1] http://yann.lecun.com/exdb/mnist/.

probability $q = \frac{i}{100}$ for the occurrence of a 1-bit. The number of bits in each of the vectors was set as $\frac{1000}{1.44} = 694$. Considering each vector as a binary number of 694 bits, each number was transformed into its Fibonacci encoding, simulating a 1000 bit output of a first encoding round. We then applied the various second round encodings of the previous section, again on randomly generated data, and recorded the actual number of written bits. The numbers were then averaged for each value of q, which yields the results plotted in Fig. 5 for values of $q \in [0.01, \frac{1}{2}]$. The figure also includes the curve of the theoretical performance of *lookahead*, in bold, which shows a good match with the simulated values. The curve is the inverse of a quadratic function, but it looks, for the given range, almost as a straight line.

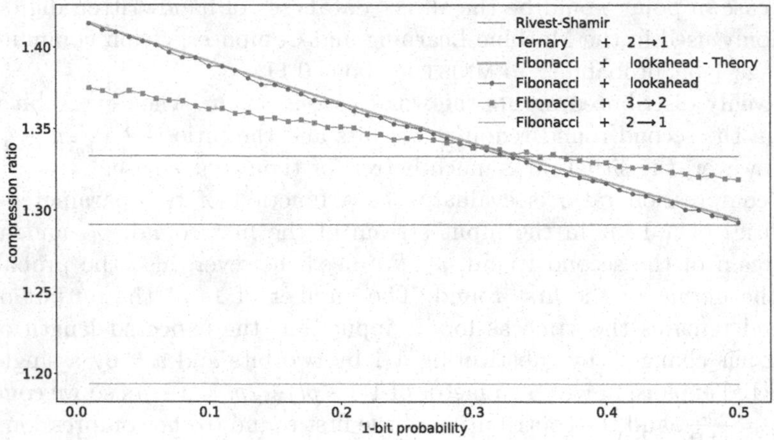

Fig. 5. Compression ratio as function of 1-bit probability.

Table 1 compares the analytically derived probabilities with the empirical occurrence probabilities on the simulated data. The first columns show the probabilities of a 1-bit, and of the pairs 00, 01 and 10, the next two columns give the performance of the 2 → 1 methods, and the last column gives the average compression ratio for $q = \frac{1}{2}$ for the lookahead method. The similarity of the two lines of the table supports the accuracy of the model assumed in our analysis.

Table 1. Comparing theoretic and simulated probabilities and compression ratios.

	1	01	10	00	Fib2–1	Ter2–1	FibLook
Theoretic	0.2764	0.2764	0.2764	0.447	1.194	1.292	1.295
Simulated	0.2759	0.2758	0.2761	0.448	1.194	1.291	1.293

The performance has also been tested on some real, not randomly generated, data. We took the first bits of each of the six categories of the Pizza & Chili

Corpus[2] and partitioned them into 100 blocks so as to let each block produce a string of 600 storage bits in a first round encoding. For RS-WOM, each block thus consisted of 400 data bits, for Fibonacci encoding, a block was of length 417 data bits and for ternary, 474 data bits (=300 trits). The bits immediately following those used for the first round were then considered as the data to be written in the second round, and we counted the number of these data bits that could be encoded. Table 2 summarizes the results.

Table 2. Comparing theoretic and real data compression ratios.

	1-bits	RS	Fib2–1	Ter2–1	FibLook	Fib3–2
Theoretic		1.333	1.194	1.292	1.311	*1.326*
Real data	0.426	1.333	1.192	1.290	1.307	1.322

The column headed 1-bits gives the average 1-bit density within the test data. The row Real data brings the empirical compression ratio for the different methods, and one can see that they very closely match the theoretical values, as if the data had been randomly generated. The Theoretic value for the Fib3 $\rightarrow$ 2 method appears in italics, because it has not been analytically derived, but obtained by simulation with $q = 0.426$.

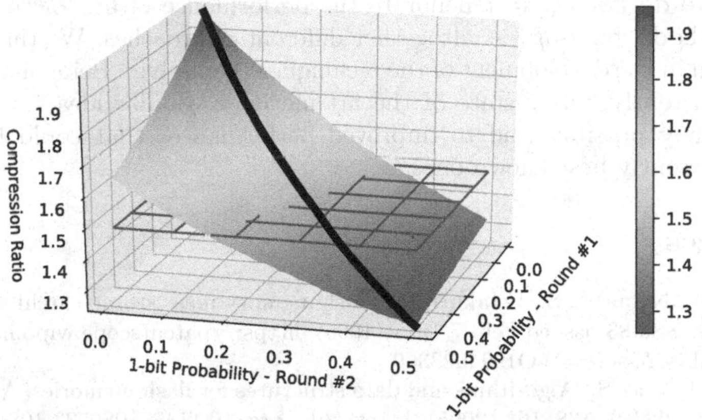

Fig. 6. Compression ratio of 2.5-ary+ lookahead as a function of the 1-bit probabilities in the first and second rounds.

Figure 6 is a 3-D plot illustrating the compression ratios for the 2.5-ary+*look-ahead* method of Sect. 3.5. To derive it, we randomly generated data with the desired probabilities for the first and second rounds and checked the resulting

[2] http://pizzachili.dcc.uchile.cl/texts.html.

compression performance. Each pair of probabilities $(p_{\mathsf{f}}, p_{\mathsf{s}})$ was tested 100 times and the results were averaged. The input probabilities are given on the x- and y-axes, and the corresponding compression ratios appear according to the scale on the z-axis. The wireframe corresponds to state of the art compression ratio, $z = 1.493$, and the black bold line crossing the surface is its intersection with the plane defined by $x = y$, corresponding to a scenario in which $p_{\mathsf{f}} = p_{\mathsf{s}}$, that is, the probabilities of a 1-bit are identical in both rounds.

5 Conclusion

We have presented several new techniques for extending context sensitive rewriting codes. Their performances are better than those of the methods of [7], but are still below the best known alternatives in the state of the art. Contrarily to other rewriting codes that are designed to yield a good compression ratio regardless of the 1-bit density of the input stream, some of the new methods presented herein take advantage of a possible non-uniformity of the input data, as may be the case for certain applications. Therefore, even though some of the compression ratios calculated above are higher than 1.493 and even than the information-theoretic upper bound of 1.585, we obviously do not claim having improved on the state of the art, since another model has been used.

It should, however, be noticed, that our challenge here is different from a situation that arises quite often in the development of new algorithms, where much effort is invested to improve a given technique, known to be currently the best. We do not try to ameliorate the performance of one of the state of the art methods, but suggest altogether different approaches. We thus see our contribution in the development of the techniques themselves. Being independent from the currently better state of the art methods, similar ideas to those we suggested may possibly lead to improved performances that could be better than the presently best known ones.

References

1. Assar, M., Nemazie, S., Estakhri, P.: Flash memory mass storage architecture. US Patent 5,388,083, issued Feb. 7 1995 (1995). https://patentscope.wipo.int/search/en/detail.jsf?docId=WO1994023369
2. Gal, E., Toledo, S.: Algorithms and data structures for flash memories. ACM Comput. Surv. **37**(2), 138–163 (2005). https://doi.org/10.1145/1089733.1089735
3. Jiang, A., Bohossian, V., Bruck, J.: Rewriting codes for joint information storage in flash memories. IEEE Trans. Inf. Theory **56**(10), 5300–5313 (2010)
4. Klein, S.T.: Should one always use repeated squaring for modular exponentiation? Inf. Process. Lett. **106**(6), 232–237 (2008). https://doi.org/10.1016/j.ipl.2007.11.016
5. Klein, S.T., Ben-Nissan, M.K.: On the usefulness of Fibonacci compression codes. Comput. J. **53**(6), 701–716 (2010). https://doi.org/10.1093/comjnl/bxp046
6. Klein, S.T., Shapira, D.: Boosting the compression of rewriting on flash memory. In: Bilgin, A., Marcellin, M.W., Serra-Sagristà, J., Storer, J.A. (eds.) DCC 2014, pp. 193–202. IEEE (2014)

7. Klein, S.T., Shapira, D.: Context sensitive rewriting codes for flash memory. Comput. J. **62**(1), 20–29 (2019). https://doi.org/10.1093/comjnl/bxy020
8. Kurkoski, B.M.: Rewriting codes for flash memories based upon lattices, and an example using the E8 lattice. In: ACTEMT 2010, pp. 1861–1865. IEEE (2010). https://doi.org/10.1109/GLOCOMW.2010.5700264
9. Rivest, R.L., Shamir, A.: How to reuse a 'write-once' memory. Inf. Control **55**(1–3), 1–19 (1982). https://doi.org/10.1016/S0019-9958(82)90344-8
10. Shpilka, A.: New constructions of WOM codes using the Wozencraft ensemble. IEEE Trans. Inf. Theory **59**(7), 4520–4529 (2013)
11. Yaakobi, E., Kayser, S., Siegel, P.H., Vardy, A., Wolf, J.K.: Codes for write-once memories. IEEE Trans. Inf. Theory **58**(9), 5985–5999 (2012)
12. Zeckendorf, E.: Représentation des nombres naturels par une somme des nombres de Fibonacci ou de nombres de Lucas. Bull. Soc. Roy. Sci. Liège **41**, 179–182 (1972)

Dolev-Yao Theory with Associative Blindpair Operators

A. Baskar[1(✉)], R. Ramanujam[2], and S. P. Suresh[3]

[1] BITS Pilani, K K Birla Goa Campus, Goa, India
abaskar@goa.bits-pilani.ac.in
[2] Institute of Mathematical Sciences, Chennai, India
[3] CMI and CNRS UMI 2000 ReLaX, Chennai, India

Abstract. In the context of modeling cryptographic tools like blind signatures and homomorphic encryption, the Dolev-Yao model is typically extended with an operator over which encryption is distributive. The intruder deduction problem has a non-elementary upper bound when the extended operator is an Abelian group operator. Here we show that the intruder deduction problem is DEXPTIME-complete when we restrict the operator to satisfy only the associative property. We propose an automata-based analysis for the upper bound and use the reachability problem for alternating pushdown systems to show the lower bound.

1 Introduction

In the use of logic as a tool for analyzing security of communication protocols, cryptography is abstracted using a term algebra. In these Dolev-Yao style models [11] for cryptographic protocols we use a term algebra containing operations like pairing, encryption, signatures, hash functions, and nonces to build terms that are sent as messages in the protocol. The adversary against a protocol is modeled as a powerful intruder who can control the entire network, and can encrypt and decrypt at will; however, the cryptographic means used are assumed to be perfect. Therefore, while the intruder may not have access to actual private keys possessed by the "honest" participants, he has access to the structural patterns of terms that may be derived from the ones sent by the participants. Since these models are used for algorithmic analysis, the following *intruder deduction problem* is of basic interest: given a finite set of terms X and a term t, is there a way for the intruder to derive t from X?

In the basic Dolev-Yao model, the main operators are pairing and encryption, but these two do not interact with each other, in the sense that the encryption of a paired term is no different from that of any other term. The Dolev-Yao model abstracts away from the details of the encryption schemes used. However, the scheme used by participants would be known to the intruder, who can well make use of this information. In Dolev-Yao theory, the terms $\{t\}_k$ and $\{t'\}_{k'}$

S. P. Suresh—Partially supported by an Infosys Grant.

M. Hospodár and G. Jirásková (Eds.): CIAA 2019, LNCS 11601, pp. 58–69, 2019.
https://doi.org/10.1007/978-3-030-23679-3_5

are assumed to be distinct, unless $t = t'$ and $k = k'$. However, this is in general not true of cryptographic schemes such as the RSA. The algebraic properties of the encryption operator may well dictate the use of an equational theory to which the intruder has access. In such a context, interaction between encryption and other operators may be important. The reader is referred to the excellent survey [10] for studies of this kind.

One way of studying such interaction is by considering an extension of the Dolev-Yao term algebra with additional operators that interact in some specific way with encryption. For instance, [12] study an Abelian group operator $+$ such that $\{t_1 + \cdots + t_n\}_k = \{t_1\}_k + \cdots + \{t_n\}_k$, i.e. encryption is homomorphic over $+$. They employ a very involved argument and prove the intruder deduction problem in the general case to be decidable with a non-elementary upper bound. They also give a DEXPTIME algorithm in the case when the operator is xor, and a PTIME algorithm in the so-called binary case.

In this paper, we study an associative blind pair operator $+$ in which encryption is distributive. This operator satisfies two equations $\{t + t'\}_k = \{t\}_k + \{t'\}_k$ and $(t_1 + t_2) + t_3 = t_1 + (t_2 + t_3)$. We show the intruder deduction problem for the Dolev-Yao term algebra with this extended operator is decidable in exponential time. The standard strategy consists of two steps. The first step is to prove the so-called **locality property** [6,8,13], if t is derivable from X, then there is a special kind of derivation (a **normal derivation**) π such that every term occurring in π comes from $S(X \cup \{t\})$, where S is a function mapping a finite set of terms to *another finite set of terms.* Typically S is the **subterm function** *st*, but in many cases it is a minor variant. The second step is using the locality property to provide a decision procedure for the intruder deduction problem.

Our system does not have an obvious locality property, so we cannot follow the standard route to decidability. The first contribution of this paper is to show a way of working around this difficulty by proving a *weak locality property*: we define a function S which maps every finite set of terms X to an *infinite* set of terms $S(X)$. We then prove all terms occurring in a normal derivation of t from X are from $S(X \cup \{t\})$, and the set of terms in $S(X \cup \{t\})$ are derivable from X is regular. This facilitates an automaton construction and yields a decision procedure for checking whether t is derivable from X. The second contribution is to settle the complexity of the intruder deduction problem by proving DEXPTIME-hardness by reduction from the reachability problem for alternating pushdown systems.

In [1], generic decidability results are given for the intruder deduction problem for convergent subterm theories and locally stable equational theories. Later in [9], similar results have been attained for monoidal theories. But our system does not belong to any of these subclasses. In [7], a generic procedure for the intruder deduction problem (deducibility) is given for arbitrary convergent equational theories. This procedure might not terminate but whenever it terminates it gives the correct answer. For the blind signature theory, this procedure terminates and it is implemented in polynomial time. But the modeling of blind signatures using the associative blind pair operator is different and hence the results in this paper. In [2], Dolev-Yao model is extended with an operator which is associative, commutative and idempotent but this operator doesn't interact with the encryption operator.

In earlier work in [5], we proposed similar system described in this paper, but we imposed a restriction on the blind pair operator: one of the components in the blind pair is always of the form n or $\{n\}_k$ where n is an atomic term and the only rule that involves distributing an encryption over a blind pair is the derivation of $[\{t\}_k, n]$ from $[t, \{n\}_{inv(k)}]$ and k. This restricted system also satisfies a locality property and using that we get a PTIME algorithm. It turns out that the considered restriction well suffices for the use of blind signatures in applications like voting protocols. In [6], the blind pair operator proposed did not have associativity property and the intruder deduction problem is DEXPTIME-complete but the operator might not satisfy associative property. The strategy is used here is similar to [3].

In Sect. 2, we present the basic definitions related to the Dolev-Yao system with the blind pair operator which is associative and in which encryption distributes. In Sect. 3, we prove a normalization result and a weak subterm property. Section 4 contains details of an automaton-based DEXPTIME decision procedure for the intruder deduction problem. Section 5 contains the DEXPTIME [4] complexity lower bound. Please refer [4] for detailed proofs.

2 The Dolev-Yao Framework and the Intruder Deduction Problem

Assume a set of basic terms $\mathcal{B}$, containing the set of keys $\mathcal{K}$. Let *inv* be a function on $\mathcal{K}$ such that $inv(inv(k)) = k$. The set of **terms** $\mathcal{T}$ is defined to be:

$$\mathcal{T} \ ::= \ m \mid (t_1, t_2) \mid \{t\}_k \mid t_1 + t_2 \ldots + t_l$$

where $m \in \mathcal{B}$, $k \in \mathcal{K}$, and $\{t, t_1, \ldots, t_l\} \subseteq \mathcal{T}$.

Definition 1. *The set of* **subterms** *of* t, $st(t)$, *is the smallest* $Y \subseteq \mathcal{T}$ *such that*

- $t \in Y$,
- *if* $(t_1, t_2) \in Y$, *then* $\{t_1, t_2\} \subseteq Y$,
- *if* $t_1 + t_2 + \cdots + t_l \in Y$, *then* $\{t_i + t_{i+1} \ldots + t_j | 1 \leq i \leq j \leq l\} \subseteq Y$, *and*
- *if* $\{t\}_k \in Y$, *then* $\{t, k\} \subseteq Y$.

The set of subterms of X, $st(X)$, *is* $\bigcup_{t \in X} st(t)$ *and its size is at most* $(\sum_{t \in X} |t|)^2$.

For simplicity, we assume henceforth that all terms are **normal**. These are terms which do not contain a subterm of the form $\{t_1 + t_2\}_k$. For a term t, we get its normal form by "pushing encryptions over blind pairs, all the way inside." Formally, it is defined as follows:

Definition 2. *The* **normal form** *of a term t, denoted by $t\downarrow$, is defined inductively as follows.*

- $m\downarrow = m$ *for* $m \in \mathcal{B}$,
- $(t_1, t_2)\downarrow = (t_1\downarrow, t_2\downarrow)$,
- $(t_1 + t_2)\downarrow = t_1\downarrow + t_2\downarrow$,
- $\{t\}_k\downarrow = \begin{cases} \{t_1\}_k\downarrow + \{t_2\}_k\downarrow, & \textit{if } t = t_1 + t_2, \textit{ for some } t_1 \textit{ and } t_2; \\ \{t\downarrow\}_k, & \textit{otherwise.} \end{cases}$

$$\frac{}{X \vdash t}\ Ax\ \ (t \in X)$$

$$\frac{X \vdash t \quad X \vdash k}{X \vdash \{t\}_k\downarrow}\ \textit{encrypt} \qquad \frac{X \vdash \{t\}_k\downarrow \quad X \vdash inv(k)}{X \vdash t}\ \textit{decrypt}$$

$$\frac{X \vdash t_0 \quad X \vdash t_1}{X \vdash (t_0, t_1)}\ \textit{pair} \qquad \frac{X \vdash (t_0, t_1)}{X \vdash t_i}\ \textit{split}_i$$

$$\frac{X \vdash t_0 \quad X \vdash t_1}{X \vdash t_0 + t_1}\ \textit{blindpair} \qquad \frac{X \vdash t_0 + t_1 \quad X \vdash t_i}{X \vdash t_{1-i}}\ \textit{blindsplit}_i (i = 0, 1)$$

synth-rules   *analz*-rules

Fig. 1. Deduction system.

The rules for deriving new terms from existing terms are given in Fig. 1. The rules on the left column is referred as *synth*-rules as the conclusion of the rules contain its premises as subterms. The rules on the right column is referred as *analz*-rules as the conclusion of the rules are subterms of the left hand premise.

We like to emphasize that the subtle difference between the *analz*-rules for the pair operator (t_0, t_1) and blind pair operator $t_0 + t_1$. If we have (t_0, t_1) then we can derive t_0 using $split_0$ rule and t_1 using $split_1$ rule. But to derive t_0 from $t_0 + t_1$ using $blindsplit_1$ rule, we also need t_1 (and similarly to derive t_1 from $t_0 + t_1$ using $blindsplit_0$ rule, we also need t_0).

Definition 3. *A* ***derivation*** *or a* ***proof*** π *of a term t from a set of terms X is a tree*

- *whose nodes are labeled by sequents of the form $X \vdash t'$ for some $t' \in \mathcal{T}$ and connected by one of the analz-rules or synth-rules in Fig. 1,*
- *whose root is labeled $X \vdash t$, and*
- *whose leaves are labeled by Ax rule in Fig. 1.*

We use $X \vdash t$ to denote that there is a proof of t from X. For a set of terms X, $cl(X) = \{t \mid X \vdash t\}$ is the **closure** *of X.*

Example 1. Let $X = \{a+b, \{b\}_k, k, inv(k)\}$ and t to be a, then the following derivation shows that $X \vdash t$.

$$\dfrac{\dfrac{\dfrac{\dfrac{}{X \vdash a+b}\,Ax \quad \dfrac{}{X \vdash k}\,Ax}{X \vdash \{a\}_k + \{b\}_k}\,encrypt \qquad \dfrac{}{X \vdash \{b\}_k}\,Ax}{X \vdash \{a\}_k}\,blindsplit \qquad \dfrac{}{X \vdash inv(k)}\,Ax}{X \vdash a}\,decrypt$$

Example 2. For the same X and t, we show a different derivation for $X \vdash t$.

$$\dfrac{\dfrac{}{X \vdash a+b}\,Ax \qquad \dfrac{\dfrac{}{X \vdash \{b\}_k}\,Ax \quad \dfrac{}{X \vdash inv(k)}\,Ax}{X \vdash b}\,decrypt}{X \vdash a}\,blindsplit$$

Definition 4. *The* ***intruder deduction problem*** *is the following: given a finite set $X \subseteq \mathcal{T}$ and $t \in \mathcal{T}$, determine whether $X \vdash t$.*

3 Weak Locality Property

As we have mentioned earlier, our derivation system lacks the locality property but we prove a weak locality property in this section and use it to solve the intruder deduction problem. Even if there are derivations of $X \vdash t$ with out the weak locality property, there will be one derivation of $X \vdash t$ with the weak locality property. Such a derivation will not have a few patterns (for example split rule will not be applied immediately after a pair rule). If any such pattern occurs, we argue there is a way to get rid of it without changing the final conclusion of the derivation. This is achieved by providing a set of transformation rules which dictate how to replace forbidden derivations by acceptable derivations. We formalize these concepts below.

Definition 5. *A* ***transformation rule*** *is a pair of proofs (π_1, π_2) such that the roots of π_1 and π_2 are the same. Any subproof that matches a pattern of π_1 is meant to be replaced by the π_2. A proof π is a* ***normal proof*** *if transformation rules in Fig. 2 cannot be applied to π. The first two transformation rules in Fig. 2 are from [6] and the last two transformation rules are included to handle the associative property of the blind pair operator. We have listed only a few transformation rules here and please refer [4] for all the rules.*

The derivation provided in Example 1 is not a normal proof as we can apply transformation rule in the third row of Fig. 2 (for blindsplit rule which is followed by the decrypt rule). On the other hand, the derivation provided in Example 2 is a normal proof as no transformation rules can be applied.

Lemma 1. *For a given $X \cup \{t\} \subseteq \mathcal{T}$, if $X \vdash t$, then there is a normal proof for $X \vdash t$.*

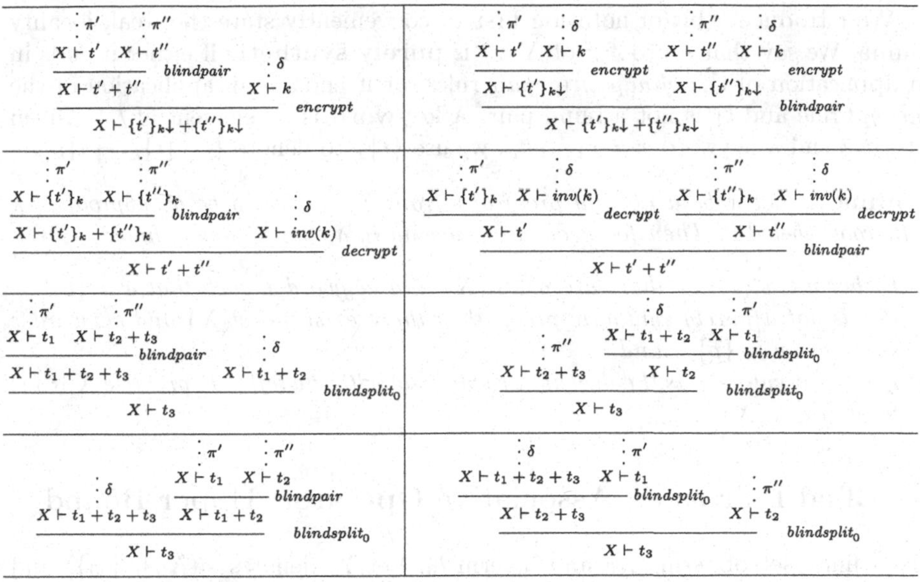

Fig. 2. Transformation rules for the associative case.

If a proof for $X \vdash t$ is not a normal proof, then we apply the transform rules in Fig. 2 as long as possible. But it is not clear whether this procedure will terminate and eventually lead to a normal proof. We define a measure for every proof such that application of transformation rule reduces the measure of the proof. This will immediately lead to that the above procedure terminates.

For every proof π, we define a measure, $d(\pi)$, recursively as follow:

- if the last rule of π is an Ax rule, $d(\pi) = 1$,
- if π has only one immediate subproof π' then $d(\pi) = d(\pi') + 1$, and
- if π has immediate subproofs π' and π'' and r is the last rule of π, then

$$d(\pi) = \begin{cases} d(\pi') + d(\pi'') + 2, & \text{if } r = \textit{blindpair}; \\ 2^{d(\pi')+d(\pi'')}, & \text{if } r = \textit{encrypt} \text{ or } \textit{decrypt}; \\ d(\pi') + d(\pi'') + 1, & \text{otherwise.} \end{cases}$$

The above definition might look cryptic at first: for instance why the encrypt/decrypt rule increases the measure exponentially. We are using the subproof δ twice on the right hand sides of the first three transformations. So additive increase will not help our objective: the measure should decrease after applying the transformation rules. But fortunately the encrypt/decrypt rule on the left hand side builds on a bigger subproof whereas the encrypt/decrypt rule on the right hand side builds on smaller subproofs. We make use of this observation and define the measure such that repeating δ on right hand side will still decrease the measure of the proof.

We introduce a bit of notation first to conveniently state the weak locality lemma. We say that a proof π of $X \vdash t$ is **purely synthetic** if either it ends in an application of the *blindpair* or *pair* rules, or it ends in an application of the *encrypt* rule and $t\downarrow$ is not a blind pair. A **keyword** is an element of $\mathcal{K}^*$. Given a term t and a keyword $x = k_1 \cdots k_n$, we use $\{t\}_x$ to denote $\{\cdots\{t\}_{k_1}\cdots\}_{k_n}$.

Lemma 2. *Let π be a normal proof of t from X, and let δ be a subproof of π with root labeled r. Then for every u occurring in δ, the following hold:*

1. *Either $u \in st(r)$, or there are $p \in st(X)$ and keyword x such that $u = \{p\}_x$,*
2. *if δ is not a purely synthetic proof, then there exist $p \in st(X)$ and keyword x such that $u = \{p\}_x$, and*
3. *If the last rule of δ is the decrypt or split rule with the left side premise $X \vdash r_1$, then $r_1 \in st(X)$.*

4 Blind Pair as an Associative Operator: Upper Bound

Fix a finite set of terms X_0 and a term t_0. Let Y_0 denotes $st(X_0 \cup \{t_0\})$ and $K_0 = Y_0 \cap \mathcal{K}$. In this section, we address the question of whether there exists a normal proof of t_0 from X_0. The weak locality property (Lemma 2) provides a key to the solution – every term occurring in such a proof is of the form $\{p\}_x$ for $p \in Y_0$ and $x \in K_0^*$.

For every $p \in Y_0$, define $\mathcal{L}_p = \{x \in K_0^* \mid X_0 \vdash \{p\}_x\}$. It is easy to see that $\mathcal{L}_p$ satisfies the following equations:

$$\text{if } x \in \mathcal{L}_p \text{ and } x \in \mathcal{L}_{p'} \text{ then } x \in \mathcal{L}_{p+p'},$$
$$\text{if } x \in \mathcal{L}_p \text{ and } x \in \mathcal{L}_{p+p'}, \text{ then } x \in \mathcal{L}_{p'},$$
$$\text{if } x \in \mathcal{L}_{p'} \text{ and } x \in \mathcal{L}_{p+p'}, \text{ then } x \in \mathcal{L}_p$$
$$kx \in \mathcal{L}_p \text{ iff } x \in \mathcal{L}_{\{p\}_k},$$
$$\text{if } x \in \mathcal{L}_p \text{ and } \varepsilon \in \mathcal{L}_k, \text{ then } xk \in \mathcal{L}_p, \text{ and}$$
$$\text{if the empty string } \varepsilon \in \mathcal{L}_{\{p\}_k} \text{ and } \varepsilon \in \mathcal{L}_{inv(k)}, \text{ then } \varepsilon \in \mathcal{L}_p.$$

If $p, p', p+p'$ are considered as states and x is accepted from p as well as p', then we want x is to be accepted from $p+p'$. To capture this we need an and edge (labeled with ϵ) from p and p' to $p+p'$. This suggests the construction of an alternating automaton $\mathcal{A}$ such that checking $X \vdash \{t\}_x$ is equivalent to checking whether there is an accepting path of x from t in $\mathcal{A}$. First we recall the definition of alternating automaton and other related notions.

Definition 6. *An* **alternating automaton** *is $\mathcal{A} = (Q, \Sigma, \hookrightarrow, F)$, where Q is a finite set of states, Σ is a finite alphabet, $\hookrightarrow \subseteq Q \times (\Sigma \cup \{\varepsilon\}) \times 2^Q$ is the transition relation, and $F \subseteq Q$ is the set of final states.*

For $q \in Q$, $a \in \Sigma \cup \{\varepsilon\}$, and $C \subseteq Q$, we use $q \overset{a}{\hookrightarrow} C$ to denote the fact that $(q, a, C) \in \hookrightarrow$. For ease of notation, we also write $q \overset{a}{\hookrightarrow} q'$ to mean $q \overset{a}{\hookrightarrow} \{q'\}$.

Given $C \subseteq Q$, *and* $x \in \Sigma^*$, *we use the notation* $q \overset{x}{\Rightarrow}_{\mathcal{A},i} C$ *iff*

- $C = \{q\}, x = \varepsilon$, *and* $i = 0$, *or*
- *there is a transition* $q \overset{a}{\hookrightarrow} \{q_1, \ldots, q_n\}$ *of* $\mathcal{A}$, $y \in \Sigma^*$, *and* $i_1, \ldots, i_n \geq 0$ *such that* $i = i_1 + \cdots + i_n + 1$ *and* $x = ay$ *and for all* $j \in \{1, \ldots, n\}$, $q_j \overset{y}{\Rightarrow}_{\mathcal{A},i_j} C_j$ *such that* $C = C_1 \cup \cdots \cup C_n$.

For $C = \{q_1, \ldots, q_m\}$ *and* $C' \subseteq Q$, *we use the notation* $C \overset{x}{\Rightarrow}_{\mathcal{A},i} C'$ *to mean that for all* $j \leq m$, *there exist* i_j *such that* $q_j \overset{x}{\Rightarrow}_{\mathcal{A},i_j} C_j$, *and* $i = i_1 + \cdots + i_m, C' = C_1 \cup \cdots \cup C_m$. *We also say* $q \overset{x}{\Rightarrow}_{\mathcal{A}} C$ *and* $C \overset{x}{\Rightarrow}_{\mathcal{A}} C'$ *to mean that there is some* i *such that* $q \overset{x}{\Rightarrow}_{\mathcal{A},i} C$ *and* $C \overset{x}{\Rightarrow}_{\mathcal{A},i} C'$, *respectively.*

We say a word x *has an accepting run from* q *iff* $q \overset{x}{\Rightarrow}_{\mathcal{A}} C$ *such that* $C \subseteq F$. *For a given* q, *is the set of words accepted by* $\mathcal{A}$ *with* q *as initial state.*

$$\mathcal{L}(\mathcal{A}, q) = \{x \in \Sigma^* \mid q \overset{x}{\Rightarrow}_{\mathcal{A}} C \text{ such that } C \subseteq F\}$$

We typically drop the subscript $\mathcal{A}$ if it is clear from the context which alternating automaton is referred to.

Now we construct an alternating automaton $\mathcal{A}$ such that $\mathcal{L}_p = \mathcal{L}(\mathcal{A}, p)$ for each $p \in Y_0$. The states of the automaton are terms from Y_0, and the transition relation is a direct transcription of the equations in 1. For instance there is an edge labeled k from t to $\{t\}_k$, and there is an edge labeled ε from t to the set $\{t + t', t'\}$. We introduce a final state f and introduce an ε-labeled edge from t to f whenever $\varepsilon \in \mathcal{L}_t$.

Definition 7. *Let* $\mathcal{A}_0$ *be given by* $(Q, \Sigma, \hookrightarrow_0, F)$ *where* $Q = Y_0 \cup \{f\}$ $(f \notin Y_0)$, $\Sigma = K_0$, $F = \{f\}$, *and* $\hookrightarrow_0$ *be the smallest subset of* $Q \times (\Sigma \cup \{\varepsilon\}) \times 2^Q$ *that satisfies the following:*

- *if* $t \in Y_0, k \in K_0$ *such that* $\{t\}_k{\downarrow} \in Y_0$, *then* $t \overset{k}{\hookrightarrow}_0 \{\{t\}_k{\downarrow}\}$.
- *if* $t, t', t'' \in Y_0$ *such that* t *is the conclusion of a blindpair or blindsplit*$_i$ *rule with premises* t' *and* t'', *then* $t \overset{\varepsilon}{\hookrightarrow}_0 \{t', t''\}$.
- *if* $t \in X_0$, *then* $t \overset{\varepsilon}{\hookrightarrow}_0 \{f\}$.
- *if* $k \in X_0 \cap K_0$, *then* $f \overset{k}{\hookrightarrow}_0 \{f\}$.

There is one issue in this automaton $\mathcal{A}_0$: if $kx \in \mathcal{L}_t$ then $x \in \mathcal{L}_{\{t\}_k}$. These cannot be represented directly by a transition in the automaton. Thus we define a revised automaton that has an edge labeled ε from $\{t\}_k$ to q whenever the original automaton has an edge labeled k from t to q. In fact, it does not suffice to stop after revising the automaton once. The procedure has to be repeated till no more new edges can be added.

Thus we define a sequence of alternating automata $\mathcal{A}_1, \mathcal{A}_2, \ldots, \mathcal{A}_i, \ldots$, each of which adds transitions to the previous one, as given by the below definition.

Definition 8. *For each* $i > 0, \mathcal{A}_i$ *is given by* $(Q, \Sigma, \hookrightarrow_i, F)$ *where* $\hookrightarrow_i$ *is the smallest subset of* $Q \times (\Sigma \cup \{\varepsilon\}) \times 2^Q$ *such that:*

1. *if* $q \overset{a}{\Rightarrow}_{i-1} C$, *then* $q \overset{a}{\hookrightarrow}_i C$.
2. *if* $\{t\}_k{\downarrow} \in Y_0$ *and* $t \overset{k}{\Rightarrow}_{i-1} C$, *then* $\{t\}_k{\downarrow} \overset{\varepsilon}{\hookrightarrow}_i C$.
3. *if* $k \in K_0$ *and* $k \overset{\varepsilon}{\Rightarrow}_{i-1} \{f\}$, *then* $f \overset{k}{\hookrightarrow}_i \{f\}$.
4. *if* $\Gamma \subseteq Y_0$, $t \in Y_0$, *and if there is an instance r of one of the rules of Fig. 1 (unary or binary) whose set of premises is (exactly)* Γ *and conclusion is* t, *then the following holds:*

$$\text{if } u \overset{\varepsilon}{\Rightarrow}_{i-1} \{f\} \text{ for every } u \in \Gamma, \text{ then } t \overset{\varepsilon}{\hookrightarrow}_i \{f\}.$$

We use $\hookrightarrow_i$ *for* $\hookrightarrow_{\mathcal{A}_i}$ *and* $\Rightarrow_i$ *for* $\Rightarrow_{\mathcal{A}_i}$

Lemma 3. *1. For all* $i \geq 0$ *and all* $a \in \Sigma \cup \{\varepsilon\}$, *the relation* $\overset{a}{\Rightarrow}_i$ *is constructible from* $\hookrightarrow_i$ *in time* $2^{O(d)}$, *where* $d = |Q|$.

2. For all $i \geq 0$ *and all* $a \in \Sigma$, *the relation* $\overset{a}{\hookrightarrow}_{i+1}$ *is constructible from* $\Rightarrow_i$ *in time* $2^{O(d)}$.

3. There exists $d' \leq d^2 \cdot 2^d$ *such that for all* $i \geq d'$, $q \in Q$, $a \in \Sigma \cup \{\varepsilon\}$, *and* $C \subseteq Q$, $q \overset{a}{\hookrightarrow}_i C$ *if and only if* $q \overset{a}{\hookrightarrow}_{d'} C$.

Theorem 1 *(***Soundness***). For any i, any* $t \in Y_0$, *and any keyword* x, *if* $t \overset{x}{\Rightarrow}_i \{f\}$, *then* $X_0 \vdash \{t\}_x{\downarrow}$.

Theorem 2 *(***Completeness***). For any* $t \in Y_0$ *and any keyword* x, *if* $X_0 \vdash \{t\}_x{\downarrow}$, *then there exists an* $i \geq 0$ *such that* $t \overset{x}{\Rightarrow}_i \{f\}$.

The number of subterms is $O(n^2)$ if X_0, t_0 is of size $O(n)$. So we have to iterate the saturation procedure at most 2^{n^2} (the number of subsets of states) times.

Theorem 3. *Given a finite* $X_0 \subseteq \mathcal{T}$ *and* $t_0 \in \mathcal{T}$, *checking whether* $X_0 \vdash t_0$ *is solvable in time* $O(2^{n^2})$ *where* $n = \sum_{t \in X_0} |t| + |t_0|$.

5 Blind Pair as an Associative Operator: Lower Bound

In this section, we reduce the reachability problem of alternating pushdown systems to the intruder deduction problem. The reduction is similar to the reduction in [6] with a few modifications.

Definition 9. *An* ***alternating pushdown system*** *(APDS) is a triple* $\mathcal{P} = (P, \Gamma, \Delta)$, *where*

- P *is a finite set of* control locations,
- Γ *is a finite* stack alphabet, *and*
- $\Delta \subseteq (P \times \Gamma^*) \times 2^{(P \times \Gamma^*)}$ *is a set of* transition rules.

We write transitions as $(a, x) \hookrightarrow \{(b_1, x_1), \ldots, (b_n, x_n)\}$. *A* configuration *is a pair* (a, x) *where* $a \in P$ *and* $x \in \Gamma^*$. *Given a set of configurations* C, *a configuration* (a, x), *and* $i \geq 0$, *we say that* $(a, x) \overset{i}{\Rightarrow}_{\mathcal{P}} C$ *iff:*

- *$(a, x) \in C$ and $i \geq 0$, or*
- *there is a transition $(a, y) \hookrightarrow \{(b_1, y_1), \ldots, (b_n, y_n)\}$ of $\mathcal{P}$, $z \in \Gamma^*$, and $i_1, \ldots, i_n \geq 0$ such that $i = i_1 + \cdots + i_n$ and $x = yz$ and for all $j \in \{1, \ldots, n\}$, $(b_j, y_j z) \overset{i_j}{\Rightarrow}_{\mathcal{P}} C$.*

We use $(a, x) \Rightarrow_{\mathcal{P}} C$ to denote $(a, x) \overset{i}{\Rightarrow}_{\mathcal{P}} C$ for some i.

Theorem 4 ([14]). *The* **reachability problem for alternating pushdown systems**, *which asks, given an APDS $\mathcal{P}$ and configurations (s, x_s) and (f, x_f), whether $(s, x_s) \Rightarrow_{\mathcal{P}} (f, x_f)$, is* DEXPTIME*-complete.*

We reduce this problem to the problem of checking whether $X \vdash t$ in our proof system, given $X \subseteq \mathcal{T}$ and $t \in \mathcal{T}$. We use $\{c\}_x \wedge \{b_1\}_{y_1} \wedge \cdots \wedge \{b_n\}_{y_n} \overset{Ass}{\Longrightarrow} \{b\}_y$, called **associative rewrite terms**, to denote the following term

$$\{b_1\}_{y_1} + \{c\}_x + \{b_2\}_{y_2} + \{c\}_x + \cdots + \{c\}_x + \{b_n\}_{y_n} + \{c\}_x + \{b\}_y + \{c\}_x + \{b_1\}_{y_1} + \{c\}_x + \{b_2\}_{y_2} + \{c\}_x + \cdots + \{c\}_x + \{b_n\}_{y_n}$$

where $c, b_1, \ldots, b_n, b$ be set of basic terms and let $x, y_1, \ldots, y_n, y$ be keywords.

Definition 10. *Suppose $\mathcal{P} = (P, \Gamma, \hookrightarrow)$ is an APDS, and (s, x_s) and (f, x_f) are two configurations of $\mathcal{P}$. The rules in $\hookrightarrow$ are numbered 1 to l.*

We define a set of terms X such that $(s, x_s) \Rightarrow_{\mathcal{P}} (f, x_f)$ iff $X \vdash \{s\}_{x_s e}$.

- *$P \cup C$ is taken to be a set of basic terms, where $C = \{c_1, \ldots c_l\}$,*
- *$\Gamma \cup \{e, d\}$ is taken to be a set of keys, such that $e, d \notin \Gamma$, and none of the keys in $\Gamma \cup \{e\}$ is an inverse of another,*
- *$X_1 = \{\{f\}_{x_f e}\} \cup \{\{c\}_d \mid c \in C\}$.*
- *$X_2 = \{\{c_i\}_d \wedge \{b_1\}_{x_1} \wedge \cdots \wedge \{b_n\}_{x_n} \overset{Ass}{\Longrightarrow} \{a\}_x \mid (a, x) \hookrightarrow_{\mathcal{P}} \{(b_1, x_1), \ldots, (b_n, x_n)\}$ is the i th rule of $\hookrightarrow\}$, and*

In the rest of the section, we assume $X = X_1 \cup X_2 \cup \Gamma \cup \{e\}$.

Lemma 4. *If $\{c\}_d \wedge \{b_1\}_{y_1} \wedge \cdots \wedge \{b_n\}_{y_n} \overset{Ass}{\Longrightarrow} \{b\}_y$ is an associative rewrite term in X_2 and $z \in \Gamma^*$ such that for all $i \leq n : X \vdash \{b_i\}_{y_i z e}$, then $X \vdash \{b\}_{yze}$.*

We can encrypt $\{c\}_d$ using the keys in ze to derive $X \vdash \{c\}_{dze}$. Using blindsplit rule on associative rewrite term, we can derive $X \vdash \{b\}_{yze}$.

Using the above lemma we can prove if $(a, x) \Rightarrow_i \{(f, x_f)\}$, then $X \vdash \{a\}_{xe}$.

Lemma 5. *For all configurations (a, x) and all $i \geq 0$, if $(a, x) \Rightarrow_i \{(f, x_f)\}$ then $X \vdash \{a\}_{xe}$.*

To prove the converse of Lemma 5, we have to prove some properties of the normal proof of $X \vdash \{a\}_{xe}$. First, we make some observations about the normal proof π of $X \vdash \{a\}_{xe}$. There are no *pair, split, decrypt* rules in π. This is easy to see from the set X and the conclusion. Most importantly, there are no *blindpair* rules in π. Since the conclusion is not a blindpair term, the transformation rules in Fig. 1 eliminate the *blindpair* rules.

Lemma 6. *Let π be a normal proof of $X \vdash \{a\}_{xe}$, for $a \in P$ and $x \in \Gamma^*$. Then any term u occurring in π is of the form $\{p\}_w$, for $p \in st(X)$ and $w \in \Gamma^* \cup \Gamma^* e$.*

The following lemma constrains the structure of rules that occur in any normal proof of $X \vdash \{a\}_{xe}$. This lemma is weaker than its counterpart in [6] as the right side premise of blindsplit may be a blindpair term.

Lemma 7. *Let π be a normal proof of $X \vdash \{a\}_{xe}$, for $a \in P$ and $x \in \Gamma^*$. Let δ be a subproof of π with root labeled r.*

1. *If the last rule of δ is an encrypt rule, then $r = \{p\}_w$ for some $p \in X$ and keyword $w \in \Gamma^* \cup \Gamma^* e$.*
2. *If the last rule of δ is a blindsplit rule, then $r = \{p\}_{we}$, where $p \in st(X)$ and $w \in \Gamma^*$.*

We now state an important property of normal proofs from rewrite systems – namely that whenever the "conclusion" of a rewrite term is provable, all the "premises" are provable too. The proof of the lemma is given in appendix.

Lemma 8. *Let π be a normal proof of $X \vdash \{a\}_{xe}$, for $a \in P$ and $x \in \Gamma^*$. Then either $\{a\}_{xe} \in X_1$ or there is a rewrite term $\{c_m\}_d \wedge \{b_1\}_{y_1} \wedge \cdots \wedge \{b_n\}_{y_n} \overset{Ass}{\Longrightarrow} \{a\}_y$ in X_2, and $z \in \Gamma^*$ such that $x = yz$, for all $i \leq n$, $\{b_i\}_{y_i ze}$ occurs in π.*

Lemma 9. *For any configuration (a, x), if there is a normal proof of $X \vdash \{a\}_{xe}$, then $(a, x) \Rightarrow_{\mathcal{P}} (f, x_f)$.*

Proof. By Lemma 8, $X \vdash \{a\}_{xe}$ means that either $\{a\}_{xe} \in X_1$ or there is an associative rewrite term $\{c\}_d \wedge \{b_1\}_{y_1} \wedge \cdots \wedge \{b_n\}_{y_n} \overset{Ass}{\Longrightarrow} \{a\}_y$ in X_2, and $z \in \Gamma^*$ such that $x = yz$ and for all $i \leq n$, $\{b_i\}_{y_i ze}$ occurs in π.

In the first case ($\{a\}_{xe} \in X_1$), $a = f$ and $x = x_f$, and it follows that $(a, x) \Rightarrow_{\mathcal{P}} (f, x_f)$. In the second case, by induction hypothesis, $(b_i, y_i z) \Rightarrow_{\mathcal{P}} (f, x_f)$, for all $i \leq n$. Combined with $(a, y) \hookrightarrow \{(b_1, y_1), \ldots, (b_n, y_n)\}$, it follows that $(a, x) = (a, yz) \Rightarrow_{\mathcal{P}} (f, x_f)$.

Theorem 5. *Given a finite $X \subseteq \mathcal{T}$ and a term $t \in \mathcal{T}$, checking whether $X \vdash t$ is* DEXPTIME*-hard.*

6 Discussion

The techniques of our paper do not seem to extend to the system with Abelian group operators, nor for slightly weaker systems where $+$ is associative and commutative, or when $+$ is a (not necessarily commutative) group operator and the term syntax allows terms of the form $-t$. The decidability results in [12] are driven by a set of normalization rules whose effect is drastically different from ours. Our rules ensure that the "width" of terms occurring in a normal proof of $X \vdash t$ is bounded by $X \cup \{t\}$. But their normalization rules ensure that the encryption depth of terms occurring in a normal proof of $X \vdash t$ is bounded by $X \cup \{t\}$. But the width of terms, represented by coefficients in the +-terms, can grow unboundedly. The rest of their decidability proof is an involved argument using algebraic methods. But the relationships between the two techniques need to be studied in more depth and might be useful to solve weaker systems and the system with an Abelian group operators. We leave this for future work.

References

1. Abadi, M., Cortier, V.: Deciding knowledge in security protocols under equational theories. Theor. Comput. Sci. **367**(1–2), 2–32 (2006). https://doi.org/10.1016/j.tcs.2006.08.032
2. Avanesov, T., Chevalier, Y., Rusinowitch, M., Turuani, M.: Satisfiability of general intruder constraints with and without a set constructor. J. Symbolic Comput. **80**, 27–61 (2017). https://doi.org/10.1016/j.jsc.2016.07.009
3. Baskar, A.: Decidability results for extended Dolev-Yao theories. Ph.D. thesis, Chennai Mathematical Institute (2011)
4. Baskar, A., Ramanujam, R., Suresh, S.: Dolev-Yao theory with associative blindpair operators, Technical report (2019). http://www.cmi.ac.in/~spsuresh/pdfs/ciaa19-tr.pdf
5. Baskar, A., Ramanujam, R., Suresh, S.P.: Knowledge-based modelling of voting protocols. In: Samet, D. (ed.) TARK 2007, pp. 62–71 (2007). https://doi.org/10.1145/1324249.1324261
6. Baskar, A., Ramanujam, R., Suresh, S.P.: A DEXPTIME-complete Dolev-Yao theory with distributive encryption. In: Hliněný, P., Kučera, A. (eds.) MFCS 2010. LNCS, vol. 6281, pp. 102–113. Springer, Heidelberg (2010). https://doi.org/10.1007/978-3-642-15155-2_11
7. Ciobâca, S., Delaune, S., Kremer, S.: Computing knowledge in security protocols under convergent equational theories. J. Autom. Reason. **48**(2), 219–262 (2012). https://doi.org/10.1007/s10817-010-9197-7
8. Comon-Lundh, H., Shmatikov, V.: Intruder deductions, constraint solving and insecurity decision in presence of exclusive or. In: LICS 2003, pp. 271–280. IEEE Computer Society (2003). https://doi.org/10.1109/LICS.2003.1210067
9. Cortier, V., Delaune, S.: Decidability and combination results for two notions of knowledge in security protocols. J. Autom. Reason. **48**(4), 441–487 (2012). https://doi.org/10.1007/s10817-010-9208-8
10. Cortier, V., Delaune, S., Lafourcade, P.: A survey of algebraic properties used in cryptographic protocols. J. Comput. Secur. **14**(1), 1–43 (2006). http://content.iospress.com/articles/journal-of-computer-security/jcs244
11. Dolev, D., Yao, A.: On the security of public-key protocols. IEEE Trans. Inf. Theory **29**(2), 198–207 (1983). https://doi.org/10.1109/TIT.1983.1056650
12. Lafourcade, P., Lugiez, D., Treinen, R.: Intruder deduction for the equational theory of Abelian groups with distributive encryption. Inf. Comput. **205**(4), 581–623 (2007). https://doi.org/10.1016/j.ic.2006.10.008
13. Rusinowitch, M., Turuani, M.: Protocol insecurity with a finite number of sessions and composed keys is NP-complete. Theor. Comput. Sci. **299**(1–3), 451–475 (2003). https://doi.org/10.1016/S0304-3975(02)00490-5
14. Suwimonteerabuth, D., Schwoon, S., Esparza, J.: Efficient algorithms for alternating pushdown systems with an application to the computation of certificate chains. In: Graf, S., Zhang, W. (eds.) ATVA 2006. LNCS, vol. 4218, pp. 141–153. Springer, Heidelberg (2006). https://doi.org/10.1007/11901914_13

Semi-linear Lattices and Right One-Way Jumping Finite Automata (Extended Abstract)

Simon Beier and Markus Holzer(✉)

Institut für Informatik, Universität Giessen,
Arndtstr. 2, 35392 Giessen, Germany
{simon.beier,holzer}@informatik.uni-giessen.de

Abstract. Right one-way jumping automata (ROWJFAs) are an automaton model that was recently introduced for processing the input in a discontinuous way. In [S. Beier, M. Holzer: Properties of right one-way jumping finite automata. In Proc. 20th DCFS, number 10952 in LNCS, 2018] it was shown that the permutation closed languages accepted by ROWJFAs are exactly those with a finite number of positive Myhill-Nerode classes. Here a Myhill-Nerode equivalence class $[w]_L$ of a language L is said to be positive if w belongs to L. Obviously, this notion of positive Myhill-Nerode classes generalizes to sets of vectors of natural numbers. We give a characterization of the linear sets of vectors with a finite number of positive Myhill-Nerode classes, which uses rational cones. Furthermore, we investigate when a set of vectors can be decomposed as a finite union of sets of vectors with a finite number of positive Myhill-Nerode classes. A crucial role is played by lattices, which are special semi-linear sets that are defined as a natural way to extend "the pattern" of a linear set to the whole set of vectors of natural numbers in a given dimension. We show connections of lattices to the Myhill-Nerode relation and to rational cones. Some of these results will be used to give characterization results about ROWJFAs with multiple initial states. For binary alphabets we show connections of these and related automata to counter automata.

1 Introduction

Semi-linear sets, Presburger arithmetic, and context-free languages are closely related to each other by the results of Ginsburg and Spanier [10] and Parikh [14]. More precisely, a set is semi-linear if and only it is expressible in Presburger arithmetic, which is the first order theory of addition. These sets coincide with the Parikh images of regular languages, which are exactly the same as the Parikh images of context-free languages by Parikh's theorem that states that the Parikh image of any context-free language is semi-linear. Since then semi-linear sets and results thereof are well known in computer science. Recently, the interest on semi-linear sets has increased significantly. On the one hand, there was renewed

M. Hospodár and G. Jirásková (Eds.): CIAA 2019, LNCS 11601, pp. 70–82, 2019.
https://doi.org/10.1007/978-3-030-23679-3_6

interest in equivalence problems on permutation closed languages [12] which obviously correspond to their Parikh-image, and on the other hand, it turned out that semi-linearity is the key to understand the accepting power of jumping finite automata, an automaton model that was introduced in [13] for discontinuous information processing. Roughly speaking, a jumping finite automaton is an ordinary finite automaton, which is allowed to read letters from anywhere in the input string, not necessarily only from the left of the remaining input. Moreover, semi-linear sets were also subject to descriptional complexity considerations in [3] and [5].

The tight relation between semi-linear sets and jumping automata is not limited to this automaton model, but also turns over to right one-way jumping automata (ROWJFAs), which were introduced in [4], as shown in [1,2]. This device moves its head from left-to-right starting from the leftmost letter in the input, reads and erases some symbols, while it jumps over others, and when it reaches the end of the input word, it returns to the beginning and continues the computation, which is executed deterministically. Most questions on formal language related problems such as inclusion problems, closure properties, and decidability of standard problems concerning ROWJFAs were answered recently in one of the papers [1,2,4]. One of the main results on these devices was a characterization of the induced language family that reads as follows: a permutation closed language L belongs to **ROWJ**, the family of all languages accepted by ROWJFAs, if and only if L can be written as the *finite union* of Myhill-Nerode equivalence classes. Observe, that the overall number of equivalence classes can be infinite. This result nicely contrasts the characterization of regular languages, which requires that the overall number of equivalence classes is finite.

In this paper we try to improve the understanding of the Myhill-Nerode equivalence relation given by a subset of $\mathbb{N}^k$ as defined in [9]. For a subset $S \subseteq \mathbb{N}$ and the induced Myhill-Nerode relation, an equivalence class is called positive if the vectors of the class lie in S. We characterize in which cases linear sets have only a finite number of positive equivalence classes in terms of rational cones, which are a special type of convex cones that are important objects in different areas of mathematics and computer science like combinatorial commutative algebra, geometric combinatorics, and integer programming. A special type of semi-linear sets called lattices is introduced. Their definition is inspired by the mathematical object of a lattice which is of great importance in geometry and group theory, see [6]. These lattices are subgroups of $\mathbb{R}^k$ that are isomorphic to $\mathbb{Z}^k$ and span the real vector space $\mathbb{R}^k$. Our semi-linear lattices are defined like linear sets, but allowing integer coefficients for the period vectors, instead of only natural numbers. However our lattices are still, per definition, subsets of $\mathbb{N}^k$. Lattices have only one positive Myhill-Nerode class and can be decomposed as a finite union of linear sets with only one positive Myhill-Nerode class. We give a characterization of the lattices that can even be decomposed as a finite union of linear sets with linearly independent period sets and only one positive Myhill-Nerode class and again get a connection to rational cones. That is why we study these objects in more detail and show that the set of vectors with only non-negative components in a linear subspace of dimension n of $\mathbb{R}^k$ spanned by a subset of $\mathbb{N}^k$ always forms a rational cone spanned by a linearly independent subset of $\mathbb{N}^k$ if and only if $n \in \{0, 1, 2, k\}$. This result has consequences for the mentioned decompositions of lattices. We show when a subset of $\mathbb{N}^k$ can be decomposed as a finite union of those subsets that have only a finite number of positive Myhill-Nerode classes. That result heavily depends on the theory of lattices.

The obtained results on lattices are applied to ROWJFAs generalized to devices with multiple initial states (MROWJFAs). This slight generalization is in the same spirit as the one for ordinary finite automata that leads to multiple entry deterministic finite automata [7]. We show basic properties of MROWJFAs and inclusion relations to families of the Chomsky hierarchy and related families. A connection between the family of permutation closed languages accepted by MROWJFAs (the corresponding language family is referred to **pMROWJ**) and lattices is shown. This connection allows us to deduce a characterization of languages in **pMROWJ** from our results about lattices and decompositions of subsets of $\mathbb{N}^k$. We also investigate the languages accepted by MROWJFAs and related languages families for the special case of a binary input alphabet and get in some cases different or stronger results than for arbitrary alphabets. We can show that each permutation closed semi-linear language (these are exactly the languages accepted by jumping finite automata) over a binary alphabet is accepted by a counter automaton. Furthermore, each language over a binary alphabet accepted by a ROWJFA is also accepted by a realtime deterministic counter automaton. Our results for lattices lead to a characterization, which is stronger than the one for arbitrary alphabets, of the languages over binary alphabets in **pMROWJ**: these are exactly the languages that are a finite union of permutation closed languages accepted by ROWJFAs, which are characterized by positive Myhill-Nerode classes as stated above.

2 Preliminaries

We use $\subseteq$ for inclusion and $\subset$ for proper inclusion of sets. For a binary relation $\sim$ let $\sim^+$ and $\sim^*$ denote the transitive closure of $\sim$ and the transitive-reflexive closure of $\sim$, respectively. In the standard manner, $\sim$ is extended to $\sim^n$, where $n \geq 0$. Let $\mathbb{Z}$ be the set of integers, $\mathbb{R}$ be the set of real numbers, and $\mathbb{N}$ ($\mathbb{R}_{\geq 0}$, respectively) be the set of integers (real numbers, respectively) which are non-negative. Let $k \geq 0$. For the set $T \subseteq \{1, 2, \ldots, k\}$ with $T = \{t_1, t_2, \ldots, t_\ell\}$ and $t_1 < t_2 < \cdots < t_\ell$ we define $\pi_{k,T} : \mathbb{N}^k \to \mathbb{N}^{|T|}$ as $\pi_{k,T}(\boldsymbol{x}_1, \boldsymbol{x}_2, \ldots, \boldsymbol{x}_k) = (\boldsymbol{x}_{t_1}, \boldsymbol{x}_{t_2}, \ldots, \boldsymbol{x}_{t_{|T|}})$. The elements of $\mathbb{R}^k$ can be partially ordered by the $\leq$-relation on vectors. For vectors $\boldsymbol{x}$ and $\boldsymbol{y}$ with $\boldsymbol{x}, \boldsymbol{y} \in \mathbb{R}^k$ we write $\boldsymbol{x} \leq \boldsymbol{y}$ if all components of $\boldsymbol{x}$ are less or equal to the corresponding components of $\boldsymbol{y}$. For a set $S \subseteq \mathbb{R}^k$ let $\mathsf{span}(S)$ be the intersection of all linear subspaces of $\mathbb{R}^k$ that are supersets of S. This vector space is also called the *linear subspace of* $\mathbb{R}^k$ spanned by S. For a linear subspace V of $\mathbb{R}^k$ let $\dim(V)$ be the dimension of V. For a finite $S \subseteq \mathbb{Z}^k$ the *rational cone spanned by* S is

$\mathsf{cone}(S) = \{\sum_{x_i \in S} \lambda_i \cdot \boldsymbol{x_i} \mid \lambda_i \in \mathbb{R}_{\geq 0}\} \subseteq \mathbb{R}^k$. A *linearly independent rational cone* in $\mathbb{R}^k$ is a set of the form $\mathsf{cone}(S)$ for a linearly independent $S \subseteq \mathbb{Z}^k$. Each rational cone is a finite union of linearly independent rational cones, see for example [15].

For a $\boldsymbol{c} \in \mathbb{N}^k$ and a finite $P \subseteq \mathbb{N}^k$ let $\mathsf{L}(\boldsymbol{c}, P) = \{\boldsymbol{c} + \sum_{x_i \in P} \lambda_i \cdot \boldsymbol{x_i} \mid \lambda_i \in \mathbb{N}\}$ and $\mathsf{La}(\boldsymbol{c}, P) = \{\boldsymbol{c} + \sum_{x_i \in P} \lambda_i \cdot \boldsymbol{x_i} \mid \lambda_i \in \mathbb{Z}\} \cap \mathbb{N}^k$. By definition, $\mathsf{L}(\boldsymbol{c}, P) \subseteq \mathsf{La}(\boldsymbol{c}, P)$. The vector c is called the *constant vector* whereas the set P is called the set of *periods* of $\mathsf{L}(\boldsymbol{c}, P)$ and of $\mathsf{La}(\boldsymbol{c}, P)$. Sets of the form $\mathsf{L}(\boldsymbol{c}, P)$, for a $\boldsymbol{c} \in \mathbb{N}^k$ and a finite $P \subseteq \mathbb{N}^k$, are called *linear* subsets of $\mathbb{N}^k$, while sets of the form $\mathsf{La}(\boldsymbol{c}, P)$ are called *lattices.* A subset of $\mathbb{N}^k$ is said to be *semi-linear* if it is a finite union of linear subsets. For a $\boldsymbol{c} \in \mathbb{N}^k$, $n \geq 0$, and $\boldsymbol{x_1}, \boldsymbol{x_2}, \ldots, \boldsymbol{x_n} \in \mathbb{N}^k$ we have that $\mathsf{La}(\boldsymbol{c}, \{\boldsymbol{x_1}, \boldsymbol{x_2}, \ldots, \boldsymbol{x_n}\})$ is equal to the set of all $\boldsymbol{y} \in \mathbb{N}^k$ such that there exists $\lambda_1, \mu_1, \lambda_2, \mu_2, \ldots, \lambda_n, \mu_n \in \mathbb{N}$ with $\boldsymbol{c} + \sum_{i=1}^{n} \lambda_i \boldsymbol{x_i} = \boldsymbol{y} + \sum_{i=1}^{n} \mu_i \boldsymbol{x_i}$, which is a Presburger set. Since the Presburger sets are exactly the semi-linear sets by [10], every lattice is semi-linear. In order to explain our definitions we give an example.

Example 1. Consider the vector $\boldsymbol{c} = (4, 4)$ and the period vectors $\boldsymbol{p_1} = (1, 2)$ and $\boldsymbol{p_2} = (2, 0)$. A graphical presentation of the linear set $\mathsf{L}(\boldsymbol{c}, P)$ with $P = \{\boldsymbol{p_1}, \boldsymbol{p_2}\}$ is given on the left of Fig. 1. The constant vector $\boldsymbol{c}$ is drawn as a dashed arrow and both periods $\boldsymbol{p_1}$ and $\boldsymbol{p_2}$ are depicted as solid arrows. The dots indicate the elements that belong to $\mathsf{L}(\boldsymbol{c}, P)$. The lattice $\mathsf{La}(\boldsymbol{c}, P)$ is drawn in the middle of Fig. 1. Again, the constant vector is dashed, while both periods are solid arrows. Since now integer coefficients are allowed, there are new elements compared to $\mathsf{L}(\boldsymbol{c}, P)$ that belong to $\mathsf{La}(\boldsymbol{c}, P)$. On the right of Fig. 1 it is shown that $\mathsf{La}(\boldsymbol{c}, P)$ can be written as a linear set by using the constant vector $\boldsymbol{0}$ and the three period vectors drawn as solid arrows, that is, $\mathsf{La}(\boldsymbol{c}, P) = \mathsf{L}(\boldsymbol{0}, \{\boldsymbol{p_1}, \boldsymbol{p_2}, \boldsymbol{p_3}\})$, where $\boldsymbol{p_3} = (0, 2)$. □

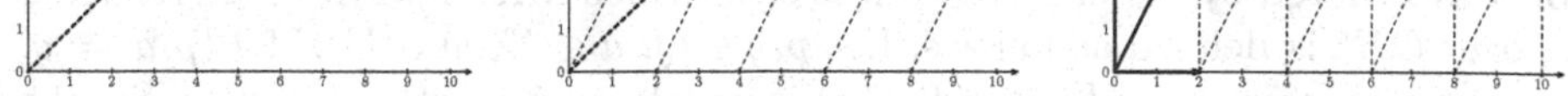

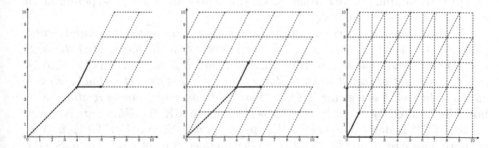

Fig. 1. The linear set $\mathsf{L}(\boldsymbol{c}, P)$ with $\boldsymbol{c} = (4, 4)$ and $P = \{\boldsymbol{p_1}, \boldsymbol{p_2}\}$, where $\boldsymbol{p_1} = (1, 2)$ and $\boldsymbol{p_2} = (2, 0)$ drawn on the left. The black dots indicate membership in $\mathsf{L}(\boldsymbol{c}, P)$. The lattice set $\mathsf{La}(\boldsymbol{c}, P)$ is depicted in the middle. Here the black dots refer to membership in $\mathsf{La}(\boldsymbol{c}, P)$. On the right a representation of $\mathsf{La}(\boldsymbol{c}, P)$ as a linear set is shown. The constant vector $\boldsymbol{0}$ is not shown and the period vectors are drawn as solid arrows.

An important result about semi-linear sets is that each semi-linear set can be written as a finite union of linear sets with linearly independent period sets [8]:

Theorem 2. *Let $k \geq 0$ and $S \subseteq \mathbb{N}^k$ be a semi-linear set. Then, there is $m \geq 0$, vectors $\mathbf{c_1}, \mathbf{c_2}, \ldots, \mathbf{c_m} \in \mathbb{N}^k$, and linearly independent sets $P_1, P_2, \ldots, P_m \subseteq \mathbb{N}^k$ such that $S = \bigcup_{i=1}^{m} \mathsf{L}(\mathbf{c}_i, P_i)$.*

Now, we recall some basic definitions from formal language theory. Let Σ be an alphabet. Then Σ^* is the set of all words over Σ, including the empty word λ. For a language $L \subseteq \Sigma^*$ define the set $\mathsf{perm}(L) = \cup_{w \in L} \mathsf{perm}(w)$, where $\mathsf{perm}(w) = \{\, v \in \Sigma^* \mid v$ is a permutation of $w \,\}$. A language L is called *permutation closed* if $L = \mathsf{perm}(L)$. The length of a word $w \in \Sigma^*$ is denoted by $|w|$. For the number of occurrences of a symbol a in w we use the notation $|w|_a$. If Σ is the ordered alphabet $\Sigma = \{a_1, a_2, \ldots, a_k\}$, the *Parikh-mapping* $\psi : \Sigma^* \to \mathbb{N}^k$ is the function defined by $w \mapsto (|w|_{a_1}, |w|_{a_2}, \ldots, |w|_{a_k})$. The set $\psi(L)$ is called the *Parikh-image* of L. A language $L \subseteq \Sigma^*$ is called *semi-linear* if its Parikh-image $\psi(L)$ is a semi-linear set.

Let M be a monoid, i.e., a set with an associative binary operation and an identity element. For a subset $L \subseteq M$ let $\sim_L$ be the *Myhill-Nerode equivalence relation* on M. So, for two elements $v, w \in M$, we have $v \sim_L w$ if, for all $u \in M$, the equivalence $vu \in L \Leftrightarrow wu \in L$ holds. For $w \in M$, we call the equivalence class $[w]_{\sim_L}$ *positive* if $w \in L$. For $k \geq 0$ and $M = \mathbb{N}^k$ the equivalence relation $\sim_L$ will be written as $\equiv_L$, because that is the notation of this relation on $\mathbb{N}^k$ in [9]. If $L \subseteq \Sigma^*$ is a permutation closed language and $v, w \in L$ we have $v \sim_L w$ if and only if $\psi(v) \equiv_{\psi(L)} \psi(w)$. So, the language L is regular if and only if $\mathbb{N}^{|\Sigma|} / \equiv_{\psi(L)}$ is finite.

Let **REG**, **DCF**, **CF**, and **CS** be the families of regular, deterministic context-free, context-free, and context-sensitive languages. Moreover, we are interested in families of permutation closed languages. These language families are referred to by a prefix **p**. E.g., **pREG** denotes the language family of all permutation closed regular languages. Let **JFA** be the family of all languages accepted by jumping finite automata, see [13]. These are exactly the permutation closed semi-linear languages.

A *right one-way jumping finite automaton with multiple initial states* (MROWJFA) is a tuple $A = (Q, \Sigma, R, S, F)$, where Q is the *finite set of states*, Σ is the *finite input alphabet*, $\Sigma \cap Q = \emptyset$, R is a *partial function* from $Q \times \Sigma$ to Q, $S \subseteq Q$ is the *set of initial or start states*, and $F \subseteq Q$ is the *set of final states*. A *configuration* of A is a string in $Q\Sigma^*$. The *right one-way jumping relation*, symbolically denoted by $\circlearrowright_A$ or just $\circlearrowright$ if it is clear which MROWJFA we are referring to, over $Q\Sigma^*$ is defined as follows. Let $p, q \in Q$, $a \in \Sigma$, $w \in \Sigma^*$. If $R(p, a) = q$, then we have $paw \circlearrowright qw$. In case $R(p, a)$ is undefined, we get $paw \circlearrowright pwa$. So, the automaton jumps over a symbol, when it cannot be read. The *language accepted* by A is

$$L_R(A) = \{\, w \in \Sigma^* \mid \exists s \in S, f \in F : sw \circlearrowright^* f \,\}.$$

We say that A *accepts* $w \in \Sigma^*$ if $w \in L_R(A)$ and that A *rejects* w otherwise. Let **MROWJ** be the family of all languages that are accepted by MROWJFAs.

Furthermore, in case the MROWJFA has a single initial state, i.e., $|S| = 1$, then we simply speak of a right one-way jumping automaton (ROWJFA) and refer to the family of languages accepted by ROWJFAs by **ROWJ**. Obviously, by definition we have $\mathbf{ROWJ} \subseteq \mathbf{MROWJ}$. We give an example of a ROWJFA:

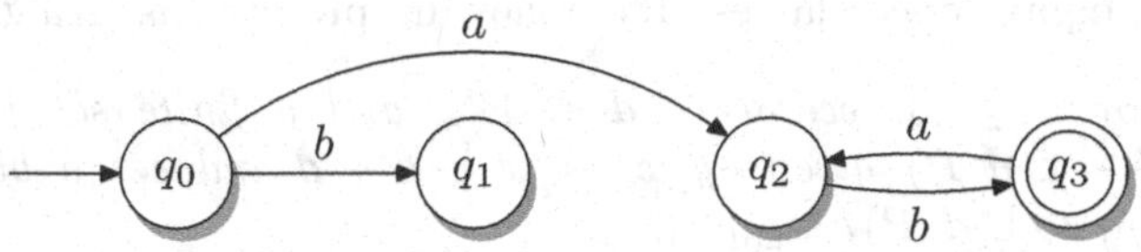

Fig. 2. The ROWJFA A.

Example 3. Let A be the ROWJFA $A = (\{q_0, q_1, q_2, q_3\}, \{a, b\}, R, q_0, \{q_3\})$, where the set R consists of the rules $q_0 b \to q_1$, $q_0 a \to q_2$, $q_2 b \to q_3$, and $q_3 a \to q_2$. The automaton A is depicted in Fig. 2. To show how ROWJFAs work, we give an example computation of A on the input $aabbba$:

$$q_0 aabbba \circlearrowright q_2 abbba \circlearrowright^2 q_3 bbaa \circlearrowright^3 q_2 abb \circlearrowright^2 q_3 ba \circlearrowright^2 q_2 b \circlearrowright q_3$$

That shows $aabbba \in L_R(A)$. Analogously, one can see that every word that contains the same number of a's and b's and that begins with an a is in $L_R(A)$. On the other hand, no other word can be accepted by A, interpreted as an ROWJFA. So, we get $L_R(A) = \{\, w \in a\{a, b\}^* \mid |w|_a = |w|_b \,\}$. Notice that this language is non-regular and not closed under permutation. □

The following characterization of permutation closed languages accepted by ROWJFAs is known from [2].

Theorem 4. *Let L be a permutation closed language. Then, the language L is in* **pROWJ** *if and only if the Myhill-Nerode relation $\sim_L$ has only a finite number of positive equivalence classes.*

3 Lattices, Linear Sets, and Myhill-Nerode Classes

Because of Theorem 4 a permutation closed language is in **ROWJ** if and only if the Parikh-image has only a finite number of positive Myhill-Nerode equivalence classes. In this section we will study these kind of subsets of $\mathbb{N}^k$. Linear sets and lattices will play a key role in our theory. We will investigate decompositions of subsets of $\mathbb{N}^k$ as finite unions of such subsets that have only a finite number of positive equivalence classes. This will lead to characterization results about the language class **pMROWJ** in the next section.

3.1 Connections Between Linear Sets and Rational Cones

It was pointed out in [11] that "rational cones in $\mathbb{R}^d$ are important objects in toric algebraic geometry, combinatorial commutative algebra, geometric combinatorics, integer programming." In the following we will see how rational cones are related to the property of linear sets to have only a finite number of positive Myhill-Nerode equivalence classes. The following property is straightforward.

Lemma 5. *For $k \geq 0$, vectors $\boldsymbol{c}, \boldsymbol{d} \in \mathbb{N}^k$, and a finite set $P \subseteq \mathbb{N}^k$ the map $\mathsf{L}(\boldsymbol{c}, P) \to \mathsf{L}(\boldsymbol{d}, P)$ given by $\boldsymbol{x} \mapsto \boldsymbol{x} - \boldsymbol{c} + \boldsymbol{d}$ induces a bijection from $\mathsf{L}(\boldsymbol{c}, P)/\equiv_{\mathsf{L}(\boldsymbol{c},P)}$ to $\mathsf{L}(\boldsymbol{d}, P)/\equiv_{\mathsf{L}(\boldsymbol{d},P)}$.* □

Next, we define two properties of subsets of $\mathbb{N}^k$ which involve rational cones. Let $k \geq 0$ and $S \subseteq \mathbb{N}^k$. Then, the set S has the *linearly independent rational cone property* if $\mathsf{span}(S) \cap (\mathbb{R}_{\geq 0})^k = \mathsf{cone}(T)$, for some a linearly independent $T \subseteq \mathbb{N}^k$. The set S has the *own rational cone property* if S is finite and it holds $\mathsf{span}(S) \cap (\mathbb{R}_{\geq 0})^k = \mathsf{cone}(S)$.

A linear set has only a finite number of positive Myhill-Nerode equivalence classes if and only if the period set has the own rational cone property:

Theorem 6. *Let $k \geq 0$ and $P \subseteq \mathbb{N}^k$ be finite. Then, $\left|\mathsf{L}(\boldsymbol{0}, P)/\equiv_{\mathsf{L}(\boldsymbol{0},P)}\right| < \infty$ if and only if P has the own rational cone property.* □

For linear sets with linearly independent periods we even get a stronger equivalence than in Theorem 6:

Corollary 7. *For $k \geq 0$ and a linearly independent $P \subseteq \mathbb{N}^k$ the following three conditions are equivalent:*

1. $\left|\mathsf{L}(\boldsymbol{0}, P)/\equiv_{\mathsf{L}(\boldsymbol{0},P)}\right| < \infty$
2. $\left|\mathsf{L}(\boldsymbol{0}, P)/\equiv_{\mathsf{L}(\boldsymbol{0},P)}\right| = 1$
3. *The set P has the own rational cone property.* □

3.2 Decompositions of Lattices

Lattices defined as subsets of $\mathbb{R}^k$ play an important rule in geometry, group theory, and cryptography, see [6]. Our lattices defined as subsets of $\mathbb{N}^k$ are a natural way to extend "the pattern" of a linear set to $\mathbb{N}^k$. Using lattices we can give a characterization in which cases arbitrary subsets of $\mathbb{N}^k$ can be decomposed as a finite union of subsets with only a finite number of positive Myhill-Nerode classes in the next subsection. This result, in turn, will enable us to prove a characterization result about MROWJFAs in the next section. In this subsection, we will show some decomposition results about lattices: it will turn out that lattices can be decomposed as a finite union of linear sets which have only one positive Myhill-Nerode equivalence class. Since each semi-linear set is the finite union of linear sets with linearly independent period sets by Theorem 2, we will investigate in which cases lattices can even be decomposed as a finite union of linear sets that have linearly independent period sets and only one positive

Myhill-Nerode equivalence class (or only a finite number of positive Myhill-Nerode equivalence classes).

For $k \geq 0$, $\boldsymbol{c}, \boldsymbol{y} \in \mathbb{N}^k$, a finite $P \subseteq \mathbb{N}^k$, and $\boldsymbol{x} \in \mathsf{La}(\boldsymbol{c}, P)$ the vector $\boldsymbol{x}+\boldsymbol{y}$ is in $\mathsf{La}(\boldsymbol{c}, P)$ if and only if $\boldsymbol{y} \in \mathsf{La}(\boldsymbol{0}, P)$. This gives us that each lattice has only one positive Myhill-Nerode equivalence class. On the other hand, each lattice is a finite union of linear sets that have only one positive Myhill-Nerode equivalence class:

Proposition 8. *Let $k \geq 0$, $\boldsymbol{c} \in \mathbb{N}^k$, and $P \subseteq \mathbb{N}^k$ be finite. Then, there is a natural number $m > 0$, $\boldsymbol{c_1}, \boldsymbol{c_2}, \ldots, \boldsymbol{c_m} \in \mathbb{N}^k$, and a finite $Q \subseteq \mathbb{N}^k$ such that $\mathsf{La}(\boldsymbol{c}, P) = \bigcup_{i=1}^{m} \mathsf{L}(\boldsymbol{c_i}, Q)$ and $\left|\mathsf{L}(\boldsymbol{0}, Q)/\equiv_{\mathsf{L}(\boldsymbol{0},Q)}\right| = 1$.* □

The linearly independent rational cone property is connected to the property of lattices to be a finite union of linear sets that have linearly independent period sets and only finitely many positive Myhill-Nerode equivalence classes:

Theorem 9. *For $k \geq 0$, $\boldsymbol{c} \in \mathbb{N}^k$, and a finite $P \subseteq \mathbb{N}^k$ the following three conditions are equivalent:*

1. *There is an $m > 0$, vectors $\boldsymbol{c_1}, \boldsymbol{c_2}, \ldots, \boldsymbol{c_m} \in \mathbb{N}^k$, and linearly independent $Q_1, Q_2, \ldots, Q_m \subseteq \mathbb{N}^k$ such that $\mathsf{La}(\boldsymbol{c}, P) = \bigcup_{i=1}^{m} \mathsf{L}(\boldsymbol{c_i}, Q_i)$ and for all $i \in \{1, 2, \ldots, m\}$ it holds $\left|\mathsf{L}(\boldsymbol{0}, Q_i)/\equiv_{\mathsf{L}(\boldsymbol{0},Q_i)}\right| < \infty$.*
2. *There is an $m > 0$, vectors $\boldsymbol{c_1}, \boldsymbol{c_2}, \ldots, \boldsymbol{c_m} \in \mathbb{N}^k$, and a linearly independent $Q \subseteq \mathbb{N}^k$ such that $\mathsf{La}(\boldsymbol{c}, P) = \bigcup_{i=1}^{m} \mathsf{L}(\boldsymbol{c_i}, Q)$ and $\left|\mathsf{L}(\boldsymbol{0}, Q)/\equiv_{\mathsf{L}(\boldsymbol{0},Q)}\right| = 1$.*
3. *The set P has the linearly independent rational cone property.* □

Because of Theorem 9 it is worthwhile to investigate the linearly independent rational cone property more. Intuitively one might think that this property always holds, but it turns out that this is only the case in dimension $k \leq 3$:

Theorem 10. *Let $k \geq 0$ and $n \in \{0, 1, \ldots, k\}$. Then, the condition that each $S \subseteq \mathbb{N}^k$ with $\dim(\mathsf{span}(S)) = n$ has the linearly independent rational cone property holds if and only if $n \in \{0, 1, 2, k\}$.* □

Thus, for $k \geq 0$ and $n \in \{0, 1, \ldots, k\}$, the condition that for all vectors $\boldsymbol{c} \in \mathbb{N}^k$ and finite sets $P \subseteq \mathbb{N}^k$ with $\dim(\mathsf{span}(P)) = n$ we get a decomposition of the set $\mathsf{La}(\boldsymbol{c}, P)$ as in Theorem 9 is equivalent to the condition $n \in \{0, 1, 2, k\}$.

3.3 A Decomposition Result About Subsets of $\mathbb{N}^k$

Having the decompositions of lattices from Subsect. 3.2, we now turn to a decomposition result about arbitrary subsets of $\mathbb{N}^k$. To state the result, we will work with quasi lattices: let $k \geq 0$ and $S \subseteq \mathbb{N}^k$. The set S is a *quasi lattice* if there is a $\boldsymbol{y} \in \mathbb{N}^k$, an $m \geq 0$, vectors $\boldsymbol{c_1}, \boldsymbol{c_2}, \ldots, \boldsymbol{c_m} \in \mathbb{N}^k$, and finite subsets $P_1, P_2, \ldots, P_m \subseteq \mathbb{N}^k$ such that the set $\{\, \boldsymbol{z} \in S \mid \boldsymbol{z} \geq \boldsymbol{y} \,\}$ is equal to $\{\, \boldsymbol{z} \in \bigcup_{j=1}^{m} \mathsf{La}(\boldsymbol{c_j}, P_j) \mid \boldsymbol{z} \geq \boldsymbol{y} \,\}$.

We can identify a pattern of two linear sets formed by three vectors that gives a sufficient condition for the property of a subset of $\mathbb{N}^k$ to not be a quasi lattice:

Lemma 11. *Let $k \geq 0$ and $S \subseteq \mathbb{N}^k$ such that there are vectors $\boldsymbol{u}, \boldsymbol{v}, \boldsymbol{w} \in \mathbb{N}^k$ with $\pi_{k,\{j\}}(\boldsymbol{v}) > 0$, for all $j \in \{1, 2, \ldots, k\}$ with $\mathsf{L}(\boldsymbol{u}, \{\boldsymbol{v}\}) \cap S = \emptyset$ and moreover $\mathsf{L}(\boldsymbol{u} + \boldsymbol{w}, \{\boldsymbol{v}, \boldsymbol{w}\}) \subseteq S$. Then, the set S is* not *a quasi lattice.* □

We call subsets of $\mathbb{N}^k$ that allow a pattern as in the above lemma anti-lattices: let $k \geq 0$ and $S \subseteq \mathbb{N}^k$. If there are vectors $\boldsymbol{u}, \boldsymbol{v}, \boldsymbol{w} \in \mathbb{N}^k$ with $\pi_{k,\{j\}}(\boldsymbol{v}) > 0$ for all $j \in \{1, 2, \ldots, k\}$ so that $\mathsf{L}(\boldsymbol{u}, \{\boldsymbol{v}\}) \cap S = \emptyset$ and $\mathsf{L}(\boldsymbol{u} + \boldsymbol{w}, \{\boldsymbol{v}, \boldsymbol{w}\}) \subseteq S$, the set S is called an *anti-lattice.* semi-linear set is a quasi lattice if and only if it is not an anti-lattice:

Proposition 12. *Let $k \geq 0$ and $S \subseteq \mathbb{N}^k$ be a semi-linear set. Then, the set S is a quasi lattice if and only if S is not an anti-lattice.* □

It follows that each subset of $\mathbb{N}^k$ which has only a finite number of positive Myhill-Nerode equivalence classes is a quasi lattice:

Corollary 13. *For a $k \geq 0$ and a subset $S \subseteq \mathbb{N}^k$ with $|S/\equiv_S| < \infty$ the set S is a quasi lattice.* □

Quasi lattices are related to the property of a subset $S \subseteq \mathbb{N}^k$ to be a finite union of subsets of $\mathbb{N}^k$ that have only a finite number of positive Myhill-Nerode equivalence classes, which holds exactly if S is a finite union of linear sets that have only one positive Myhill-Nerode equivalence class:

Theorem 14. *For a $k \geq 0$ and a subset $S \subseteq \mathbb{N}^k$ the following three conditions are equivalent:*

1. *There is an $m \geq 0$ and subsets $S_1, S_2, \ldots, S_m \subseteq \mathbb{N}^k$ such that $S = \bigcup_{j=1}^m S_j$ and for each $j \in \{1, 2, \ldots, m\}$ we have $\left|S_j/\equiv_{S_j}\right| < \infty$.*
2. *There is an $m \geq 0$ and linear sets $L_1, L_2, \ldots, L_m \subseteq \mathbb{N}^k$ such that $S = \bigcup_{j=1}^m L_j$ and for each $j \in \{1, 2, \ldots, m\}$ we have $\left|L_j/\equiv_{L_j}\right| = 1$.*
3. *For all subsets $T \subseteq \{1, 2, \ldots, k\}$ and vectors $\boldsymbol{x} \in \mathbb{N}^{|T|}$ it holds that the set $\pi_{k,\{1,2,\ldots,k\}\setminus T}(\{\, \boldsymbol{z} \in S \mid \pi_{k,T}(\boldsymbol{z}) = \boldsymbol{x} \,\})$ is a quasi lattice.* □

In dimension $k \leq 3$ we can strengthen the second condition of Theorem 14, while we can weaken the third condition in dimension $k \leq 2$:

Corollary 15. *For a $k \in \{0, 1, 2, 3\}$ and a subset $S \subseteq \mathbb{N}^k$ the conditions from Theorem 14 are equivalent to the following condition. There is a number $m \geq 0$, vectors $\mathbf{c_1}, \mathbf{c_2}, \ldots, \mathbf{c}_m \in \mathbb{N}^k$, and linearly independent sets $P_1, P_2, \ldots, P_m \subseteq \mathbb{N}^k$ such that it holds $S = \bigcup_{j=1}^m \mathsf{L}(\mathbf{c}_j, P_j)$ and for each $j \in \{1, 2, \ldots, m\}$ we have $\left|\mathsf{L}(\mathbf{0}, P_j)/\equiv_{\mathsf{L}(\mathbf{0}, P_j)}\right| = 1$. For a $k \in \{0, 1, 2\}$ and a subset $S \subseteq \mathbb{N}^k$ the conditions from Theorem 14 are equivalent to the condition that S is a semi-linear set and a quasi lattice.* □

4 Right One-Way Jumping Finite Automata with Multiple Initial States

In this section we investigate MROWJFAs. To get results about these devices we use results from Subsect. 3.3.

4.1 Results for Arbitrary Alphabets

First, some basic properties are given. Directly from the definition of MROWJFAs we get that the unary languages in **MROWJ** are exactly the unary regular languages and that **MROWJ** consists exactly of the finite unions of languages from **ROWJ**. However, it is not clear that every language from **pMROWJ** is a finite union of languages from **pROWJ**. From [2] we know that a^* and the language $\{ w \in \{a,b\}^* \mid |w|_a = |w|_b \}$ are in **ROWJ**, but the union of these two sets is not in **ROWJ**. Together with the properties of **ROWJ** shown in [2] and [4], this gives us: we have **REG** $\subset$ **ROWJ** $\subset$ **MROWJ** and also **pREG** $\subset$ **pROWJ** $\subseteq$ **pMROWJ**. The family **MROWJ** is incomparable to **DCF** and to **CF**. Each language in **MROWJ** is semi-linear and contained in the complexity classes **DTIME**(n^2) and **DSPACE**(n). We get **pMROWJ** $\nsubseteq$ **CF** and **pMROWJ** $\subseteq$ **JFA** $\subset$ **pCS**. The letter-bounded languages contained in **MROWJ** are exactly the regular letter-bounded languages.

Now, we will study the language class **pMROWJ** in more detail. The foundation for this will be the next result.

Theorem 16. *The Parikh-image of each language in* **pMROWJ** *is a quasi lattice.* □

Because the Parikh-image of $\{ w \in \{a,b\}^* \mid |w|_a \neq |w|_b \}$ is an anti-lattice, this language is not in **MROWJ**. Thus, we have **pMROWJ** $\subset$ **JFA** and that the family **pMROWJ** is incomparable to **pDCF** and to **pCF**.

To get more detailed results about **pMROWJ**, we define the language operation of *disjoint quotient* of a language $L \subseteq \Sigma^*$ with a word $w \in \Sigma^*$ as follows:

$$\begin{aligned} L/^d w &= \{ v \in \Sigma^* \mid vw \in L, \forall a \in \Sigma : (|v|_a = 0 \vee |w|_a = 0) \} \\ &= (L/w) \cap \{ a \in \Sigma \mid |w|_a = 0 \}^*. \end{aligned}$$

From Theorem 4 we get that the family **pROWJ** is closed under the operations of quotient with a word and disjoint quotient with a word. Let Σ be an alphabet, $\Pi \subseteq \Sigma$, and $L \subseteq \Sigma^*$ be in **MROWJ**. Then, it is easy to see that $L \cap \Pi^*$ is also in **MROWJ**. Thus, we get that if **pMROWJ** is closed under the operation quotient with a word, then **pMROWJ** is also closed under disjoint quotient with a word.

Theorem 4 gives a characterization of the language class **pROWJ** in terms of the Myhill-Nerode relation. The next Corollary is a result in the same spirit for the language class **pMROWJ**. Theorems 4, 14, and 16 give us a characterization of all languages L for which each disjoint quotient of L with a word is contained in **pMROWJ**:

Corollary 17. *For an alphabet Σ and a permutation closed language $L \subseteq \Sigma^*$ the following conditions are equivalent:*

1. *For all $w \in \Sigma^*$ the language $L/^d w$ is in* **pMROWJ**.
2. *There is an $n \geq 0$ and $L_1, L_2, \ldots, L_n \subseteq \Sigma^*$ with $L_1, L_2, \ldots, L_n \in$* **pROWJ** *and $L = \bigcup_{i=1}^{n} L_i$.*

3. *There is an* $n \geq 0$ *and permutation closed languages* $L_1, L_2, \ldots, L_n \subseteq \Sigma^*$ *such that* $L = \bigcup_{i=1}^{n} L_i$ *and for all* $i \in \{1, 2, \ldots, n\}$ *the language* L_i *has only a finite number of positive Myhill-Nerode equivalence classes.*
4. *There is an* $m \geq 0$ *and linear sets* $L_1, L_2, \ldots, L_m \subseteq \mathbb{N}^{|\Sigma|}$ *such that* $\psi(L) = \bigcup_{j=1}^{m} L_j$ *and for each* $j \in \{1, 2, \ldots, m\}$ *we have* $|L_j/\equiv_{L_j}| = 1$.
5. *For all subsets* $T \subseteq \{1, 2, \ldots, |\Sigma|\}$ *and vectors* $\boldsymbol{x} \in \mathbb{N}^{|T|}$ *it holds that the set* $\pi_{|\Sigma|, \{1,2,\ldots,|\Sigma|\} \setminus T}\left(\{\, \boldsymbol{z} \in \psi(L) \mid \pi_{|\Sigma|,T}(\boldsymbol{z}) = \boldsymbol{x} \,\}\right)$ *is a quasi lattice.* □

For ternary alphabets we can weaken the first condition of the previous corollary, by the fact that the family **JFA** is closed under the operation of disjoint quotient, and strengthen its fourth condition by Corollary 15:

Corollary 18. *For an alphabet* Σ *with* $|\Sigma| = 3$ *and a permutation closed language* $L \subseteq \Sigma^*$ *the following two conditions are equivalent:*

1. *For all unary* $w \in \Sigma^*$ *the language* $L/^d w$ *is in* **pMROWJ**.
2. *There is a number* $m \geq 0$, *vectors* $\boldsymbol{c_1}, \boldsymbol{c_2}, \ldots, \boldsymbol{c_m} \in \mathbb{N}^3$, *and linearly independent sets* $P_1, P_2, \ldots, P_m \subseteq \mathbb{N}^3$ *such that* $\psi(L) = \bigcup_{j=1}^{m} \mathsf{L}(\boldsymbol{c_j}, P_j)$ *and for each* $j \in \{1, 2, \ldots, m\}$ *we have* $\left|\mathsf{L}(\boldsymbol{0}, P_j)/\equiv_{\mathsf{L}(\boldsymbol{0},P_j)}\right| = 1$. □

From Theorem 4 and Corollary 17 we get that the condition that each language from **pMROWJ** is a finite union of languages from **pROWJ** is equivalent to the condition that the family **pMROWJ** is closed under the operation of quotient with a word and to the condition that the family **pMROWJ** is closed under the operation of disjoint quotient with a word.

Consider an alphabet Σ and a language $L \subseteq \Sigma^*$. If for all $w \in \Sigma^*$ the language $L/^d w$ is in **pMROWJ**, then the language L is contained in the complexity class **DTIME**(n), as the next result shows:

Lemma 19. *Let* Σ *be an alphabet,* $n > 0$, *and* $L_1, L_2, \ldots, L_n \subseteq \Sigma^*$ *be in* **pROWJ**. *Then, there is a one-way* $(n \cdot |\Sigma|)$*-head DFA with endmarker accepting* $\bigcup_{j=1}^{n} L_i$. □

4.2 Results for Binary Alphabets

Now, we will investigate **MROWJ** and related language families for binary alphabets. It turns out that for some problems we get different or stronger results than for arbitrary alphabets. From the next theorem it follows that for binary alphabets **pCF** = **JFA**, whereas for arbitrary alphabets it holds **pCF** ⊂ **JFA**.

Theorem 20. *Each permutation closed semi-linear language over a binary alphabet is accepted by a counter automaton.* □

For binary alphabets we have **pROWJ** ⊂ **pDCF**, while for arbitrary alphabets **pROWJ** is incomparable to **pDCF** and to **pCF**:

Proposition 21. *Each language over a binary alphabet in* **pROWJ** *is accepted by a realtime deterministic counter automaton.* □

For the family **pMROWJ** we get the following results. Notice that for arbitrary alphabets **pMROWJ** and **pCF** are incomparable.

Corollary 22. *For binary alphabets it holds that* **pROWJ** $\subset$ **pMROWJ**, *that* **pMROWJ** *is incomparable to* **pDCF**, *and that* **pMROWJ** $\subset$ **JFA** $=$ **pCF**. □

If the languages do not need to be closed under permutation, we get for binary alphabets the same inclusion relations between **ROWJ**, **MROWJ**, and **DCF** as for arbitrary alphabets:

Lemma 23. *For binary alphabets* **ROWJ** $\subset$ **MROWJ**. *The families* **ROWJ** *and* **MROWJ** *are both incomparable to* **DCF** *over binary alphabets.* □

Theorems 4 and 16, Proposition 12, and Corollary 15 imply a characterization of the languages in **pMROWJ** over a binary alphabet, which is stronger than the statement for arbitrary alphabets in Corollary 17, because we do not need to consider disjoint quotients of a language with a word here.

Corollary 24. *Let Σ be an alphabet with $|\Sigma| = 2$ and $L \subseteq \Sigma^*$ be a permutation closed language. Then, the following conditions are equivalent:*

1. *Language L is in* **pMROWJ**.
2. *There is an $n \geq 0$ and $L_1, L_2, \ldots, L_n \subseteq \Sigma^*$ with $L_1, L_2, \ldots, L_n \in$* **pROWJ** *and $L = \bigcup_{i=1}^{n} L_i$.*
3. *There is an $n \geq 0$ and permutation closed languages $L_1, L_2, \ldots, L_n \subseteq \Sigma^*$ such that $L = \bigcup_{i=1}^{n} L_i$ and for all $i \in \{1, 2, \ldots, n\}$ the language L_i has only a finite number of positive Myhill-Nerode equivalence classes.*
4. *There is a number $m \geq 0$, vectors $\mathbf{c}_1, \mathbf{c}_2, \ldots, \mathbf{c}_m \in \mathbb{N}^2$, and linearly independent sets $P_1, P_2, \ldots, P_m \subseteq \mathbb{N}^2$ such that $\psi(L) = \bigcup_{j=1}^{m} \mathsf{L}(\mathbf{c}_j, P_j)$ and for each $j \in \{1, 2, \ldots, m\}$ we have $\left|\mathsf{L}(\mathbf{0}, P_j)/\equiv_{\mathsf{L}(\mathbf{0}, P_j)}\right| = 1$.*
5. *The Parikh-image of L is a semi-linear set and a quasi lattice.*
6. *The Parikh-image of L is a semi-linear set and not an anti-lattice.* □

From Corollary 24 it follows that each language from **pMROWJ** over a binary alphabet is a finite union of permutation closed languages accepted by a realtime deterministic counter automaton.

5 Conclusions

We have investigated ROWJFAs with multiple initial states and showed inclusion and incomparability results of the induced language family by using results on semi-linear sets and generalizations thereof. In order to complete the picture of these new language family it remains to study closure properties and decision problems for these devices and moreover to investigate nondeterministic variants of ROWJFAs in general.

References

1. Beier, S., Holzer, M.: Decidability of right one-way jumping finite automata. In: Hoshi, M., Seki, S. (eds.) DLT 2018. LNCS, vol. 11088, pp. 109–120. Springer, Cham (2018). https://doi.org/10.1007/978-3-319-98654-8_9
2. Beier, S., Holzer, M.: Properties of right one-way jumping finite automata. In: Konstantinidis, S., Pighizzini, G. (eds.) DCFS 2018. LNCS, vol. 10952, pp. 11–23. Springer, Cham (2018). https://doi.org/10.1007/978-3-319-94631-3_2
3. Beier, S., Holzer, M., Kutrib, M.: On the descriptional complexity of operations on semilinear sets. In: Csuhaj-Varjú, E., Dömösi, P., Vaszil, G. (eds.) AFL 2017. EPTCS, vol. 252, pp. 41–55. Debrecen, Hungary (2017). https://doi.org/10.4204/EPTCS.252.8
4. Chigahara, H., Fazekas, S., Yamamura, A.: One-way jumping finite automata. Int. J. Found. Comput. Sci. **27**(3), 391–405 (2016). https://doi.org/10.1142/S0129054116400165
5. Chistikov, D., Haase, C.: The taming of the semi-linear set. In: Chatzigiannakis, I., Mitzenmacher, M., Rabani, Y., Sangiorgi, D. (eds.) ICALP 2016. LIPIcs, vol. 55, pp. 128:1–128:13 (2016). https://doi.org/10.4230/LIPIcs.ICALP.2016.128
6. Conway, J., Horton, S., Neil, J.A.: Sphere Packings, Lattices and Groups, Grundlehren der Mathematischen Wissenschaften, vol. 290, 3rd edn. Springer, New York (1999). https://doi.org/10.1007/978-1-4757-6568-7
7. Gill, A., Kou, L.T.: Multiple-entry finite automata. J. Comput. System Sci. **9**(1), 1–19 (1974). https://doi.org/10.1016/S0022-0000(74)80034-6
8. Ginsburg, S., Spanier, E.H.: Bounded ALGOL-like languages. Trans. Am. Math. Soc. **113**, 333–368 (1964). https://doi.org/10.2307/1994067
9. Ginsburg, S., Spanier, E.H.: Bounded regular sets. Proc. Am. Math. Soc. **17**(5), 1043–1049 (1966). https://doi.org/10.1090/S0002-9939-1966-0201310-3
10. Ginsburg, S., Spanier, E.H.: Semigroups, Presburger formulas, and languages. Pac. J. Math. **16**(2), 285–296 (1966). https://doi.org/10.2140/pjm.1966.16.285
11. Gubeladze, J., Michalek, M.: The poset of rational cones. Pac. J. Math. **292**(1), 103–115 (2018). https://doi.org/10.2140/pjm.2018.292.103
12. Haase, C., Hofman, P.: Tightening the complexity of equivalence problems for commutative grammars. In: Ollinger, N., Vollmer, H. (eds.) STACS 2016. LIPIcs, vol. 47, pp. 41:1–41:14 (2016). https://doi.org/10.4230/LIPIcs.STACS.2016.41
13. Meduna, A., Zemek, P.: Jumping finite automata. Int. J. Found. Comput. Sci. **23**(7), 1555–1578 (2012). https://doi.org/10.1142/S0129054112500244
14. Parikh, R.J.: On context-free languages. J. ACM **13**(4), 570–581 (1966). https://doi.org/10.1145/321356.321364
15. Studený, M.: Convex cones in finite-dimensional real vector spaces. Kybernetika **29**(2), 180–200 (1993). http://www.kybernetika.cz/content/1993/2/180

Z-Automata for Compact and Direct Representation of Unranked Tree Languages

Johanna Björklund[1], Frank Drewes[1(✉)], and Giorgio Satta[2]

[1] Department of Computing Science, Umeå University, Umeå, Sweden
{johanna,drewes}@cs.umu.se

[2] Department of Information Engineering, University of Padua, Padua, Italy
satta@dei.unipd.it

Abstract. Unranked tree languages are valuable in natural language processing for modelling dependency trees. We introduce a new type of automaton for unranked tree languages, called Z-automaton, that is tailored for this particular application. The Z-automaton offers a compact form of representation, and unlike the closely related notion of stepwise automata, does not require a binary encoding of its input. We establish an arc-factored normal form, and prove the membership problem of Z-automata in normal form to be in $O(mn)$, where m is the size of the transition table of the Z-automaton and n is the size of the input tree.

1 Introduction

Unranked tree languages (UTLs) have been studied since the 60s, most notably as a formal model for the document markup language XML [1,5]. The present work is motivated by their use as a representation for dependency trees, a model for natural language syntax widespread in natural language processing [7]. A *dependency tree* for a sentence is, simply put, an unranked tree structure whose nodes are the lexical items of the sentence and whose arcs represent binary grammatical relations such as subject, direct object, modifier, and so on; see Fig. 1 for an example. As an alternative to the traditional phrase structure trees generated by context-free grammars, dependency trees are more flexible in the design of statistical syntactic models, and provide a better trade-off between expressivity and computational efficiency. Here we focus on projective dependency trees, roughly speaking, trees whose arcs do not cross each other when drawn in the semi-plane above the input sentence. While the analysis of phrase structure trees by bottom-up tree automata, regular and context-free tree grammars, and tree-adjoining grammars is standard, no similarly convenient devices are commonly used for dependency trees. This article takes a first step in this direction.

Computer Science literature contains a number of formalisms for representing UTLs [3,8]. The best known is probably the unranked tree automaton (UTA) of Brüggemann-Klein, Murata, and Wood [1]. The transitions in a UTA are similar to those in a bottom-up tree automaton, but the domain of the transition

M. Hospodár and G. Jirásková (Eds.): CIAA 2019, LNCS 11601, pp. 83–94, 2019.
https://doi.org/10.1007/978-3-030-23679-3_7

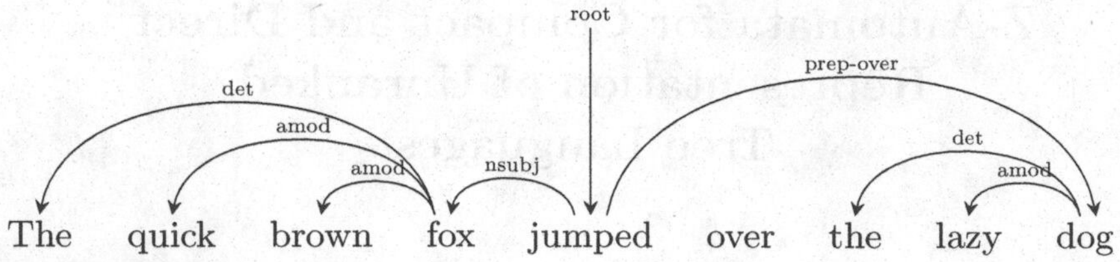

Fig. 1. The dependency analysis assigned by the Stanford parser to the sentence 'The quick brown fox jumped over the lazy dog.'

function consists of pairs of an input symbol and a regular language of states. Unfortunately, as shown in [11], UTA do not yield unique minimal deterministic UTA. Moreover, even when the string languages are represented by DFAs, the minimization problem is NP-complete. Martens and Niehren [10] therefore propose *stepwise tree automata* (STA) which process binarized encodings of unranked tree automata. Bottom-up (bu-) deterministic stepwise automata have the advantage of having a canonical form, and being more succinct than bu-deterministic tree automata over the first-child next-sibling encoding. Nonetheless, stepwise automata are not natural devices for linguistic purposes, since the binary encoding obfuscates the syntactic representation. There are also logic formalisms for (weighted) unranked tree languages. In [4], Droste and Vogler provide a weighted monadic second order logic for unranked trees and introduce the notion of weighted UTA. Again, the theories of ranked and unranked tree languages differ, this time in that weighted UTA and a syntactically restricted weighted MSO-logic for unranked trees have the same expressive power in case the semiring is commutative, but not in general.

As an alternative to these formalisms, we propose Z-automata. In its canonical computations, a Z-automaton visits the input tree bottom-up in an order resembling a zed-shaped motion, alternating horizontal moves and vertical moves. Z-automata have the same expressive power as UTA and STA. They combine the best aspects of both: The representation is arguably as natural as UTA, and as compact as STA. To our knowledge, Z-automata are also the first formal device for dependency trees using latent variables. Our long-term objective is to provide transducers that translate dependency syntactic trees into graph-based structures, representing the semantics of the input sentence. The use by Z-automata of rules whose left-hand sides may refer to components at differing tree depths make the formalism more appropriate as a basis for syntax-semantic translation, similarly to the tree transducers developed in [9].

2 Preliminaries

General Notation. The set of natural numbers is denoted by $\mathbb{N}$, and $\mathbb{N}_+ = \mathbb{N} \setminus \{0\}$. For $n \in \mathbb{N}$ the set $\{1, \ldots, n\}$ is abbreviated to $[n]$. In particular, $[0] = \emptyset$. The set of all strings over a set S is written S^*, ε is the empty string, $S^+ = S^* \setminus \{\varepsilon\}$, and 2^S is the powerset of S. Given a string w, we write $[w]$ for the set of its elements, i.e., the smallest set S such that $w \in S^*$. Given a string s and a set of strings S, we denote by $s \cdot S$ the set $\{ss' \mid s' \in S\}$.

Trees. Let Σ be an alphabet. We define the set T_Σ of *(unranked) trees* over Σ as usual. It is the smallest set such that, for all $f \in \Sigma$ and $t_1, \ldots, t_n \in \mathrm{T}_\Sigma$ ($n \in \mathbb{N}$), we have $f(t_1, \ldots, t_n) \in \mathrm{T}_\Sigma$. In particular $f()$, which we abbreviate by f, is in T_Σ. (This is the base case of the inductive definition.)

A *ranked alphabet* Σ is an alphabet additionally equipped with a function $\#\colon \Sigma \to \mathbb{N}$. For $f \in \Sigma$, the value $\#(f)$ is called the rank of f. For any $n \geq 0$, we denote by Σ_n the set of all symbols of rank n from Σ. If Σ is ranked, then T_Σ is restricted so that $f(t_1, \ldots, t_n) \in \mathrm{T}_\Sigma$ only if $n = \#(f)$. Thus, in this case T_Σ becomes a set of *ranked trees.*

In both cases, the *nodes* of a tree are identified by their Gorn addresses, which are strings in $\mathbb{N}_+^*$: the root has the address ε, and if α is the address of a node in t_i then $i\alpha$ is the address of that node in $f(t_1, \ldots, t_n)$. The label of node α in t is denoted by $t(\alpha)$, and the set of all nodes of t is $N(t)$. For $\Sigma' \subseteq \Sigma$, the set of all nodes $\alpha \in N(t)$ with $t(\alpha) \in \Sigma'$ is denoted by $N_{\Sigma'}(t)$. A node $\alpha \in N(t)$ is a *leaf* if $\alpha 1 \notin N(t)$, and is *internal* otherwise. The *size* of t is $|t| = |N(t)|$.

We denote a subset $\{\alpha_1, \ldots, \alpha_k\}$ of the set of nodes of a tree t as $(\alpha_1, \ldots, \alpha_k)$ if we wish to indicate that $\alpha_1, \ldots, \alpha_k$ are listed in lexicographic order.

Let $\square \notin \Sigma$ be a special symbol. A *context* is a tree $c \in \mathrm{T}_{\Sigma \cup \{\square\}}$ such that c contains exactly one occurrence of $\square$, and this occurrence is a leaf. Given such a context and a tree t, we let $c[t]$ denote the tree obtained from c by replacing $\square$ with t. Formally, $c[t] = t$ if $c = \square$, and otherwise $c[t] = f(s_1, \ldots, s_{i-1}, s_i[t], s_{i+1}, \ldots, s_n)$, where $c = f(s_1, \ldots, s_n)$ and $s_i \in \mathrm{T}_{\Sigma \cup \{\square\}}$ is the context among $s_1, \ldots, s_n$. For contexts $c \neq \square$, the notation $c[t]$ is extended in the obvious way to $c[t_1, \ldots, t_k]$ for trees $t_1, \ldots, t_k$ ($k \in \mathbb{N}$). It yields the tree obtained by inserting the string of subtrees $t_1, \ldots, t_k$ at the position marked by $\square$ (which is indeed a tree as we only use it if $c \neq \square$). To be precise, if $c = f(s_1, \ldots, s_n)$ with $n > 0$ and s_i is the context among $s_1, \ldots, s_n$, then

$$c[t_1, \ldots, t_k] = \begin{cases} f(s_1, \ldots, s_{i-1}, t_1, \ldots, t_k, s_{i+1}, \ldots, s_n), & \text{if } s_i = \square; \\ f(s_1, \ldots, s_{i-1}, s_i[t_1, \ldots, t_k], s_{i+1}, \ldots, s_n), & \text{otherwise.} \end{cases}$$

Ranked Tree Automata. A *ranked bottom-up tree automaton* (TA) is a tuple $A = (Q, \Sigma, R, F)$ where Q is a finite set of states, Σ is a ranked input alphabet, R is a finite set of transition rules, and $F \subseteq Q$ is a set of accepting (final) states. Each transition rule is a triple of the form $f(q_1, \ldots, q_n) \to q$ where $q_1, \ldots, q_n, q \in Q$, $f \in \Sigma$, and $\#(f) = n$. The TA is *deterministic* if all distinct transition rules have distinct left-hand sides.

Let $t \in \mathrm{T}_{\Sigma \cup Q}$. A transition rule $f(q_1, \ldots, q_n) \to q$ is *applicable* to t, if t can be written as $t = c[f(q_1, \ldots, q_n)]$. If so, then there is a computation step $t \to_A \bar{t} = c[q]$. A tree $t \in \mathrm{T}_\Sigma$ is *accepted*, or *recognized*, by A if there is a string of computation steps $t \to_A^* q$, for some $q \in F$. The *language* accepted by A, denoted $\mathcal{L}(A)$, is the set of all trees in T_Σ that A accepts.

3 Z-Automata

A *Z-automaton* is a quadruple $A = (\Sigma, Q, R, F)$ consisting of

- a finite input alphabet Σ;
- a finite set Q of *states* which is disjoint with Σ;
- a finite set R of *transition rules*, each of the form $s \to q$ consisting of a left-hand side $s \in \mathrm{T}_{\Sigma \cup Q}$ and a right-hand side $q \in Q$;
- a finite set $F \subseteq Q$ of accepting states.

Let $t \in \mathrm{T}_{\Sigma \cup Q}$. A transition rule $s \to q$ is *applicable* to t, if t can be written as $t = c[f(t_1, \ldots, t_n)]$, such that $s = f(t_1, \ldots, t_k)$ for some $k \leq n$. If so, then there is a computation step $t \to_A \bar{t} = c[q(t_{k+1}, \ldots, t_n)]$. A tree $t \in \mathrm{T}_\Sigma$ is *accepted*, or *recognized*, by A if there is a sequence of computation steps $t \to_A^* q$, for some $q \in F$. The *language* accepted by A, denoted $\mathcal{L}(A)$, is the set of all trees in T_Σ that A accepts. The automaton A is *deterministic* if there do not exist distinct transition rules $s \to q$ and $t \to p$ in R such that $s \to q$ is applicable to t. We note that this condition is sufficient to guarantee that if a node n in the input tree is processed by some rule $s \to q \in R$, then there is no competing rule $t \to p \in R$ that could also have been applied to process n.

Example 1. Let $A = (Q, \Sigma, R, f)$, where $\Sigma = \{a, b, c\}$, $Q = \bigcup_{x \in \Sigma} \{p_x, q_x\}$, $F = \{p_x \mid x \in \Sigma\}$, and R is given as follows, where x and y range over Σ:

$$\begin{array}{llllllll}
x(y) & \to q_x & x(p_y) & \to q_x & & & & \\
q_x(y) & \to q_x & q_x(p_y) & \to q_x & & & & \\
x(x, y) & \to p_x & x(p_x, y) & \to p_x & x(x, p_y) & \to p_x & x(p_x, p_y) & \to p_x \\
q_x(x, y) & \to p_x & q_x(p_x, y) & \to p_x & q_x(x, p_y) & \to p_x & q_x(p_x, p_y) & \to p_x \,.
\end{array}$$

The language recognized by A is the set of all unranked trees over the alphabet Σ, in which the second-to-last child of every internal node carries the same label as the node itself.

The state p_x is used to mark a node originally labelled x, whose subtree have successfully been checked. The first transition rule of the table lets us start the processing by selecting a left-most arc between a leaf labelled $y \in \Sigma$ and its parent labelled $x \in \Sigma$, removing the leaf and turning the label x of the parent into q_x to remember its label. The second transition rule of the first line is similar, for the recursive case where the leaf represents an already processed subtree. The second line just steps through the children of a node labelled q_x, allowing to skip them one by one if they are leaves with labels in $\Sigma \cup \{p_y \mid y \in \Sigma\}$. Line three allows us to nondeterministically replace a node α labelled x and its two leftmost children by p_x if these children are leaves and the label of the first child matches x. Line four is similar, but for q_x instead of x. Thus, these transition rules "guess" that there are no more children to the right. Should the guess be wrong, the automaton will not be able to complete the processing of the subtree rooted at α, because p_x is a leaf wherever it occurs in a transition rule in R.

Figure 2 shows an accepting computation of A on an input tree. The computation starts by processing the right-most subtree. Intuitively, the states labelling

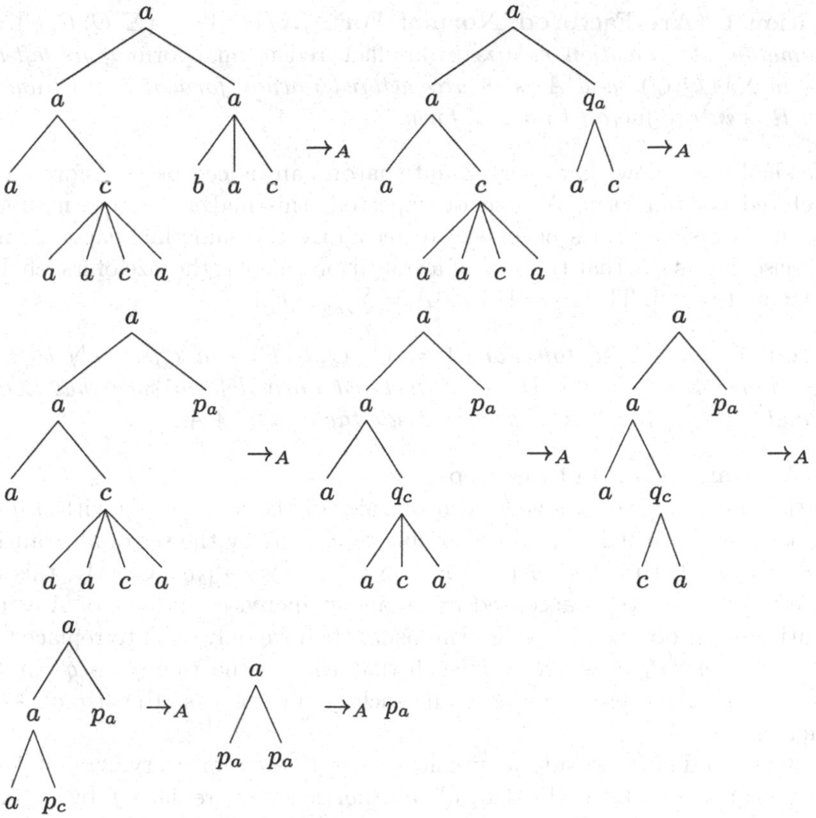

Fig. 2. A sample computation of the Z-automaton A of Example 1. The automaton accepts all unranked trees over the alphabet $\{a, b, c\}$, in which every internal node has the same label as its second-to-last child.

an internal node α, take the role of internal states in a computation of a string automaton processing the children of α. As this subtree is well-formed with respect to $\mathcal{L}(A)$ and its root is labelled by a, it is eventually labelled by p_a. At this point, the computation must also process the left subtree, before it can continue upwards. As also this subtree is well-formed and its root is labelled a, it eventually results in the state p_a. In the final step of the computation, the automaton replaces the remaining structure by p_a, thus accepting the tree.

Using one additional state r_x for each $x \in \Sigma$, and a new accepting state p, an alternative set of transition rules exploits that we can turn individual input symbols into states:

$$\begin{array}{cccc} x \to p_x & x \to q_x & & \\ q_x(p_y) \to q_x & q_x(p_x) \to r_x & r_x(p_y) \to p_x & r_x(p_y) \to p\,. \end{array}$$

These transition rules are in fact in a particular normal form, that simplifies many of the upcoming arguments.

Definition 1 (Arc-Factored Normal Form). *Let $A = (\Sigma, Q, R, F)$ be a Z-automaton. A transition rule is in* arc-factored normal form *if its left-hand side is in $\Sigma \cup Q(Q)$, and A is in arc-factored normal form if every transition rule in R is in arc-factored normal form.*

We shall now show that every Z-automaton can indeed be transformed into arc-factored normal form. As can be expected, this makes a larger number of states and transition rules necessary to recognize the same language. To make this precise, let us say that the *size* of a transition rule r is the size of its left-hand side, denoted by $|r|$. The size of A is $|A| = \sum_{r \in R} |r|$.

Theorem 1. *Every Z-automaton $A = (\Sigma, Q, R, F)$ can effectively be transformed into a Z-automaton B in arc-factored normal form such that $\mathcal{L}(B) = \mathcal{L}(A)$ and $|B| \leq 4|A|^2$. If A is deterministic then $|B| \leq 4|A|$.*

Proof. We transform A in three steps:

In the first step, we remove transition rules of the form $p \to q$ with $p, q \in Q$. We do this by the usual procedure: simply replace R by the set of all transition rules $t \to q'$ such that $t \to q$ is in R, $t \notin Q$, and $q \to_A^* q'$. Clearly, this does not affect the set of trees accepted by A, and it increases the size of A at most quadratically. If, however, A is deterministic, then we only need to replace $t \to q$ by $t \to q'$ for $q \to_A^* q'$ where q' is such that there is no rule $q' \to q''$ in R (if such q' exists). As there is at most one such q', in this case the size of A does not increase at all.

In the second step, we add a transition rule $f \to q_f$ for every symbol $f \in \Sigma$, where q_f is a fresh state added to Q. Furthermore, we replace f by q_f in the left-hand side of every ordinary transition rule in R of size larger than 1. Clearly, this does not affect the language recognized by A. Of course, the introduction of new states and transition rules can be restricted to those symbols which actually occur in a left-hand side, which means that at most $|A|$ transition rules are added.

The third and final step is slightly more technical, and easiest to describe in an iterative manner. However, the intuition is rather straightforward: instead of consuming an entire left-hand side $s \in \mathrm{T}_Q$ in one step, the arcs are consumed one by one, using auxiliary states.

Formally, as long as A is not in arc-factored normal form, select any transition rule $s \to q$ such that $|s| > 2$. Then s has the form $c[q_1(q_2, t_1, \ldots, t_n)]$ for some context c, states q_1, q_2, and trees $t_1, \ldots, t_n$ ($n \geq 0$). We decompose the transition rule into one that consumes $q_1(q_2)$, resulting in a new state $q_{1;2}$, and one that consumes $c[q_{1;2}(t_1, \ldots, t_n)]$. Thus, the first of these transition rules is in arc-factored normal form and the second is of size one less than the original transition rule. Let n be the type of q_1 and α its address in s (i.e., α is the address of $\square$ in c). Then the first transition rule is $q_1(q_2) \to q_{1;2}$. The second transition rule is $c[q_{1;2}(t_1, \ldots, t_n)] \to q$.

It should be clear that this procedure of splitting the original transition rule $s \to q$ into two does not change the language recognized by A. Moreover, $\sum_{r \in R, |r| > 2} |r|$ is reduced by one each time a transition rule is split in this way.

Thus, the process terminates and yields a Z-automaton in arc-factored normal form of size $\leq 4|A|^2$ or, if A is deterministic, of size $\leq 4|A|$. □

Once the automaton is in arc-factored normal form, we can use the standard powerset construction to make it deterministic.

Lemma 1. *There is an algorithm that turns a Z-automaton A into a deterministic Z-automaton B in arc-factored normal form such that $\mathcal{L}(A) = \mathcal{L}(B)$.*

Proof (sketch). Let $A = (\Sigma, Q, R, F)$ be a Z-automaton. Without loss of generality, we may assume that A is in arc-factored normal form. For $t \in \Sigma \cup Q(Q)$, let $R(t) = \{q \in Q \mid (t \to q) \in R\}$. We let $B = (\Sigma, 2^Q, R_1 \cup R_2, F')$, where

$$R_1 = \bigcup_{f \in \Sigma} \{f \to R(f)\},$$

$$R_2 = \bigcup_{P_1, P_2 \subseteq Q} \{P_1(P_2) \to \bigcup_{p_1 \in P_1, p_2 \in P_2} R(p_1(p_2))\},$$

and $F' = \{P \subseteq Q \mid P \cap F \neq \emptyset\}$. Clearly, B is in arc-factored normal form, and hence also deterministic because transition rules in arc-factored normal form violate the determinism requirement only if their left-hand sides are equal.

It is furthermore straightforward to verify that A and B are language equivalent, which completes the proof sketch. □

Naturally, the determinisation according to the previous lemma may take exponential time, simply because the size of the output Z-automaton B has exponentially many states.

4 Equivalence to Stepwise Tree Automata

As we shall see, Z-automata accept the same family of unranked regular tree languages as unranked tree automata [1] and stepwise automata [2]. The latter operates on binary encodings of the input tree. This encoding makes use of an auxiliary symbol @, used as a binary operator over trees, that extends the tree t_1 in its first argument by adding the tree t_2 in its second argument as the right-most direct child of the root of t_1. A sample encoding is shown in Fig. 3.

Definition 2 (Binary Encoding). *Given an (unranked) alphabet Σ, we denote by $\Sigma_@$ the alphabet $\Sigma \cup \{@\}$, viewed as a ranked alphabet in which the symbols in Σ are taken to have rank 0, and the symbol @ to have rank 2. For every tree $t = f(t_1, \ldots, t_n) \in \mathrm{T}_\Sigma$, the function $tree_@(t) : \mathrm{T}_\Sigma \to \mathrm{T}_{\Sigma_@}$ is given by*

$$tree_@(t) = \begin{cases} f, & \text{if } n = 0; \\ @(tree_@(f(t_1, \ldots, t_{n-1})), tree_@(t_n)), & \text{otherwise.} \end{cases}$$

We extend $tree_@$ to tree languages: for all $L \subseteq \mathrm{T}_\Sigma$, $tree_@(L) = \{tree_@(t) \mid t \in L\}$.

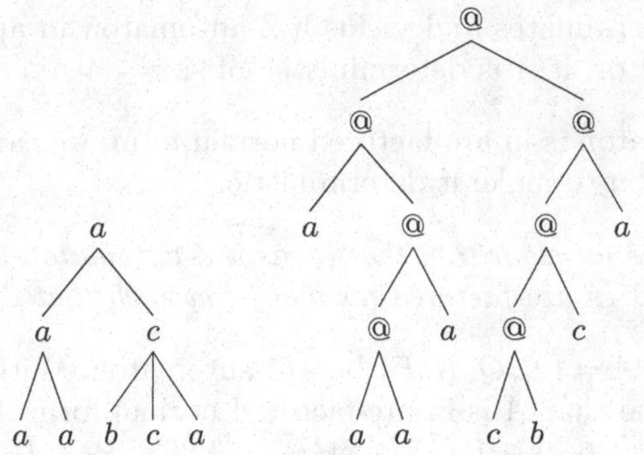

Fig. 3. The input tree t over the alphabet $\{a, b, c\}$ used in Example 1 and its binary encoding $tree_@(t)$.

It is not difficult to check that $tree_@$ is a bijection between T_Σ and $\mathrm{T}_{\Sigma_@}$.

A stepwise tree automaton is simply a ranked bottom-up tree automaton that receives as inputs binary encodings of unranked trees.

Definition 3 (Stepwise Automaton [2]**).** *A stepwise tree automaton (STA) $M = (Q, \Sigma, R, F)$ is a ranked bottom-up tree automaton over $\Sigma_@$. Consequently, every transition rule in R is of the form $a \to q$ or $@(p, p') \to q$ where $a \in \Sigma$ is a symbol of rank* 0, *and $q, p, p' \in Q$.*

In their arc-factored normal form, Z-automata can be understood as a syntactic variation of stepwise tree automata, and these in turn are bottom-up (ranked) tree automata. This link between the devices means that Z-automata can be firmly grounded on the well-developed theory of regular tree languages.

Definition 4 (Related Automata). *A Z-automaton $A = (\Sigma, Q, R, F)$ in arc-factored normal form and an STA $M_A = (Q, \Sigma_@, P, Q)$, are* related *if*

- *$a \to q \in P$ if and only if $a \to q \in R$, for every $a \in \Sigma$ and $q \in Q$, and*
- *$@(p, p') \to q \in P$ if and only if $p(p') \to q \in R$, for every $p, p', q \in Q$.*

As can be expected, a Z-automaton and a stepwise tree automaton that are related recognize the same language. For a given a Z-automaton or STA A with state set Q, and a tree t, we denote by $eval(A, t) = \{q \in Q \mid t \to_A^* q\}$ the set of states reached by A on input t.

Theorem 2. *Let $A = (\Sigma, Q, R, F)$ be a Z-automaton in arc-factored normal form and $M_A = (Q, \Sigma_@, P, Q)$ an STA, such that A and M_A are related. Then $\mathcal{L}(M_A) = tree_@(\mathcal{L}(A))$, and M_A is deterministic if and only if A is.*

Proof. Clearly, the automaton M_A is deterministic if and only if A is. To prove that $\mathcal{L}(M_A) = tree_@(\mathcal{L}(A))$, we show that $eval(M_A, tree_@(t)) = eval(A, t)$ for every tree $t \in \mathrm{T}_\Sigma$. We prove this by induction on the structure of the trees. Let $t = f(t_1, \dots, t_n) \in \mathrm{T}_\Sigma$.

If $q \in eval(A, t)$, then we have the following cases:

- If $n = 0$, then there is a transition rule $f \to q \in R$, and by construction, $f \to q \in P$ so $q \in eval(M_A, tree_@(t))$.
- If $n = 1$, then there is a $p \in Q$ and a $p' \in eval(A, t_1)$ such that $f \to p$ and $p(p') \to q \in R$. By the induction hypothesis, $eval(M_A, tree_@(t_1)) = eval(A, t_1)$ and by construction, both $f \to p$ and $@(p, p') \to q$ are in P, so $q \in eval(M_A, tree_@(t))$.
- If $n > 1$, then there is a $p \in eval(A, f(t_1, \dots, t_{n-1}))$ and a $p' \in eval(A, t_n)$ such that $p(p') \to q \in R$. By the induction hypothesis,

$$eval(M_A, tree_@(f(t_1, \dots, t_{n-1}))) = eval(A, f(t_1, \dots, t_{n-1})),$$

  and $eval(M_A, tree_@(t_n)) = eval(A, t_n)$, and by construction $@(p, p') \to q \in P$, so again $q \in eval(M_A, tree_@(t))$.

The other direction is obtained by the reversed reasoning, using the same three cases. □

This bridge between Z-automata and STA has several immediate implications, summarised in Corollaries 1 and 2.

Corollary 1. *For an unranked tree language L, the following are equivalent:*

1. *L is recognized by a Z-automaton.*
2. *L is recognized by a UTA.*
3. *$tree_@(L)$ is recognized by an STA.*

Corollary 2. *The following properties hold for Z-automata:*

1. *The family of tree languages accepted by Z-automata is closed under union, intersection, and complement.*
2. *Deterministic Z-automata are an equally succinct representation of unranked tree languages as deterministic STA, and exponentially more succinct than deterministic UTA [11].*

Item 2 of Corollary 2 means that given a deterministic Z-automaton A with n states, a minimal deterministic UTA for $\mathcal{L}(A)$ may have $O(2^n)$ states. However, given a deterministic UTA B with m states, it is always possible to find a deterministic Z-automaton for $\mathcal{L}(B)$ with $O(m)$ states.

Theorem 3. *For every Z-automaton A, there is a unique minimal deterministic Z-automaton B in arc-factored normal form such that $\mathcal{L}(A) = \mathcal{L}(B)$. If A is deterministic, then B can be computed in time $O(m \log n)$, where m and n are the size of the transition table and the number of states of A, respectively.*

Proof. Let $A = (\Sigma, Q, R, F)$ be a Z-automaton, which we may, without loss of generality, assumed to be in arc-factored normal form. Let M_A be the STA related to A. We note that both can be viewed as ordered labelled hypergraphs with node set Q and hyperedge set R. A hyperedge corresponding to

$r = (a \to q)$ is labelled with a and incident with q. A hyperedge corresponding to $r = (@(p, p') \to q)$ or $r = (p(p') \to q)$ is labelled with @ and incident with $pp'q$. For each $q \in F$, there is an additional hyperedge labelled '!' incident with q (where $! \notin \Sigma$). Obviously, the hypergraph representations of A and A_M are isomorphic, and both automata are uniquely determined by the hypergraph.

Let B be the Z-automaton A_N, where N is the result of minimizing the stepwise tree automaton A_M using the forward-bisimulation algorithm of [6], which coincides with standard minimization on deterministic tree automata. For binary trees, the time complexity of this algorithm is $O(m \log n)$. Since related automata recognize the same language, have the same number of states, and are either both deterministic, or both non-deterministic, we have that B is a deterministic Z-automaton with the same number of states as A_N, and such that $\mathcal{L}(B) = \mathcal{L}(N) = \mathcal{L}(M_A) = \mathcal{L}(A)$.

Suppose that there is another deterministic Z-automaton C with strictly fewer states than B recognizing the same language. In this case, the deterministic stepwise tree automaton M_C would be language equivalent to N, but have fewer states. This is not possible by the correctness of the minimization algorithm in [6]. Hence, B has a minimal number of states.

Finally assume that there is another deterministic Z-automaton C with the same number of states as B that is, when viewed as a hypergraph, not isomorphic to B. Then B_M and C_M are not isomorphic to each other, as they are isomorphic to B and C, respectively. This contradicts the uniqueness of the minimal deterministic STA.

Hence, B is the unique minimal deterministic Z-automaton. □

5 Left-to-Right Bottom-Up Derivations

The Z-automata semantics given in Sect. 3 allows transition rules to be applied wherever they apply in an intermediate tree t. As we shall see, we can restrict applications to the two lowest nodes along the left-most path of t, without loss of expressive power.

Definition 5 (LRBU Derivation). *Let $A = (\Sigma, Q, R, F)$ be a Z-automaton in arc-factored normal form, and let $s \in \mathrm{T}_\Sigma$. A computation is* left-to-right-bottom-up *(LRBU) if, in every step $t \to_A t'$ of the computation, one of the following holds. If α is the left-most leaf of t, then either*

1. *$t(\alpha) \in \Sigma$ and the transition rule is applied at node α or*
2. *$t(\alpha) \in Q$ and the transition rule is applied at the parent of α.*

We let $\mathcal{L}_{lrbu}(A) = \{t \in \mathrm{T}_\Sigma \mid t \to_A^* q$ by an LRBU computation for a $q \in F\}$.

Note that, in the second case above, the transition rule applied to the parent of α can either be of the form $a \to q$ or of the form $p(p') \to q$.

Theorem 4. *For every Z-automaton A in arc-factored normal form, we have $\mathcal{L}(A) = \mathcal{L}_{lrbu}(A)$.*

Proof. Let $A = (\Sigma, Q, R, F)$ be a Z-automaton in arc-factored normal form, and let $t \in \mathrm{T}_\Sigma$. We show that A has an accepting computation on t if and only if it has an accepting LRBU computation on t. The 'if' direction is trivial. The 'only if' direction is proved by induction on the structure of t. We argue that every computation of A ending in a state $q \in Q$ can be turned into an LRBU computation ending in the same state.

If $|t| = 1$ then this is trivially true because the computation already is LRBU. If $|t| \geq 2$, then t can be obtained from two trees $s, s' \in \mathrm{T}_\Sigma$ by adding s' as the rightmost child of the root of s. Since t is accepted by A, there is an accepting computation π of A on t. This computation, restricted to the transition rule applications at nodes in s and s' in the obvious way, yields subcomputations $s \to_A^* p$ and $s' \to_A^* p'$, for some $p, p' \in Q$. Since the computation accepts t, its last step is of the form $p(p') \to_A q$ for a state $q \in F$. By the induction hypothesis, there are LRBU computations μ and μ' on s and s', respectively, that accomplish the same. We can thus construct an accepting LRBU computation on t by first applying μ to t, then μ' to the subtree s' of t, and finally the transition rule $p(p') \to q$ to the remaining tree $p(p')$. □

From Theorems 4, 5 follows:

Theorem 5. *The membership problem for Z-automata in arc-factored normal form is in $O(mn)$, where m is the number of transition rules and n is the size of the input tree.*

Proof (Sketch). Let $A = (\Sigma, Q, R, F)$ be a Z-automaton in arc-factored normal form. To decide whether an input tree $t \in \mathrm{T}_\Sigma$ is in $\mathcal{L}(A)$, the automaton is applied to t by performing LRBU computations on t. At every step, it uses on-the-fly subset construction to check what transition rules in R are applicable at the last two nodes of the leftmost path of the intermediate tree. The time needed to consume one edge of t is thus in $O(|R|)$, and there are $|t| = n$ edges to consume. □

6 Conclusion

We have introduced a new type of automaton for unranked tree languages, the Z-automaton, and shown it to be equivalent to the UTA and STA. Z-automata offer a more compact form of representation than UTA, and avoid the binary encoding used by STA. We have also provided a normal form and a standard left-to-right bottom-up (LRBU) mode of derivations that although syntactically more restrictive, retain the expressive power of the original device.

Given the close relation between Z-automata, STA, and bottom-up ranked tree automata, we expect the majority of the results pertaining to the latter models to carry over. However, in some situations, the time and space complexities may be affected. A further investigation in this direction is left for future work, as is the study of logical characterizations.

Acknowledgment. We thank the reviewers for carefully reading the manuscript. In particular, we thank one reviewer who pointed out a flaw in the original version of Theorem 1.

References

1. Brüggemann-Klein, A., Murata, M., Wood, D.: Regular tree and regular hedge languages over unranked alphabets: version 1. Techcial report HKUST-TCSC-2001-0, The Hong Kong University of Science and Technology (2001). http://repository.ust.hk/ir/Record/1783.1-738
2. Carme, J., Niehren, J., Tommasi, M.: Querying unranked trees with stepwise tree automata. In: van Oostrom, V. (ed.) RTA 2004. LNCS, vol. 3091, pp. 105–118. Springer, Heidelberg (2004). https://doi.org/10.1007/978-3-540-25979-4_8
3. Comon, H., et al.: Tree automata techniques and applications. http://www.grappa.univ-lille3.fr/tata. Accessed 12 Oct 2007
4. Droste, M., Vogler, H.: Weighted logics for unranked tree automata. Theory Comput. Syst. **48**(1), 23–47 (2011). https://doi.org/10.1007/s00224-009-9224-4
5. Gécseg, F., Steinby, M.: Tree Automata. Akadémiai Kiadó, Budapest (1984). https://arxiv.org/abs/1509.06233
6. Högberg, J., Maletti, A., May, J.: Backward and forward bisimulation minimization of tree automata. Theor. Comput. Sci. **410**(37), 3539–3552 (2009). https://doi.org/10.1016/j.tcs.2009.03.022. Preliminary version. In: CIAA 2007
7. Kübler, S., McDonald, R., Nivre, J.: Dependency Parsing. Morgan and Claypool Publishers, New York (2009). https://doi.org/10.2200/S00169ED1V01Y200901HLT002
8. Libkin, L.: Logics for unranked trees: an overview. Log. Methods Comput. Sci. **2**(3), 1–31 (2006). https://doi.org/10.2168/LMCS-2(3:2)2006
9. Maletti, A., Graehl, J., Hopkins, M., Knight, K.: The power of extended top-down tree transducers. SIAM J. Comput. **39**(2), 410–430 (2009). https://doi.org/10.1137/070699160
10. Martens, W., Niehren, J.: Minimizing tree automata for unranked trees. In: Bierman, G., Koch, C. (eds.) DBPL 2005. LNCS, vol. 3774, pp. 232–246. Springer, Heidelberg (2005). https://doi.org/10.1007/11601524_15
11. Martens, W., Niehren, J.: On the minimization of XML schemas and tree automata for unranked trees. J. Comput. System Sci. **73**(4), 550–583 (2007). https://doi.org/10.1016/j.jcss.2006.10.021

A Benchmark Production Tool for Regular Expressions

Angelo Borsotti[1], Luca Breveglieri[1(✉)], Stefano Crespi Reghizzi[1,2], and Angelo Morzenti[1]

[1] Politecnico di Milano, 20133 Milan, Italy
angelo.borsotti@mail.polimi.it,
{luca.breveglieri,stefano.crespireghizzi,angelo.morzenti}@polimi.it
[2] CNR-IEIIT, 20133 Milan, Italy

Abstract. We describe a new tool, named *REgen*, that generates regular expressions (RE) to be used as test cases, and that generates also synthetic benchmarks for exercising and measuring the performance of RE-based software libraries and applications. Each *group* of REs is randomly generated and satisfies a user-specified set of constraints, such as length, nesting depth, operator arity, repetition depth, and syntax tree balancing. In addition to such parameters, other features are chosen by the tool. An RE group may include REs that are ambiguous, or that define the same regular language but differ with respect to their syntactic structure. A *benchmark* is a collection of RE groups that have a user-specified numerosity and distribution, together with a representative sample of texts for each RE in the collection. We present two generation algorithms for RE groups and for benchmarks. Experimental results are reported for a large benchmark we used to compare the performance of different RE parsing algorithms. The tool *REgen* and the RE benchmark are publicly available and fill a gap in supporting tools for the development and evaluation of RE applications.

Keywords: Regular expression generation · Benchmark for regular expressions · Regular expression tool

1 Introduction

Regular expressions (RE) are a widely applied language definition model. Actually the term RE refers not only to the Kleene formal model, but also to programming notations like that of the *Java.regexp* library, which we generically call *technical RE* [2]. Many algorithms and software libraries using REs, referred to as *RE SW*, continue to be developed for many purposes, e.g., string matching, text editing, code inspection, intrusion detection, etc. Our focus is on those RE SW that not just recognize regular sets of strings, but also assign them a structure, i.e., do parsing. Quite often, the REs in such applications are ambiguous, therefore a string can be parsed in many different ways.

M. Hospodár and G. Jirásková (Eds.): CIAA 2019, LNCS 11601, pp. 95–107, 2019.
https://doi.org/10.1007/978-3-030-23679-3_8

The development and evaluation of RE SW would benefit from using large collections of REs, but surprisingly we could not find any available one, which we needed for measuring the performance of different RE parsing algorithms, including our own [1]. This motivated the design and implementation of a new tool, called *REgen*, to produce customizable RE collections, as well as string samples of the corresponding regular languages. By using the tool, we synthesized a large RE benchmark, described in Sect. 4, that we used for an objective comparison of RE parsing algorithms. However, *REgen* is not biased towards a specific RE SW and is planned as a general-purpose customizable tool.

Related Work. We briefly consider two research directions, and why they could not be exploited here. First, string generation programs driven by a given context-free (CF) grammar have been used, at least since the '80s, to produce input data for testing compilers, e.g., [3], and other software systems, e.g., [7]. Such generator algorithms are typically guided by simple criteria, such as the minimal coverage criterion, ensuring that all CF rules are used to produce a minimal set of strings. Of course, most produced strings, though syntactically correct, are illegal input data for the SW system under test; they may help debugging, but they are not intended for evaluating SW execution performance. In practice, compiler evaluation relies on big hand-written language-specific benchmarks, e.g., SPEC for the C language. Our tool is also driven by a CF grammar, namely the meta-grammar of REs, but it essentially differs because *REgen* has a meta-level and a terminal level. At meta-level, each output string is a *generated RE* (*GRE*), and is used at terminal level to drive the text generation component of *REgen*, which creates a set of *generated texts* (*GT*).

Second, our project objectives differ from those of more theoretical research on RE enumeration, although enumeration algorithms may seem to address similar requirements as our meta-language level. The RE enumeration procedure in [5] is actually targeted at enumerating regular languages rather than REs, thus it carefully avoids generating two equivalent REs, whereas for a tool like ours, generating also equivalent GREs is acceptable and even desirable, e.g., to evaluate how the structure of equivalent REs impacts on SW performance.

Paper Contributions. The design of a new tool for generating REs and the corresponding texts raised various technical questions for which existing systems did not offer ready solutions. Since the range of RE SW is ill-defined and open, we decided that our tool should be *customizable*, so that the future users of *REgen* will be able to match the features of the GRE benchmarks, with the typical properties of the REs occurring in, say, a code inspection versus a web searching application. For instance, the REs used in text searching typically have a very small nesting level for the star (more generally, repetition) operator. Unfortunately, we could not find any established classification of REs oriented towards their application domains, and we had to examine the following question: how to select a not too large set of parameters that would allow to classify REs according to flexible empirical criteria. We started from the classical parameters such as RE length and star (better, repetition) depth, then we added and experimented others, later described in the paper, such as the maximal arity of an operator (*or* and *dot*). Other parameters specify that certain combinations of operations are forbidden. Another interesting structural parameter is whether the RE tree is balanced or not; we found that it is better to separate the generation algorithms for the two cases. Clearly, the RE parameters we have identified and included in the current tool are just a well-thought initial model, which is open to revision and tuning to better adjust to unanticipated use cases.

The main output of our research is the specification and implementation of the *REgen* tool, which actually includes two generator levels, GRE and GT. The GRE generator is the innovative and major component, while the GT generator is indispensable but more traditional. More precisely, the tool consists of three parts. Part one outputs a single GRE compliant with user-specified or default parameter values, thus, by repeated application with fixed values, it generates a random *group* of GREs that fulfill identical constraints. Part two repeatedly applies Part one, each time with stepping parameter values, and thus outputs a random collection of GRE groups, to be called a *benchmark*, which has user-specified features. Part three works on a given GRE and produces a representative sample of GTs, with a user-specified length and numerosity.

By using *REgen*, a large RE benchmark has been created, and we report the main measurements of the GREs and GTs, and the tool execution times. Moreover, we have further analyzed the GREs for the following important properties that are not controlled by the current input parameters: the ambiguity of GREs, and how many GREs present in the benchmark define nondisjoint languages.

The Java code of *REgen* and the benchmark are available at the URL http://github.com/FLC-project/REgen, and they will hopefully serve software developers and formal language researchers.

Paper Organization. Section 2 contains the basic definitions of GREs and their operators and abstract syntax trees, followed by the input parameters that constrain tree shape and contents. Section 3 outlines the generation algorithms. Section 4 presents some quantitative aspects of the benchmark generated. The Conclusion hints to future developments.

2 Basic Definitions

The notions we use are standard in formal language theory. First, we define the RE family to be considered. A *generated RE* (*GRE*) is a string over an alphabet $\Omega = M \uplus \Sigma$, where set M contains the metasymbols and set Σ, called the text alphabet, contains the terminals that may occur in a *generated text* (*GT*). The GRE structure is better represented by an *abstract syntax tree* (*AST*). Table 1 and the examples in Fig. 1 should give a sufficient idea of the language of GREs, denoted L_{GRE}, and also of the ASTs. To denote a GRE we use letters such as e, f, e_1, ...; the empty string is ε. Notice that rule 5 in Table 1 defines the *repetition* operation, which contains rules 5.1, 5.2 and 5.3 as special cases.

Definition 1 (AST). *Let $e \in L_{GRE}$, the corresponding AST, denoted e_T, has the structure and node labels specified in Table 1.* □

Table 1. Components and rules of a GRE and the corresponding AST tree.

#	Rules defining GRE e	Node label of the corresponding AST
1	$e = \varepsilon$	Leaf node with label ε (empty string)
2	$e = a \in \Sigma$	Leaf node with label a (terminal character)
3	$e = e_1 \mid e_2 \mid \ldots \mid e_k \quad k \geq 2$	Inner node with label "$\mid$" and k children
4	$e = e_1 \cdot e_2 \cdot \ldots \cdot e_k \quad k \geq 2$	Inner node with label "$\cdot$" and k children
5	$e = e_1^{i,j} \quad 0 \leq i < j \leq \infty$	Inner node with label i, j and one child e_1
5.1	$e = e_1^*$ same as $e_1^{0,\infty}$	Inner node with label "$*$" and one child e_1
5.2	$e = e_1^+$ same as $e_1^{1,\infty}$	Inner node with label "$+$" and one child e_1
5.3	$e = e_1^?$ same as $e_1^{0,1}$	Inner node with label "$?$" and one child e_1

See the examples in Fig. 1. An internal node of an AST belongs to the types:

$$type = \{ \overbrace{union \mid, \ concatenation \cdot}^{\text{non-unary}}, \ \overbrace{repetition \, (\min \ldots \max)}^{\text{unary}} \}$$

As said, the *iterators* star "$*$" and cross "$+$", and the *optionality* operator "$?$", are subcases of repetition nodes, with the values already shown in Table 1.

The language defined by a GRE e is denoted $L(e) \subseteq \Sigma^*$, and to prevent confusion, its sentences are called *generated texts* (GT). The GREs e and f (Fig. 1) are *weakly equivalent* since $L(e) = L(f)$. Yet, since GRE f assigns to the text $a\,b\,a\,b$ a syntax tree (ST) different from the two trees assigned to the same string by GRE e (in Fig. 1, middle right), the two GREs e and f are not interchangeable when they are used for string matching or searching.

In Table 2 we list and describe the parameters and choices the user may enter, to customize the collection of GREs produced by *REgen*; some parameters are illustrated in Fig. 1 (bottom). The current selection of parameters tries to balance the complication of having too many generation parameters and the flexibility needed for tayloring GREs to specific applications.

3 The RE Generator

The goal of the *RE generator* is to produce a set of possibly very many GREs that match the parameter values specified by the user or by default. This is achieved through iteratively executing a procedure that generates random REs. Such a procedure is designed to produce, with a very high probability, a distinct RE at each invocation, so as to minimize the likelihood of discarding duplicates.

More precisely, the RE generator produces a set of ASTs, called a *group*, such that for all ASTs in the same group, the *primary* parameters of Table 2 take the same values, e.g., all ASTs are balanced or all are unbalanced. However, as it would be detrimental that all ASTs have the same frontier length, we decided that the number φ of leaves is not fixed, but that it ranges in the same interval.

$e = (\,(a^{+} \mid b\,a \mid a\,b\,a)^{+} \mid \varepsilon\,)\,b$ $\qquad$ $f = (a^{+} \mid b\,a \mid a\,b\,a)^{*}\,b$

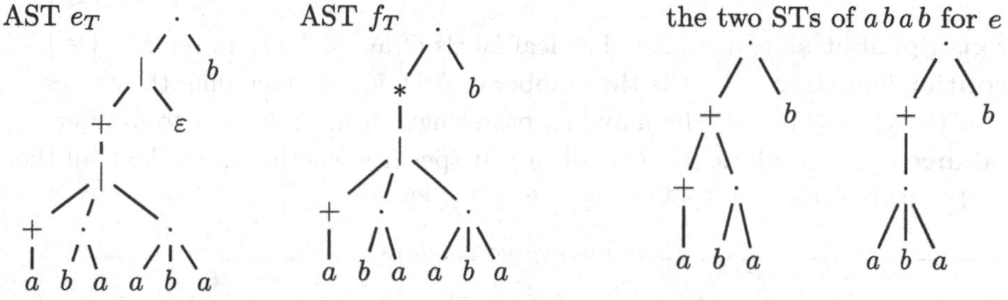

parameter types for AST	*parameter values for the AST e_T*
text alphabet size	$\alpha = 2$ (alphabet $\Sigma = \{\, a,\; b \,\}$)
frontier length	$\varphi = 8$ (frontier $a\,b\,a\,a\,b\,a\,\varepsilon\,b$)
tree depth	$\tau\,(e_T) = \max\,(5, 5, 5, 5, 5, 5, 2, 1) = 5$
balanced or unbalanced	$\beta =$ *unbalanced*
associative-operator degrees (in left-to-right top-down order)	$\delta_{\cdot} = 2 \;\; \delta_{\mid} = 2 \;\; \delta_{\mid} = 3 \;\; \delta_{\cdot} = 2 \;\; \delta_{\cdot} = 3$ $\delta = \max\,(\delta_{\cdot},\, \delta_{\mid}) = 3$
repetition depth (paths listed from left to right)	$\rho = 2 \;\; \rho = 1 \;\; \ldots \;\; \rho = 1 \;\; \rho = 0 \;\; \rho = 0$
forbidden (parent, child) pair	('|', '|') $\quad$ ('.', '.') $\quad$ (*unary, unary*)

Fig. 1. Top: GREs e and f (a and b are arbitrary terminals). Middle left: the ASTs e_T and f_T of e and f. Middle right: the syntax trees in $T\,(e)$ of the text $a\,b\,a\,b$, where in the left ST the higher node "+" has two children, since there are two iterations. Bottom: values of the main parameters of e_T; in the last row, the (parent, child) pairs that do not occur in e_T are listed as forbidden.

Thus, a *group* is qualified by the following parameter values. The text alphabet Σ (thus its cardinality $\alpha = |\,\Sigma\,|$) and the balance parameter β have fixed values. The tree depth τ ranges over an interval (min and max may coincide), and $\delta_{\cdot}$ has a fixed value, which specifies the interval $[2 \ldots \delta_{\cdot}]$; the case of $\delta_{\mid}$ is identical. In the GREs, we rule out the occurrence of immediately nested unary operators, since they are idempotent (in an obvious sense) and it is unlikely that any RE SW needs to discriminate between the sub-REs, say, $(e)^{*}$ and $\big((e)^{*}\big)^{?}$.

Though two ASTs in the same group have the same parameters, they may differ for the choice of internal node types and labels. To produce a wider variety of ASTs, the generator is repeatedly invoked with different parameter settings, thus resulting in a set of groups, which we call a *collection*.

First, we describe at a high-level the RE generation algorithm, which is actually split into two parts for balanced and unbalanced trees.

Table 2. Main GRE parameters to drive the generator.

primary parameters

text alphabet size $\alpha = |\Sigma|$. The leaf labels of an AST are in set $\Sigma \cup \{ \varepsilon \}$.
frontier length $\varphi \geq 1$. It is the number of AST leaves, including the ε ones.
tree depth $\tau \geq 0$. It is the maximal path length from AST root to frontier.
balanced or unbalanced β (boolean). It specifies whether in an AST all the paths from root to frontier have the same length.

secondary parameters

associative-operator degree $\delta_{\bullet}$, $\delta_{|} \geq 2$. They denote the max bounds on the numbers of child nodes of a concatenation and a union node, respectively. We set $\delta = \max\left(\delta_{\bullet}, \delta_{|}\right)$. In Fig. 1 their values are listed for each node.
repetition depth $\rho \geq 0$. For a path from node to leaf, it specifies the number of repetition nodes that occur on that path.
forbidden parent-child (relation) This binary relation in *type* × *type* specifies the pairs of parent-child node types that must not occur in an AST.

Balanced Tree Generation Algorithm. First, we state and prove a property, used in the algorithm, about the number of leaves in a balanced tree. In the coming discussion, we set $\delta = \max\left(\delta_{\bullet}, \delta_{|}\right)$.

Proposition 1 (relation between leaf number and operator degree). *Consider the root-to-leaf paths in a balanced tree. Define the (non-empty) set* $\{ \langle i, n_i \rangle \mid \; 1 \leq i \leq \delta \}$, *where* $n_i \geq 0$ *is the number of degree-i nodes on a given such path; therefore, the tree depth is* $\tau = \sum_{1 \leq i \leq \delta} n_i$. *If such a set is the same on all root-to-leaf paths, then the following relation holds for the tree leaf number:*

$$\varphi = 1^{n_1} \cdot 2^{n_2} \cdot \ldots \cdot \delta^{n_\delta} = \prod_{1 \leq i \leq \delta} i^{n_i}$$

□

Proof. The proof is by induction on the tree depth τ.

Base Step. Consider the (elementary) tree with a single node, thus $\tau = 0$ and $\varphi = 1$. Then, $n_i = 0$ for $1 \leq i \leq \delta$, and the above relation trivially holds.

Inductive Step. For any k with $1 \leq k \leq \delta$, consider $k \geq 1$ trees $t_1, \ldots, t_k$ that have equal depth $\tau \geq 1$ and the same set $\{ \langle i, n_i \rangle \mid \; 1 \leq i \leq \delta \}$ of numbers n_i of degree-i nodes on any root-to-node path. By the inductive hypothesis, all such trees have the same leaf number $\varphi = \prod_{1 \leq i \leq \delta} i^{n_i}$. Build a (balanced) tree $\hat{t}$ with a new root of degree $k \geq 1$ and append the trees $t_1, \ldots, t_k$ to this root. For tree $\hat{t}$, the set of the numbers $\hat{n}_i$ of degree-i nodes on any root-to-node path, i.e., $\{ \langle i, \hat{n}_i \rangle \mid \; 1 \leq i \leq \delta \}$, is identical on all such paths, with $\hat{n}_k = n_k + 1$

and $\hat{n}_i = n_i$ for every $i \neq k$. By construction, the leaf number of $\hat{t}$ is $\hat{\varphi} = k\varphi = k \cdot 1^{n_1} \cdot \ldots \cdot \delta^{n_\delta} = 1^{n_1} \cdot \ldots \cdot k \cdot k^{n_k} \cdot \ldots \cdot \delta^{n_\delta} = 1^{n_1} \cdot \ldots \cdot k^{n_k+1} \cdot \ldots \cdot \delta^{n_\delta} = \prod_{1 \leq i \leq \delta} i^{\hat{n}_i}$. Thus, tree $\hat{t}$ satisfies the above relation. □

We outline the recursive procedure that builds an AST, in the top-down order:

1 Randomly generate a factorization of parameter φ according to Proposition 1, i.e., generate a set of pairs $\langle$ node-number, degree-value $\rangle$:

$$\left\{ \langle i, n_i \rangle \mid (1 \leq i \leq \delta) \wedge (n_i \geq 0) \wedge \left(\tau = \sum_{1 \leq i \leq \delta} n_i\right) \wedge \left(\varphi = \prod_{1 \leq i \leq \delta} i^{n_i}\right) \right\} \quad (1)$$

2. In any order, build a child node, then recursively build the child subtrees.

As the algorithm recurs down on a root-to-leaf path, it carries over as a procedure parameter the list of the degrees chosen for the nodes created on that path.

We discuss some special cases occurring in the preceding algorithm. Since the range of values of the secondary parameters $\delta_{\bullet}$ and $\delta_{|}$ is typically quite restricted, for certain values of the primary parameter φ there may not be any factorization (1); for instance, when $\varphi = 69 = 3 \times 23$ and $\delta < 23$. In such cases, the following heuristics is applied: parameter φ is decreased by a few units, then a balanced tree is built and is adjusted to the original value of φ by attaching the few missing nodes to the tree bottom branches. Therefore, all the generated ASTs are balanced and every root-to-leaf path comprises the same number of nodes for any degree, except possibly for the two last tree levels. We note that such adjustments are possible because an exact compliance with the parameter values is not required for a benchmark generator. On the other hand, a formal enumeration algorithm, e.g., [5], is subjected to much stricter requirements.

Unbalanced Tree Generation Algorithm. Unbalanced trees are also generated top-down, by means of a recursive procedure that combines the primary parameters for the frontier length φ and tree depth τ, thus achieving a large variety of tree shapes. The procedure repeatedly executes the following two phases:

1. For an internal node, starting from the root, randomly elect one of the child nodes as *distinguished*, which will be the root of the deepest subtree that has the maximum number of leaves. The total leaf number N (initially $N = \varphi$ for the root of the whole tree) is partitioned, and a fixed fraction of leaves, equal to $\left[\frac{N}{F} \right]$ for a certain F, is assigned to such a child node, while the remaining $N - \left[\frac{N}{F} \right]$ leaves are randomly distributed to the other siblings.
2. Iterate phase 1 at the next tree level. Notice that the number of leaves assigned to the current distinguished child node decreases with the distance of the node from the root, according to a geometric progression.

To satisfy the tree depth parameter τ, the equality $F = \sqrt[\tau]{\varphi}$ must hold. The maximum node degree δ must agree with F as well, hence also with the frontier length φ and the tree depth τ from which F derives, to ensure that the distinguished child node is assigned a leaf number greater than all those of the other siblings. Since the number of siblings is at most $\delta - 1$ and in total they have $N - \left\lceil \frac{N}{F} \right\rceil$ leaves, for the above condition to be satisfiable, this (properly rounded) inequality must hold: $\frac{N}{F} > \left(N - \frac{N}{F} \right) / \left(\delta - 1 \right)$. It follows $\delta > F$. This constraint is easily satisfied in all the practical cases. For instance, with $\varphi = 100$ and $\tau = 5$, it holds $F = 2.512$, and the maximum node degree is constrained to $\delta > 2$. Therefore, all the generated ASTs have one or more root-to-leaf paths of the desired length, and all the other paths are shorter. Moreover, the degree of all the nodes is within the limit δ.

$$\alpha = 4 \quad \beta = balanced \quad \varphi = 12 \quad \tau = 4 \quad \delta = 3 \quad (\text{in } (1) \ n_1 = 1 \quad n_2 = 2 \quad n_3 = 1)$$

$$(a^+ \mid b^?)\,(db)^* \,(a^* \mid d^{4,8}) \mid (ba \mid a\,d \mid bc)^+ \quad \left((dc)^+ \mid a^*b^+\right)\left((ca) \mid (db)\right)^* \left((c \mid a)^{3,7} \mid d^*a^+\right)$$

$$\alpha = 5 \quad \beta = unbalanced \quad \varphi = 13 \quad \tau = 4 \quad \delta = 3 \qquad (F = 1,8988)$$

$$(b \mid d \mid c)\,(ac \mid b \mid d) \mid a^+ \,(e \mid c \mid a)\,(c \mid e) \qquad \left((dac) \mid b\right)\left(da\,(b \mid c) \mid ab \mid c\right)(ab)^*$$

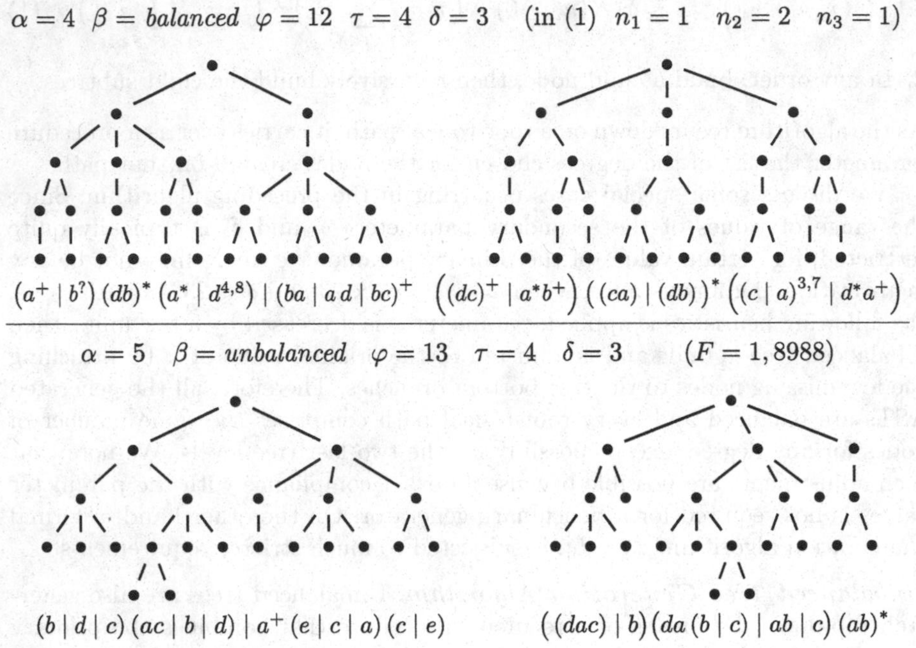

Fig. 2. Sample REs in two GRE *groups* identified by their primary parameters. The ASTs are simplified to show only the levels and highlight the balanced (top) vs. unbalanced (bottom) structure.

Group Production. As said, the GREs of a *group* are obtained by repeatedly invoking the random generation procedure with fixed primary parameter values. Due to randomness, it may happen that two identical GREs are produced, and a check is performed to avoid duplicates in the same group. We have experimentally found that duplications occur in a negligible number of cases and do not affect the generation speed. Figure 2 shows a few GREs with their ASTs, generated for two *groups* identified by the listed parameter values.

In the current version of *REgen*, the RE generator does not have any way to enforce that the generated RE is ambiguous or not. Such a control, if required, is currently performed off-line by another part of the tool, see later. We have found that a significant portion of GREs is ambiguous, typically about 60%.

Printing GREs as Formulas. The ASTs must be eventually converted into a textual form suitable for the intended RE SW. We do not describe the simple conversion, and just comment on the introduction of parentheses into a GRE. Parentheses serve two purposes: to enforce an operator evaluation priority and, for *technical* REs such as Posix, also to identify the sub-REs that have to be matched with the source text (this use is known as *capturing*). When converting an AST into a formula, *REgen* always prints the priority parentheses. In addition, if a sub-RE has to be "captured", an embracing parenthesis pair is printed, even if it is unnecessary for priority. To know when, the new boolean parameter *capturing* is affixed to all the internal AST nodes.

3.1 Benchmark Production

In our setting, a (synthetic) *benchmark* is a large set of GREs, each one accompanied by a set of texts. More precisely, a benchmark is structured as one or more *collections* of groups, each *group* being a randomly generated set of REs that have the same user-specified primary parameters.

Since benchmarks can be generated for different and unforeseen RE SW, it would be unwise to fix any general properties for benchmarks. The case of a benchmark of broad interest, used to evaluate RE parsing SW, is described in detail in Sect. 4. The benchmark comprises many groups of GREs of increasing length, and each GRE is accompanied by a set of texts of increasing length. The wide range of GRE lengths allowed us to measure and plot the time an RE parsing algorithm takes to "compile" an RE, as a function of its length. Moreover, the text parsing time depends on both the text length and the RE length; to compare such times, our benchmark contains a large and diversified corpus of GREs and texts.

Notice that generating a few short REs and texts is simple, but doing so for long and significantly different REs and texts may run into time and memory limits. The naive approach based on enumerating REs by increasing length, and then selecting the few of them that fit the given criteria, is too slow to be feasible. In other words, an ideal requirement for an efficient generator is that only the REs that fit the benchmark objectives be generated, thus avoiding the production of REs that would be later discarded. Our tool approaches such an ideal and produces tolerably few unfit REs.

Text Generation Algorithm. Given an RE e, our tool randomly computes one or more generated texts GT $x \in L(e)$ by two simple procedures. The first procedure has two parameters, the RE e and the length ℓ of the text to be generated, and it produces just one GT x with length $|x| \approx \ell$. The second procedure is used to generate many GTs organized into a finite collection $\mathcal{C} = \{ G_1, G_2, \ldots, G_g \}$ of *text groups*, i.e., $G_i \subset L(e)$, each group containing about the same number of texts. The length of the text increases from one group to the next, as specified by one of the input parameters, which are the following: the RE e, the number g of groups, the group size $|G_i|$, and the *step* $s > 0$. Then, each GT group comprises GTs with approximately the following lengths:

$$\forall x \in G_1 \ \ |x| \in [0 \ldots s] \qquad \forall i \geq 2 \ \ \forall x \in G_i \ \ |x| \in \big[(i-1) \cdot s + 1 \ldots i \cdot s\big]$$

In this way, a user can customize the text lengths of a GT collection and so produce groups that include a statistically significant sample of texts within specified length intervals. Concerning the GT generation algorithm, it suffices to say that it operates in two phases:

1. Given a GRE e, encoded by the AST, the generator tabulates, for each subtree corresponding to a sub-RE e_j, the min and max lengths of a text in $L(e_j)$.
2. For each length ℓ, the GTs are top-down recursively computed by visiting their inner nodes and, for each node, by randomly partitioning the text length and distributing the resulting parts to its child nodes; details are omitted.

Last, notice that the GT collection is neither intended nor guaranteed to cover all the possible choices of the given RE, since *REgen* is not a test case generator for verifying SW systems. However, since the GTs are randomly generated, the benchmark can be dimensioned to be statistically significant.

4 Experimental Results

By using *REgen*, we have generated a large benchmark, which we needed for a related project, where we had developed a new deterministic parsing algorithm for ambiguous REs [1]. We wanted to objectively compare its speed against other existing algorithms, such as the RE2 library. The few collections of REs we could find, though too small for such a purpose, provided an initial indication of the kind of REs to be considered for a benchmark. Since the RE parsers are not biased towards specific uses of REs, we needed to exert them on an RE mix covering large intervals of essentially all the parameters listed in Table 2.

Some relevant features of such a benchmark are shown in Table 3 and are commented below. There are two collections of ten groups, one unbalanced and the other balanced, and each group contains one hundred GREs. The group parameters, which control the GRE generation, have the following values. The frontier length φ ranges from 1 to 100, increasing by 10 in each group; the depth τ ranges from 2 to 5; the repetition depth (in particular the star and cross depths) is limited only by τ; and the operator arity δ is unlimited. The following operator pairs are forbidden for parent-child nodes: ('|', '|'), ('·', '·') and (*unary*, *unary*). The text letters are taken from the alphanumeric alphabet (62 characters). The benchmark size in terms of GREs, which is of 2,000 REs totalizing about 280,000 characters, is much larger than any existing collection.

Next, we look at other properties. Through an external ambiguity detection algorithm [1], we analyzed the GREs. In Table 3, the *ambiguous* row counts the number of ambiguous GREs, with the rather surprising result that 59% unbalanced and 67% balanced GREs are ambiguous. Of course, having a large percentage of ambiguous REs was very desirable for evaluating the parsers.

In each *collection*, we also checked the presence of GREs defining the same language, and we found almost none of them. A plausible explanation is that the

Table 3. Benchmark for the performance evaluation of RE parsing algorithms.

Applies to	Benchmark feature	Collection 1	Collection 2
Generated regular expression (GRE)	Balancing	Unbalanced	Balanced
	Total number of GREs	1,000	1,000
	N. of groups of GREs	10	10
	N. of ambiguous GREs	596	677
	N. of weakly equiv. GREs	6	2
	N. of overlapping GREs	544	666
	N. of discarded GREs	0	486
	Total GRE length	125,165 char	154,436 char
Gen. text (GT)	Number of texts	99,730	99,820
	Total GT length	45,081,981 char	45,155,166 char
GRE+GT	CPU generation time	33 s	37 s

generated corpus, though large, is very small compared to the huge generation space, so that the generation algorithms effectively produce random GREs. On the other hand, the number of GREs that define non-disjoint languages is much higher: 54% unbalanced and 66% balanced GREs define a language that overlaps the language of another GRE in the same collection.

In the row *discarded*, the unbalanced generator always ends successfully, whereas the balanced one creates 49% GREs that fail to have the required frontier length φ. This is plausibly due to the length constraint imposed by Proposition 1 for a given depth. This notwithstanding, collection generation is fast (see below). Then, we comment the results for GTs. We wanted to plot the execution times of different parsing algorithms on texts of length in $1 \ldots 100$. Moreover, to improve measurement accuracy, the number of GTs in each length class must be uniform and sufficiently large. Initially, this was problematic, since the *density function* [8] of regular languages for most GREs is a high-order polynomial or exponential. Therefore, for a given GRE, the population of shorter GTs was often scarce. To increase the number of short texts, we gathered the GTs of identical length coming from different GREs present in the benchmark, thus obtaining an adequate and uniform number of GTs for all the lengths.

REgen is fast enough for a practical use. Table 3 reports the CPU time[1] to generate the benchmark, including both GREs and GTs, but excluding the time for testing GRE ambiguity and language disjointness, performed off-line.

Based on such an experience, we anticipate that it will be easier and faster to generate customized benchmarks for RE applications more specialized than RE parsing. For instance, REs for text or pattern searching are typically simpler and have a low nesting operator degree, in particular for repetition operators.

[1] On an AMD Athlon dual-core processor with 2.00 GB RAM and 2.20 GHz clock.

5 Conclusion

Since no previous work on RE generation systems was available, in order to make a well-thought design of *REgen* we initially considered a wide range of RE parameters. Then, we experimented with tool prototypes for different input parameters, and we compared the generation times and the sensitivity of the generated GRE corpus to various parameters. Eventually, we selected the parameters listed in this paper. With such a selection, *REgen* is capable of producing a satisfactory variety of GREs, and is fast. Yet the current choice is by no means final, and further experience will be important. We hope that this tool and the benchmark will serve the scientific and technical communities.

Future Developments. The percentage of ambiguous GREs in the benchmark is likely to be significant for some RE SW, such as those for searching, but currently it is not an input parameter to *REgen*. To add it to the parameters, we need to study how to efficiently incorporate an ambiguity test, such as [6], into the RE generator. A different possibility would be to incorporate an NFA generation algorithm (see [4] and its references) into *REgen*, and then to compute one or more REs for the language recognized. At last, a promising parameter for a future investigation is the RE *density function* [8]. By using the formal results in that paper, one might engineer a generator to produce GREs with specified density functions, say, polynomial. Yet the interplay between GRE density and ambiguity remains to be clarified: in our setting, it seems more appropriate to define for an RE a density function representing, for any length value, the number of syntax trees, instead of the number of texts as done in [8].

References

1. Borsotti, A., Breveglieri, L., Crespi Reghizzi, S., Morzenti, A.: From ambiguous regular expressions to deterministic parsing automata. In: Drewes, F. (ed.) CIAA 2015. LNCS, vol. 9223, pp. 35–48. Springer, Cham (2015). https://doi.org/10.1007/978-3-319-22360-5_4
2. Câmpeanu, C., Salomaa, K., Yu, S.: Regex and extended regex. In: Champarnaud, J.-M., Maurel, D. (eds.) CIAA 2002. LNCS, vol. 2608, pp. 77–84. Springer, Heidelberg (2003). https://doi.org/10.1007/3-540-44977-9_7
3. Celentano, A., Crespi Reghizzi, S., Della Vigna, P., Ghezzi, C., Granata, G., Savoretti, F.: Compiler testing using a sentence generator. Softw. Pract. Exp. **10**, 897–918 (1980). https://doi.org/10.1002/spe.4380101104
4. Héam, P.-C., Joly, J.-L.: On the uniform random generation of non deterministic automata up to isomorphism. In: Drewes, F. (ed.) CIAA 2015. LNCS, vol. 9223, pp. 140–152. Springer, Cham (2015). https://doi.org/10.1007/978-3-319-22360-5_12
5. Lee, J., Shallit, J.: Enumerating regular expressions and their languages. In: Domaratzki, M., Okhotin, A., Salomaa, K., Yu, S. (eds.) CIAA 2004. LNCS, vol. 3317, pp. 2–22. Springer, Heidelberg (2005). https://doi.org/10.1007/978-3-540-30500-2_2
6. Sulzmann, M., Lu, K.Z.M.: Derivative-based diagnosis of regular expression ambiguity. Int. J. Found. Comput. Sci. **28**(5), 543–562 (2017)

7. Sutton, M., Greene, A., Amini, P.: Fuzzing: Brute Force Vulnerability Discovery. Addison-Wesley, Boston (2007)
8. Szilard, A., Yu, S., Zhang, K., Shallit, J.: Characterizing regular languages with polynomial densities. In: Havel, I.M., Koubek, V. (eds.) MFCS 1992. LNCS, vol. 629, pp. 494–503. Springer, Heidelberg (1992). https://doi.org/10.1007/3-540-55808-X_48

New Algorithms for Manipulating Sequence BDDs

Shuhei Denzumi(✉)

The University of Tokyo, Hongo 7-3-1, Bunkyo, Tokyo 113-8656, Japan
denzumi@mist.i.u-tokyo.ac.jp

Abstract. Sequence binary decision diagram (SeqBDD) is a data structure to represent and manipulate sets of strings. This is a variant of zero-suppressed binary decision diagram (ZDD) that manipulates combinatorial sets. Nowadays, binary decision diagrams (BDDs) and its family have been recognized as an important data structure to manipulate discrete structures. SeqBDD has some set manipulation operations inherited from ZDD, but the number of the operations is not enough to deal with a wide variety of requests in string processing area. In this paper, we propose 50 new algorithms for manipulating SeqBDDs. We divide the operations into three categories and list up them. We also analyzed the time and space complexities of some new algorithms.

Keywords: Manipulation algorithm · Operation · Sequence binary decision diagram · Data structure · Complexity

1 Introduction

Constructing indices that store sets of strings in compact space is a fundamental problem in computer science, and have been extensively studied in the decades [4,8–10,12,19]. Examples of compact string indices include: tries [1,9], finite automata and transducers [10,13]. By the rapid increase of massive amounts of sequential data such as biological sequences, natural language texts, and sensing data stream, these compact string indices have attracted much attention and gained more importance in many string processing applications [9,12]. In such applications, an index not only has to compactly store sets of strings for *searching*, but also has to efficiently manipulate them with various set operations. For example, the most basic operations are *union, intersection*, *difference*, and *concatenation*. *Minimal acyclic deterministic finite automata* (*minimal ADFAs*) [9,10,13] are one of such index structures that fulfill the above requirements based on finite automata theory, and have been used in many sequence processing applications [15,19]. However, the algorithms to manipulate them is complicated because of the multiple branching of the underlying directed acyclic graph structure.

To overcome this problem, Loekito *et al.* [14] proposed *sequence binary decision diagrams* (*SeqBDDs*), which is a compact representation of finite sets of

M. Hospodár and G. Jirásková (Eds.): CIAA 2019, LNCS 11601, pp. 108–120, 2019.
https://doi.org/10.1007/978-3-030-23679-3_9

strings along with algorithms for manipulation operations. A SeqBDD is a vertex-labeled graph structure, which resembles an acyclic DFA in binary form (left-child, right-sibling representation [6]) with associated minimization rules for sharing siblings as well as children that are different from ones for a minimal ADFA. Due to these minimization rules, a SeqBDD can be more compact than an equivalent ADFA [11]. Novel features of the SeqBDDs are their abilities to share equivalent subgraphs and reuse results of intermediate computation between different multiple SeqBDDs. These characteristics allow us to avoid redundant generation of vertices and computation. In 2014, SeqDD, a variant of SeqBDD, was proposed by Alhakami, Ciardo and Chrobak [2]. However, they did not propose manipulating algorithms.

SeqBDD is a member of decision diagram family. Binary decision diagram (*BDD*) [5] is proposed by Bryant to manipulate Boolean functions. There are some studies about relationships between BDDs and Automata [7,17]. The most fundamental operations for string sets, such as union, intersection, and difference, are implemented by the almost same algorithms on *zero-suppressed BDD* (*ZDD*) [18] which is a variant of BDD and manipulates sets of combinations. ZDD has much more operations to manipulate sets of combinations. Since SeqBDD can be said as a child of ZDD, it inherits some operations from ZDD. However, it is not enough to manipulate sets of combinations because we can define much more operations for string sets than sets of combinations due to the differences between combinations and strings. SeqBDD did not have even fundamental operations such as concatenation. Size of a combination is bounded by the size of the universal set, but length of a string is not bounded by the size of the alphabet. A combination does not have order between its elements, but a string has order between its symbols. For example, a combination $\{a, b, c\}$ equals to $\{b, c, a\}$, $\{c, b, a\}$, and $\{a, b, c, b, a\}$, but a string *abc* is not equal to *bca*, *cba*, and *abcba*. In addition, we can distinguish substrings such as prefixes, suffixes, substrings, and subsequences even though they are the same as string. In this paper, we propose 50 new operations on SeqBDD. Almost all algorithms can be implemented as simple recursive algorithms. The collection of manipulation operations will be useful to implement various string applications on the top of SeqBDDs. The organization of this paper is as follows. In Sect. 2, we introduce our notation and data structures, operations, and techniques used throughout this paper. In Sect. 3, we propose new operations and analyze their complexities.

2 Preliminary

Let $\Sigma = \{a, b, \ldots\}$ be a countable alphabet of *symbols*. We assume that the symbols of Σ are ordered by a precedence $\prec_\Sigma$ such as $a \prec_\Sigma b \prec_\Sigma \cdots$ in a standard way. Let $s = a_1 \cdots a_n$, $n \geq 0$, be a *string* over Σ. For every $i = 1, \ldots, n$, we denote by $\alpha[i] = a_i$ the i-th symbol of α. We denote by $|\alpha| = n$ the *length* of α. The *empty string*, a string of length zero, is denoted by ε. We denote by Σ^* the set of all strings of length $n \geq 0$. For two strings α and β, we denote the *concatenation* of α and β by $\alpha \cdot \beta$ or $\alpha\beta$. If $\zeta = \alpha\beta\gamma$ for some possibly empty

Attribute	Terminal	Nonterminal
zero	null	$zero(v)$
one	null	$one(v)$
label	$\top$	$label(v)$
val	$value(v)$	null

Fig. 1. The attribute values for a vertex v.

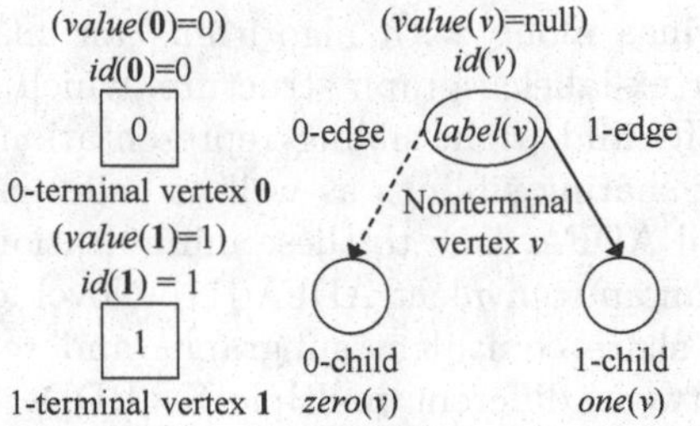

Fig. 2. The 0-terminal, 1-terminal and nonterminal vertices.

strings α, β, and γ, we refer to α, β, and γ as a *prefix*, *factor*, and *suffix* of ζ, respectively. For a string ζ of length n and $1 \le i_1 < i_2 < \cdots < i_k \le n$, we refer to $\zeta[i_1]\zeta[i_2]\cdots\zeta[i_k]$ as a *subsequence* of ζ. A *reverse* of ζ is $\zeta^R = \zeta[|\zeta|]\cdots\zeta[1]$.

A *language* on an alphabet Σ is a set $L \subseteq \Sigma^*$ of strings on Σ. A *finite language* of size $m \ge 0$ is just a finite set $L = \{\alpha_1, \ldots, \alpha_m\}$ of m strings on Σ. A finite language L is referred to as a *string set*. We define the *cardinality* of L by $|L| = m$, the *total length* of L by $||L|| = \sum_{\alpha \in L} |\alpha|$, and the *maximal string length* of L by $\mathsf{maxlen}(L) = \max\{\, |\alpha| \mid \alpha \in L \,\}$. The *empty language* of cardinality 0 is denoted by $\emptyset$. For languages $L, M \subseteq \Sigma^*$, we define the following binary operations, called *Boolean set operations*: the *union* $L \cup M$, the *intersection* $L \cap M$, the *difference* $L \backslash M$, the *symmetric difference* $L \oplus M = (L\backslash M) \cup (M \backslash L)$, the *concatenation* $L \cdot M = \{\, \alpha\beta \mid \alpha \in L, \beta \in M \,\}$ as usual.

2.1 Sequence Binary Decision Diagrams

In this subsection, we give the SeqBDD, introduced by Loekito *et al.* [14], as our graphical representation of a finite language. Then, we show its canonical form. A vertex v in a SeqBDD is represented by a structure with the attributes *id*, *label*, *zero*, *one*, and *value*. We have two types of vertices, called *nonterminal* and *terminal vertices*, both of which are represented by the same type of struct, but the attribute values for a vertex v depend on its vertex type, as given in Fig. 1. A graphical explanation of the correspondence between the attribute values and the vertex type is given in Fig. 2.

Definition 1 (Sequence BDD) [14]. *A* sequence binary decision diagram *(a SeqBDD) is a multi-rooted, vertex-labeled, directed graph $G = (V, E)$ with $R \subseteq V$ satisfying the following:*

- *V is a vertex set containing two types of vertices known as terminal and nonterminal vertices. Each has certain attributes, id, label, zero, one, and value. The respective attributes are shown in Fig. 1.*
- *There are two types of terminal vertices, called* 1-terminal *and* 0-terminal *vertices, respectively. A SeqBDD may have at most one 0-terminal and at most one 1-terminal: (1) A* terminal vertex *v has as an attribute $value(v) \in$*

$\{0, 1\}$, *indicating whether it is a 1-terminal or a 0-terminal, denoted by* **1** *or* **0**, *respectively. v has an attribute label*$(v) = \top$ *the special* null symbol $\top \notin \Sigma$, *which is larger than any symbol in* Σ, *i.e.,* $c \prec_\Sigma \top$ *for any* $c \in \Sigma$. *The equality* $=_\Sigma$ *and the strict total order* $\prec_\Sigma$ *are defined on* $\Sigma \cup \{\top\}$; *(2) A* nonterminal vertex v *has as attributes a symbol label*$(v) \in \Sigma$ *called the* label, *and two children, one*(v) *and zero*$(v) \in V$, *called the 1-child and 0-child. We refer to the pair of corresponding outgoing edges as the 1-edge and 0-edge from* v. *We define the* attribute triple *for* v *by triple*$(v) = \langle label(v), zero(v), one(v)\rangle$. *For distinct vertices* u *and* v, $id(u) \neq id(v)$ *holds.*

- *We assume that the graph is* acyclic *in its 1- and 0-edges. That is, there exists some partial order* $\prec_V$ *on vertices of* V *such that* $v \prec_V zero(v)$ *and* $v \prec_V one(v)$ *for any nonterminal* v.
- *Furthermore, we assume that the graph must be* ordered *in its 0-edges, that is, for any nonterminal vertex* v, *if zero*(v) *is also nonterminal, we must have label*$(v) \prec_\Sigma label(zero(v))$, *where* $\prec_\Sigma$ *is the strict total order on symbols of* $\Sigma \cup \{\top\}$. *The graph is not necessarily ordered in its 1-edges.*
- R *is a set of roots. All vertices in* V *are reachable from at least one vertex in* R.

For any vertex v in a SeqBDD G, the *subgraph rooted by* v is defined as the graph consisting of v and all its descendants. A SeqBDD is called *single-rooted* if it has exactly one root, and *multi-rooted* otherwise. We define the *size* of the graph rooted by a vertex v, denoted by $|v|$, as the number of its nonterminals reachable from v. By definition, the graph consisting of a single terminal vertex, **0** or **1**, is a SeqBDD of size zero. A graph G is called *single-rooted*. In this paper, we identify a single-rooted SeqBDD and its root vertex name. Multi-rooted graphs are useful in the shared SeqBDD environment described in Subsect. 2.2.

Now, we give the semantics of a SeqBDD.

Definition 2 (The Language Represented by a Single-Rooted Seq BDD). *In a single-rooted SeqBDD* G, *a vertex* v *in* G *denotes a finite language* $L_G(v)$ *on* Σ *defined recursively as:*

1. *If* v *is a terminal vertex,* $L_G(v)$ *is the trivial language defined as: (i) if value*$(v) = 1$, $L_G(v) = \{\varepsilon\}$, *and (ii) if value*$(v) = 0$, $L_G(v) = \emptyset$.
2. *If* v *is a nonterminal vertex,* $L_G(v)$ *is the finite language* $L_G(v) = (label(v) \cdot L_G(one(v))) \cup L_G(zero(v))$.

For example, the SeqBDD in Fig. 3 represents languages $L(r_1) = \{$aaba, aabc, aac, abba, abbc, abc, acc, adc, bba, bbc, bc, cc, dc$\}$ and $L(r_2) = \{$abba, abbc, abc, acc, adc, bbba, bbbc, bbc, bcc, bdc, cc, dc$\}$.

We write $L(v)$ for $L_G(v)$ if the underlying graph G is clearly understood. Moreover, if G is a SeqBDD with the single root $r \in R$, we write $L(G)$ for $L_G(r)$. We say that G is a *SeqBDD for* L if $L = L(G)$.

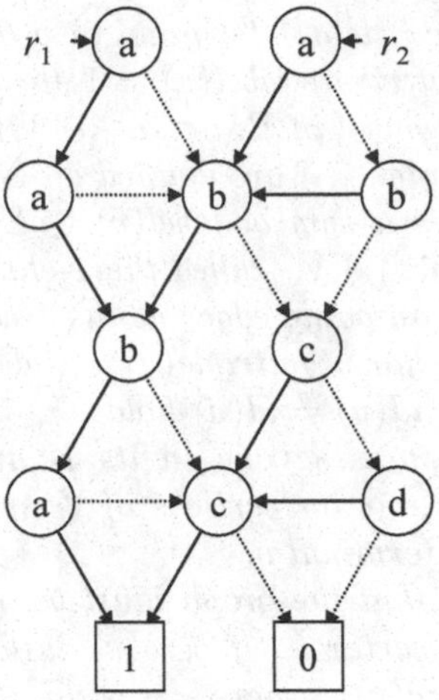

Fig. 3. An example of a SeqBDD in a shared environment. Nonterminal vertices are drawn as cercles with their labels. Terminal vertices are drawn as squares with their values. 1-edges and 0-edges are drawn as solid arrows and dotted arrows, respectively.

2.2 Shared SeqBDDs

We can use a multi-rooted SeqBDD G as a persistent data structure for storing and manipulating a collection of more than one set of strings on an alphabet Σ. In an environment, we can create a new subgraph by combining one or more existing subgraphs in G in an arbitrary way. As an invariant, all subgraphs in G are maintained as minimal. A *shared SeqBDD environment* is a 4-tuple $\mathcal{E} = (G, R, \mathit{uniqtable}, \mathit{memocache})$ consisting of a multi-rooted SeqBDD G with a vertex set V, a root vertex set R, and two hash tables *uniqtable* and *memocache*, explained below. If two tables are clearly understood from context, we identify $\mathcal{E}$ with the underlying graph G by omitting tables.

The first table *uniqtable*, called the *unique vertex table*, assigns a nonterminal vertex $v = \mathit{uniqtable}(a, v_0, v_1)$ of G to a given triple $\tau = \langle a, v_0, v_1\rangle$ of a symbol and a pair of vertices in G. This table is maintained such that it is a function from all triples τ to the nonterminal vertex v in G such that $\mathit{triple}(v) = \tau$. If such a node does not exist, *uniqtable* returns *null*. When we want to get a vertex with a certain attribute triple $\langle a, v_0, v_1\rangle$, we first check whether such a vertex already exists or not by querying the *uniqtable*. If such a vertex exists, we use the vertex returned from the *uniqtable*. Otherwise, we create a new vertex with the attribute triple and register it to the *uniqtable*. The operation $\mathsf{Getvertex}(a, v_0, v_1)$ executes this process. Due to this process, we can avoid generating redundant equivalent vertices. Consequently, the SeqBDD is kept minimal even though it is multi-rooted.

The second table *memocache*, called the *operation cache*, is used for a user to memorize the invocation pattern "$\mathit{op}(x_1, \ldots, x_k)$" of a user-defined operation *op* and the associated return value $u = op(v_1, \ldots, v_k)$, where each v_i, $i = 1, \ldots, n$ is an argument of the operation. An argument can be a symbol, a natural number, or an existing vertex in G. We assume that the hash tables *uniqtable* and *memocache* are global variables in $\mathcal{E}$, and initialized to the empty tables when $\mathcal{E}$ is initialized.

Figure 3 shows that two SeqBDDs rooted by r_1 and r_2 share their equivalent subgraphs. In a shared environment, we can deal with multiple SeqBDDs in minimal form by using *uniqtable*, and reuse computational results of operations for some vertex when we want to execute the same operation for the same vertex by referring *memocache*. For example, assume that we compute $\mathsf{Card}(r_1)$, $\mathsf{Card}(v)$ is called for each descendant of r_1 during the recursive process. (Note that $|L(v)| = |L(zero(v))| + |L(one(v))|$.) If we compute $\mathsf{Card}(r_2)$ after obtaining the result of $\mathsf{Card}(r_1)$, during the computation of the cardinality of r_2, we need to continue recursive calls $\mathsf{Card}(zero(v))$ and $\mathsf{Card}(one(v))$ only at each nonterminal vertex v that is a descendant of r_2 but not a descendant of r_1 because the *memocache* remembers the result $\mathsf{Card}(v)$.

2.3 Operations

We view a symbolic manipulation program as executing a sequence of commands that build up representations of languages and that determine various properties about them. For example, suppose we wish to construct the representation of the language computed by a data mining program. At this point, we can test various properties of the language, such as to list some member, to list all members, and to test some string for membership.

Here, we will present algorithms to perform basic operations on sets of strings represented as SeqBDD. Table 1 summarizes operations of SeqBDDs. This table contains some new operations. Rev, LRotate, and RRotate are new ones and can be used to find palindromes and Lyndon words [16]. These basic operations can be combined to perform a wide variety of operations on sets of strings. We can construct a SeqBDD that represents a given language in $O(||L||)$ time. Aoki *et al.* proposed a more efficient algorithm to construct a SeqBDD representing a set of reversed strings [3]. Our algorithms utilize techniques commonly used in BDD and ZDD algorithms such as ordered traversal, table look-up, and vertex encoding. As the table shows, most of the algorithms have time complexity proportional to the size of the SeqBDDs being manipulated. Hence, as long as the languages of interest can be represented by reasonably small SeqBDD such that used for speech recognition [19], our algorithms are quite efficient.

These algorithms are implemented as simple recursive algorithms. Such style of algorithms are commonly used on other decision diagrams because it has the following nice properties:

- Speeding up by memoization: Sharing intermediate results between different execution of operations for SeqBDDs rooted by different vertices.

Table 1. SeqBDD basic operations.

Name	Output	Time & space complexity
0	The 0-terminal vertex	O(1)
1	The 1-terminal vertex	O(1)
Getvertex(a, v_0, v_1)	A SeqBDD vertex r such that $label(r) = a$, $zero(r) = v_0$, $one(v) = v_1$	O(1)
Build(α)	A SeqBDD vertex r such that $L(r) = \{\alpha\}$	O($\lvert\alpha\rvert$)
Onset(u, a)	A SeqBDD vertex r such that $L(r) = \{\alpha \mid a\alpha \in L(u)\}$	O($\lvert\Sigma\rvert$)
Offset(u, a)	A SeqBDD vertex r such that $L(r) = \{b\alpha \mid b\alpha \in L(u), b \neq a\}$	O($\lvert\Sigma\rvert$)
Member(u, α)	$\alpha \in L(v)$?	O($\lvert\Sigma\rvert\lvert\alpha\rvert$)
AddStr(v, α)	A SeqBDD vertex r such that $L(r) = L(v) \cup \{\alpha\}$	O($\lvert\Sigma\rvert\lvert\alpha\rvert$)
DelStr(v, α)	A SeqBDD vertex r such that $L(r) = L(v) \backslash \{\alpha\}$	O($\lvert\Sigma\rvert\lvert\alpha\rvert$)
Union(u, v)	A SeqBDD vertex r such that $L(r) = L(u) \cup L(v)$	O($\lvert u\rvert\lvert v\rvert$)
Intersection(u, v)	A SeqBDD vertex r such that $L(r) = L(u) \cap L(v)$	O($\lvert u\rvert\lvert v\rvert$)
Difference(u, v)	A SeqBDD vertex r such that $L(r) = L(u) \backslash L(v)$	O($\lvert u\rvert\lvert v\rvert$)
SymDiff(u, v)	A SeqBDD vertex r such that $L(r) = L(u) \oplus L(v)$	O($\lvert u\rvert\lvert v\rvert$)
Equal(u, v)	$L(u) = L(v)$?	O(1)
IsSubset(u, v)	$L(u) \subseteq L(v)$?	O($\lvert u\rvert\lvert v\rvert$)
Count(u)	the number of nodes $\lvert u\rvert$	O($\lvert u\rvert$)
Card(u)	$\lvert L(u)\rvert$	O($\lvert u\rvert$)
TotalLen(u)	$\sum_{\alpha \in L(u)} \lvert\alpha\rvert$	O($\lvert u\rvert$)
MinLen(u)	$\min_{\alpha \in L(u)}\{\lvert\alpha\rvert\}$	O($\lvert u\rvert$)
MaxLen(u)	$\max_{\alpha \in L(u)}\{\lvert\alpha\rvert\}$	O($\lvert u\rvert$)
Print1(v)	Some string of $L(v)$	O(maxlen($L(v)$))
PrintAll(v)	$L(v)$	O($\lvert L(v)\rvert$maxlen($L(v)$))
Random(u)	A string $\alpha \in L(u)$ chosen uniformly at random	O($\lvert u\rvert$)
All1()	$\{a \mid a \in \Sigma\}$	O($\lvert\Sigma\rvert$)
Alln()	A SeqBDD vertex r such that $L(r) = \{a_1 \cdots a_n \mid a_1, \ldots, a_n \in \Sigma\}$	O($n\lvert\Sigma\rvert$)
HeadRemove(u)	$\{\alpha \mid a \in \Sigma, a\alpha \in L(u)\}$	O($2^{2^{\lvert u\rvert}}$)
TailRemove(u)	$\{\alpha \mid a \in \Sigma, \alpha a, \in L(u)\}$	O($\lvert u\rvert$)
Rev(u)	A SeqBDD vertex r such that $L(r) = \{\alpha^R \mid \alpha \in L(u)\}$	N/A
LRotate(u)	A SeqBDD vertex r such that $L(r) = \{\alpha a \mid a\alpha \in L(u), a \in \Sigma\} \cup (L(u) \cap \{\epsilon\})$	O($\lvert u\rvert^2$)
RRotate(u)	A SeqBDD vertex r such that $L(r) = \{a\alpha \mid \alpha a \in L(u), a \in \Sigma\} \cup (L(u) \cap \{\epsilon\})$	N/A

- Easy implementation: From a long history of research of automata, we can find a more efficient algorithm for each operation. However, implementing the best algorithms is generally difficult. Simple algorithms are valuable to make libraries in order to accept various requests for manipulation on sets of strings.

Therefore, implementing various operations in a simple recursive manner is important to obtain the above properties even though there are more efficient problem-specific algorithms.

3 SeqBDD Manipulation Operations

In this section, we list up new SeqBDD operations. We categorize the algorithms into the following three groups:

- Combination: Combine multiple SeqBDDs.
- Enumeration: Enumerate all strings that satisfy some condition.
- Retrieval: Retrieve strings which satisfy some conditions from a given set.

All of the following algorithms use *uniqtable* and *memocache* as global variables. We can define operations not included in the following tables, but we only consider operations that we can provide their algorithms.

3.1 Combination Operations

Combination operations are listed in Table 2. Basic Boolean set operations are in the table of basic operations. Concat, OverlapConcat, LDiv, RDiv, CDiv, LRem, RRem, and CRem are algebraic operations. These operations can be used to construct SeqBDDs for given regular languages and decompose SeqBDDs into several languages. LExistDiv, RExistDiv, CExistDiv, LExistRem, RExistRem, and CExistRem is variants of LDiv, RDiv, CDiv, LRem, RRem, and CRem that can be obtained by switching the quantifiers from $\forall$ to $\exists$ in the definition of operations. PrefAssign, SuffAssign, and FactAssign construct SeqBDDs by replacing prefixes, suffixes, and factors of $L(u)$ that is included in $L(v)$ by the language $L(w)$, respectively. Separate computes all factors of $L(u)$ that can be obtained by considering strings in $L(v)$ as delimiters of strings in $L(u)$.

3.2 Enumeration Operations

Enumeration operations are listed in Table 3. For given a string $\alpha \in \Sigma^*$, we define $Prefix(\alpha)$ is the set of all prefixes of α, $Suffix(\alpha)$ is the set of all suffixes of α, $Factor(\alpha)$ is the set of all factors of α, and $Subseq(\alpha)$ is the set of all subsequence of α. Also, we define $PropPrefix(\alpha) = Prefix(\alpha)\backslash\{\alpha\}$, $PropSuffix(\alpha) = Suffix(\alpha)\backslash\{\alpha\}$, $PropFactor(\alpha) = Factor(\alpha)\backslash\{\alpha\}$, and $PropSubseq(\alpha) = Subseq(\alpha)\backslash\{\alpha\}$. We use "?" as a wild card in the algorithm HammDistWild and EditDistWild. Pref, Suff, Fact, Subseq. PropPref, PropSuff, PropFact, PropSubseq construct SeqBDDs that can be used as indices. HammDist, EditDist, HammDistWild. EditDistWild are applied to approximate indices and matching problems. These algorithms are useful to generate all candidates to be processed explicitly.

Table 2. SeqBDD combination operations.

Name	Output	Time & space complexity
Concat(u, v)	A SeqBDD vertex r such that $L(r) = \{\alpha\beta \mid \alpha \in L(u), \beta \in L(v)\}$	$O(\|u\|^2 2^{2\|v\|})$
OverlapConcat$_{i,j,k}$ (u, v)	A SeqBDD vertex r such that $L(r) = \{\alpha\beta\gamma \mid \alpha\beta \in L(u), \beta\gamma \in L(v), \|\alpha\| \geq i, \|\beta\| \geq j, \|\gamma\| \geq k\}$	N/A
LDiv(u, v)	A SeqBDD vertex r such that $L(r) = \{\gamma \mid \forall\beta \in L(v), \beta\gamma \in L(u)\}$	$O(\|v\|2^{2\|u\|})$
RDiv(u, v)	A SeqBDD vertex r such that $L(r) = \{\alpha \mid \forall\beta \in L(v), \alpha\beta \in L(u)\}$	$O(\|u\|\|v\|)$
CDiv(u, v)	A SeqBDD vertex r such that $L(r) = \{\alpha\gamma \mid \forall\beta \in L(v), \alpha\beta\gamma \in L(u)\}$	$O(2^{2\|u\|\|v\|})$
LRem(u, v)	A SeqBDD vertex r such that $L(r) = \{\zeta \mid \zeta \in L(u), \exists\beta \in L(v), \zeta \neq \beta\gamma, \forall\gamma \in \Sigma^*\}$	$O(\|u\|\|v\|^3 2^{2\|u\|})$
RRem(u, v)	A SeqBDD vertex r such that $L(r) = \{\zeta \mid \zeta \in L(u), \exists\beta \in L(v), \zeta \neq \alpha\beta, \forall\alpha \in \Sigma^*\}$	$O(\|u\|\|v\|2^{2\|u\|})$
CRem(u, v)	A SeqBDD vertex r such that $L(r) = \{\zeta \mid \zeta \in L(u), \exists\beta \in L(v), \zeta \neq \alpha\beta\gamma, \forall\alpha, \gamma \in \Sigma^*\}$	N/A
LExistDiv(u, v)	A SeqBDD vertex r such that $L(r) = \{\gamma \mid \exists\beta \in L(v), \beta\gamma \in L(u)\}$	$O(\|v\|2^{2\|u\|})$
RExistDiv(u, v)	A SeqBDD vertex r such that $L(r) = \{\alpha \mid \exists\beta \in L(v), \alpha\beta \in L(u)\}$	$O(\|u\|\|v\|)$
CExistDiv(u, v)	A SeqBDD vertex r such that $L(r) = \{\alpha_0 \cdots \alpha_n \mid \exists\beta_1, \ldots, \beta_n \in L(v), \alpha_0\beta_1\alpha_1 \cdots \beta_n\alpha_n \in L(u), L(v) \cap Factor(\alpha_i) = \emptyset, i = 0, \ldots, n\}$	N/A
LExistRem(u, v)	A SeqBDD vertex r such that $L(r) = \{\zeta \mid \zeta \in L(u), \beta \in L(v), \zeta \neq \beta\gamma, \forall\gamma \in \Sigma^*\}$	$O(\|v\|2^{2\|u\|})$
RExistRem(u, v)	A SeqBDD vertex r such that $L(r) = \{\zeta \mid \zeta \in L(u), \beta \in L(v), \zeta \neq \alpha\beta, \forall\alpha \in \Sigma^*\}$	$O(\|u\|\|v\|)$
CExistRem(u, v)	A SeqBDD vertex r such that $L(r) = \{\zeta \mid \zeta \in L(u), \beta \in L(v), \beta \notin Factor(\zeta)\}$	N/A
PrefAssign(u, v, w)	A SeqBDD vertex r such that $L(r) = \{\zeta\gamma \mid \exists\beta \in L(v), \beta\gamma \in L(u), \zeta \in L(w)$, **or** $\beta \in L(v), \zeta\gamma \in L(u), \beta \notin Prefix(\zeta\gamma)\}$	$O(\|v\|2^{2\|u\|\|w\|})$
SuffAssign(u, v, w)	A SeqBDD vertex r such that $L(r) = \{\alpha\zeta \mid \exists\beta \in L(v), \alpha\beta \in L(u), \zeta \in L(w)$, **or** $\beta \in L(v), \alpha\zeta \in L(u), \beta \notin Suffix(\alpha\zeta)\}$	$O(\|v\|2^{2\|u\|\|w\|})$
FactAssign(u, v, w)	A SeqBDD vertex r such that $L(r) = \{\alpha_0\zeta\alpha_1 \cdots \zeta\alpha_n \mid (\exists\beta_1, \ldots, \beta_n \in L(v), \alpha_0\beta_1\alpha_1 \cdots \beta_n\alpha_n \in L(u), L(v) \cap Factor(\alpha_i) = \emptyset, i = 0, \ldots, n, \zeta_1, \ldots, \zeta_n \in L(w))$, **or** $(\beta \in L(v), \alpha_0 \in L(u), \beta \notin Factor(\alpha_0))\}$	$O(\|v\|2^{2\|u\|\|w\|})$
Separate(u, v)	A SeqBDD vertex r such that $L(r) = \{\alpha_i \mid \exists\beta_1, \ldots, \beta_n \in L(v), \alpha_0\beta_1\alpha_1 \cdots \beta_n\alpha_n \in L(u), L(v) \cap Factor(\alpha_i) = \emptyset, i = 0, \ldots, n$ $\alpha_0 \in L(u), \beta \in L(v), \beta \notin Factor(\alpha_0), i = 0\}$.	N/A

Table 3. SeqBDD enumeration operations.

Name	Output	Time & space complexity
Pref(u)	A SeqBDD vertex r such that $L(r) = \bigcup_{\alpha \in L(u)} Prefix(\alpha)$.	$O(\|u\|)$
Suff(u)	A SeqBDD vertex r such that $L(r) = \bigcup_{\alpha \in L(u)} Suffix(\alpha)$.	$O(\|u\|^2)$
Fact(u)	A SeqBDD vertex r such that $L(r) = \bigcup_{\alpha \in L(u)} Factor(\alpha)$.	$O(\|u\|^2)$
Subseq(u)	A SeqBDD vertex r such that $L(r) = \bigcup_{\alpha \in L(u)} Subseq(\alpha)$.	$O(2^{2\|u\|})$
PropPref(u)	A SeqBDD vertex r such that $L(r) = \bigcup_{\alpha \in L(u)} PropPrefix(\alpha)$.	$O(\|u\|)$
PropSuff(u)	A SeqBDD vertex r such that $L(r) = \bigcup_{\alpha \in L(u)} PropSuffix(\alpha)$.	$O(\|u\|^2)$
PropFact(u)	A SeqBDD vertex r such that $L(r) = \bigcup_{\alpha \in L(u)} PropFactor(\alpha)$.	$O(\|u\|^2)$
PropSubseq(u)	A SeqBDD vertex r such that $L(r) = \bigcup_{\alpha \in L(u)} PropSubseq(\alpha)$.	$O(2^{2\|u\|})$
HammDist(u, d)	A SeqBDD vertex r consists of strings within Hamming distance d from $\alpha \in L(u)$.	N/A
EditDist(u, d)	A SeqBDD vertex r consists of strings within edit distance d from $\alpha \in L(u)$.	N/A
HammDistWild(u, d)	A SeqBDD vertex r consists of strings within Hamming distance d from $\alpha \in L(u)$ allowing use of wild cards.	N/A
EditDistWild(u, d)	A SeqBDD vertex r consists of strings within edit distance d from $\alpha \in L(u)$ allowing use of wild cards.	N/A

3.3 Retrieval Operations

Retrieval operations are listed in Table 4. Shorter, Longer, Just, Shortest, and Longest derive languages consisting of strings of desired length. ExistPref, ExistSuff, ExistFact, and ExistSubseq retrieve strings that have some string in $L(v)$ as their prefixes, suffixes, factors, and subsequences, respectively. PrefMaximal, SuffMaximal, FactMaximal, SubseqMaximal, PrefMinimal, SuffMinimal, FactMinimal, and SubseqMinimal can find maximal or minimal strings among their prefixes, suffixes, factors, and subsequences, respectively.

3.4 Complexity Analyses

In this subsection, we describe how the complexities in the above tables are calculated. For basic set operations such as Union, Intersection, and Difference for

Table 4. SeqBDD retrieval operations.

Name	Output	Time & space complexity
Shorter(u, l)	A SeqBDD vertex r such that $L(r) = \{\alpha \mid \alpha \in L(u), \lvert\alpha\rvert \le l\}$.	$O(l\lvert u\rvert)$
Longer(u, l)	A SeqBDD vertex r such that $L(r) = \{\alpha \mid \alpha \in L(u), l \le \lvert\alpha\rvert\}$.	$O(l\lvert u\rvert)$
Just(u, l)	A SeqBDD vertex r such that $L(r) = \{\alpha \mid \alpha \in L(u), l = \lvert\alpha\rvert\}$.	$O(l\lvert u\rvert)$
Shortest(u)	A SeqBDD vertex r such that $L(r) = \{\alpha \mid \alpha \in L(u), \lvert\alpha\rvert = min_{\beta \in L(u)}\{\lvert\beta\rvert\}\}$.	$O(\lvert u\rvert)$
Longest(u)	A SeqBDD vertex r such that $L(r) = \{\alpha \mid \alpha \in L(u), \lvert\alpha\rvert = max_{\beta \in L(u)}\{\lvert\beta\rvert\}\}$.	$O(\lvert u\rvert)$
ExistPref(u, v)	A SeqBDD vertex r such that $L(r) = \{\alpha \mid \alpha \in L(u), \exists\beta \in L(v), \beta \in Prefix(\alpha)\}$.	$O(\lvert u\rvert\lvert v\rvert)$
ExistSuff(u, v)	A SeqBDD vertex r such that $L(r) = \{\alpha \mid \alpha \in L(u), \exists\beta \in L(v), \beta \in Suffix(\alpha)\}$.	$O(\lvert u\rvert\lvert v\rvert)$
ExistFact(u, v)	A SeqBDD vertex r such that $L(r) = \{\alpha \mid \alpha \in L(u), \exists\beta \in L(v), \beta \in Factor(\alpha)\}$.	$O(\lvert u\rvert\lvert v\rvert)$
ExistSubseq(u, v)	A SeqBDD vertex r such that $L(r) = \{\alpha \mid \alpha \in L(u), \exists\beta \in L(v), \beta \in Subseq(\alpha)\}$.	$O(\lvert u\rvert 2^{2\lvert v\rvert})$
PrefMaximal(u)	A SeqBDD vertex r such that $L(r) = \{\alpha \mid \alpha, \beta \in L(u), \alpha \ne \beta, \alpha \notin Prefix(\beta)\}$.	$O(\lvert u\rvert^2)$
SuffMaximal(u)	A SeqBDD vertex r such that $L(r) = \{\alpha \mid \alpha, \beta \in L(u), \alpha \ne \beta, \alpha \notin Suffix(\beta)\}$.	$O(\lvert u\rvert^3)$
FactMaximal(u)	A SeqBDD vertex r such that $L(r) = \{\alpha \mid \alpha, \beta \in L(u), \alpha \ne \beta, \alpha \notin Factor(\beta)\}$.	$O(\lvert u\rvert^3)$
SubseqMaximal(u)	A SeqBDD vertex r such that $L(r) = \{\alpha \mid \alpha, \beta \in L(u), \alpha \ne \beta, \alpha \notin Subseq(\beta)\}$.	$O(\lvert u\rvert 2^{2\lvert u\rvert})$
PrefMinimal(u)	A SeqBDD vertex r such that $L(r) = \{\alpha \mid \alpha, \beta \in L(u), \alpha \ne \beta, \beta \notin Prefix(\alpha)\}$.	$O(\lvert u\rvert^3)$
SuffMinimal(u)	A SeqBDD vertex r such that $L(r) = \{\alpha \mid \alpha, \beta \in L(u), \alpha \ne \beta, \beta \notin Suffix(\alpha)\}$.	$O(\lvert u\rvert^3)$
FactMinimal(u)	A SeqBDD vertex r such that $L(r) = \{\alpha \mid \alpha, \beta \in L(u), \alpha \ne \beta, \beta \notin Factor(\alpha)\}$.	$O(\lvert u\rvert^4)$
SubseqMinimal(u)	A SeqBDD vertex r such that $L(r) = \{\alpha \mid \alpha, \beta \in L(u), \alpha \ne \beta, \beta \notin Subseq(\alpha)\}$.	$O(\lvert u\rvert^2 2^{2\lvert u\rvert^2})$
ComnPref(u)	A SeqBDD vertex r such that $L(r) = \bigcap_{\alpha \in L(u)} Prefix(\alpha)$.	$O(\lvert u\rvert)$

vertices u and v, its time and space complexities are $O(|u||v|)$ because possible function calls with different pair of vertices are at most $O(|u||v|)$, and function calls with the same arguments are processed in constant time thanks to the memoization technique. As a result, the size of output SeqBDD is also $O(|u||v|)$ [11]. Consequently, if we continue Union or Intersection k times for vertices reachable from v, the complexity becomes $O(|v|^{k+1})$. Note that each vertex in the resultant

SeqBDD can be written as a combination of $k+1$ vertices of v's descendants. If the number of repetition k is not fixed, each vertex in the output SeqBDD can be written as combination of all v's descendants. Therefore, complexity becomes $O(2^{2|v|})$ in such cases. Note that the size of output SeqBDD is $O(2^{|v|})$. If each output vertex can be written as a result of computing $|v|$ vertices combined by j non-commutative operations, its complexity is $O(\sum_{i=1}^{|v|} j^{i-1} i!)$. The complexities in the tables are obtained from the above observations. For operations with more complicated algorithms, we could not calculate complexities and the time & space complexity columns of such operations are N/A.

4 Conclusion

In this paper, we proposed 50 new algorithms for manipulating SeqBDDs. All of our algorithms are written as recursive algorithms with memoization. Due to intermediate results sharing caused by memoization technique, the total computation time of multiple executions of the same operation will be faster when dealing with multi-rooted SeqBDD in a shared environment. For future work, we implement the algorithms proposed in this paper. The complexity analyses can be improved. We should consider combining our algorithms with existing problem-specific efficient algorithms. We will be able to define more operations and give algorithms for them.

References

1. Aho, A.V., Hopcroft, J.E., Ullman, J.D.: The Design and Analysis of Computer Algorithms. Addison-Wesley, Boston (1974)
2. Alhakami, H., Ciardo, G., Chrobak, M.: Sequence decision diagrams. In: Moura, E., Crochemore, M. (eds.) SPIRE 2014. LNCS, vol. 8799, pp. 149–160. Springer, Cham (2014). https://doi.org/10.1007/978-3-319-11918-2_15
3. Aoki, H., Yamashita, S., Minato, S.: An efficient algorithm for constructing a sequence binary decision diagram representing a set of reversed sequences. In: Hong, T., et al. (eds.) Proceedings of 2011 IEEE International Conference on Granular Computing, pp. 54–59. IEEE Computer Society (2011). https://doi.org/10.1109/GRC.2011.6122567
4. Blumer, A., Blumer, J., Haussler, D., Ehrenfeucht, A., Chen, M.T., Seiferas, J.I.: The smallest automaton recognizing the subwords of a text. Theoret. Comput. Sci. **40**, 31–55 (1985). https://doi.org/10.1016/0304-3975(85)90157-4
5. Bryant, R.E.: Graph-based algorithms for Boolean function manipulation. IEEE Trans. Comput. **C–35**(8), 677–691 (1986). https://doi.org/10.1109/TC.1986.1676819
6. Bubenzer, J.: Minimization of acyclic DFAs. In: Holub, J., Žďárek, J. (eds.) Proceedings of Prague Stringology Conference 2011, pp. 132–146. Czech Technical University (2011). http://www.stringology.org/event/2011/p12.html
7. Champarnaud, J.M., Pin, J.E.: A maxmin problem on finite automata. Discrete Appl. Math. **23**(1), 91–96 (1989). https://doi.org/10.1016/0166-218X(89)90037-1
8. Crochemore, M.: Transducers and repetitions. Theoret. Comput. Sci. **45**(1), 63–86 (1986). https://doi.org/10.1016/0304-3975(86)90041-1

9. Crochemore, M., Hancart, C., Lecroq, T.: Algorithms on Strings. Cambridge University Press, Cambridge (2007)
10. Daciuk, J., Mihov, S., Watson, B.W., Watson, R.: Incremental construction of minimal acyclic finite state automata. Comput. Linguist. **26**(1), 3–16 (2000). https://doi.org/10.1162/089120100561601
11. Denzumi, S., Yoshinaka, R., Arimura, H., Minato, S.: Sequence binary decision diagram: minimization, relationship to acyclic automata, and complexities of Boolean set operations. Discrete Appl. Math. **212**, 61–80 (2016). https://doi.org/10.1016/j.dam.2014.11.022
12. Gusfield, D.: Algorithms on Strings, Trees, and Sequences: Computer Science and Computational Biology. Cambridge University Press, Cambridge (1997)
13. Hopcroft, J.E., Motwani, R., Ullman, J.D.: Introduction to Automata Theory, Languages, and Computation, 3rd edn. Addison-Wesley, Boston (2006)
14. Loekito, E., Bailey, J., Pei, J.: A binary decision diagram based approach for mining frequent subsequences. Knowl. Inf. Syst. **24**(2), 235–268 (2010). https://doi.org/10.1007/s10115-009-0252-9
15. Lucchesi, C.L., Kowaltowski, T.: Applications of finite automata representing large vocabularies. Softw. Pract. Exp. **23**(1), 15–30 (1993). https://doi.org/10.1002/spe.4380230103
16. Lyndon, R.C.: On Burnside's problem. Trans. Am. Math. Soc. **77**(2), 202–215 (1954)
17. Michon, J.-F., Champarnaud, J.-M.: Automata and binary decision diagrams. In: Champarnaud, J.-M., Ziadi, D., Maurel, D. (eds.) WIA 1998. LNCS, vol. 1660, pp. 178–182. Springer, Heidelberg (1999). https://doi.org/10.1007/3-540-48057-9_15
18. Minato, S.: Zero-suppressed BDDs for set manipulation in combinatorial problems. In: Dunlop, A.E. (ed.) Proceedings of 30th Design Automation Conference, pp. 272–277. ACM Press (1993). https://doi.org/10.1145/157485.164890
19. Mohri, M., Moreno, P., Weinstein, E.: Factor automata of automata and applications. In: Holub, J., Žd'árek, J. (eds.) CIAA 2007. LNCS, vol. 4783, pp. 168–179. Springer, Heidelberg (2007). https://doi.org/10.1007/978-3-540-76336-9_17

A Simple Extension to Finite Tree Automata for Defining Sets of Labeled, Connected Graphs

Akio Fujiyoshi[1] and Daniel Průša[2](✉)

[1] Department of Computer and Information Sciences, Ibaraki University, 4-12-1 Nakanarusawa, Hitachi, Ibaraki 316-8511, Japan
akio.fujiyoshi.cs@vc.ibaraki.ac.jp

[2] Faculty of Electrical Engineering, Czech Technical University, Karlovo náměstí 13, 121 35 Prague 2, Czech Republic
prusapa1@fel.cvut.cz

Abstract. This paper introduces spanning tree automata (ST automata) usable for defining sets of labeled, connected graphs. The automata are simply obtained by extending ordinary top-down finite tree automata for labeled, ordered trees. It is shown that ST automata can define any finite set of labeled, connected graphs, and also some subclasses of infinite sets of graphs that can represent the structure of chemical molecules. Although the membership problem for ST automata is NP-complete, an efficient software was developed which supports a practical use of ST automata in chemoinformatics as well as in other fields.

Keywords: Automata theory · Tree automaton · Graph automaton · NP-completeness · Chemoinformatics

1 Introduction

Formal grammars, finite automata and regular expressions are powerful tools for defining sets of strings over a finite alphabet [10,11]. For defining sets of labeled, ordered trees, we have tree grammars and finite tree automata as well [2,4,8,13]. How about for defining sets of graphs? Monadic second-order logic (MSOL) has been studied for describing graph properties [6]. There are many studies of graph grammars [14]. As for practical tools like context-free grammars and regular expressions, however, there is no common idea. This paper suggests the use of finite tree automata with a simple extension for defining sets of graphs.

Simple but powerful tools for defining a set of labeled, connected graphs has been requested in the field of chemoinformatics [3]. Pharmaceutical companies and research laboratories have to claim their intellectual property on chemical

A. Fujiyoshi—Supported by JSPS KAKENHI Grant Number JP18H01036.
D. Průša—Supported by the Czech Science Foundation grant 19-21198S.

M. Hospodár and G. Jirásková (Eds.): CIAA 2019, LNCS 11601, pp. 121–132, 2019.
https://doi.org/10.1007/978-3-030-23679-3_10

structures of new medicine by applying for patents. Chemical structure formulas of molecules are labeled, connected graphs, where vertices are labeled as the name of atoms and edges are labeled as the type of bonds. To protect the intellectual property of new medicine, not only the exact chemical structure of new medicine but also similar chemical structures must be explicitly claimed in a patent application because a chemical compound with a similar chemical structure usually has a similar chemical property. The most popular way for this purpose is using a Markush structure. A Markush structure is a graphical diagram with expressions in a natural language commonly used in patent claims, firstly used in January, 1923. Because of the limitation of its expressive power, the range of a Markush structure often becomes too broad and contains many unrelated chemical compounds [15]. However, a substitutable method has not been invented so far, and Markush structures are continuously used for almost 100 years.

This paper introduces spanning tree automata (ST automata) for defining sets of labeled, connected graphs. ST automata are simply obtained by extending ordinary top-down finite tree automata for labeled, ordered trees. The idea behind this extension is based on a very simple fact: "Any connected graph with cycles becomes a tree if we break all cycles." As shown in Fig. 1, by choosing an edge from each cycle and inserting two virtual vertices at the middle of the edges, a tree is obtained. We call this tree an extended spanning tree. An ST automaton may be viewed as a finite tree automaton that accepts extended spanning trees instead of labeled, connected graphs.

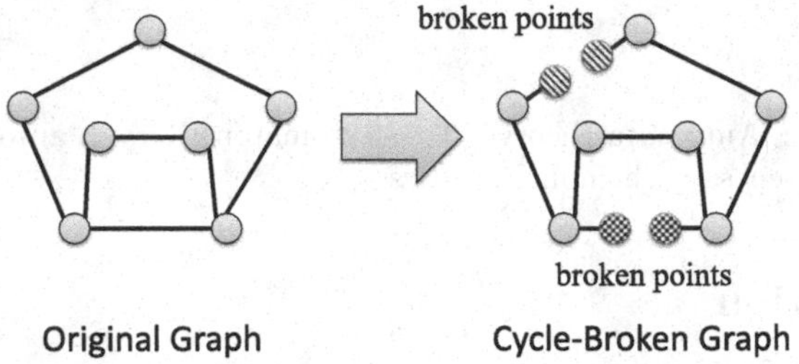

Fig. 1. Obtaining an extended spanning tree.

The goal of the paper is to demonstrate that the proposed ST automata (defined in Sect. 3) are a practical tool which can be applied to describe and analyse structures important for chemoinformatics and other fields. It is shown that ST automata can define any finite set of labeled, connected graphs (Sect. 4). The ability to define infinite sets of graphs is strengthened after introducing a variant of ST automata working over breadth-first search spanning trees only (Sect. 5). Although the membership problem for ST automata is NP-complete, we were able to develop an implementation efficient enough to find subgraphs accepted by an ST automaton in graphs induced by real data. The implementation extends the algorithm in [7] proposed for finding a spanning tree accepted by a finite tree automaton in a graph of treewidth 2. A report on the newly developed software and performed experiments is available in Sect. 6.

2 Preliminaries

A *graph* is an ordered pair $G = (V, E)$, where V is a finite set of *vertices*, and E is a set of unordered pairs of distinct vertices, called *edges*. An edge $\{u, v\} \in E$ is written as uv or vu. A vertex $u \in V$ is *adjacent* to another vertex $v \in V$ if an edge uv is in E. For $v \in V$, we define $N(v) = \{u \mid u \in V$ and u is adjacent to $v\}$, and $|N(v)|$ is called the *degree* of v.

For vertices $u, v \in V$, a *path* of *length* $n \geq 0$ from u to v is a sequence of vertices $v_1, \ldots, v_{n+1}$ where $u = v_1$, $v = v_{n+1}$, for all $1 \leq i \leq n$, v_i is adjacent to v_{i+1}, and $v_1, v_2, \ldots, v_{n+1}$ are all distinct except that v_1 may equal to v_{n+1}. The *distance* between $u, v \in V$ in G, denoted $d_G(u, v)$, is the length of a shortest path from u to v. A *cycle* is a path of positive length from v to v for some $v \in V$. Graph G is *acyclic* if there is no cycle in G. Graph G is *connected* if there is a path from u to v for any pair of distinct vertices $u, v \in V$.

A *tree* is a connected, acyclic graph. A vertex of a tree is called a *node*. A *rooted tree* is a pair (T, r) such that T is a tree, and r is a node of T. The node r is called the *root*. In a rooted tree, we assume that the edges have a natural direction away from the root. The *parent* of a node v is the node adjacent to v on the path from the root to v. Note that every node except the root has a unique parent. The *children* of a node v are the nodes whose parent is v. A node without any children is called a *leaf*.

Let Σ be a finite set of *vertex labels*, and let Γ be a finite set of *edge labels*. A *vertex labeling* of G is a function $\sigma : V \to \Sigma$, and a *edge labeling* of G is a function $\gamma : E \to \Gamma$. A *labeled* graph over Σ and Γ is a quadruple $G = (V, E, \sigma, \gamma)$. In this paper, we assume every graph to be connected and labeled, and a graph implies a labeled, connected graph unless otherwise stated. We use letters in Roman alphabet $A, a, B, b, C, c, \ldots$ for vertex labels and numerical digits $1, 2, 3, \ldots$ for edge labels.

Let $G = (V, E, \sigma, \gamma)$ be a graph over Σ and Γ, and let $B \subseteq E$ be a subset of edges such that $T = (V, E \setminus B)$ is a tree. B is called a set of *non-tree edges*. An *extended spanning tree* of G decided by B is a tree $T = (V', E', \sigma', \gamma')$ over Σ and Γ defined as follows:

- $V' = V \cup \{b_u, b_v \mid b = uv \in B\}$, where b_u and b_v are new vertices not included in V, called *virtual vertices* for a non-tree edge b.
- $E' = (E \setminus B) \cup \{ub_u, vb_v \mid b = uv \in B\}$.
- $\sigma' : V' \to \Sigma$ is such that, for each $v \in V$, $\sigma'(v) = \sigma(v)$, and, for each $v \in V' \setminus V$, $\sigma'(v)$ is set to undefined.
- $\gamma' : E' \to \Gamma$ is such that, for each $e \in E$, $\gamma'(e) = \gamma(e)$, and, for each $b = uv \in B$, $\gamma'(ub_u) = \gamma'(vb_u) = \gamma(b)$.

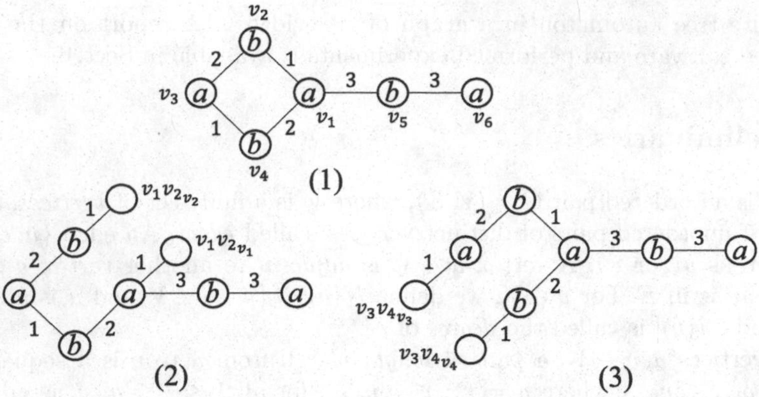

Fig. 2. (1) The graph G, (2) the extended spanning tree decided by B_1, and (3) the extended spanning tree decided by B_2.

Example 1. Let $G = (V, E, \sigma, \gamma)$ be a graph over $\Sigma = \{a, b\}$, $\Delta = \{1, 2, 3\}$, where

$$\begin{aligned} V &= \{v_1, v_2, v_3, v_4, v_5, v_6\}, \\ E &= \{v_1v_2, v_1v_4, v_1v_5, v_2v_3, v_3v_4, v_5v_6\}, \\ \sigma &= \{(v_1, a), (v_2, b), (v_3, a), (v_4, b), (v_5, b), (v_6, a)\}, \text{ and} \\ \delta &= \{(v_1v_2, 1), (v_1v_4, 2), (v_1v_5, 3), (v_2v_3, 2), (v_3v_4, 1), (v_5v_6, 3)\}. \end{aligned}$$

For the graph G, $B_1 = \{v_1v_2\}$ and $B_2 = \{v_3v_4\}$ are two of the sets of non-tree edges. The graph G and the extended spanning trees decided by B_1 and B_2 are illustrated in Fig. 2.

3 Spanning Tree Automata for Labeled, Connected Graphs

A spanning tree automaton is defined as an extension of the well-known nondeterministic top-down finite tree automaton for labeled, ordered trees [4]. Instead of graphs, an ST automaton deals with their extended spanning trees.

3.1 Definitions

A *spanning tree automaton (ST automaton)* is a 6-tuple $A = (Q, \Sigma, \Gamma, q_0, P, R)$ where:

- Q is a finite set of *states*,
- Σ is an alphabet of *vertex labels*,
- Γ is an alphabet of *edge labels*,
- $q_0 \in Q$ is the *initial state*,
- P is a set of unordered pairs of states, called *acceptable state matchings*, and
- R is a finite set of *transition rules* of the form

$$q(f(c_1, c_2, \ldots, c_n)) \to f(q_1(c_1), q_2(c_2), \ldots, q_n(c_n))$$

where $n \geq 0$, $f \in \Sigma$, $q, q_1, q_2, \ldots, q_n \in Q$, and $c_1, c_2, \ldots, c_n \in \Gamma$. The number n is called the *width* of a transition rule. When $n = 0$, we write $q(f) \to f$ instead of $q(f()) \to f()$.

Let $A = (Q, \Sigma, \Gamma, q_0, P, R)$ be an ST automaton, let $G = (V, E, \sigma, \gamma)$ be a graph, let $T = (V', E', \sigma', \gamma')$ be an extended spanning tree of G decided by a set of non-tree edges B, and let $r \in V$ be a vertex of G. A *state mapping* on T is a function $\mu : V' \to Q$. A state mapping μ on the rooted tree (T, r) is *acceptable* by A if the following conditions hold:

- $\mu(r) = q_0$, i.e., a state mapped to the root is always the initial state,
- for each node $v \in V'$ with n $(n > 0)$ children $v_1, v_2, \ldots, v_n$, if $\sigma(v) = f$, $\mu(v) = q$, $\gamma(vv_1) = c_1$, $\gamma(vv_2) = c_2$, $\ldots$, $\gamma(vv_n) = c_n$, and $\mu(v_1) = q_1$, $\mu(v_2) = q_2$, $\ldots$, $\mu(v_n) = q_n$, then R contains the following transition rule:

$$q(f(c_1, c_2, \ldots, c_n)) \to f(q_1(c_1), q_2(c_2), \ldots, q_n(c_n)),$$

- for each leaf $v \in V$, if $\sigma(v) = f$ and $\mu(v) = q$, then R contains the following transition rule:

$$q(f) \to f,$$

- and for each $b = uv \in B$, $\{\mu(b_u), \mu(b_v)\} \in P$, i.e., the states mapped to the virtual vertices for b must be in acceptable state matchings.

The graph G is *accepted* by A if an extended spanning tree T decided by some set of non-tree edges B exists, a state mapping μ on T exists, a vertex $r \in V$ exists, and μ on (T, r) is acceptable by A.

The set of graphs *defined* by an ST automaton A is the set accepted by A.

Example 2. $A = (Q, \Sigma, \Gamma, q_0, P, R)$ is an example of an ST automaton, where $Q = \{q_0, q_1, q_2, q_3\}$, $\Sigma = \{a, b\}$, $\Gamma = \{1, 2, 3\}$, $P = \{\{q_1, q_1\}, \{q_1, q_2\}\}$, and R consists of transition rules:

$$q_0(a(1,2,3)) \to a(q_1(1), q_2(2), q_3(3)), \quad q_1(a(2)) \to a(q_2(2)),$$
$$q_2(b(1)) \to b(q_1(1)), \quad q_3(b(3)) \to b(q_3(3)), \quad q_3(a) \to a.$$

Consider the graph G and its non-tree edge set B_1 in Example 1. Let G' be the extended spanning tree of G decided by B_1. Consider the following state mapping μ on G':

$$\mu = \{(v_1, q_0), (v_2, q_2), (v_3, q_1), (v_4, q_2), (v_5, q_3), (v_6, q_3), (v_1v_{2v_1}, q_1), (v_1v_{2v_2}, q_1)\}.$$

The state mapping μ on (G', v_1) is illustrated in Fig. 3. The graph G is accepted by A because μ on (G', v_1) is acceptable by A. Note that the pair of states mapped to the virtual vertices for v_1v_2 is $\{q_1, q_1\}$, and it is in P.

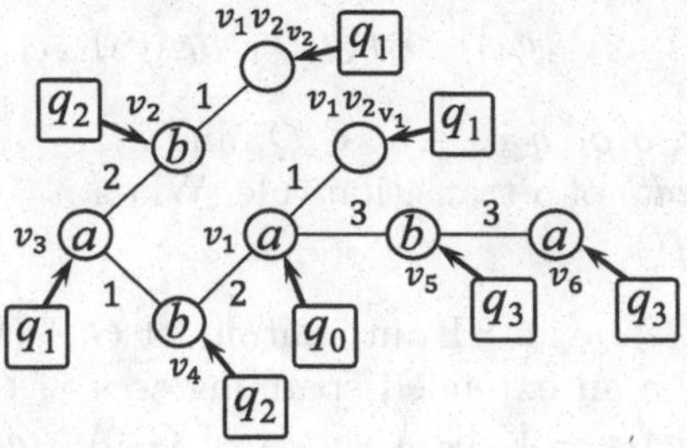

Fig. 3. The state mapping μ on (G', v_1).

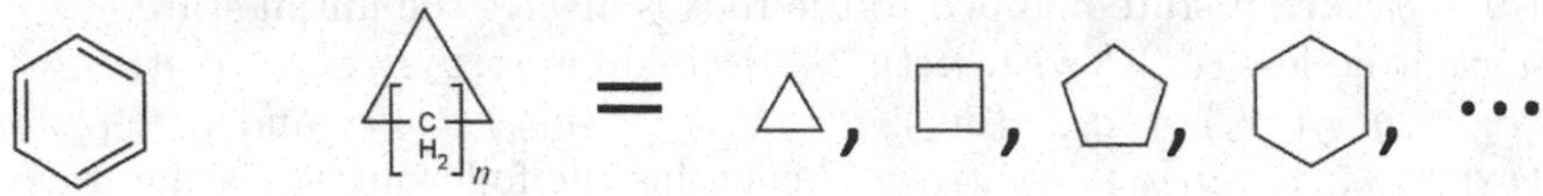

(a) (b)

Fig. 4. Chemical structural formulas of (a) benzene and (b) cycloalkanes.

3.2 Examples of Spanning Tree Automata

Example 3. We present two ST automata defining a set of chemical structural formulas. One defines the chemical structural formula of benzene as illustrated in Fig. 4a, and the other defines the cycloalkanes as illustrated in Fig. 4b. In a chemical structural formula, carbon atoms are implied to be located at the vertices of line segments, and hydrogen atoms attached to carbon atoms are omitted.

We set $\Sigma = \{C\}$ and $\Gamma = \{1, 2\}$, where the vertex label C stands for a carbon atom, and the edge labels 1 and 2 stand for a single bond and a double bond, respectively.

The following is an ST automaton that defines a chemical structural formula of benzene: $A = (Q, \Sigma, \Gamma, q_0, P, R)$, where $Q = \{q_0, q_1, q_2, q_3, q_4, q_5, q_6\}$, $P = \{\{q_6, q_6\}\}$ and R consists of transition rules:

$$q_0(C(1,2)) \to C(q_1(1), q_6(2))\,, \quad q_1(C(2)) \to C(q_2(2))\,, \quad q_2(C(1)) \to C(q_3(1))\,,$$
$$q_3(C(2)) \to C(q_4(2))\,, \quad q_4(C(1)) \to C(q_5(1))\,, \quad q_5(C(2)) \to C(q_6(2))\,.$$

The following is an ST automaton that defines chemical structural formulae of the cycloalkanes: $A = (Q, \Sigma, \Gamma, q_0, P, R)$, where $Q = \{q_0, q_1, q_2, q_3\}$, $P = \{\{q_3, q_3\}\}$ and R consists of transition rules:

$$q_0(C(1,1)) \to C(q_1(1), q_3(1))\,, \quad q_1(C(1)) \to C(q_2(1))\,,$$
$$q_2(C(1)) \to C(q_2(1))\,, \quad q_2(C(1)) \to C(q_3(1))\,.$$

4 Properties of Spanning Tree Automata

Lemma 1. *For any graph G there is an ST automaton A defining the set $\{G\}$.*

Proof. Suppose that $G = (V, E, \sigma, \gamma)$, a graph over Σ and Γ, is given. Let B be a set of non-tree edges of G, and let $G' = (V', E', \sigma', \gamma')$ be the extended spanning tree of G decided by B. Choose any vertex $r \in V$ for the root.

We can construct an ST automaton $A = (Q, \Sigma, \Gamma, q_0, P, R)$ as follows:

- $Q = \{\hat{v} \mid v \in V\} \cup \{\hat{p} \mid p \in B\}$,
- $q_0 = \hat{r}$,
- $P = \{\{\hat{p}, \hat{p}\} \mid p \in B\}$, and
- for each $v \in V$, R has the following transition rule:

$$\hat{v}(f(c_1, c_2, \ldots, c_n)) \to f(q_1(c_1), q_2(c_2), \ldots, q_n(c_n))$$

where v has n children $v_1, v_2, \ldots, v_n$ in the rooted tree (G', r), $f = \sigma(v)$, and, for $1 \leq i \leq n$, if $v_i = p_v$ for some $p = uv \in B$, then $c_i = \gamma(uv)$ and $q_i = \hat{p}$, otherwise $c_i = \gamma(vv_i)$ and $q_i = \hat{v}_i$.

An acceptable state mapping μ on (G', r) can be obtained as follows: For $v \in V$, $\mu(v) = \hat{v}$, and, for $p = uv \in B$, $\mu(p_u) = \mu(p_v) = \hat{p}$.

Clearly, the ST automaton A precisely defines the set $\{G\}$. □

Lemma 2. *The class of sets of graphs accepted by ST automata is effectively closed under union.*

Proof. Let $A = (Q, \Sigma, \Gamma, q_0, P, R)$ and $A' = (Q', \Sigma', \Gamma', q_0', P', R')$ be ST automata. We may assume that $Q \cap Q' = \emptyset$. We consider an ST automaton $A'' = (Q'', \Sigma'', \Gamma'', q_0'', P'', R'')$ defined as follows:

- $Q'' = Q \cup Q' \cup \{q_0''\}$, where q_0'' is a new state,
- $\Sigma'' = \Sigma \cup \Sigma'$,
- $\Gamma'' = \Gamma \cup \Gamma'$,
- $P'' = P \cup P'$, and
- $R'' = R \cup R' \cup \{r'' \mid r \in R \cup R'$, q_0 or q_0' appears on the left-hand side of r, and r'' is obtained by replacing q_0 or q_0' on the left-hand side of r with $q_0''\}$.

Clearly, a graph G is accepted by A'' if and only if G is accepted by either A or A'. □

Theorem 1. *For any finite set of graphs, we can construct an ST automaton that defines it.*

Proof. The theorem clearly follows from Lemmas 1 and 2. □

Because the membership problem for ST automata includes the graph isomorphism problem, it is at least GI-hard. Its NP-completeness is obtained by the reduction from the Hamiltonian cycle problem with vertex degree at most 3 [9]. When a graph with degree at most 3 has a Hamiltonian cycle, (1) the graph has no vertex of degree 0 or 1, (2) for each vertex of degree 2, both edges connected to the vertex belong to the Hamiltonian cycle, and (3) for each vertex of degree 3, two edges connected to the vertex belong to the Hamiltonian cycle but the remaining edge does not and is adjacent to another vertex of degree 3.

Theorem 2. *The membership problem for ST automata is NP-complete.*

Proof. Consider the ST automaton $A = (Q, \Sigma, \Gamma, q_0, P, R)$, where $Q = \{q_0, q_1, q_2\}$, $\Sigma = \{a\}$, $\Gamma = \{1\}$, $P = \{\{q_1, q_1\}, \{q_2, q_2\}\}$ and R consists of transition rules:

$$q_0(a(1,1)) \to a(q_1(1), q_1(1)), \quad q_0(a(1,1,1)) \to a(q_1(1), q_1(1), q_2(1)),$$
$$q_1(a(1)) \to a(q_1(1)), \quad q_1(a(1,1)) \to a(q_1(1), q_2(1)).$$

It is clear that A accepts a graph with degree at most 3 that has a Hamiltonian cycle. Since the Hamiltonian cycle problem with vertex degree at most 3 is NP-hard, this problem is also NP-hard.

On the other hand, given a graph G, we can nondeterministically obtain a set of non-tree edges B, an extended spanning tree G' decided by B, a state mapping μ on G', a vertex $r \in V$, and check if μ on (G', r) is acceptable by A in polynomial time. Thus the problem is in the class NP. □

5 Breadth-First Search Spanning Tree Automata

ST automata can define some infinite sets of graphs, like the set of chemical structural formulas of cycloalkanes shown in Example 3. On the other hand, it is not difficult to find infinite sets of graphs impossible for any ST automaton to define. For example, there is no ST automaton accepting any set of graphs where the graph maximum degree is not bounded. This might not seem too restrictive as vertex degrees of chemical structures are usually bounded. However, there is a more limiting restriction which comes from the observation that if an ST automaton A accepts a graph whose number of minimum cycles is greater than the number of acceptable state matchings of A, then some pairs of virtual vertices are mapped in the same state matching. Consequences are demonstrated by the following example.

Example 4. The set of chemical structural formulas for benzene and acenes, shown in Fig. 5, cannot be defined by any ST automaton.

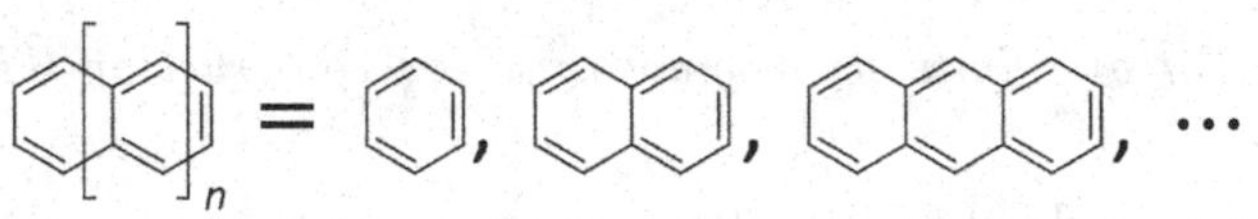

Fig. 5. Chemical structural formulas for benzene and acenes.

There is no limit for the number of minimum cycles of the defined graphs. From this reason, for any ST automaton A, there is a graph G in the defined set such that its number of minimum cycles exceeds the number of acceptable state matchings of the automaton. If two pairs of virtual vertices (uv_u, uv_v) and (st_s, st_t) are mapped to the same state matching, and u, v, s, t are all distinct, then another graph obtained from G by removing the edges uv and st and adding the new edges ut and vs is accepted by A. However, the newly obtained graph is not a chemical structural formula for an acene anymore.

To handle chained structures like acenes by ST automata, we introduce a variant of the automata working over extensions of breadth-first search (BFS, [5]) spanning trees only. A breadth-first search spanning tree automaton (BFS-ST automaton) is a six-tuple $A = (Q, \Sigma, \Gamma, q_0, P, R)$ where the components have the same meaning as in the case of the ST automaton defined in Subsect. 3.1.

A graph $G = (V, E, \delta, \gamma)$ is accepted by A if G has a BFS spanning tree $T = (V, E_T)$ rooted in a vertex r (i.e., for all $v \in V$, it holds that $d_G(r, v) = d_T(r, v)$) such that the pair (T', r), where T' is the extended spanning tree decided by $E \setminus E_T$, is accepted by A for some state mapping μ.

We give a characterization of a certain family of infinite sets of graphs accepted by BFS-ST automata, which includes the set of graphs representing benzene and acenes. The idea behind the family is (1) to take a word w from a regular language, (2) to substitute graphs for symbols of w (where occurrences of the same symbol are substituted by isomorphic graphs), and (3) to combine neighboring graphs by merging some of their predefined pairs of vertices. A detailed description of this construction follows.

Let Σ and Γ be finite sets of vertex and edge labels, respectively. We say that $C = (V, E, \sigma, \gamma, \boldsymbol{V}^+, \boldsymbol{V}^-)$ is a *graph component* over (Σ, Γ) if $C' = (V, E, \sigma, \gamma)$ is a labeled, connected graph over Σ, and Γ, $\boldsymbol{V}^+$ and $\boldsymbol{V}^-$ are non-empty vectors of distinct elements of V, there is no edge in E connecting a pair of vertices from $\boldsymbol{V}^-$, and there is an integer $d \geq 1$ such that $\forall u \in \boldsymbol{V}^+, \forall v \in \boldsymbol{V}^- : d'_C(u, v) \in \{d, d+1\}$. An example of graph components is given in Fig. 6.

Let L be a regular language over an alphabet Σ_1. Let FIRST$(L) \subseteq \Sigma_1$ be the set of symbols that begin a word from L, and FOLLOW$(L, a) \subseteq \Sigma_1$ be the set of symbols $b \in \Sigma_1$ for which there is a word in L in which b follows after a.

A *component substitution function* π is a function assigning to each symbol of Σ_1 a graph component over (Σ, Γ). Let $\pi(a) = C_a = (V_a, E_a, \sigma_a, \gamma_a, \boldsymbol{V}_a^+, \boldsymbol{V}_a^-)$ for each $a \in \Sigma_1$. We say π is *compatible* with L iff for all $a \in \Sigma_1$, $b \in$ FOLLOW(L, a), it holds that $|\boldsymbol{V}_a^-| = |\boldsymbol{V}_b^+|$, and, for all $a \in$ FIRST(L), it holds that $|\boldsymbol{V}_a^+| = 1$. Note that $|\boldsymbol{v}|$ denotes the dimension of a vector $\boldsymbol{v}$.

For a π compatible with L, we define $\mathcal{G}(L, \pi)$ to be the set of graphs $G(w, \pi)$ where $w = a_1 \ldots a_n$, with $a_i \in \Sigma_1$, is a non-empty word from L and the graph $G(w, \pi) = (V, E, \sigma, \gamma)$ is constructed as follows. Let $C_i = (V_i, E_i, \sigma_i, \gamma_i, \boldsymbol{V}_i^+, \boldsymbol{V}_i^-)$ be a graph component isomorphic to $\pi(a_i)$. Assume that $V_i \cap V_j = \emptyset$ for all $1 \leq i < j \leq n$. Treat vectors of distinct elements as sets and define a mapping

$$\nu : \bigcup_{i=1}^{n} V_i \rightarrow \bigcup_{i=1}^{n} V_i \setminus \bigcup_{i=1}^{n-1} \boldsymbol{V}_i^-$$

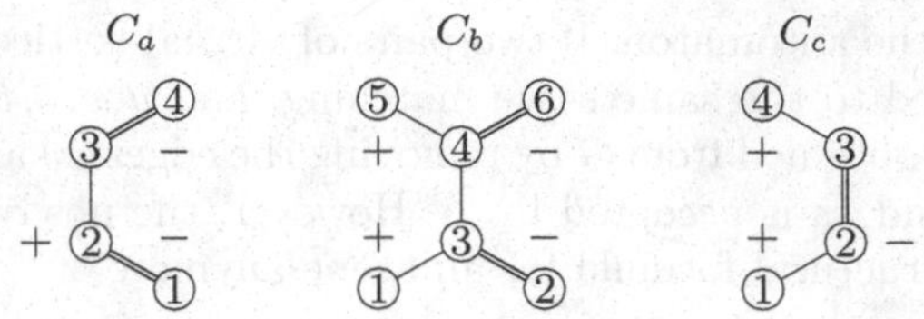

Fig. 6. Graph components $C_s = (V_s, E_s, \sigma_s, \gamma_s, \boldsymbol{V}_s^+, \boldsymbol{V}_s^-)$, $s \in \{a, b, c\}$, where it holds that $\boldsymbol{V}_a^+ = (2)$, $\boldsymbol{V}_a^- = (1, 4)$, $\boldsymbol{V}_b^+ = (1, 5)$, $\boldsymbol{V}_b^- = (2, 6)$, $\boldsymbol{V}_c^+ = (1, 4)$ and $\boldsymbol{V}_c^- = (2)$. Vertices of the sets $\boldsymbol{V}_s^+$ and $\boldsymbol{V}_s^-$ are distinguished by symbols + and −, respectively. We define $\gamma_s : E_s \to \{0, 1\}$ where labels 0 and 1 represent single and double bonds, respectively.

fulfilling: if v is the j-th component of $\boldsymbol{V}_i^-$, where $i < n$, then $\nu(v)$ equals the j-th component of $\boldsymbol{V}_{i+1}^+$, otherwise $\nu(v) = v$. Then, $V = \bigcup_{i=1}^n V_i \setminus \bigcup_{i=1}^{n-1} \boldsymbol{V}_i^- = \{\nu(v) \mid v \in \bigcup_{i=1}^n V_i\}$, $E = \{\{\nu(u), \nu(v)\} \mid \{u, v\} \in \bigcup_{i=1}^n E_i\}$, and $\sigma(\nu(v)) = \sigma_i(v)$, $\gamma(\{\nu(u), \nu(v)\}) = \gamma_i(\{u, v\})$ for all $v \in V_i$, $\{u, v\} \in E_i$, $i = 1, \ldots, n$.

Example 5. Let L be a regular language over $\Sigma_1 = \{a, b, c\}$ defined by the regular expression ab^*c. Let $\pi : \Sigma_1 \to \{C_a, C_b, C_c\}$ be a component substitution function such that $\pi(a) = C_a$, $\pi(b) = C_b$, $\pi(c) = C_c$ where the graph components are those shown in Fig. 6. Observe that π is compatible with L. Then, $\mathcal{G}(L, \pi)$ is a set of graphs that represent benzene and acenes.

Theorem 3. *For any regular language L over Σ_1 and any component substitution function $\pi : \Sigma_1 \to \mathcal{C}$, where $\mathcal{C}$ is a set of graph components over (Σ, Γ) and π is compatible with L, there is a BFS-ST automaton A accepting $\mathcal{G}(L, \pi)$.*

We omit the proof of this theorem because of lack of space.

6 Implementation and Experiments

For practical use of ST automata, a search software which for a given dataset of graphs finds subgraphs accepted by an ST automaton was developed. It allows to search for acceptable subgraphs of the maximum or minimum size. The source code of the software, written in the C++ programming language, is available on the web site: http://apricot.cis.ibaraki.ac.jp/CBGfinder/.

The graphset-subgraph matching algorithm used in the software is an extension of the algorithm described in [7], which was designed to find a spanning tree accepted by a finite tree automaton in an input graph of treewidth 2. The new algorithm was developed based on the original one with the following extensions: (1) It searches for graphs defined by ST or BFS-ST automata instead of spanning trees defined by tree automata. (2) It is optionally able to search for subgraphs and induced subgraphs (defined by an ST or BFS-ST automaton) in a given input graph. (3) There is no limit on the input graph treewidth.

The algorithm is dynamic programming based and works in a bottom-up manner to construct an acceptable state mapping. Partial solutions established

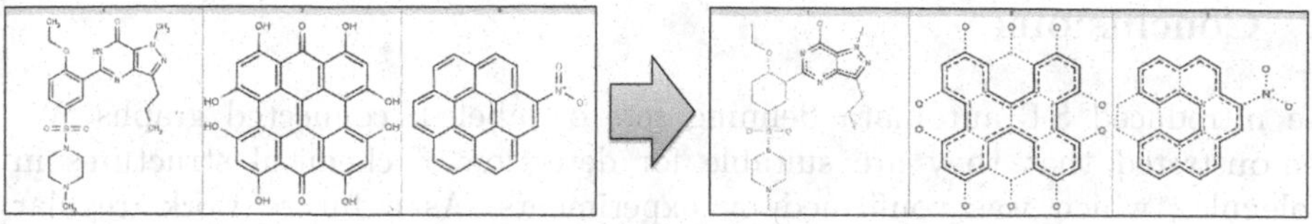

Fig. 7. Longest aromatic cycles detected by the search software. Three samples of input molecules are shown on the left. All parts of the found longest aromatic cycles are highlighted by the dashed line segments on the right.

over subgraphs are combined to reach a global solution. For a graph $G = (V, E)$ and an ST automaton A, the maximum number of partial solutions over a subgraph is $T = (r \cdot 2^{width} \cdot tw)^{tw}$, where tw is the treewidth of G, r is the number of transition rules of A, and $width$ is the maximum width of a transition rule. It can be derived that the space complexity is $O(|E| \cdot T)$, and the time complexity is $O(|E| \cdot T^2 \cdot \log(T))$. Note that these estimates are theoretical upper bounds, the actual space consumptions and running times are typically lower due to pruning many of the partial solutions that do not extend to larger ones.

To demonstrate a practical usage of the software, an evaluation was conducted to find the longest aromatic cycle of each molecule stored in the ChEMBL database. ChEMBL is a database of bioactive drug-like small molecules maintained by the European Bioinformatics Institute. 635,933 molecules are stored in ChEMBL version 8. Among them, 87 molecules containing a fullerene structure are excepted because their treewidth is too big. The number of atoms (bonds) of a molecule varies from 1 (0) to 878 (895) and is 32.02 (34.46) on average. An ST automaton defining the set of aromatic cycles was used.

As a result, among 635,846 molecules, 580,354 molecules were accepted with largest aromatic cycles detected, and 55,492 molecules without aromatic cycles were rejected. The evaluation was finished in 353.4 s in total (0.55 ms per item on average). The molecule which took the longest time (0.028 s) was the rightmost one in Fig. 7. The specification of the machine used for the experiment is as follows: Intel core i5-5200U (2.20GHz) CPU, 8 GB RAM, and Microsoft Windows 7 (64Bit) OS.

The software can be used not only for chemoinformatics but also for various NP-hard graph problems such as subgraph isomorphism, travelling salesman, longest path, feedback vertex set, Steiner tree, and so on.

To demonstrate this, we briefly report on the Third Parameterized Algorithms and Computational Experiments Challenge (PACE 2018) competition [12], in which the software participated in Track B. The task was to compute an optimal Steiner tree of a given graph within a given time limit on the same public environment. For this competition, a well-known speed-up technique [1] was implemented. The software correctly solved 49 out of 100 competition instances, despite it is not fully optimized for this particular task (for comparison, the best five participating systems solved 92, 77, 58, 52 and 52 instances, respectively).

7 Conclusions

We introduced ST automata defining sets of labeled, connected graphs. We demonstrated that they are suitable for detection of chemical structures in molecules, which was confirmed by experiments. As a future work, regular expressions for the automata should be considered. It would also be beneficial to identify broader subclasses of sets of graphs defined by BFS-ST automata.

References

1. Bodlaender, H.L., Cygan, M., Kratsch, S., Nederlof, J.: Deterministic single exponential time algorithms for connectivity problems parameterized by treewidth. Inf. Comput. **243**, 86–111 (2015). https://doi.org/10.1016/j.ic.2014.12.008
2. Brainerd, W.S.: Tree generating regular systems. Inf. Control **14**(2), 217–231 (1969). https://doi.org/10.1016/S0019-9958(69)90065-5
3. Brown, N.: Chemoinformatics-an introduction for computer scientists. ACM Comput. Surv. **41**(2), 8:1–8:38 (2009). https://doi.org/10.1145/1459352.1459353
4. Comon, H., et al.: Tree automata techniques and applications (2007). http://tata.gforge.inria.fr/. Accessed 12 Oct 2007
5. Cormen, T.H., Leiserson, C.E., Rivest, R.L., Stein, C.: Introduction to Algorithms, 3rd edn. MIT Press, Cambridge (2009). http://mitpress.mit.edu/books/introduction-algorithms
6. Courcelle, B., Engelfriet, J.: Graph Structure and Monadic Second-Order Logic - A Language-Theoretic Approach, Encyclopedia of Mathematics and its Applications, vol. 138. Cambridge University Press, Cambridge (2012)
7. Fujiyoshi, A.: A practical algorithm for the uniform membership problem of labeled multidigraphs of tree-width 2 for spanning tree automata. Int. J. Found. Comput. Sci. **28**(5), 563–582 (2017). https://doi.org/10.1142/S012905411740007X
8. Fujiyoshi, A., Kasai, T.: Spinal-formed context-free tree grammars. Theory Comput. Syst. **33**(1), 59–83 (2000). https://doi.org/10.1007/s002249910004
9. Garey, M., Johnson, D., Stockmeyer, L.: Some simplified NP-complete graph problems. Theoret. Comput. Sci. **1**(3), 237–267 (1976). https://doi.org/10.1016/0304-3975(76)90059-1
10. Hopcroft, J.E., Ullman, J.D.: Introduction to Automata Theory, Languages and Computation. Addison-Wesley, Reading (1979)
11. Kleene, S.C.: Representation of events in nerve nets and finite automata. In: Shannon, C.E., McCarthy, J. (eds.) Automata Studies, pp. 3–42. Princeton University Press, Princeton (1951)
12. PACE 2018. https://pacechallenge.org/2018/steiner-tree/
13. Rounds, W.C.: Mapping and grammars on trees. Math. Syst. Theory **4**(3), 257–287 (1970). https://doi.org/10.1007/BF01695769
14. Rozenberg, G., Ehrig, H., Engels, G., Kreowski, H., Montanari, U. (eds.): Handbook of Graph Grammars and Computing by Graph Transformations, Volume 1–3. World Scientific (1997–1999)
15. Sibley, J.F.: Too broad generic disclosures: a problem for all. J. Chem. Inf. Comput. Sci. **31**(1), 5–9 (1991). https://doi.org/10.1021/ci00001a002

Composition Closure of Linear Weighted Extended Top-Down Tree Transducers

Zoltán Fülöp[1] and Andreas Maletti[2(✉)]

[1] Department of Foundations of Computer Science, University of Szeged, Árpád tér 2, Szeged 6720, Hungary
fulop@inf.u-szeged.hu

[2] Department of Mathematics and Computer Science, Universität Leipzig, PO Box 100 920, 04009 Leipzig, Germany
maletti@informatik.uni-leipzig.de

Abstract. Linear weighted extended top-down tree transducers with regular look-ahead and with weights from a semiring are formal models that are used in syntax-based statistical machine translation. The composition hierarchies of some restricted versions of such weighted tree transducers (also without regular look-ahead) are considered. In particular, combinations of the restrictions of ε-freeness (all rules consume input), nondeletion, and strictness (all rules produce output) are considered. The composition hierarchy is shown to be finite for all but one ε-free variant of these weighted transducers over any commutative semiring.

1 Introduction

Linear extended top-down tree transducers (l-xt) were introduced (under a different name) and investigated already in [1]. We present them in the framework of synchronous grammars [3] since in syntax-based statistical machine translation these transducers are applied, and since we utilize some results of [6,14]. An l-xt M has a finite set of states and finitely many rules of the form $\langle \ell, q, r\rangle$, where q is a state and the left- and right-hand side ℓ and r are trees, which may also contain state-labeled leaves such that each state in r also occurs in ℓ. Linearity requires that each state occurs at most once both in ℓ and in r. In particular, in ε-rules the left-hand side ℓ and in non-strict rules the right-hand side r is just a state. The semantics of M is defined by means of synchronous rewriting using the derivation relation $\Rightarrow$. It is defined over sentential forms, which are triples (ξ, L, ζ) consisting of trees ξ and ζ with state-labeled leaves and a set L of links. A link is a pair (u, v) of positions pointing to occurrences of the same state in the trees ξ and ζ, respectively. A rule $\langle \ell, q, r\rangle$ can be applied to a sentential form (ξ, L, ζ) if there is a link $(u, v) \in L$ such that u and v point to an occurrence of the state q. In this case we write $(\xi, L, \zeta) \Rightarrow (\xi', L', \zeta')$, where

Z. Fülöp—Supported by NKFI grant K 108 448 and by grant 20391-3/2018/FEKUSTRAT of the Ministry of Human Capacities, Hungary.

A. Maletti—Partially supported by the DFG research training group 1763 'QuantLA'.

M. Hospodár and G. Jirásková (Eds.): CIAA 2019, LNCS 11601, pp. 133–145, 2019.
https://doi.org/10.1007/978-3-030-23679-3_11

the sentential form (ξ', L', ζ') is obtained by replacing the linked occurrences of q in ξ and ζ by ℓ and r, respectively. In addition, L is updated to include links induced by occurrences of the same state in ℓ and r. The initial sentential form is $(q_0, \{(\varepsilon, \varepsilon)\}, q_0)$, in which q_0 is the initial state of M, and we apply derivation steps until no occurrences of linked states remain. Any remaining (unlinked) state occurrence in the input tree t can then be replaced by an arbitrary tree. An instance of t is obtained by replacing all state occurrences and $I(t)$ is the set of all instances of t. The tree transformation induced by M consists of all pairs (t', u) such that $(q_0, \{(\varepsilon, \varepsilon)\}, q_0) \Rightarrow^* (t, \emptyset, u)$ and $t' \in I(t)$. In order to increase their expressive power, l-xt can be equipped with regular look-ahead [4], which restricts the instances $I(t)$ such that an unlinked occurrence of a state q can only be replaced by an element of a given regular tree language $c(q)$. We abbreviate 'l-xt with regular look-ahead' by l-xt^{R}.

Weighted l-xt^{R}, abbreviated by l-wxt^{R}, are able to express quantitative properties of the tree transformations [7,13,14,16]. In an l-wxt^{R} a weight from a semiring $\mathbb{K}$ is associated to each rule, and these rule weights are multiplied in a derivation. Provided that several derivations exist, these derivation weights are summed up. In this manner, an l-wxt^{R} M assigns a weight $\|M\|_{\mathbb{K}}(t, u) \in \mathbb{K}$ to each pair (t, u) of trees. It turned out that both l-wxt and l-wxt^{R} over the probabilistic semiring can serve as formal models of tree transformations which are used in syntax-based statistical machine translation [10,12].

We focus on the composition closure of l-wxt and l-wxt^{R} without ε-rules ($\not\varepsilon$l-wxt and $\not\varepsilon$l-wxt^{R}, respectively) and some of their restricted subclasses because compositions of weighted tree transformations induced by them can be defined in terms of finite sums. Our motivation is that complex systems are often specified in terms of compositions of simpler tree transformations [17], which are easier to develop, train, and maintain [12]. More precisely, let $\mathcal{C}$ be a class of weighted tree transformations (e.g. the class of all weighted tree transformations induced by $\not\varepsilon$l-wxt^{R}). The composition hierarchy of $\mathcal{C}$ is $\mathcal{C} \subseteq \mathcal{C}^2 \subseteq \mathcal{C}^3 \subseteq \cdots$, where $\mathcal{C}^n$ denotes the n-fold composition of $\mathcal{C}$. It is either infinite (i.e., $\mathcal{C}^n \subsetneq \mathcal{C}^{n+1}$ for all n) or finite (i.e., $\mathcal{C}^n = \mathcal{C}^{n+1}$ for some n). In the latter case, the minimal such n is interesting since all compositions can be reduced to this length.

The additional standard restrictions we consider are strictness ('s'), which requires that the right-hand side r is not a single state, and nondeletion ('n'), which means that each state in the left-hand side ℓ occurs also in the right-hand side r, in both cases for each rule $\langle \ell, q, r \rangle$ of the $\not\varepsilon$l-wxt^{R}. Thus, for instance $\not\varepsilon$sl-wxt^{R} abbreviates the expression 'strict $\not\varepsilon$l-wxt^{R}'. The class of all weighted tree transformations induced by certain kind of $\not\varepsilon$l-wxt^{R} is denoted by typesetter letters so for instance $\not\varepsilon\mathtt{sl\text{-}WXT}^{\mathtt{R}}(\mathbb{K})$ stands for the set of all weighted tree transformations computable by $\not\varepsilon$sl-wxt^{R} over the semiring $\mathbb{K}$. We consider the composition hierarchies of the classes $\not\varepsilon\mathtt{nsl\text{-}WXT}(\mathbb{K})$, which is also investigated in [15], and $\not\varepsilon\mathtt{sl\text{-}WXT}(\mathbb{K})$, $\not\varepsilon\mathtt{sl\text{-}WXT}^{\mathtt{R}}(\mathbb{K})$, $\not\varepsilon\mathtt{l\text{-}WXT}^{\mathtt{R}}(\mathbb{K})$, and $\not\varepsilon\mathtt{l\text{-}WXT}(\mathbb{K})$. As main result we show that the composition hierarchies of these classes collapse at levels 2, 2, 2, 3, and 4, respectively, for an arbitrary commutative semiring $\mathbb{K}$ (cf. Theorem 16). We achieve our results by lifting the results [1, Theorem 6.2] and

[6, Theorems 26, 31, 33, 34], where it is shown that the corresponding hierarchies in the unweighted cases collapse at the same levels. To this end, we decompose an $\not\varepsilon$l-wxt^{R} into a weighted relabeling that handles all weights and nondeterminism, and a BOOLEAN functional unambiguous $\not\varepsilon$l-wxt^{R} (cf. Lemma 12). Moreover, we show that we can compose any such relabeling to the right of any l-wxt^{R} (cf. Lemma 13). These two constructions together will allow us to take all $\not\varepsilon$l-wxt^{R} in a composition chain into a particularly simple normal form (cf. Theorem 14). After some additional technical tailoring, we can utilize the mentioned results [1,6] and lift them to the corresponding weighted devices over any commutative semiring.

2 Preliminaries

We let $\mathbb{N} = \{0, 1, 2, \dots\}$ and $[n] = \{i \in \mathbb{N} \mid 1 \leq i \leq n\}$ for every $n \in \mathbb{N}$. For sets S and T, we let $2^S = \{S' \mid S' \subseteq S\}$, and we identify $S = \{s\}$ with the element s. Moreover, $T^S = \{f \mid f \colon S \to T\}$, and $|S|$ is the cardinality of S. For every $R \subseteq S \times T$, we let $\mathrm{dom}(R) = \{s \mid \exists t \in T \colon (s,t) \in R\}$ and $\mathrm{range}(R) = \{t \mid \exists s \in S \colon (s,t) \in R\}$. The *composition* of R with $R' \subseteq T \times U$ is $R \,; R' = \{(s,u) \mid \exists t \in T \colon (s,t) \in R,\ (t,u) \in R'\}$. Given $n \in \mathbb{N}$, we let S^n be the n-fold CARTESIAN product of S with itself and $S^* = \bigcup_{n \in \mathbb{N}} S^n$ is the set of all *words* over S. The *length* $|w|$ of $w \in S^n$ is n. The empty word () is also denoted by ε. The *concatenation* of $v, w \in S^*$ is $v.w$ or vw.

A *ranked alphabet* (Σ, rk) consists of a nonempty, finite set Σ and $\mathrm{rk} \colon \Sigma \to \mathbb{N}$, which we omit whenever it is obvious. We let $\Sigma^{(n)} = \{\sigma \in \Sigma \mid \mathrm{rk}(\sigma) = n\}$ for every $n \in \mathbb{N}$. In the following, Σ, Δ, and Γ are arbitrary ranked alphabets. Let V be a set with $V \cap \Sigma = \emptyset$. The set $T_\Sigma(V)$ of Σ" *trees indexed by* V is defined in the usual way, and we let $T_\Sigma = T_\Sigma(\emptyset)$. If $t \in T_\Sigma(V)$ is given as $t = \sigma(t_1, \dots, t_n)$, then we often omit the obvious quantification that $n \in \mathbb{N}$, $\sigma \in \Sigma^{(n)}$, and $t_1, \dots, t_n \in T_\Sigma(V)$. The map $\mathrm{pos} \colon T_\Sigma(V) \to 2^{(\mathbb{N}^*)}$ assigning *positions* is inductively defined for all $t \in T_\Sigma(V)$ by $\mathrm{pos}(t) = \{\varepsilon\}$ if $t \in V$ and $\mathrm{pos}(t) = \{\varepsilon\} \cup \{i.w \mid i \in [n],\ w \in \mathrm{pos}(t_i)\}$ if $t = \sigma(t_1, \dots, t_n)$. The *size* $|t|$ of a tree $t \in T_\Sigma(V)$ is $|\mathrm{pos}(t)|$. The *label* of t at $w \in \mathrm{pos}(t)$ is $t(w)$ and the *subtree* of t *rooted at* w is $t|_w$. For every set $D \subseteq \Sigma \cup V$ of labels, we let $\mathrm{pos}_D(t) = \{w \in \mathrm{pos}(t) \mid t(w) \in D\}$. The tree t is *linear* (resp. *nondeleting*) in $V' \subseteq V$ if $|\mathrm{pos}_v(t)| \leq 1$ (resp., $|\mathrm{pos}_v(t)| \geq 1$) for every $v \in V'$. We let $T_\Sigma^{\mathrm{lin}}(V)$ be the set of all trees of $T_\Sigma(V)$ that are linear in V. Moreover, $\mathrm{var}(t) = \{v \in V \mid \mathrm{pos}_v(t) \neq \emptyset\}$. We use the countably infinite set $X = \{x_i \mid i \in \mathbb{N}\}$ and $X_n = \{x_i \mid i \in [n]\}$ for every $n \in \mathbb{N}$. For every $n \in \mathbb{N}$, we define the set $C_\Sigma(X_n) = \{t \in T_\Sigma^{\mathrm{lin}}(X_n) \mid \mathrm{var}(t) = X_n\}$ of *n-contexts* and the set $\widehat{C_\Sigma}(X_n) = \{t \in C_\Sigma(X_n) \mid$ the order of variables in t is $x_1, \dots, x_n\}$ of *straight n-contexts*. Let $X' \subseteq X$ and $\theta \colon X' \to T_\Sigma$. Each such mapping θ extends to a mapping $(\cdot)\theta \colon T_\Sigma(X) \to T_\Sigma(X)$ such that for all $t \in T_\Sigma(X)$ we have $t\theta = t$ if $t \in X \setminus X'$, $t\theta = \theta(t)$ if $t \in X'$, and $t\theta = \sigma(t_1\theta, \dots, t_n\theta)$ if $t = \sigma(t_1, \dots, t_n)$. Given $t \in T_\Sigma(X)$ and $t_1, \dots, t_n \in T_\Sigma$, we write $t[t_1, \dots, t_n]$ for $t\theta$, where $\theta \colon X_n \to T_\Sigma$ is given by $\theta(x_i) = t_i$ for every $i \in [n]$. Moreover, for every $t \in T_\Sigma$ and $k \in \mathbb{N}$, let

$$\operatorname{decomp}(t) = \bigcup_{n \in \mathbb{N}} \{(c, t_1, \ldots, t_n) \in \widehat{C_\Sigma}(X_n) \times (T_\Sigma)^n \mid t = c[t_1, \ldots, t_n]\}$$

and $\operatorname{subst}_k(t) = \{(u, \theta) \in T_\Sigma^{\text{lin}}(X_k) \times (T_\Sigma)^{\text{var}(u)} \mid t = u\theta\}$. Note that both $\operatorname{decomp}(t)$ and $\operatorname{subst}_k(t)$ are finite sets.

As weight structures we use commutative semirings [9,11]. Formally, a *commutative semiring* is an algebraic structure $\mathbb{K} = (K, +, \cdot, 0, 1)$ such that $(K, +, 0)$ and $(K, \cdot, 1)$ are commutative monoids, $\cdot$ distributes over finite sums, and for all $a \in K$ we have $a \cdot 0 = 0$. Given a mapping $f \colon S \to K$, it is BOOLEAN if $\operatorname{range}(f) \subseteq \{0, 1\}$, and its *support* $\operatorname{supp}(f)$ is $\operatorname{supp}(f) = \{s \in S \mid f(s) \neq 0\}$. Any map $L \colon T_\Sigma \to K$ is a *weighted tree language.*

We will often utilize the BOOLEAN semiring $\mathbb{B} = (\{0, 1\}, \vee, \wedge, 0, 1)$, which is used to model the unweighted case, and the semiring $\mathbb{N} = (\mathbb{N}, +, \cdot, 0, 1)$. For the rest of this contribution, let $\mathbb{K} = (K, +, \cdot, 0, 1)$ be a commutative semiring.

A *weighted tree automaton* is a tuple $A = (Q, \Sigma, Q_0, \mathrm{wt})$, in which Q is a finite set of states, and $Q_0 \subseteq Q$ is a set of initial states, Σ is a ranked alphabet of input symbols, and $\mathrm{wt} \colon (\bigcup_{n \in \mathbb{N}} Q^n \times \Sigma^{(n)} \times Q) \to K$ is a weight assignment to transitions. It is BOOLEAN if the weight assignment 'wt' is BOOLEAN, and it is *(bottom-up) deterministic* if $q = q'$ for all $(q_1, \ldots, q_n, \sigma, q), (q_1, \ldots, q_n, \sigma, q') \in \operatorname{supp}(\mathrm{wt})$. The semantics $\|A\|_{\mathbb{K}} \colon T_\Sigma \to K$ of A is $\|A\|_{\mathbb{K}}(t) = \sum_{q \in Q_0} \|A\|_{\mathbb{K}}^q(t)$ for every $t \in T_\Sigma$, where the map $\|A\|_{\mathbb{K}}^q \colon T_\Sigma \to K$ is inductively defined for every $q \in Q$ and tree $t = \sigma(t_1, \ldots, t_n)$ by $\|A\|_{\mathbb{K}}^q(t) = \sum_{q_1, \ldots, q_n \in Q} \mathrm{wt}(q_1, \ldots, q_n, \sigma, q) \cdot \prod_{i=1}^n \|A\|_{\mathbb{K}}^{q_i}(t_i)$. A weighted tree language $L \colon T_\Sigma \to K$ is ($\mathbb{K}$-)*regular* if there exists a weighted tree automaton A such that $L = \|A\|_{\mathbb{K}}$. The class of all such regular weighted tree languages is denoted by $\mathrm{REG}_\Sigma(\mathbb{K})$. For a BOOLEAN deterministic weighted tree automaton A the weighted tree languages $\|A\|_{\mathbb{K}}$ and $\|A\|_{\mathbb{K}}^q$ for all $q \in Q$ are obviously BOOLEAN. The regular weighted tree languages are closed under the weighted relabelings [7, Theorem 5.3], which we introduce next.

A weighted tree transformation is a mapping $\tau \colon T_\Sigma(V) \times T_\Delta(V) \to K$. The domain '$\operatorname{dom}(\tau)$' and range '$\operatorname{range}(\tau)$' for a weighted tree transformation $\tau \colon T_\Sigma(V) \times T_\Delta(V) \to K$ are simply defined by $\operatorname{dom}(\tau) = \operatorname{dom}(\operatorname{supp}(\tau))$ and $\operatorname{range}(\tau) = \operatorname{range}(\operatorname{supp}(\tau))$. The transformation τ is *functional* (resp., *finitary*), if $\{u \mid (t, u) \in \operatorname{supp}(\tau)\}$ contains at most one element (resp., is finite) for every $t \in T_\Sigma(V)$. For a functional τ, its support $\operatorname{supp}(\tau)$ is a partial function.

A *weighted relabeling* is a mapping $\nu \colon \Sigma \times \Delta \to K$ such that $\nu(\sigma, \delta) = 0$ for all $\sigma \in \Sigma$ and $\delta \in \Delta$ with $\operatorname{rk}(\sigma) \neq \operatorname{rk}(\delta)$. Each weighted relabeling $\nu \colon \Sigma \times \Delta \to K$ extends to a finitary weighted tree transformation $\overline{\nu} \colon T_\Sigma(V) \times T_\Delta(V) \to K$, which is given as follows: for all variables $v, v' \in V$, trees $t = \sigma(t_1, \ldots, t_n) \in T_\Sigma(V)$, and $u = \delta(u_1, \ldots, u_k) \in T_\Delta(V)$, we define $\overline{\nu}(v, u) = \overline{\nu}(t, v') = 0$ and

$$\overline{\nu}(v, v') = \begin{cases} 1, & \text{if } v = v'; \\ 0, & \text{otherwise,} \end{cases} \qquad \overline{\nu}(t, u) = \begin{cases} \nu(\sigma, \delta) \cdot \prod_{i=1}^n \overline{\nu}(t_i, u_i), & \text{if } n = k; \\ 0, & \text{otherwise.} \end{cases}$$

Note that the weighted tree transformation $\overline{\nu}$ is finitary. Since $\overline{\nu}$ and ν coincide on $\Sigma^{(0)} \times \Delta^{(0)}$, we will not distinguish carefully between them and use just ν

for both. In fact, for all $t \in T_\Sigma(V)$, $u \in T_\Delta(V)$, and each $(c', u_1, \ldots, u_n) \in \text{decomp}(u)$

$$\nu(t, u) = \sum_{(c, t_1, \ldots, t_n) \in \text{decomp}(t)} \nu(c, c') \cdot \prod_{i=1}^{n} \nu(t_i, u_i) \ . \tag{1}$$

There is actually at most one decomposition of t in (1) that yields a non-zero weight for the sum (since the shapes of c and c' and similarly t_i and u_i need to coincide for all $i \in [n]$). The analogous property holds provided that a decomposition of t is given. The class of all weighted tree transformations induced by weighted relabelings is denoted by $\texttt{WREL}(\mathbb{K})$.

Given a finitary weighted tree transformation $\tau \colon T_\Sigma \times T_\Delta \to K$ and a weighted tree language $L \colon T_\Delta \to K$, we can define the pre-image $\tau^{-1}(L) \colon T_\Sigma \to K$ of L via τ for every $t \in T_\Sigma$ by $\big(\tau^{-1}(L)\big)(t) = \sum_{u \in T_\Delta} \tau(t, u) \cdot L(u)$. Given another weighted tree transformation $\tau' \colon T_\Delta \times T_\Gamma \to K$, we define the *composition* $\tau \,;\, \tau' \colon T_\Sigma \times T_\Gamma \to K$ of τ *followed by* τ' for every $t \in T_\Sigma$ and $v \in T_\Gamma$ as $\big(\tau;\tau'\big)(t, v) = \sum_{u \in T_\Delta} \tau(t, u) \cdot \tau'(u, v)$. Given classes $\mathcal{C}, \mathcal{C}'$ of tree transformations, we let $\mathcal{C} \,;\, \mathcal{C}' = \{\tau \,;\, \tau' \mid \tau \in \mathcal{C},\, \tau' \in \mathcal{C}'\}$. We also write $\tau \,;\, L$ instead of $\tau^{-1}(L)$ for a weighted relabeling τ and a weighted tree language $L \colon T_\Delta \to K$.

Theorem 1 ([7, Theorem 5.1]). For every weighted relabeling $\tau \in \texttt{WREL}(\mathbb{K})$ of type $\tau \colon T_\Sigma \times T_\Delta \to K$ and regular weighted tree language $L \in \texttt{REG}_\Delta(\mathbb{K})$, the weighted tree language $\tau^{-1}(L)$ is again regular [i.e., $\tau^{-1}(L) \in \texttt{REG}_\Sigma(\mathbb{K})$].

3 Transformational Model

A *linear weighted extended top-down tree transducer with regular look-ahead* (for short: l-wxt^{R}) over $\mathbb{K}$ [14] is a tuple $M = (Q, \Sigma, \Delta, q_0, R, \text{wt}, c)$, in which

- Q is a finite set of *states*, and $q_0 \in Q$ is an *initial state*,
- Σ and Δ are ranked alphabets of *input* and *output symbols*, respectively,
- $R \subseteq T_\Sigma^{\text{lin}}(Q) \times Q \times T_\Delta^{\text{lin}}(Q)$ is a finite set of *rules* such that $\text{var}(r) \subseteq \text{var}(\ell)$ and $\{\ell, r\} \not\subseteq Q$ for every rule $\langle \ell, q, r \rangle \in R$,
- $\text{wt} \colon R \to K$ is a *weight assignment* to the rules, and
- $c \colon Q \to \texttt{REG}_\Sigma(\mathbb{K})$ is a regular weighted *look-ahead* for each state.

To save parentheses, we will write c^q instead of $c(q)$ for every state $q \in Q$.

Next, we recall some common restrictions of the general model that have already been discussed in [7]. The l-wxt^{R} M is

- *ε-free* (resp., *strict*), if $\ell \notin Q$ (resp., $r \notin Q$) for every rule $\langle \ell, q, r \rangle \in R$,
- *nondeleting*, if $\text{var}(\ell) = \text{var}(r)$ for every rule $\langle \ell, q, r \rangle \in R$,
- BOOLEAN, if 'wt' and c^q are BOOLEAN for every state $q \in Q$,
- an *l-wxt* (i.e., without look-ahead) if $c^q(t) = 1$ for every state $q \in Q$ and tree $t \in T_\Sigma$, and
- an *l-wt*^{R} (i.e., non-extended) if $\text{pos}_\Sigma(\ell) = \{\varepsilon\}$ for every rule $\langle \ell, q, r \rangle \in R$.

Next we recall the semantics of an l-wxt^{R} $M = (Q, \Sigma, \Delta, q_0, R, \mathrm{wt}, c)$, which is the weighted tree transformation $\|M\|^q_{\mathbb{K}} : T_\Sigma \times T_\Delta \to K$ defined inductively for every $t \in T_\Sigma$ and $u \in T_\Delta$ by

$$\|M\|^q_{\mathbb{K}}(t, u) = \sum_{\substack{(\ell, t_1, \ldots, t_n) \in \mathrm{decomp}(t) \\ (r, \theta) \in \mathrm{subst}_n(u) \\ q_1, \ldots, q_n \in Q \\ \rho = \langle \ell[q_1, \ldots, q_n], q, r[q_1, \ldots, q_n] \rangle \in R}} \mathrm{wt}(\rho) \cdot \Big(\prod_{x_i \in \mathrm{var}(r)} \|M\|^{q_i}_{\mathbb{K}}(t_i, x_i\theta) \Big) \cdot \Big(\prod_{x_i \in \mathrm{var}(\ell) \setminus \mathrm{var}(r)} c^{q_i}(t_i) \Big) . \quad (2)$$

Using our remarks about $\mathrm{decomp}(t)$ and $\mathrm{subst}_n(u)$, all sets used in the index of the sum are finite, so the sum has only finitely many summands. Since we have $\langle \ell[q_1, \ldots, q_n], q, r[q_1, \ldots, q_n] \rangle \in R$, we know that $\ell \notin Q$ or $r \notin Q$. Consequently, $|t_i| < |t|$ or $|x_i\theta| < |u|$ for every $i \in [n]$ with $x_i \in \mathrm{var}(r)$, which proves that the recursion is well-founded. Besides the rule weight $\mathrm{wt}(\rho)$, we multiply the weights $\|M\|^{q_i}_{\mathbb{K}}(t_i, x_i\theta)$ of the recursive processing of those subtrees t_i that are further processed. The subtrees that are not further processed contribute their look-ahead weight $c^{q_i}(t_i)$. The semantics $\|M\|_{\mathbb{K}} : T_\Sigma \times T_\Delta \to K$ is then given for every $t \in T_\Sigma$ and $u \in T_\Delta$ by $\|M\|_{\mathbb{K}}(t, u) = \|M\|^{q_0}_{\mathbb{K}}(t, u)$. For nondeleting l-wxt^{R} the rightmost product in (2) yields 1, hence nondeleting l-wxt^{R} and nondeleting l-wxt are equally expressive. An l-wxt^{R} M is *functional* if $\|M\|_{\mathbb{K}}$ is functional. We note that each l-wxt^{R} M that is ε-free or functional induces a finitary $\|M\|_{\mathbb{K}}$. Next we relate l-wxt^{R} over the semiring $\mathbb{N}$ and l-wxt^{R} over $\mathbb{K}$. For this, we recall that $\mathbb{N}$ is the initial commutative semiring, so there exists a unique homomorphism [9,11] from $\mathbb{N}$ to $\mathbb{K}$, i.e., a mapping $h : \mathbb{N} \to K$ with $h(0) = 0$, $h(1) = 1$, $h(n + n') = h(n) + h(n')$, and $h(n \cdot n') = h(n) \cdot h(n')$ for all $n, n' \in \mathbb{N}$.

Lemma 2. Let $M = (Q, \Sigma, \Delta, q_0, R, \mathrm{wt}, c)$ be an l-wxt^{R} over the semiring $\mathbb{N}$ of nonnegative integers, and let $h : \mathbb{N} \to K$ be the unique semiring homomorphism from $\mathbb{N}$ to $\mathbb{K}$. Then $h(\|M\|_{\mathbb{N}}(t, u)) = \|M'\|_{\mathbb{K}}(t, u)$ for all $(t, u) \in T_\Sigma \times T_\Delta$, where $M' = (Q, \Sigma, \Delta, q_0, R, \mathrm{wt}', c')$ is the l-wxt^{R} over the semiring $\mathbb{K}$ with $\mathrm{wt}'(\rho) = h(\mathrm{wt}(\rho))$ and $(c')^q(t) = h(c^q(t))$ for all $\rho \in R$, $q \in Q$, and $t \in T_\Sigma$.

We abbreviate the properties of l-wxt^{R} as follows: '$\not\varepsilon$' = ε-free, 's' = strict, 'n' = nondeleting, 'B' = Boolean, 'f' = functional. We use these shorthands with the stems 'l-wxt^{R}', 'l-wxt', 'l-wt^{R}', and 'l-wt' to talk about an l-wxt^{R}, l-wxt, l-wt^{R}, or l-wt that additionally has the abbreviated properties attached as a prefix. For example, Bnl-wxt stands for "Boolean nondeleting l-wxt". We use the same abbreviations with the stem (i.e., the material behind the hyphen) in typesetter letters (and the semiring $\mathbb{K}$ in parentheses) for the corresponding classes of induced weighted tree transformations. For instance, `nl-WXT`($\mathbb{K}$) stands for the set of all weighted tree transformations computable by nl-wxt.

Utilizing the bimorphism characterizations of [7, Section 4] and the closure of the regular tree languages under linear homomorphisms [8, Theorem II.4.16], we easily obtain that both the domain as well as the range of each such transducer are regular, which we utilize without explicit mention.

Lemma 3. For every $\tau \in \texttt{l-WXT}^{\texttt{R}}(\mathbb{B})$ both $\text{dom}(\tau)$ and $\text{range}(\tau)$ are regular.

Finally, we recall the results for the composition hierarchies of the unweighted tree transformation classes, which we lift to the weighted case in Sect. 5.

Theorem 4 (see [1, Theorem 6.2] **and** [6, Theorems 26, 31, 33, 34]**).**

$$\not\varepsilon\texttt{nsl-WXT}(\mathbb{B})^3 = \not\varepsilon\texttt{nsl-WXT}(\mathbb{B})^2 \quad (3a)$$

$$\not\varepsilon\texttt{sl-WXT}(\mathbb{B})^3 = \not\varepsilon\texttt{sl-WXT}(\mathbb{B})^2 \quad (3b) \qquad \not\varepsilon\texttt{sl-WXT}^{\texttt{R}}(\mathbb{B})^3 = \not\varepsilon\texttt{sl-WXT}^{\texttt{R}}(\mathbb{B})^2 \quad (3d)$$

$$\not\varepsilon\texttt{l-WXT}(\mathbb{B})^5 = \not\varepsilon\texttt{l-WXT}(\mathbb{B})^4 \quad (3c) \qquad \not\varepsilon\texttt{l-WXT}^{\texttt{R}}(\mathbb{B})^4 = \not\varepsilon\texttt{l-WXT}^{\texttt{R}}(\mathbb{B})^3 \quad (3e)$$

Additionally, the classes of (3b) and (3d) as well as (3c) and (3e) coincide.

4 Faithful Representation

In this section, we deal with the question in which cases unweighted transducers faithfully represent certain Boolean weighted transducers (note that the weighted tree transformation induced by a Boolean l-wxt^{R} might not be Boolean). Moreover, we consider for which such transducers M another such transducer M' exists, which induces a partial function $\|M'\|_{\mathbb{B}} \subseteq \|M\|_{\mathbb{B}}$ with the same domain as $\|M\|_{\mathbb{B}}$. We start with the definition of unambiguous l-wxt^{R}. To this end, we reinterpret Boolean l-wxt^{R} over the semiring $\mathbb{K}$, which anyway only use the neutral elements 0 and 1, as Boolean l-wxt^{R} over the semiring $\mathbb{N}$ of nonnegative integers by identifying the neutral elements 0 and 1 in $\mathbb{K}$ and $\mathbb{N}$. Thus, given a Boolean l-wxt^{R} M (over $\mathbb{K}$), we write $\|M\|_{\mathbb{N}}$ for its semantics in the semiring of nonnegative integers. We also reinterpret M over the Boolean semiring $\mathbb{B}$ and write $\|M\|_{\mathbb{B}}$. Over the Boolean semiring $\mathbb{B}$, we sometimes identify mappings $f\colon S \to \{0,1\}$ with their support $\text{supp}(f)$ and vice versa, so $\|M\|_{\mathbb{B}}\colon T_\Sigma \times T_\Delta \to \{0,1\}$ is identified with $\|M\|_{\mathbb{B}} \subseteq T_\Sigma \times T_\Delta$ for a Boolean l-wxt^{R} M.

Definition 5. Let $M = (Q, \Sigma, \Delta, q_0, R, \text{wt}, c)$ be a Boolean l-wxt^{R} over $\mathbb{K}$ and $L \subseteq T_\Sigma$. We say that M is *unambiguous on* L if $\|M\|_{\mathbb{N}}(t,u) \in \{0,1\}$ for every $(t,u) \in L \times T_\Delta$ (i.e., the mapping $\|M\|_{\mathbb{N}}$ restricted to $L \times T_\Delta$ is Boolean). In the case of $L = T_\Sigma$, we also say that M is *unambiguous.*

Lemma 6. Let $M = (Q, \Sigma, \Delta, q_0, R, \text{wt}, c)$ be a Boolean l-wxt^{R} over $\mathbb{K}$ that is unambiguous on $L \subseteq T_\Sigma$. Then $\|M\|_{\mathbb{K}}(t,u) = \|M\|_{\mathbb{B}}(t,u)$ for all $(t,u) \in L \times T_\Delta$.

Next we consider how Boolean weighted tree transformations behave under composition. We will identify another restriction, functionality, that is required for the faithful representation via unweighted composition.

Lemma 7. Let $\tau\colon T_\Sigma \times T_\Delta \to K$ and $\tau'\colon T_\Delta \times T_\Gamma \to K$ be Boolean weighted tree transformations. If τ is functional, then $\tau\,;\tau' = \text{supp}(\tau)\,;\text{supp}(\tau')$.

With this knowledge we are now ready to state the main lemma of this section. Given BOOLEAN transducers that additionally obey certain functionality and unambiguity restrictions, the computation inside the BOOLEAN semiring faithfully represents the computation in the semiring $\mathbb{K}$. We recall that the neutral element of composition is the identity mapping $\mathrm{id}_{T_\Sigma} = \{(t,t) \mid t \in T_\Sigma\}$ of the correct set T_Σ, whose range is clearly T_Σ.

Lemma 8. Let $n \geq 1$ be an integer and $M_i = (Q_i, \Sigma_i, \Sigma_{i+1}, q_i^0, R_i, \mathrm{wt}_i, c_i)$ be a BOOLEAN l-wxt$^\mathrm{R}$ for every $i \in [n]$. If (i) M_i is unambiguous on

$$\mathrm{range}(\|M_1\|_\mathbb{K} \,;\cdots;\, \|M_{i-1}\|_\mathbb{K})$$

and (ii) $\|M_1\|_\mathbb{K} \,;\cdots;\, \|M_{i-1}\|_\mathbb{K}$ is functional for every $i \in [n]$, then

$$\|M_1\|_\mathbb{K} \,;\cdots;\, \|M_n\|_\mathbb{K} = \|M_1\|_\mathbb{B} \,;\cdots;\, \|M_n\|_\mathbb{B} \;.$$

We identify a weighted tree transformation over $\mathbb{B}$ with its support for the rest of this section. A *uniformizer* [2] of a tree transformation $\tau \subseteq T_\Sigma \times T_\Delta$ is a partial function $f\colon T_\Sigma \to T_\Delta$ such that $f \subseteq \tau$ and $\mathrm{dom}(f) = \mathrm{dom}(\tau)$. In other words, a uniformizer of τ is a maximal partial function contained in τ. We start with a simple proposition that shows how uniformizers behave under composition.

Lemma 9 ([2, Lemma 24]). Let $n \geq 1$ be an integer, $\Sigma_1, \ldots, \Sigma_{n+1}$ be ranked alphabets, and $\tau_i \subseteq T_{\Sigma_i} \times T_{\Sigma_{i+1}}$ and $f_i\colon T_{\Sigma_i} \to T_{\Sigma_{i+1}}$ be tree transformations for all $i \in [n]$. If

1. $\mathrm{range}(\tau_j) \subseteq \mathrm{dom}(\tau_{j+1})$ for all $1 \leq j \leq n-1$ and
2. f_i is a uniformizer for τ_i for all $i \in [n]$,

then $f = f_1 \,;\cdots;\, f_n$ is a uniformizer for $\tau = \tau_1 \,;\cdots;\, \tau_n$ and $\mathrm{dom}(\tau) = \mathrm{dom}(\tau_1)$. If additionally τ is functional, then $f = \tau$.

Finally, we need two results from the theory of unweighted tree transducers. The first statement establishes the existence of uniformizers of tree transformations induced by $\not\varepsilon$l-wxt$^\mathrm{R}$ over $\mathbb{B}$.

Lemma 10 (variant of [5, Lemma]**).** For every $w \subseteq \{\mathtt{n}, \mathtt{s}\}$, each tree transformation of $w\not\varepsilon\mathtt{l}$-$\mathtt{WXT}^\mathtt{R}(\mathbb{B})$ has a uniformizer in $w\not\varepsilon\mathtt{fl}$-$\mathtt{WXT}^\mathtt{R}(\mathbb{B})$.

The second statement builds also on [5, Lemma], which essentially says that functional top-down tree transducers can be determinized provided that they have regular look-ahead. We utilize the same idea to prove a corresponding lemma, where we use unambiguity instead of determinism. The lemma shows that we can remove ambiguity from a functional l-wxt$^\mathrm{R}$ over $\mathbb{B}$. We use the shorthand 'u' to abbreviate 'unambiguous'.

Lemma 11. $w\mathtt{fl}$-$\mathtt{WXT}^\mathtt{R}(\mathbb{B}) = w\mathtt{ful}$-$\mathtt{WXT}^\mathtt{R}(\mathbb{B})$ for all $w \subseteq \{\not\varepsilon, \mathtt{n}, \mathtt{s}\}$.

5 Main Results

We start with a construction that shows that a weighted relabeling can be separated from an ε-free l-wxt^{R} that handles all the weights and the nondeterminism leaving a Boolean functional ε-free l-wxt^{R} that is also unambiguous.

Lemma 12. For all $w \subseteq \{\mathtt{n}, \mathtt{s}\}$

$$w\not\varepsilon\texttt{l-WXT}^{\texttt{R}}(\mathbb{K}) \subseteq \texttt{WREL}(\mathbb{K}) \, ; w\not\varepsilon\texttt{Bful-WXT}^{\texttt{R}}(\mathbb{K})$$
$$w\not\varepsilon\texttt{l-WXT}(\mathbb{K}) \subseteq \texttt{WREL}(\mathbb{K}) \, ; w\not\varepsilon\texttt{Bful-WXT}(\mathbb{K}) \ .$$

Proof. Let $M = (Q, \Sigma, \Delta, q_0, R, \mathrm{wt}, c)$ be an arbitrary ε-free l-wxt^{R}. Since we also need access to the transitions of a weighted tree automaton computing the regular look-ahead, let $A = (Q', \Sigma, Q'_0, \underline{\mathrm{wt}})$ be a weighted tree automaton such that $Q \subseteq Q'$ and $\|A\|^q_{\mathbb{K}} = c^q$ for every $q \in Q$ (e.g., we can take the disjoint union of the weighted tree automata computing c^q for all $q \in Q$). Let $P = R \cup \mathrm{supp}(\underline{\mathrm{wt}})$ be the set of all rules and transitions used in M and A. We first construct the ranked alphabet (Σ', rk') consisting of the symbols $\Sigma' = \Sigma \cup (\Sigma \times P)$ such that $\mathrm{rk}'(\sigma) = \mathrm{rk}(\sigma)$ and $\mathrm{rk}'(\langle \sigma, \rho \rangle) = \mathrm{rk}(\sigma)$ for every $\sigma \in \Sigma$ and $\rho \in P$. Next, we construct the weighted relabeling $\nu \colon \Sigma \times \Sigma' \to K$ as follows: $\nu(\sigma, \sigma') = \delta_{\sigma\sigma'}$ and

$$\nu(\sigma, \langle \sigma', \rho \rangle) = \begin{cases} \delta_{\sigma\sigma'} \cdot \mathrm{wt}(\rho), & \text{if } \rho \in R; \\ \delta_{\sigma\sigma'} \cdot \underline{\mathrm{wt}}(\rho), & \text{if } \rho \in \mathrm{supp}(\underline{\mathrm{wt}}) \end{cases}$$

for all $\sigma, \sigma' \in \Sigma$ and $\rho \in P$, where $\delta_{\sigma\sigma'}$ is the usual Kronecker delta. In other words, the relabeling either (i) keeps the symbol or (ii) keeps the input symbol, but annotates a rule or transition and charges the corresponding weight. Intuitively, the relabeling annotates the rules and transitions to be executed, but the relabeling does not ensure that the annotation can actually be executed at the annotated position. This check and the execution are performed by the Boolean ε-free l-wxt^{R} $M' = (Q, \Sigma', \Delta, q_0, R', \mathrm{wt}', \underline{c})$, to which the Boolean weighted tree automaton $A' = (Q', \Sigma', Q'_0, \underline{\mathrm{wt}'})$ is associated via $\underline{c}^q = \|A'\|^q_{\mathbb{K}}$ for every state $q \in Q$. We set

- $\rho' = \langle \langle \ell(\varepsilon), \rho \rangle (\ell|_1, \dots, \ell|_{\mathrm{rk}(\sigma)}), q, r \rangle \in R'$ and $\mathrm{wt}'(\rho') = 1$ for every rule $\rho = \langle \ell, q, r \rangle \in R$,
- $\underline{\mathrm{wt}'}(q'_1, \dots, q'_n, \langle \sigma, \rho \rangle, q') = 1$ for every $\rho = (q'_1, \dots, q'_n, \sigma, q') \in \mathrm{supp}(\underline{\mathrm{wt}})$, and
- no additional rules are in R' and $\underline{\mathrm{wt}'}(\rho) = 0$ for all other transitions ρ.

Note that $\ell(\varepsilon) \in \Sigma$ in the first item because M is ε-free. Hence M' is ε-free. Moreover, A' is deterministic and both M' and A' are Boolean because $\underline{c}^q = \|A'\|^q_{\mathbb{K}}$ is also Boolean. So the constructed l-wxt^{R} M' is Boolean and ε-free. Moreover, it inherits the properties 'nondeleting' and 'strict' from M. If M has trivial look-ahead c, then we set $\underline{c}$ to the trivial look-ahead for $T_{\Sigma'}$ for the statements on l-wxt. Finally, it is straightforward to establish that M' is functional and unambiguous as it can at most execute the annotated rules and transitions (and can perform this in at most one fashion).

It remains to prove that $\|M\|_{\mathbb{K}} = \nu \mathbin{;} \|M'\|_{\mathbb{K}}$, for which we first prove that $\|M\|_{\mathbb{K}}^{q} = \nu \mathbin{;} \|M'\|_{\mathbb{K}}^{q}$ for every $q \in Q$ and $\|A\|_{\mathbb{K}}^{q'} = \nu \mathbin{;} \|A'\|_{\mathbb{K}}^{q'}$ for every $q' \in Q'$. These proofs can be found in the appendix.

We prove that we can compose any such relabeling to the right of any l-wxt^{R}.

Lemma 13. For all $w \subseteq \{\mathtt{n}, \mathtt{s}\}$

$$w\not\varepsilon\mathtt{l\text{-}WXT}^{\mathtt{R}}(\mathbb{K}) \mathbin{;} \mathtt{WREL}(\mathbb{K}) \subseteq w\not\varepsilon\mathtt{l\text{-}WXT}^{\mathtt{R}}(\mathbb{K})$$
$$w\not\varepsilon\mathtt{l\text{-}WXT}(\mathbb{K}) \mathbin{;} \mathtt{WREL}(\mathbb{K}) \subseteq w\not\varepsilon\mathtt{l\text{-}WXT}(\mathbb{K})\ .$$

Proof. Let $M = (Q, \Sigma, \Delta, q_0, R, \mathrm{wt}, c)$ be an ε-free l-wxt^{R} and $\nu \colon \Delta \times \Delta' \to K$ be a weighted relabeling. We construct the l-wxt^{R} $M' = (Q, \Sigma, \Delta', q_0, R', \mathrm{wt}', c)$ such that $\langle \ell, q, r' \rangle \in R'$ and $\mathrm{wt}'(\langle \ell, q, r' \rangle) = \sum_{\langle \ell, q, r'' \rangle \in R} \mathrm{wt}(\langle \ell, q, r'' \rangle) \cdot \nu(r'', r')$ for every translation rule $\langle \ell, q, r \rangle \in R$ and $r' \in T_{\Delta'}(Q)$ with $\nu(r, r') \neq 0$. No additional rules are in R'. Since the left-hand sides and the shape of the right-hand sides remains the same, it is clear that M' inherits the properties 'ε-free', 'nondeleting', and 'strict' directly from M. Since the look-ahead coincides these results also hold for l-wxt.

It remains to prove that $\|M\|_{\mathbb{K}} \mathbin{;} \nu = \|M'\|_{\mathbb{K}}$, which we prove again with the help of $\|M\|_{\mathbb{K}}^{q} ; \nu = \|M'\|_{\mathbb{K}}^{q}$ for every $q \in Q$. The proof details are in the appendix.

We now have the two ingredients that allow us to normalize composition chains of ε-free l-wxt^{R}.

Theorem 14. For all $n \geq 1$ and $w \subseteq \{\mathtt{n}, \mathtt{s}\}$

$$w\not\varepsilon\mathtt{l\text{-}WXT}^{\mathtt{R}}(\mathbb{K})^{n} \subseteq \mathtt{WREL}(\mathbb{K}) \mathbin{;} w\not\varepsilon\mathtt{Bful\text{-}WXT}^{\mathtt{R}}(\mathbb{K})^{n}$$
$$w\not\varepsilon\mathtt{l\text{-}WXT}(\mathbb{K})^{n} \subseteq \mathtt{WREL}(\mathbb{K}) \mathbin{;} w\not\varepsilon\mathtt{Bful\text{-}WXT}(\mathbb{K})^{n}\ .$$

Proof. We prove the statements by induction on n. For $n = 1$, they are proved in Lemma 12. Suppose that the property holds for $n \geq 1$. Then using Lemmas 12 and 13 and the induction hypothesis in sequence we obtain

$$w\not\varepsilon\mathtt{l\text{-}WXT}^{\mathtt{R}}(\mathbb{K})^{n+1} \subseteq w\not\varepsilon\mathtt{l\text{-}WXT}^{\mathtt{R}}(\mathbb{K})^{n} \mathbin{;} \mathtt{WREL}(\mathbb{K}) \mathbin{;} w\not\varepsilon\mathtt{Bful\text{-}WXT}^{\mathtt{R}}(\mathbb{K})$$
$$\subseteq w\not\varepsilon\mathtt{l\text{-}WXT}^{\mathtt{R}}(\mathbb{K})^{n} \mathbin{;} w\not\varepsilon\mathtt{Bful\text{-}WXT}^{\mathtt{R}}(\mathbb{K}) \subseteq \mathtt{WREL}(\mathbb{K}) \mathbin{;} w\not\varepsilon\mathtt{Bful\text{-}WXT}^{\mathtt{R}}(\mathbb{K})^{n+1}$$

and the same reasoning proves the statement also for l-wxt.

Finally, we compose a weighted relabeling to the left of an ε-free l-wxt^{R} to eliminate the weighted relabeling again.

Lemma 15. $\mathtt{WREL}(\mathbb{K}) \mathbin{;} w\not\varepsilon\mathtt{l\text{-}WXT}^{\mathtt{R}}(\mathbb{K}) \subseteq w\not\varepsilon\mathtt{l\text{-}WXT}^{\mathtt{R}}(\mathbb{K})$ for all $w \subseteq \{\mathtt{n}, \mathtt{s}\}$.

Proof. Let $\nu \colon \Sigma \times \Sigma' \to K$ be a weighted relabeling, $M = (Q, \Sigma', \Delta, q_0, R, \mathrm{wt}, c)$ be an arbitrary ε-free l-wxt^{R}. The ε-free l-wxt^{R} $M' = (Q, \Sigma, \Delta, q_0, R', \mathrm{wt}', \underline{c})$ is given by $\langle \ell', q, r \rangle \in R'$ and $\mathrm{wt}'(\langle \ell', q, r \rangle) = \sum_{\langle \ell'', q, r \rangle \in R} \nu(\ell', \ell'') \cdot \mathrm{wt}(\langle \ell'', q, r \rangle)$ for every rule $\rho = \langle \ell, q, r \rangle \in R$ and $\ell' \in T_{\Sigma}(Q)$ with $\nu(\ell', \ell) \neq 0$. No additional rules are in R'. In addition, we let $\underline{c}^q = \nu \,;\, c^q$ for every $q \in Q$, which is regular by Theorem 1. Obviously, the constructed l-wxt^{R} M' is ε-free, and it inherits the properties 'nondeleting' and 'strict' from M.

To prove that $\nu \,;\, \|M\|_{\mathbb{K}} = \|M'\|_{\mathbb{K}}$, we first prove that $\nu \,;\, \|M\|^q_{\mathbb{K}} = \|M'\|^q_{\mathbb{K}}$ for every $q \in Q$. Both proofs can be found in the appendix.

Now we are ready to state and prove our main results.

Theorem 16.

$$\not\varepsilon\texttt{nsl-WXT}(\mathbb{K})^3 = \not\varepsilon\texttt{nsl-WXT}(\mathbb{K})^2 \quad (4a)$$

$$\not\varepsilon\texttt{sl-WXT}(\mathbb{K})^3 = \not\varepsilon\texttt{sl-WXT}(\mathbb{K})^2 \quad (4b) \qquad \not\varepsilon\texttt{sl-WXT}^{\mathtt{R}}(\mathbb{K})^3 = \not\varepsilon\texttt{sl-WXT}^{\mathtt{R}}(\mathbb{K})^2 \quad (4d)$$

$$\not\varepsilon\texttt{l-WXT}(\mathbb{K})^5 = \not\varepsilon\texttt{l-WXT}(\mathbb{K})^4 \quad (4c) \qquad \not\varepsilon\texttt{l-WXT}^{\mathtt{R}}(\mathbb{K})^4 = \not\varepsilon\texttt{l-WXT}^{\mathtt{R}}(\mathbb{K})^3 \quad (4e)$$

Additionally, the classes of (4b) and (4d) as well as (4c) and (4e) coincide.

Proof. All the right-to-left inclusions are trivial. The left-to-right inclusions are shown as follows. To prove (4a), let $\tau \in \not\varepsilon\texttt{nsl-WXT}(\mathbb{K})^3$ be of type $\tau\colon T_\Sigma \times T_\Delta \to K$. According to Theorem 14 there exist a weighted relabeling $\nu\colon \Sigma \times \Sigma' \to K$ and $\tau'\colon T_{\Sigma'} \times T_\Delta \to K$ such that $\tau = \nu \,;\, \tau'$ and $\tau' \in \not\varepsilon\texttt{nsBful-WXT}(\mathbb{K})^3$. Since the composition of functional weighted tree transformations is naturally again functional, we can apply Lemma 8 to obtain that $\tau' \in \not\varepsilon\texttt{nsful-WXT}(\mathbb{B})^3$. Using (3a), we obtain $\tau' \in \not\varepsilon\texttt{nsl-WXT}(\mathbb{B})^2$. Let $\tau' = \tau'_1 \,;\, \tau'_2$ with $\tau'_1, \tau'_2 \in \not\varepsilon\texttt{nsl-WXT}(\mathbb{B})$. Next we restrict the range of τ'_1 to the regular tree language $\mathrm{dom}(\tau'_2)$. In this way, we obtain the tree transformation $\tau''_1 \in \not\varepsilon\texttt{nsl-WXT}(\mathbb{B})$. Clearly, $\tau''_1 \,;\, \tau'_2 = \tau'_1 \,;\, \tau'_2$. Using Lemma 10 we additionally obtain uniformizers $f''_1, f''_2 \in \not\varepsilon\texttt{nsfl-WXT}(\mathbb{B})$ for τ''_1 and τ'_2, respectively. Since τ' is functional, we fulfill all the requirements of Lemma 9 and we can conclude that $f''_1 \,;\, f''_2 = \tau''_1 \,;\, \tau'_2 = \tau'_1 \,;\, \tau'_2 = \tau'$. Hence $\tau' \in \not\varepsilon\texttt{nsfl-WXT}(\mathbb{B})^2$. With the help of Lemma 11 we obtain $\tau' \in \not\varepsilon\texttt{nsful-WXT}(\mathbb{B})^2$, which immediately also yields $\tau' \in \not\varepsilon\texttt{nsBful-WXT}(\mathbb{K})^2$ by Lemma 8. Finally, we utilize Lemma 15 to show that $\tau = \nu \,;\, \tau' \in \not\varepsilon\texttt{nsl-WXT}(\mathbb{K})^2$ as desired.

This approach works in the same manner for (4d) and (4e). However, instead of (3a), we use the results (3d) and (3e), respectively.

To prove (4b) we proceed in the same manner as in case (4a) and obtain that $\tau = \nu \,;\, \tau'$, where ν is a weighted relabeling and $\tau' \in \not\varepsilon\texttt{sful-WXT}(\mathbb{B})^3$. Then we use

$$\not\varepsilon\texttt{sl-WXT}(\mathbb{B})^3 = \not\varepsilon\texttt{nsl-WXT}(\mathbb{B}) \,;\, \not\varepsilon\texttt{sl-WXT}^{\mathtt{R}}(\mathbb{B})$$

from [6, Theorem 20], and again as in the proof of case (4a) we obtain the statement $\tau' \in \not\varepsilon\texttt{nsBful-WXT}(\mathbb{K}) \,;\, \not\varepsilon\texttt{sBful-WXT}^{\mathtt{R}}(\mathbb{K})$. It is well-known that regular look-ahead can be simulated by a nondeleting, strict, and linear weighted top-down tree transducer. Thus, we obtain that τ' is an element of

$$\not\varepsilon\texttt{nsBful-WXT}(\mathbb{K}) \,;\, \not\varepsilon\texttt{sBful-WXT}^{\mathtt{R}}(\mathbb{K}) \subseteq \not\varepsilon\texttt{nsl-WXT}(\mathbb{K}) \,;\, \texttt{nsl-WT}(\mathbb{K}) \,;\, \not\varepsilon\texttt{sl-WXT}(\mathbb{K})$$
$$\subseteq \not\varepsilon\texttt{nsl-WXT}(\mathbb{K}) \,;\, \not\varepsilon\texttt{sl-WXT}(\mathbb{K}) \subseteq \not\varepsilon\texttt{sl-WXT}(\mathbb{K})^2,$$

where the second inclusion is due to [13, Theorem 8]. Then by Lemma 15 we obtain that $\tau \in \not\varepsilon\texttt{sl-WXT}(\mathbb{K})^2$.

Finally, for (4c) we also proceed as usual: $\tau = \nu \mathbin{;} \tau'$, where ν is a weighted relabeling and $\tau' \in \not\varepsilon\texttt{ful-WXT}(\mathbb{B})^5$. We continue with

$$\not\varepsilon\texttt{l-WXT}(\mathbb{B})^5 = \not\varepsilon\texttt{l-WXT}(\mathbb{B})^4 \subseteq \not\varepsilon\texttt{l-WXT}^{\texttt{R}}(\mathbb{B})^4 \subseteq \texttt{l-WT}^{\texttt{R}}(\mathbb{B}) \mathbin{;} \not\varepsilon\texttt{sl-WXT}^{\texttt{R}}(\mathbb{B})^2 \enspace ,$$

where the first equality is by (3c) and the second inclusion is due to [6, Theorem 24]. Continuing on as before, we arrive at

$$\tau' \in \texttt{Bful-WT}^{\texttt{R}}(\mathbb{K}) \mathbin{;} \not\varepsilon\texttt{sBful-WXT}^{\texttt{R}}(\mathbb{K})^2 \enspace .$$

Removing the regular look-ahead with the constructions already mentioned, we obtain

$$\tau' \in \texttt{nsl-WT}(\mathbb{K}) \mathbin{;} \texttt{l-WT}(\mathbb{K}) \mathbin{;} \not\varepsilon\texttt{sl-WXT}(\mathbb{K})^2 \subseteq \not\varepsilon\texttt{l-WXT}(\mathbb{K})^4$$

and then by Lemma 15 we conclude that $\tau \in \not\varepsilon\texttt{l-WXT}(\mathbb{K})^4$. The final equalities between the classes of (4b) and (4d) as well as (4c) and (4e) follow directly from the presented arguments.

References

1. Arnold, A., Dauchet, M.: Morphismes et bimorphismes d'arbres. Theor. Comput. Sci. **20**(1), 33–93 (1982). https://doi.org/10.1016/0304-3975(82)90098-6
2. Benedikt, M., Engelfriet, J., Maneth, S.: Determinacy and rewriting of functional top-down and MSO tree transformations. J. Comput. Syst. Sci. **85**, 57–73 (2017). https://doi.org/10.1016/j.jcss.2016.11.001
3. Chiang, D.: An introduction to synchronous grammars. In: Calzolari, N., Cardie, C., Isabelle, P. (eds.) Proceedings of 44th Annual Meeting ACL. Association for Computational Linguistics (2006). Part of a tutorial given with Kevin Knight. https://www3.nd.edu/~dchiang/papers/synchtut.pdf
4. Engelfriet, J.: Top-down tree transducers with regular look-ahead. Math. Syst. Theory **10**(1), 289–303 (1977). https://doi.org/10.1007/BF01683280
5. Engelfriet, J.: On tree transducers for partial functions. Inf. Process. Lett. **7**(4), 170–172 (1978). https://doi.org/10.1016/0020-0190(78)90060-1
6. Engelfriet, J., Fülöp, Z., Maletti, A.: Composition closure of linear extended top-down tree transducers. Theory Comput. Syst. **60**(2), 129–171 (2017). https://doi.org/10.1007/s00224-015-9660-2
7. Fülöp, Z., Maletti, A., Vogler, H.: Weighted extended tree transducers. Fund. Inform. **111**(2), 163–202 (2011). https://doi.org/10.3233/FI-2011-559
8. Gécseg, F., Steinby, M.: Tree Automata, 2nd edn. Akadémiai Kiadó, Budapest (1984). https://arxiv.org/abs/1509.06233
9. Golan, J.S.: Semirings and Their Applications. Kluwer Academic, Dordrecht (1999). https://doi.org/10.1007/978-94-015-9333-5
10. Graehl, J., Knight, K., May, J.: Training tree transducers. Comput. Linguist. **34**(3), 391–427 (2008). https://doi.org/10.1162/coli.2008.07-051-R2-03-57
11. Hebisch, U., Weinert, H.J.: Semirings - Algebraic Theory and Applications in Computer Science. Series in Algebra. World Scientific, Singapore (1998). https://doi.org/10.1142/3903

12. Knight, K., Graehl, J.: An overview of probabilistic tree transducers for natural language processing. In: Gelbukh, A. (ed.) CICLing 2005. LNCS, vol. 3406, pp. 1–24. Springer, Heidelberg (2005). https://doi.org/10.1007/978-3-540-30586-6_1
13. Lagoutte, A., Maletti, A.: *Survey*: weighted extended top-down tree transducers part III—composition. In: Kuich, W., Rahonis, G. (eds.) Algebraic Foundations in Computer Science. LNCS, vol. 7020, pp. 272–308. Springer, Heidelberg (2011). https://doi.org/10.1007/978-3-642-24897-9_13
14. Maletti, A.: The power of weighted regularity-preserving multi bottom-up tree transducers. Int. J. Found. Comput. Sci. **26**(7), 987–1005 (2015). https://doi.org/10.1142/S0129054115400109
15. Maletti, A.: Compositions of tree-to-tree statistical machine translation models. In: Brlek, S., Reutenauer, C. (eds.) DLT 2016. LNCS, vol. 9840, pp. 293–305. Springer, Heidelberg (2016). https://doi.org/10.1007/978-3-662-53132-7_24
16. Maletti, A., Graehl, J., Hopkins, M., Knight, K.: The power of extended top-down tree transducers. SIAM J. Comput. **39**(2), 410–430 (2009). https://doi.org/10.1137/070699160
17. May, J., Knight, K., Vogler, H.: Efficient inference through cascades of weighted tree transducers. In: Hajič, J., Carberry, S., Clark, S., Nivre, J. (eds.) Proceedings of 48th Annual Meeting ACL, pp. 1058–1066. Association for Computational Linguistics (2010). http://www.aclweb.org/anthology/P10-1108

A General Architecture of Oritatami Systems for Simulating Arbitrary Finite Automata

Yo-Sub Han[1], Hwee Kim[2], Yusei Masuda[3], and Shinnosuke Seki[3,4](✉)

[1] Department of Computer Science, Yonsei University,
50 Yonsei-Ro, Seodaemum-Gu, Seoul 03722, Republic of Korea
[2] Department of Mathematics and Statistics, University of South Florida,
4202, E. Fowler Ave., Tampa, FL 33620, USA
[3] Department of Computer and Network Engineering,
University of Electro-Communications,
1-5-1 Chofugaoka, Chofu, Tokyo 182-8585, Japan
s.seki@uec.ac.jp
[4] École Normale Supérieure de Lyon,
46 allée d'Italie, 69007 Lyon, France

Abstract. In this paper, we propose an architecture of oritatami systems with which one can simulate an arbitrary nondeterministic finite automaton (NFA) in a unified manner. The oritatami system is known to be Turing-universal but the simulation available so far requires 542 bead types and $O(t^4 \log^2 t)$ steps in order to simulate t steps of a Turing machine. The architecture we propose employs only 329 bead types and requires just $O(t|Q|^4|\Sigma|^2)$ steps to simulate an NFA with a state set Q working on a word of length t over an alphabet Σ.

1 Introduction

Transcription (Fig. 1) is a process in which from a template DNA sequence, its complementary RNA sequence is synthesized by an *RNA polymerase* letter by letter. The product RNA sequence (*transcript*) is folding upon itself into a structure while being synthesized. This phenomenon called *cotranscriptional folding* has proven programmable by Geary, Rothemund, and Andersen in [6], in which they programmed an RNA rectangular tile as a template DNA sequence in the sense that the transcript synthesized from this template folds cotranscriptionally into that specific RNA tile highly probably *in vitro*. As cotranscriptional folding

This work is supported primarily by JSPS-NRF Bilateral Program No. YB29004 to Han and Seki, the Basic Science Research Program (NRF-2018R1D1A1A09084107) to Han, JSPS KAKENHI Grant-in-Aids for Young Scientists (A) No. 16H05854 and for Challenging Research (Exploratory) No. 18K19779 to Seki, and JST Program to Disseminate Tenure Tracking System, MEXT, Japan No. 6F36 to Seki.
Kim is also supported by NIH R01GM109459, NSF's CCF01526485, DMS-1800443, the Southeast Center for Mathematics and Biology, and the NSF-Simons Research Center for Mathematics of Complex Biological Systems (DMS-1764406, 594594).

M. Hospodár and G. Jirásková (Eds.): CIAA 2019, LNCS 11601, pp. 146–157, 2019.
https://doi.org/10.1007/978-3-030-23679-3_12

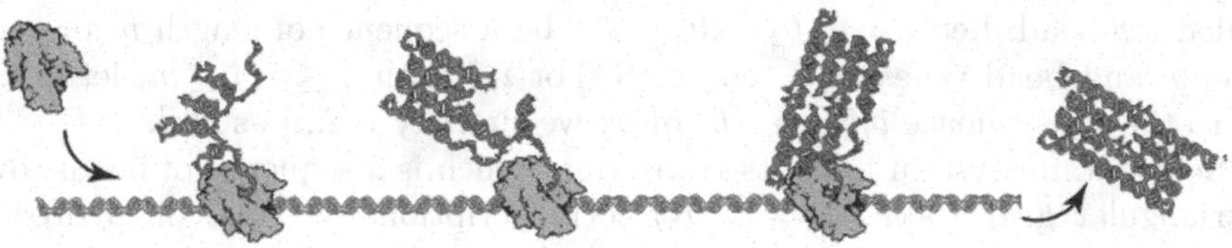

Fig. 1. RNA origami, a novel self-assembly technology by cotranscriptional folding [6]. RNA polymerase (orange complex) attaches to an artificial template DNA sequence (gray spiral) and synthesizes the complementary RNA sequence (blue sequence), which folds into a rectangular tile while being synthesized. (Color figure online)

has turned out to play significant computational roles in organisms (see, e.g., [10]), a next step is to program computation in cotranscriptional folding.

Oritatami is a mathematical model proposed by Geary et al. [4] to understand computational aspects of cotranscriptional folding. This model has recently enabled them to prove that cotranscriptional folding is actually Turing universal [5]. Their Turing-universal oritatami system Ξ_{TU} adopts a periodic transcript[1] whose period consists of functional units called *modules*. Some of these modules do computation by folding into different shapes, which resembles somehow computation by cotranscriptional folding in nature [10]. Being thus motivated, the study of cotranscriptional folding of shapes in oritatami was initiated by Masuda, Seki, and Ubukata in [9] and extended independently by Domaine et al. [2] as well as by Han and Kim [7] further. In [9], an arbitrary finite portion of the Heighway dragon fractal was folded by an oritatami system Ξ_H. The Heighway dragon can be described as an automatic sequence [1], that is, as a sequence producible by a deterministic finite automaton with output (DFAO) in an algorithmic manner. The system Ξ_{HD} involves a module that simulates a 4-state DFAO A_{HD} for the Heighway dragon. The Turing-universal system was not embedded into Ξ_{HD} in place for this module primarily because it may fold into different shapes even on inputs of the same length and secondly because it employs unnecessarily many 542 types of abstract molecules (*bead*) along with an intricate network of interactions (rule set) among them. Their implementation of the DFAO module however relies on the cycle-freeness of A_{HD} too heavily to be generalized for other DFAs; let alone for nondeterministic FAs (NFAs).

In this paper, we propose an architecture of oritatami system that allows for simulating an arbitrary NFA using 329 bead types. In order to run an NFA over an alphabet Σ with a state set Q on an input of length t, it takes $O(t|Q|^4|\Sigma|^2)$ steps. In contrast, the system Ξ_{TU} requires $O(t^4 \log^2 t)$ steps to simulate t steps of a Turing machine. A novel feature of technical interest is that all the four modules of the architecture share a common interface ((2) in Sect. 3).

2 Preliminaries

Let B be a set of types of abstract molecules, or *beads*, and B^* be the set of finite sequences of beads including the empty sequence λ. A bead of type $b \in B$

[1] A periodic transcript is likely to be able to be transcribed from a circular DNA [3].

is called a b-bead. Let $w = b_1 b_2 \cdots b_n \in B^*$ be a sequence of length n for some integer n and bead types $b_1, \ldots, b_n \in B$. For i, j with $1 \leq i, j \leq n$, let $w[i..j]$ refer to the subsequence $b_i b_{i+1} \cdots b_j$ of w; we simplify $w[i..i]$ as $w[i]$.

The oritatami system folds its transcript, which is a sequence of beads, over the triangular grid graph $\mathbb{T} = (V, E)$ cotranscriptionally based on hydrogen-bond-based interactions (*h-interaction* for short) which the system allows for between beads of particular types placed at the unit distance. When beads form an h-interaction, we say informally they are *bound*. The i-th point of a directed path $P = p_1 p_2 \cdots p_n$ in $\mathbb{T}$ is referred to as $P[i]$, that is, $P[i] = p_i$. A *(finite) conformation* C is a triple (P, w, H) of a directed path P in $\mathbb{T}$, $w \in B^*$ of the same length as P, and a set of h-interactions $H \subseteq \big\{\{i, j\} \bigm| 1 \leq i, i{+}2 \leq j, \{P[i], P[j]\} \in E\big\}$. This is to be interpreted as the sequence w being folded in such a manner that its i-th bead is placed at the i-th point of the path P and the i-th and j-th beads are bound iff $\{i, j\} \in H$. A symmetric relation $R \subseteq B \times B$ called *rule set* governs which types of two beads can form an h-interaction between. An h-interaction $\{i, j\} \in H$ is *valid with respect to* R, or *R-valid*, if $(w[i], w[j]) \in R$. A conformation is R-valid if all of its h-interactions are R-valid. For $\alpha \geq 1$, a conformation is *of arity* α if it contains a bead that forms α h-interactions and none of its beads forms more. By $\mathcal{C}_{\leq \alpha}$, we denote the set of all conformations of arity at most α.

An oritatami system grows conformations by elongating them according to its own rule set R. Given an R-valid finite conformation $C_1 = (P, w, H)$, we say that another conformation C_2 is its *elongation by a bead of type* $b \in B$, written as $C_1 \xrightarrow{R}_b C_2$, if $C_2 = (Pp, wb, H \cup H')$ for some point p not along the path P and possibly-empty set of h-interactions $H' \subseteq \big\{\{i, |w|+1\} \bigm| 1 \leq i < |w|, \{P[i], p\} \in E, (w[i], b) \in R\big\}$. Observe that C_2 is also R-valid. This operation is recursively extended to the elongation by a finite sequence of beads as: $C \xrightarrow{R}{}^*_\lambda C$ for any conformation C; and $C_1 \xrightarrow{R}{}^*_{wb} C_2$ for conformations C_1, C_2, a finite sequence of beads $w \in \Sigma^*$, and a bead $b \in \Sigma$ if there is a conformation C' such that $C_1 \xrightarrow{R}{}^*_w C'$ and $C' \xrightarrow{R}_b C_2$.

A finite *oritatami system* is a tuple $\Xi = (R, \alpha, \delta, \sigma, w)$, where R is a rule set, α is an arity, $\delta \geq 1$ is a parameter called *delay*, σ is an R-valid initial conformation of arity at most α called *seed*, upon which its finite transcript $w \in B^*$ is to be folded by stabilizing beads of w one at a time so as to minimize energy collaboratively with its succeeding $\delta{-}1$ nascent beads. The *energy* of a conformation $C = (P, w, H)$, denoted by $\Delta G(C)$, is defined to be $-|H|$; that is, more h-interactions make a conformation more stable. The set $\mathcal{F}(\Xi)$ of conformations *foldable* by this system is recursively defined as: the seed σ is in $\mathcal{F}(\Xi)$; and provided that an elongation C_i of σ by the prefix $w[1..i]$ be foldable (i.e., $C_0 = \sigma$), its further elongation C_{i+1} by the next bead $w[i{+}1]$ is foldable if

$$C_{i+1} \in \mathop{\arg\min}_{\substack{C \in \mathcal{C}_{\leq\alpha} s.t. \\ C_i \xrightarrow{R}_{w[i+1]} C}} \min\Big\{\Delta G(C') \Bigm| C \xrightarrow{R}{}^*_{w[i+2...i+k]} C', k \leq \delta, C' \in \mathcal{C}_{\leq\alpha}\Big\}. \quad (1)$$

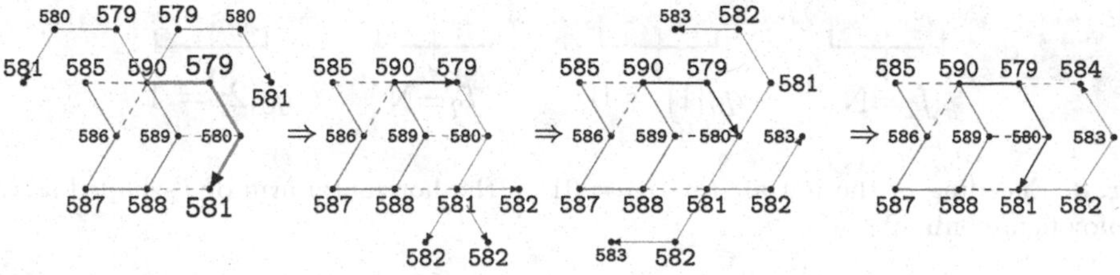

Fig. 2. Growth (folding) of a spacer of glider shape (g-spacr). The rule set R to fold this is $\{(579, 584), (580, 589), (581, 588), (582, 587), (583, 586), (585, 590), (586, 590)\}$. (Color figure online)

We say that the bead $w[i+1]$ and the h-interactions it forms are *stabilized* (not nascent any more) according to C_{i+1}. Note that an arity-α oritatami system cannot fold any conformation of arity larger than α. The system Ξ is *deterministic* if for all $i \geq 0$, there exists at most one C_{i+1} that satisfies (1). An oritatami system is *cyclic* if its transcript admits a period shorter than the half of itself.

Example 1 (g-spacer). Let us provide an example of deterministic oritatami system that folds into a *glider* motif, which will be used as a component called *g-spacer* in Sect. 3. Consider a delay-3 oritatami system whose transcript w is a repetition of 579−580−$\cdots$−590 and rule set R is as captioned in Fig. 2. Its seed, colored in red, can be elongated by the first three beads $w[1..3] =$ 579−580−581 in various ways, only three of which are shown in Fig. 2 (left). The rule set R allows $w[1]$ to be bound to 584, $w[2]$ to 589, and $w[3]$ to 588, but 584-bead is not around. In order for both $w[2]$ and $w[3]$ to be thus bound, the nascent fragment $w[1..3]$ must be folded as bolded in Fig. 2 (left). According to this most stable elongation, the bead $w[1] =$ 579 is stabilized to the east of the previous 580-bead. Then $w[4] =$ 582 is transcribed. It is capable of binding to a 587-bead but no such bead is reachable, and hence, this newly-transcribed bead cannot override the "bolded" decision. Therefore, $w[2]$ is also stabilized according to this decision along with its bond with the 589-bead. The next bead $w[5] =$ 583 cannot override the decision, either, and hence, $w[3]$ is stabilized along with its bond with the 588-bead as shown in Fig. 2 (right).

3 Architecture

We shall propose an architecture of a nondeterministic cyclic oritatami system Ξ that simulates at delay 3 an NFA $A = (Q, \Sigma, q_0, Acc, f)$, where Q is a finite set of states, Σ is an alphabet, $q_0 \in Q$ is the initial state, $Acc \subseteq Q$ is a set of accepting states, and $f : Q \times \Sigma \to 2^Q$ is a nondeterministic transition function. What the architecture actually simulates is rather its modification $A_\$ = (Q \cup \{q_{Acc}\}, \Sigma \cup \{\$\}, q_0, \{q_{Acc}\}, f \cup f_\$)$, where $f_\$: (Q \cup \{q_{Acc}\}) \times (\Sigma \cup \{\$\}) \to 2^{Q \cup \{q_{Acc}\}}$ is defined over Σ exactly same as f, and moreover, $f_\$(q, \$) = \{q_{Acc}\}$ for all $q \in Acc$. Note that $w \in L(A)$ iff $w\$ \in L(A_\$)$. For the sake of upcoming arguments, we regard the transition function $f \cup f_\$$ rather as a set of transitions $\{f_1, f_2, \cdots, f_n\}$, where

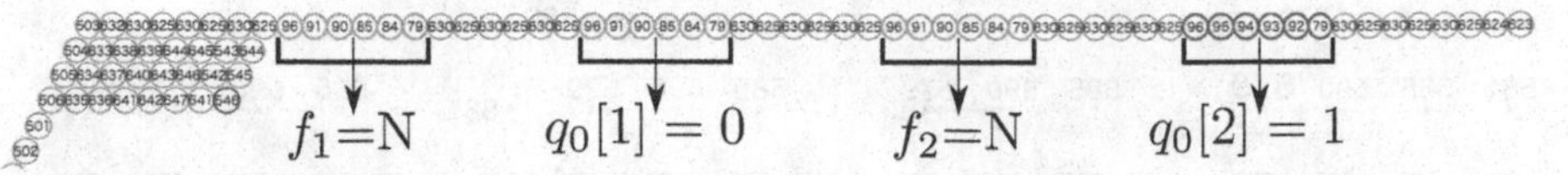

Fig. 3. Encoding of the initial state $q_0 = 01$ on the horizontal arm of Γ-shaped seed. (Color figure online)

f_k is a triple (o_k, a_k, t_k), meaning that reading a_k in the state o_k (origin) causes a transition to t_k (target). Note that $n = O(|Q|^2|\Sigma|)$.

The architecture assumes that each state q is uniquely assigned with an n-bit binary sequence, whose i-th bit from most significant bit (MSB) is referred to as $q[i]$. It also assumes a unique m-bit binary sequence for each letter $a \in \Sigma$, whose ℓ-th bit from MSB is referred to as $a[\ell]$, where $m = \lceil \log |\Sigma| \rceil$.

3.1 Overview

Seed. The seed of Ξ is of Γ shape (Fig. 3). Below its horizontal arm is encoded the initial state q_0 in the following format:

$$\bigodot_{k=1}^{n} \left(x_{f_k} \to (\mathsf{630} \to \mathsf{625} \to)^3 z_{q_0[k]} \to (\mathsf{630} \to \mathsf{625} \to)^3 \right) \mathsf{624} \to \mathsf{623}, \tag{2}$$

where $z_0 = \mathsf{96} \to \mathsf{91} \to \mathsf{90} \to \mathsf{85} \to \mathsf{84} \to \mathsf{79}$, $z_1 = \mathsf{96} \to \mathsf{95} \to \mathsf{94} \to \mathsf{93} \to \mathsf{92} \to \mathsf{79}$, and for some bead types $b, c \in B$, the arrow $b \to c$ (resp. $\nearrow, \nwarrow, \leftarrow, \swarrow, \searrow$) implies that a c-bead is located to the eastern (resp. north-eastern, north-western, western, south-western, and south-eastern) neighbor of a b-bead. Note that the seed and Module 4, which we shall explain soon, initialize all the variables $f_1, \dots, f_n$ to N by having a sequence x_N of bead types be exposed to the corresponding positions $x_{f_1}, \cdots, x_{f_n}$, where $x_N = z_0$ while $x_Y = z_1$, which is not used here but shall be used later. An input word $u = b_1 b_2 \cdots$ is encoded on the right side of its vertical arm (see [8], which is an arXiv version of this paper, for its illustration as well as for other figures omitted due to space constraint) as:

$$\bigodot_{j=1}^{|u|} \left((y_{sp} \swarrow)^{2|f|-1} \bigodot_{\ell=1}^{m} (y_{b_i[\ell]} \swarrow y_{sp} \swarrow)(y_{sp} \swarrow)^{2+2|f|} \right), \tag{3}$$

where $y_{sp} = y_1 = \mathsf{501} \swarrow \mathsf{502} \swarrow \mathsf{503} \swarrow \mathsf{504} \swarrow \mathsf{505} \swarrow \mathsf{506}$ and $y_0 = \mathsf{501} \swarrow \mathsf{502} \swarrow \mathsf{503} \swarrow \mathsf{504} \swarrow \mathsf{507} \swarrow \mathsf{508}$.

The first period of the transcript of Ξ starts folding at the top left corner of the seed, or more precisely, as to succeed its last bead 540 circled in blue in Fig. 3. It folds into a parallelogram macroscopically by folding in a zigzag manner microscopically (zig ($\hookrightarrow$) and zag ($\hookleftarrow$) are both of height 3) while reading the current (initial) state q_0 from above and the first letter b_1 from left, and outputs one of the states in $f(q_0, b_1)$, say q_1, nondeterministically below in the format (2). All the states in $f(q_0, b_1)$ are chosen equally probably. The folding ends at the bottom left corner of the parallelogram. The next period likewise reads the state q_1 and next letter b_2, and outputs a state in $f(q_1, b_2)$ nondeterministically below the parallelogram it has folded. Generally speaking, for $i \geq 2$, the i-th period simulates a nondeterministic transition from the state q_{i-1}, output by the previous period, on the letter b_i.

Modules. One period of the transcript is semantically factorized into four functional subsequences called modules. All these modules fold into a parallelogram of width $\Theta(n)$ and of respective height $6 \times 2n$, $6 \times 2m$, 6×2, and $6 \times 2n$ (recall one zigzag is of height 6); that is, the first module makes $2n$ zigzags, for example. These parallelograms pile down one after another. One period thus results in a parallelogram of width and height both $\Theta(n)$. Their roles are as follows:

Module 1 extracts all the transitions that originate at the current state;
Module 2 extracts all the transitions that read the current letter among those chosen by Module 1;
Module 3 nondeterministically chooses one state among those chosen by Module 2, if any, or halts the system otherwise;
Module 4 outputs the chosen state downward.

In this way, these modules filter candidates for the next transition, and importantly, through a common interface, which is the format (2).

3.2 Implementation

Let us assume that the transcript has been folded up to its $(i-1)$-th period successfully into a parallelogram, which outputs the state q_{i-1} below, and the next period reads the letter b_i. See Figs. 4, 6, 8, and 11 for an example run.

Bricks. All the modules (more precisely, their transcripts) consist of functional submodules. Each submodule expects several surrounding environments. A conformation that the submodule takes in such an expected environment is called a *brick* [5]. On the inductive assumption that all the previous submodules have folded into a brick, a submodule never encounters an unexpected environment, and hence, folds into a brick. Any expected environment exposes 1-bit information b below and a submodule enters it in such a manner that its first bead is placed either 1-bead below y (*starting at the top*) or 3-beads below y (*at the bottom*). Hence, in this paper, a brick of a module X is denoted as $X_{-\mathrm{hy}}$, where $\mathrm{h} \in \{\mathrm{t}, \mathrm{b}\}$ indicates whether this brick starts at the top or bottom and y is the input from above.

Spacers and Turners. The transcript of a zig or a zag is a chain of submodules interleaved by a structural sequence called a *spacer*. A spacer keeps two continuous submodules far enough horizontally so as to prevent their interference. We employ spacers that fold into a parallelogram (p-spacer) or glider (g-spacer, Fig. 2) of height 3. They start and end folding at the same height (top or bottom) in order to propagate 1-bit of information. The spacer and its 1-bit carrying capability are classical, found already in the first oritatami system [4].

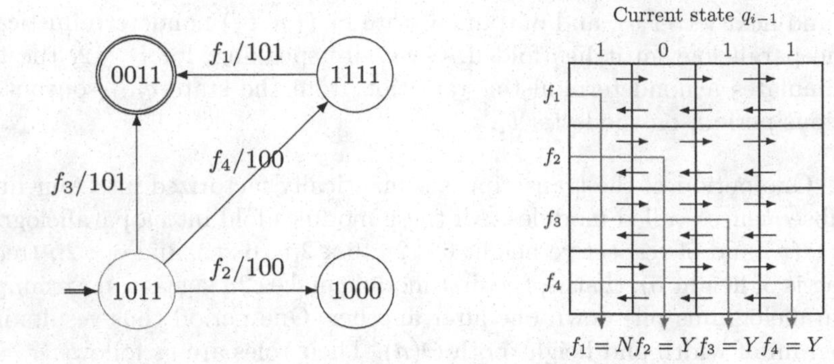

Fig. 4. Example run of the proposed architecture. (Left) A 4-state FA with 4 transitions f_1, f_2, f_3, f_4 to be simulated, which is obtained from a 3-state FA with the 2 transitions f_2 and f_4 in the way explained in the main text, that is, by adding a new accepting sink state 0011 and transitions f_1, f_3 on the special letter \$, encoded as 101. (Right) Outline of the flow of 1-bit information of whether each of the transitions originates from the current state 1011 or not through Module 1.

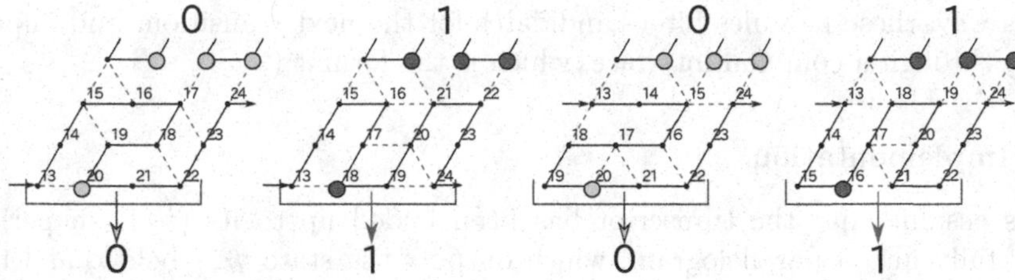

Fig. 5. The four bricks of A_1, that is, $A_{1\text{-}0\text{b}}, A_{1\text{-}1\text{b}}, A_{1\text{-}0\text{t}}$, and $A_{1\text{-}1\text{t}}$.

After a zig is transcribed a structural submodule called *turner*. Its role is to fold so as to guide the transcript to the point where the next zag is supposed to start. Likewise, a zag is followed by a turner for the next zig. Some turners play also a functional role.

Module 1 (origin state checker; see Fig. 4*)* folds into $2n$ zigzags. Recall that all the n variables $f_1, f_2, \ldots, f_n$ have been set to N by the seed or Module 4 in the previous period. The $(2k-1)$-th zigzag checks whether the origin o_k of the k-th transition f_k is equal to q_{i-1} or not, and if so, it sets the variable f_k to Y. Every other zigzag (2nd, 4th, and so on) just formats these variables as well as the z-variables (for the current state in (2)) using two submodules P_{zig} and P_{zag} (their bricks are illustrated in [8]); this is a common feature among all the four modules. The transcript for such a *formatting* zig (resp. zag) is a chain of $2n$ instances of P_{zig} (resp. P_{zag}), unless otherwise noted.

The transcript for the $(2k-1)$-th zig is semantically represented as $\odot_{j=1}^{n}(A' A_{o_k[j]})$ for submodules A', A_0, A_1. The zig starts folding at the bottom. The n instances of A' propagate $f_1, \ldots, f_n$ downward using the four bricks, all of which end folding at the same height as they start. See Fig. 5 for the four bricks of A_1; for those of A_0 as well as of A', see [8]. $A_{o_k[j]}$ checks whether $o_k[j] = q_{i-1}[j]$ or not when it starts at the bottom; it ends at the bottom if these bits are equal, or top otherwise. Starting at the top, it certainly ends at the top. In any case, it propagates $q_{i-1}[j]$ downward. The zig thus ends at the bottom iff $o_k = q_{i-1}$. The succeeding turner admits two conformations to let the next zag start either at the bottom if $o_k = q_{i-1}$, or top otherwise.

The transcript for the next zag is $B^{2n-2k+1}B'B^{2k-2}$ for submodules B, whose blocks are illustrated in [8], and B'. It is transcribed from right to left so that B' can read f_k. B' is in fact just a g-spacer shown in Fig. 2. This glider exposes below the bead-type sequence 590-585-584-579 if it starts folding at the bottom, or 588-587-582-581 otherwise; the former and latter shall be formatted into x_Y and x_N, respectively, by the next zigzag.

The variables $f_1, \ldots, f_n$ are updated in this way and output below in the format (2) along with the current state q_{i-1}, which is not used any more though.

Module 2 (input letter checker; see Fig. 6) folds into $2m$ zigzags; recall $m = \lceil \log |\Sigma| \rceil$. The ℓ-th bit of the input letter b_i is read by the turner between the $(2\ell-2)$-th zag and $(2\ell-1)$-th zig and the bit lets this zig start at the top if it is 0, or bottom if it is 1. Recall that f_k reads a_k for all $1 \leq k \leq n$. The ℓ-th bit of these letters is encoded in the transcript for the $(2\ell-1)$-th zig as $C_{a_1[\ell]}C_{a_2[\ell]} \cdots C_{a_n[\ell]}$ using submodules C_0 and C_1. All the bricks of C_0 and C_1 start and end at the same height, as suggested in Fig. 7; thus propagating $b_i[\ell]$ throughout the zig. Starting at the top (i.e., $b_i[\ell] = 0$), C_0 takes the brick $C_{0-\mathrm{Nt}}$ if it reads N from above or $C_{0-\mathrm{Yt}}$ if it reads Y; these bricks output N and Y downward, respectively; thus propagating the x-variables downward. On the other hand, if it starts at the bottom (i.e., $b_i[\ell] = 1$), C_0 certainly takes $C_{0-*\mathrm{b}}$ and outputs N downward. C_1 propagates what it reads downward by the bricks $C_{1-\mathrm{Nb}}, C_{1-\mathrm{Yb}}$ (see [8]) if $b_i[\ell] = 1$ while it outputs N downward by $C_{1-*\mathrm{t}}$ if $b_i[\ell] = 0$. Functioning in this way, the submodules $C_{a_1[j]}, \ldots, C_{a_n[j]}$ compare the letters that $f_1, \ldots, f_n$ read with b_i and filter those with unmatching j-th bit out. The next zag propagates the result of this filtering downward using B's.

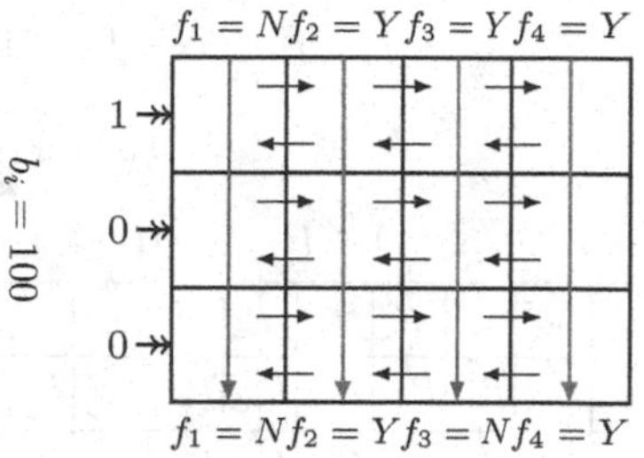

Fig. 6. Example run of the oritatami system constructed according to the proposed architecture in order to simulate the FA in Fig. 4. Here Module 2 filters transitions f_2, f_3, f_4 chosen by Module 1 further depending on whether each of them reads the letter 100 or not; thus f_3 is out.

Module 3 (nondeterministic choice of the next transition; see Fig. 8) folds into just 2 zigzags. Each transition $f_k = (o_k, a_k, t_k)$ has been checked whether $o_k = q_{i-1}$ in Module 1 and whether $a_k = b_i$ in Module 2, and the variable f_k is set to Y iff f_k passed both the checks, that is, proved *valid*. The first zig marks the valid transition with smallest subscript by setting its variable to Y' using a submodule D. This submodule was invented in [9] for the same purpose, and

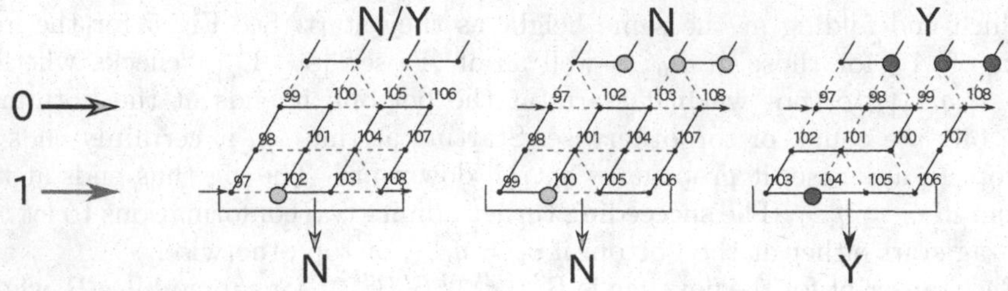

Fig. 7. The three bricks of C_0, that is, $C_{0-*\mathrm{b}}, C_{0-\mathrm{Nt}}$, and $C_{0-\mathrm{Yt}}$.

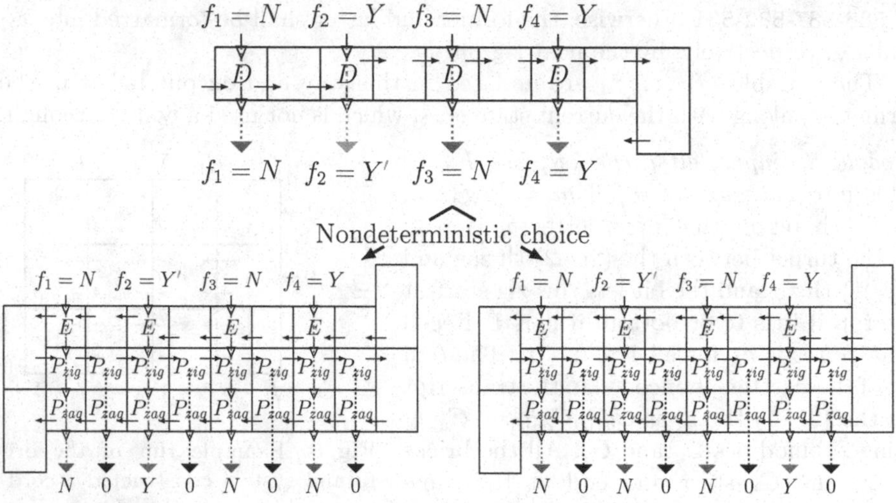

Fig. 8. Example run of Module 3, in which the transitions that have proved valid in Modules 1 and 2 (f_2 and f_4 here) are chosen nondeterministically.

hence, we just mention a property that its four bricks (see [8]) ensure this zig to end at the bottom if none of the transition has proven valid. In that case, the succeeding turner is geometrically trapped as in Fig. 9 and the system halts.

The transcript for the first zag consists of n instances of a submodule E. The five bricks of E are shown in Fig. 10. The zag starts folding at the bottom. When an E starts at the bottom and reads Y from above, it folds into the brick $E_{-\mathrm{YbY}}$ or $E_{-\mathrm{YbN}}$ in Fig. 10 nondeterministically, which amounts to choosing the corresponding valid transition or not. Observe that $E_{-\mathrm{YbY}}$ ends at the top, notifying the succeeding E's that the decision has been already made. When starting at the top, E takes no brick but $E_{-*\mathrm{t}}$, which outputs N no matter what it reads. The brick $E_{-\mathrm{Y'b}}$ and Y' (marked Y) prevent the oritatami system from not choosing any valid transition; that is, if an E starts at the bottom (meaning that none of the valid transitions has been chosen yet) and reads Y' from above, it deterministically folds into $E_{-\mathrm{Y'b}}$, which outputs Y.

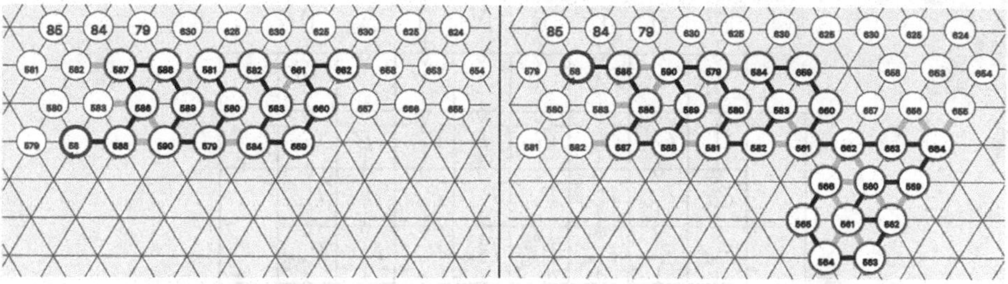

Fig. 9. Turner from the first zig of Module 3 to the first zag. (Left) It is trapped geometrically in the pocket of the previous turner and halts the system if it starts folding at the bottom. (Right) It is not trapped and lets the next zag be transcribed.

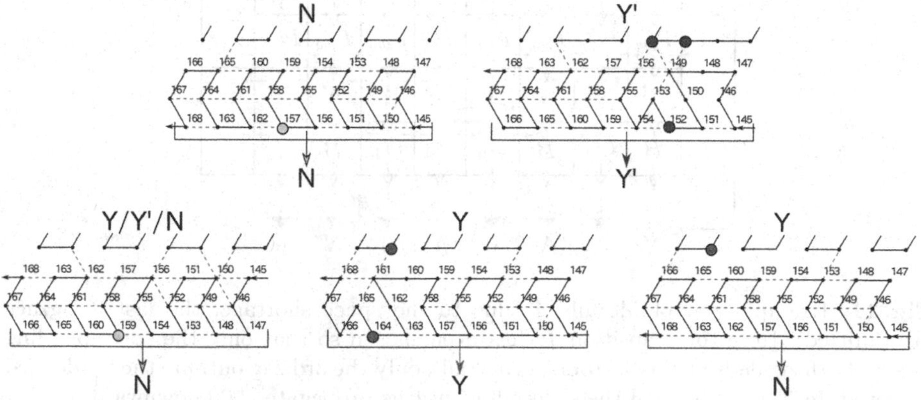

Fig. 10. The five bricks of E: (Top) $E_{-\mathrm{Nb}}$ and $E_{-\mathrm{Y'b}}$; (Bottom) $E_{-*\mathrm{t}}, E_{-\mathrm{YbY}}$, and $E_{-\mathrm{YbN}}$. Note that $E_{-\mathrm{YbY}}$ and $E_{-\mathrm{YbN}}$ are chosen nondeterministically and equally probably.

The transcript of the next zig differs from that of normal formatting zig in that every other instance of P_{zig} is replaced by a spacer. This replacement allows the n instances of P_{zag} responsible for the z-variables to take their "default" brick $P_{\mathrm{zag-0b}}$, which outputs 0. This is a preprocess for Module 4 to set these variables to the target state of the transition chosen.

Module 4 (outputting the target state of the transition chosen; see Fig. 11*)* folds into $2n$ zigzags. Its $(2k-1)$-th zig checks whether f_k was chosen or not, and if it was, the next zag sets $z_{q_i[j]}$ to $t_k[j]$ (recall t_k is the target of f_k).

The transcript for the $(2k-1)$-th zig is represented semantically as

$$(A'A')^{k-1}A_1A'(A'A')^{n-k}. \tag{4}$$

Observe that the sole A_1 is positioned so as to read the 1-bit of whether f_k was chosen or not. The zig starts at the bottom. Since A' always start and end at the same height, the A_1 starts at the bottom. It ends at the bottom if it reads Y, or top otherwise (Fig. 5). The succeeding turner is functional, which lets the next

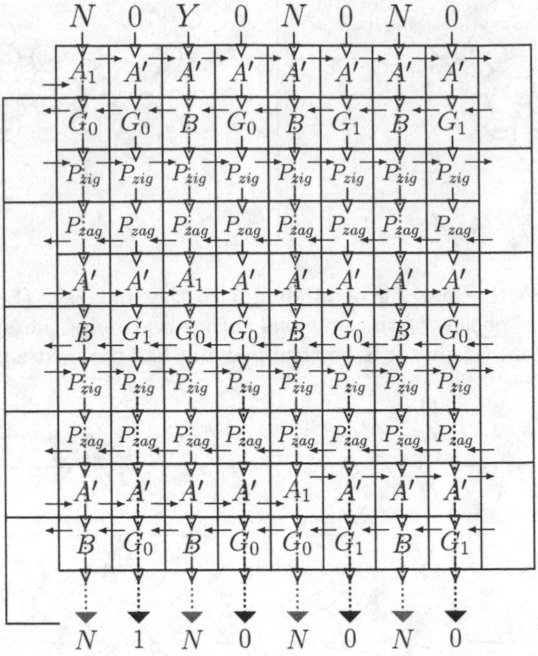

Fig. 11. Example run of Module 4 (due to the space shortage, the last 3 zigzags are omitted). Here the transition f_2 has been chosen so that only the corresponding $(2{\times}2{-}1)$-th zig ends at the bottom. As a result, only the 3rd zag outputs the hardcoded target state 1000 below. All the succeeding zigzags propagate 1000 downward.

zag start at the bottom if the previous zig has ended at the bottom, or at the top otherwise. In this way, the $(2k{-}1)$-th zag starts at the bottom iff Module 3 has chosen f_k.

The transcript for the $(2k{-}1)$-th zag is represented semantically as

$$\left(\bigodot_{j=n}^{k+1}(G_{t_k[j]}B)\right)G_{t_k[k]}G_0\left(\bigodot_{j=k-1}^{1}(G_{t_k[j]}B)\right). \tag{5}$$

All the bricks of submodules G_0 and G_1 (see [8]) start and end at the same height; thus propagating the 1-bit of whether f_k was chosen or not (bottom means chosen) through this zag. Note that this transcript is transcribed from right to left so that these G_0's and G_1's read z-variables. G_0 and G_1 just copy what they read downward if they start at the top, that is, in all zags but the one corresponding to the chosen transition. In the "chosen" zag, they rather output 0 and 1 downward, respectively. Comparing (4) with (5), we can observe that below the sole instance of A_0 is transcribed an instance of G_0. This G_0 plays a different role from other G_0's in the zag. The A_1 above outputs Y or N depending on whether f_k was chosen or not. If it outputs Y, then the $(2k{-}1)$-th zag starts at the bottom as just mentioned, and the sole brick of G_0 that starts at the bottom outputs $0 = N$. Otherwise, G_0 just propagates its output $0 = N$ downward. In this way, all the x-variables are initialized to N for the sake of succeeding period.

3.3 Verification

Using a simulator developed for [9], we have checked for each submodule that it folds as expected in all the expected environments. An expected environment can be described in terms of bricks of surrounding submodules. Folding of a submodule into a brick in an environment causes a transition to another environment for the next submodule. Such transitions combine all the expected environments together into one closed system called brick automaton, whose vertices are expected environments described in terms of surrounding bricks. The automaton is too large to be included here; see [8].

References

1. Allouche, J.P., Shallit, J.: Automatic Sequences: Theory, Applications, Generalizations. Cambridge University Press, Cambridge (2003)
2. Demaine, E.D., et al.: Know when to fold 'Em: self-assembly of shapes by folding in Oritatami. In: Doty, D., Dietz, H. (eds.) DNA 2018. LNCS, vol. 11145, pp. 19–36. Springer, Cham (2018). https://doi.org/10.1007/978-3-030-00030-1_2
3. Geary, C.W., Andersen, E.S.: Design principles for single-stranded RNA Origami structures. In: Murata, S., Kobayashi, S. (eds.) DNA 2014. LNCS, vol. 8727, pp. 1–19. Springer, Cham (2014). https://doi.org/10.1007/978-3-319-11295-4_1
4. Geary, C.W., Meunier, P., Schabanel, N., Seki, S.: Programming biomolecules that fold greedily during transcription. In: MFCS 2016. LIPIcs, vol. 58, pp. 43:1–43:14. Schloss Dagstuhl - Leibniz-Zentrum fuer Informatik (2016)
5. Geary, C.W., Meunier, P., Schabanel, N., Seki, S.: Proving the Turing universality of Oritatami co-transcriptional folding. In: Hsu, W., Lee, D., Liao, C. (eds.) ISAAC 2018. LIPIcs, vol. 123, pp. 23:1–23:13. Schloss Dagstuhl - Leibniz-Zentrum fuer Informatik (2018). https://doi.org/10.4230/LIPIcs.ISAAC.2018.23
6. Geary, C.W., Rothemund, P.W.K., Andersen, E.S.: A single-stranded architecture for cotranscriptional folding of RNA nanostructures. Science **345**(6198), 799–804 (2014). https://doi.org/10.1126/science.1253920
7. Han, Y.-S., Kim, H.: Construction of geometric structure by Oritatami system. In: Doty, D., Dietz, H. (eds.) DNA 2018. LNCS, vol. 11145, pp. 173–188. Springer, Cham (2018). https://doi.org/10.1007/978-3-030-00030-1_11
8. Han, Y., Kim, H., Masuda, Y., Seki, S.: A general architecture of Oritatami systems for simulating arbitrary finite automata (2019). http://arxiv.org/abs/1904.10174
9. Masuda, Y., Seki, S., Ubukata, Y.: Towards the algorithmic molecular self-assembly of fractals by cotranscriptional folding. In: Câmpeanu, C. (ed.) CIAA 2018. LNCS, vol. 10977, pp. 261–273. Springer, Cham (2018). https://doi.org/10.1007/978-3-319-94812-6_22
10. Watters, K., Strobel, E.J., Yu, A.M., Lis, J.T., Lucks, J.B.: Cotranscriptional folding of a riboswitch at nucleotide resolution. Nat. Struct. Mol. Biol. **23**(12), 1124–1133 (2016). https://doi.org/10.1038/nsmb.3316

Descriptional Complexity of Power and Positive Closure on Convex Languages

Michal Hospodár(✉)

Mathematical Institute, Slovak Academy of Sciences,
Grešákova 6, 040 01 Košice, Slovakia
hosmich@gmail.com

Abstract. We study the descriptional complexity of the k-th power and positive closure operations on the classes of prefix-, suffix-, factor-, and subword-free, -closed, and -convex regular languages, and on the classes of right, left, two-sided, and all-sided ideal languages. We show that the upper bound kn on the nondeterministic complexity of the k-th power in the class of regular languages is tight for closed and convex classes, while in the remaining classes, the tight upper bound is $k(n-1)+1$. Next we show that the upper bound n on the nondeterministic complexity of the positive closure operation in the class of regular languages is tight in all considered classes except for classes of factor-closed and subword-closed languages, where the complexity is one. All our worst-case examples are described over a unary or binary alphabet, except for witnesses for the k-th power on subword-closed and subword-convex languages which are described over a ternary alphabet. Moreover, whenever a binary alphabet is used for describing a worst-case example, it is optimal in the sense that the corresponding upper bounds cannot be met by a language over a unary alphabet. The most interesting result is the description of a binary factor-closed language meeting the upper bound kn for the k-th power. To get this result, we use a method which enables us to avoid tedious descriptions of fooling sets. We also provide some results concerning the deterministic state complexity of these two operations on the classes of free, ideal, and closed languages.

1 Introduction

The nondeterministic state complexity of a regular language is the smallest number of states in any nondeterministic finite automaton (with a unique initial state) recognizing this language. The nondeterministic state complexity of a regular operation is the number of states that are sufficient and necessary in the worst case to accept the language resulting from this operation, considered as a function of the nondeterministic state complexities of the operands.

The nondeterministic state complexity of basic regular operations such as union, intersection, concatenation, and positive closure, has been investigated by

Research supported by VEGA grant 2/0132/19 and grant APVV-15-0091.

M. Hospodár and G. Jirásková (Eds.): CIAA 2019, LNCS 11601, pp. 158–170, 2019.
https://doi.org/10.1007/978-3-030-23679-3_13

Holzer and Kutrib [13]. The binary witnesses for complementation and reversal were described by Jirásková [19]. The k-th power operation on nondeterministic automata was studied by Domaratzki and Okhotin [10]. The nondeterministic state complexity of operations on prefix-free and suffix-free languages was examined by Han et al. [11,12] and by Jirásková et al. [20,22]. The results of these papers were improved and new results on nondeterministic complexity were obtained in a series of papers by Mlynárčik et al. In [21], complementation on prefix-free, suffix-free, and non-returning languages was investigated. Complementation on factor-free, subword-free, and ideal languages was considered in [25], basic operations (intersection, union, concatenation, Kleene star, reversal, complementation) on closed and ideal languages in [15], and basic operations on free and convex languages in [16]. The results of these papers were summarized in the journal version [18]. Let us mention that the (deterministic) state complexity in all above mentioned classes were considered by Brzozowski et al. for basic operations [2–4] and by Čevorová for the second power, the square operation [6,7].

In this paper, we investigate the nondeterministic state complexity of the k-th power and positive closure operations on subclasses of convex languages. For both operations and all considered subclasses, we provide a tight upper bound on its nondeterministic state complexity. Except for two cases in which our witnesses are ternary, all the witnesses are described over a binary or unary alphabet. Moreover, whenever a binary alphabet is used, it is always optimal in the sense that the corresponding upper bound cannot be met by any unary language.

2 Preliminaries

We assume that the reader is familiar with basic notions in formal languages and automata theory. For details and all the unexplained notions, the reader may refer to [14,29,30]. Let Σ be a finite non-empty alphabet of symbols. Then Σ^* denotes the set of strings over the alphabet Σ including the empty string ε. A language is any subset of Σ^*.

A *nondeterministic finite automaton* (NFA) is a quintuple $A = (Q, \Sigma, \cdot, s, F)$ where Q is a finite non-empty set of *states*, Σ is a finite non-empty *input alphabet*, $s \in Q$ is the *initial* state, $F \subseteq Q$ is the set of *final* (or *accepting*) states, and $\cdot\colon Q \times \Sigma \to 2^Q$ is the *transition function* which can be extended to the domain $2^Q \times \Sigma^*$ in the natural way. The *language accepted* (or *recognized*) by the NFA A is defined as $L(A) = \{w \in \Sigma^* \mid s \cdot w \cap F \neq \emptyset\}$. An NFA is a (partial) *deterministic finite automaton* (DFA) if $|q \cdot a| \leq 1$ for each q in Q and each a in Σ.

We say that (p, a, q) is a transition in NFA A if $q \in p \cdot a$. We also say that the state q has an *in-transition* on symbol a, and the state p has an *out-transition* on symbol a. An NFA is *non-returning* if its initial state does not have any in-transitions, and it is *non-exiting* if each its final state does not have any out-transitions. To *omit* a state in an NFA means to remove it from the set of states and to remove all its in-transitions and out-transitions from the transition function. To *merge* two states means to replace them by a single state with all in-transitions and out-transitions of the original states.

Let $A = (Q, \Sigma, \cdot, s, F)$ be an NFA and $X, Y \subseteq Q$. We say that X is *reachable* in A if there is a string w in Σ^* such that $X = s \cdot w$. Next, we say that Y is *co-reachable* in A if Y is reachable in the reversed automaton A^R obtained from A by reversing all the transitions, and by swapping the roles of the initial and final states.

The nondeterministic state complexity of a regular language L, denoted $\text{nsc}(L)$, is the smallest number of states in any NFA for L. To provide lower bounds on nondeterministic state complexity, we use the fooling set method described below. A set of pairs of strings $\{(x_i, y_i) \mid i = 1, 2, \ldots, n\}$ is called a *fooling set for a language* L if for each i, j in $\{1, 2, \ldots, n\}$, (1) $x_i y_i \in L$, and (2) if $i \neq j$, then $x_i y_j \notin L$ or $x_j y_i \notin L$.

Lemma 1 (cf. [1, Lemma 1]**).** *Let $\mathcal{F}$ be a fooling set for a regular language L. Then every* NFA *for L has at least $|\mathcal{F}|$ states.* □

A slightly modified definition of the fooling set results in the notion of a *fooling set for an automaton* (cf. [17]).

Definition 2 ([17, Definition 2])**.** *A set of pairs $\{(X_i, Y_i) \mid i = 1, 2, \ldots, n\}$ is called a* fooling set for an NFA A *if for each i, j in $\{1, 2, \ldots, n\}$,*

(1) X_i is reachable and Y_i is co-reachable in A,
(2) $X_i \cap Y_i \neq \emptyset$, and
(3) if $i \neq j$, then $X_i \cap Y_j = \emptyset$ or $X_j \cap Y_i = \emptyset$.

A fooling set for an NFA A of size n exists if and only if a fooling set for the language $L(A)$ exists. The next lemma provides a useful way to to get a lower bound on the size of nondeterministic finite automata.

Lemma 3 (Greater-Smaller Lemma). *Let $n \geq m \geq 2$. Let A be an* NFA *with the state set $\{1, 2, \ldots, n\}$ and $\{(X_i, Y_i) \mid i = 1, 2, \ldots, m\}$ be a set of pairs of subsets of the state set of an* NFA *A such that for each i in $\{1, 2, \ldots, m\}$*

(1) X_i is reachable and Y_i is co-reachable in A,
(2) $i \in X_i \cap Y_i$, and
(3) $X_i \subseteq \{i, i+1, \ldots, n\}$ and $Y_i \subseteq \{1, 2, \ldots, i\}$.

Then every NFA *for $L(A)$ has at least m states.*

Proof. Since X_i is reachable, there is a string x_i which sends the initial state of A to the set X_i. Since Y_i is co-reachable, there is a string y_i which is accepted by A from every state in Y_i and rejected from every other state. Since $X_i \cap Y_i = \{i\}$, the string $x_i y_i$ is in $L(A)$. Let $i \neq j$. Without loss of generality, we have $i > j$. Then $X_i \cap Y_j = \emptyset$, so $x_i y_j$ is not in $L(A)$. Thus the set $\{(X_i, Y_i) \mid i = 1, 2, \ldots, m\}$ is a fooling set for A, so the set $\{(x_i, y_i) \mid i = 1, 2, \ldots, m\}$ is a fooling set for $L(A)$. Hence every NFA for $L(A)$ has at least m states by Lemma 1. □

If $u, v, w, x \in \Sigma^*$ and $w = uxv$, then u is a *prefix* of w, x is a *factor* of w, and v is a *suffix* of w. If $w = u_0 v_1 u_1 \cdots v_n u_n$, where $u_i, v_i \in \Sigma^*$, then $v_1 v_2 \cdots v_n$ is a *subword* of w. A prefix v (suffix, factor, subword) of w is *proper* if $v \neq w$.

A language L is *prefix-free* if $w \in L$ implies that no proper prefix of w is in L; it is *prefix-closed* if $w \in L$ implies that each prefix of w is in L; and it is *prefix-convex* if $u, w \in L$ and u is a prefix of w imply that each string v such that u is a prefix of v and v is a prefix of w is in L. Suffix-, factor-, and subword-free, -closed, and -convex languages are defined analogously. A language is a right (respectively, left, two-sided, all sided) *ideal* if $L = L\Sigma^*$ (respectively, $L = \Sigma^* L, L = \Sigma^* L \Sigma^*, L = L \sqcup\!\sqcup \Sigma^*$ where $L \sqcup\!\sqcup \Sigma^*$ is the language obtained from L by inserting any number of symbols to any string in L). Notice that the classes of free, closed, and ideal languages are subclasses of convex languages.

It is known that if a language is prefix-free, then every minimal NFA for it is non-exiting, and if a language is suffix-free, then every minimal NFA for it is non-returning [11,12]. Next, if a language is a right (left) ideal, then it is accepted by a minimal NFA such that its unique final (initial) state has a loop on each symbol and no other out-transitions (in-transitions) [18, Proposition 12]. Finally, an NFA with all states final accepts a prefix-closed language, for an NFA A if every string which is accepted from any state of A is also accepted from the initial state of A then $L(A)$ is suffix-closed, and if a language is prefix-closed and suffix-closed, then it is factor-closed [18, Proposition 13].

3 Results on Nondeterministic State Complexity

In this section, we examine the nondeterministic state complexity of the k-th power and positive closure on subclasses of convex languages. To get upper bounds, we use automata characterizations of languages in considered classes. To get lower bounds, we use the fooling set method given by Lemma 1 or, in the case of binary factor-closed languages, its simplification given by Lemma 3.

The nondeterministic state complexity of the k-th power on regular languages is kn if $k \geq 2$ and $n \geq 2$ [10, Theorem 3]. The next theorem shows that there is a smaller upper bound for the classes of free and ideal languages.

Theorem 4 (Power on free and ideal languages: Upper bounds). *Let n and k be positive integers. Let L be a prefix-free or suffix-free, or right or left ideal language accepted by an* NFA *with n states. Then L^k is accepted by an* NFA *with at most $k(n-1)+1$ states.*

Proof. We may assume that an NFA for a prefix-free language L is non-exiting and has a unique final state. To get an NFA for L^k, we take k copies of a minimal NFA for L and we merge the final state in the j-th copy with the initial state in the $(j+1)$-th copy. The initial state of the resulting NFA is the initial state in the first copy, and its unique final state is the final state in the k-th copy.

Now consider right ideals. We may assume that an NFA for a right ideal L has a loop on each symbol in its unique final state which has no other out-transitions. The construction of an NFA for L^k is the same as for prefix-free languages.

If L is suffix-free, then we may assume that a minimal NFA for L is non-returning. To get an NFA for L^k, we take k copies of a minimal NFA for L. For each symbol a and every final state p in the j-th copy with $1 \leq j \leq k-1$, we make the state p non-final and add the transitions (p, a, q) whenever there is a transition on a to q from the initial state in the $(j+1)$-th copy. Next, we omit the unreachable initial state of the $(j+1)$-th copy.

Finally, we may assume that a minimal NFA for a left ideal language L has a loop on each symbol in its initial state which has no other in-transitions. The construction of an NFA for L^k is the same as for suffix-free languages except that we add a loop on each symbol in p.

In all four cases, we get an NFA for L^k with $k(n-1)+1$ states. □

Theorem 5 (Power: Lower bounds). *Let $k \geq 2$ and $n \geq 2$.*

(a) There exists a unary subword-free language L accepted by an n-state NFA *such that every* NFA *for L^k has at least $k(n-1)+1$ states.*
(b) There exists a unary all-sided ideal language L accepted by an n-state NFA *such that every* NFA *for L^k has at least $k(n-1)+1$ states.*
(c) There exists a ternary subword-closed language L accepted by an n-state NFA *such that every* NFA *for L^k has at least kn states.*
(d) There exists a binary factor-closed language L accepted by an n-state NFA *such that every* NFA *for L^k has at least kn states.*

Proof.

(a) Let $L = \{a^{n-1}\}$, which is accepted by an n-state NFA. We have $L^k = \{a^{k(n-1)}\}$ and the set $\{(a^i, a^{k(n-1)-i}) \mid 0 \leq i \leq k(n-1)\}$ is a fooling set for L^k. By Lemma 1, every NFA for L^k has at least $k(n-1)+1$ states.
(b) Let $L = \{a^i \mid i \geq n-1\}$, which is accepted by an n-state NFA. We have $L^k = \{a^i \mid i \geq k(n-1)\}$ and the same set as above is a fooling set for L^k.
(c) Let $L = \{b^* a^i c^* \mid 0 \leq i \leq n-1\}$. For each j with $1 \leq j \leq k$, consider the set of pairs $\mathcal{F}_j = \{((ba^{n-1}c)^{j-1}ba^i, a^{n-1-i}c(ba^{n-1}c)^{k-j}) \mid 0 \leq i \leq n-1\}$. We have $(ba^{n-1}c)^k \in L^k$. Next $L^k \subseteq (b^*a^*c^*)^k$, and moreover, no string with more than $k(n-1)$ occurrences of a is in L^k. Thus the set $\bigcup_{j=1}^{k} \mathcal{F}_j$ is a fooling set for L^k of size kn, so every NFA for L^k has at least kn states by Lemma 1.
(d) Let L be the set of strings over $\{a, b\}$ whose every factor in a^* is of length at most $n-1$. Since every factor of every string in L is also in L, L is factor-closed. The language L is accepted by the partial DFA A shown in Fig. 1. Consider the kn-state partial DFA D consisting of k copies of A connected through the transition on a going from the last state of the j-th copy to the second state of the $(j+1)$-th copy; an example for $k=3$ is shown in

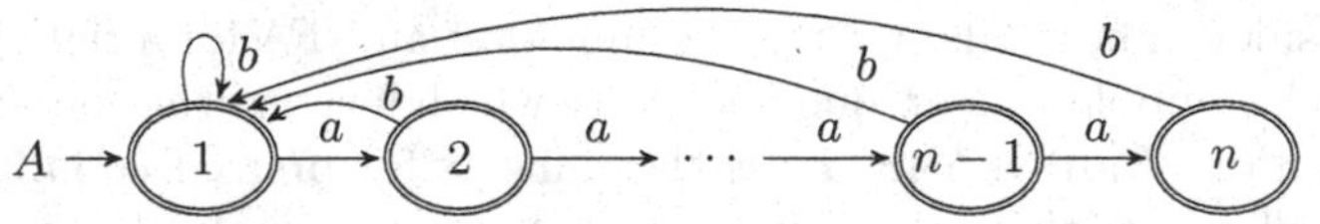

Fig. 1. A binary factor-closed witness for the k-th power meeting the bound kn.

Fig. 2. The partial DFA D accepts the language L^k. Now we prove that D is a minimal NFA for L^k. For $i = 1, 2, \ldots, kn$, let $X_i = \{i\}$ and $Y_i = \{1, 2, \ldots, i\}$. Notice that each set X_i with $i \notin \{jn+1 \mid 1 \leq j \leq k-1\}$ is reachable in D by a string in a^*; each set X_i with $i \in \{jn+1 \mid 1 \leq j \leq k-1\}$ is reachable in D by a string in a^*b; each set Y_i with $i \notin \{jn \mid 1 \leq j \leq k-1\}$ is co-reachable in D since it is reachable in D^R by a string in a^*; each set Y_i with $i \in \{jn \mid 1 \leq j \leq k-1\}$ is co-reachable in D since it is reachable in D^R by a string in a^*b. Moreover, we have $i \in X_i \cap Y_i$, $X_i \subseteq \{i, i+1, \ldots, kn\}$, and $Y_i \subseteq \{1, 2, \ldots, i\}$, so the sets X_i and Y_i satisfy the conditions of Lemma 3 (Greater-Smaller Lemma). Hence D is a minimal NFA for L^k, which proves the lower bound kn. □

The next theorem shows that two symbols are necessary to meet the bound kn.

Theorem 6 (Power on unary convex languages). *Let L be a unary convex language accepted by an* NFA *with n states. Then L^k is accepted by an* NFA *with $k(n-1)+1$ states. There exists a unary closed language L accepted by an n-state* NFA *such that every* NFA *for L^k has at least $k(n-1)+1$ states.*

Proof. If L is infinite, then $L = \{a^i \mid i \geq n-1\}$, so $L^k = \{a^i \mid i \geq k(n-1)\}$. If L is finite, then the length of the longest string in L is at most $n-1$, so the length of the longest string in L^k is at most $k(n-1)$. In both cases, the language L^k is accepted by an NFA with $k(n-1)+1$ states. For the lower bound, consider the subword-closed language $L = \{a^i \mid 0 \leq i \leq n-1\}$. Then we have $L^k = \{a^i \mid 0 \leq i \leq k(n-1)\}$, and hence $\text{nsc}(L^k) = k(n-1)+1$. □

Now we consider the operation of positive closure. The upper bound on nondeterministic state complexity of positive closure on regular languages is n [13, Theorem 9] since we can get an NFA for L^+ from an NFA for L by adding the transition (q, a, s) whenever there is a transition (q, a, f) for a final state f. The

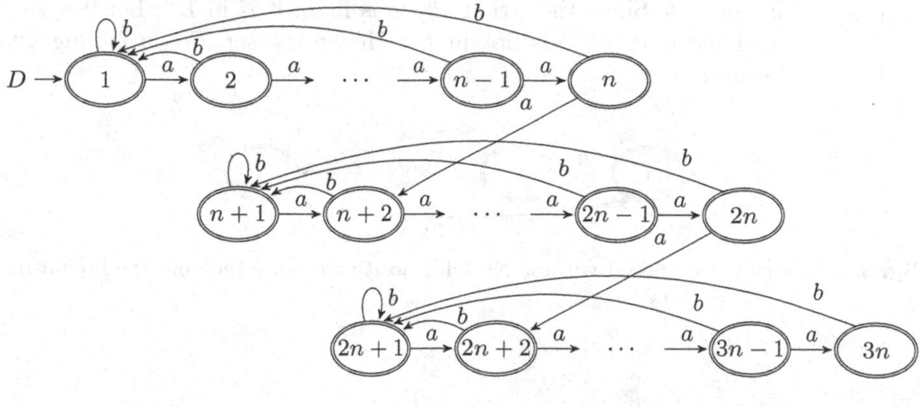

Fig. 2. A partial DFA for $L(A)^3$ where A is shown in Fig. 1.

next theorem shows that this upper bound is tight in all the classes of free and ideal, so also convex languages, and on the classes of prefix-closed and suffix-closed languages. It also proves that the positive closure of every factor-closed language is of complexity one, cf. [15, Theorem 8].

Theorem 7 (Positive closure on factor-closed languages: Upper bound). *Let L be a factor-closed language. Then L^+ is accepted by a one-state* NFA. □

Since every subword-closed language is also factor-closed, the upper bound 1 on nondeterministic state complexity of positive closure holds also for subword-closed languages, and it is met by $\{\varepsilon\}$. For other subclasses, the regular upper bound n holds, and the next theorem provides the matching lower bounds.

Theorem 8 (Positive closure: Lower bounds). *There exists*

(a) a unary subword-free (so, subword-convex) language L
(b) a unary all-sided ideal language L
(c) a binary prefix-closed language L
(d) a binary suffix-closed language L

accepted by an n-state NFA *such that every* NFA *for L^+ has at least n states.*

Proof.

(a) Let $L = \{a^{n-1}\}$, which is accepted by an n-state NFA. We have $L^+ = \{a^{k(n-1)} \mid k \geq 1\}$ and the set $\{(a^i, a^{n-1-i}) \mid 0 \leq i \leq n-1\}$ is a fooling set for L^+ of size n. By Lemma 1, every NFA for L^+ has at least n states.
(b) Let $L = \{a^i \mid i \geq n-1\}$, which is accepted by an n-state NFA. We have $L^+ = L$ and the same set as above is a fooling set for L^+ of size n.
(c) Let L be the language accepted by the NFA shown in Fig. 3. Notice that each state of this NFA is final, hence L is prefix-closed. Consider the set of pairs of strings $\mathcal{F} = \{(a^i, a^{n-1-i}b) \mid 0 \leq i \leq n-1\}$ of size n. We have $a^i a^{n-1-i} b = a^{n-1} b$. Since the string $a^{n-1}b$ is in L, it is in L^+. Let $0 \leq i < j \leq n-1$. Then $a^i a^{n-1-j} b$ is not in L^+. Hence the set $\mathcal{F}$ is a fooling set for L^+ of size n.

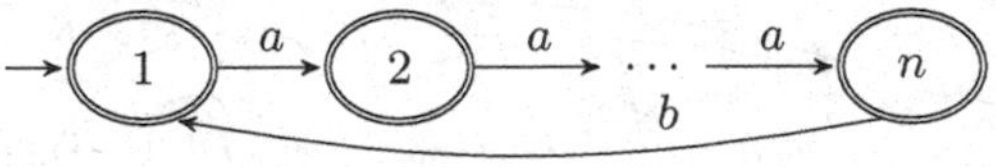

Fig. 3. A binary prefix-closed witness NFA for positive closure meeting the bound n.

(d) Let L be the language accepted by the NFA shown in Fig. 4. Notice that only strings beginning with a are accepted from non-initial states, and for every aw accepted from a non-initial state we have $w \in L$, hence L is suffix-closed. Since the initial state is a unique final state, we have $L = L^+$. Consider the set of pairs of strings $\mathcal{F} = \{(ba^i, a^{n-1-i}) \mid 0 \leq i \leq n-1\}$ of size n. We have $ba^i a^{n-1-i} = ba^{n-1}$, which is in L^+. Let $0 \leq i < j \leq n-1$. Then $ba^i a^{n-1-j}$ is not in L^+. Hence the set $\mathcal{F}$ is a fooling set for L^+ of size n. □

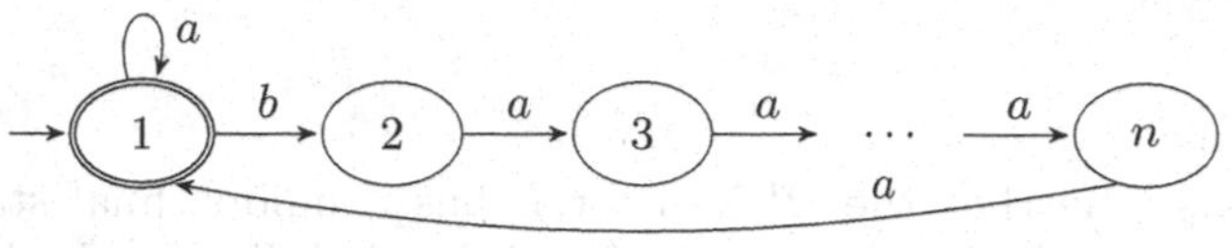

Fig. 4. A binary suffix-closed witness NFA for positive closure meeting the bound n.

4 Results on Deterministic State Complexity

The (deterministic) state complexity of a regular language L, $\text{sc}(L)$, is the smallest number of states in any DFA for L. The deterministic state complexity of square on convex languages was considered by Čevorová [6,7] who obtained tight upper bounds in all subclasses of free, ideal, and closed languages. We use some of her results in the proof of the following theorem.

Theorem 9. *Let $n \geq 2$. Let L be a language over Σ with $\text{sc}(L) \leq n$. Then*

(a) if L is prefix-free, then $\text{sc}(L^k) \leq k(n-2)+2$, and this bound is met by a unary subword-free language;
(b) if L is left ideal, then $\text{sc}(L^k) \leq k(n-1)+1$, and this bound is met by a unary all-sided ideal language;
(c) if L is right ideal, then $\text{sc}(L^k) \leq n + (k-1)2^{n-2}$, and this bound is met if $|\Sigma| \geq 2$;
(d) if L is factor-closed, then $\text{sc}(L^k) \leq k(n-1)+1$, and this bound is met by a binary subword-closed language. □

The upper bound for concatenation on suffix-closed languages is $(m-1)n+1$ [4, Theorem 3(2)], which implies the upper bound on square $(n-1)n+1$ and on the k-th power $(n-1)n^{k-1}+1$. However, the actual state complexity of square is $\frac{1}{2}(n^2+n)-1$ [7, Theorem 3.12]. The ternary witness from [7] gives the resulting complexity 16 with $n=5$, $k=2$, 25 with $n=5$, $k=3$, and 38 with $n=5$, $k=4$. It is possible that Čevorová's witness does not work for $k \geq 3$. Since we do not know the upper bound, this problem remains open.

Now we are going to examine the positive closure on DFAs accepting free, ideal, and closed languages. Since $\varepsilon \in L$ implies $L^+ = L^*$, the known results on Kleene star on closed languages [4,8] hold also for positive closure.

Theorem 10. *Let $n \geq 2$. Let L be a language over Σ with $\mathrm{sc}(L) \leq n$. Then*

(a) If L is prefix-free, then $\mathrm{sc}(L^+) \leq n$, and the bound is met by binary subword-free language.
(b) If L is suffix-free, then $\mathrm{sc}(L^+) \leq 2^{n-2}+1$, and the bound is tight if $|\Sigma| \geq 2$.
(c) If L is right or left ideal, then $\mathrm{sc}(L^+) \leq n$, and the bound is met by a unary all-sided ideal language.
(d) If L is prefix-closed, then $\mathrm{sc}(L^+) \leq 2^{n-2}+1$, and the bound is tight if $|\Sigma| \geq 2$.
(e) If L is suffix-closed, then $\mathrm{sc}(L^+) \leq n$, and the bound is tight if $|\Sigma| \geq 2$.
(f) If L is factor-closed, then $\mathrm{sc}(L^+) \leq 2$, and the bound is met by a unary subword-closed language.

Proof.

(a) We may assume that the DFA A for L has a unique final state f which goes to the non-final sink state d on each symbol. To get the DFA for L^+, it is enough to replace each transition (f, a, d) by $(f, a, s \cdot a)$ where s is the initial state and $\cdot$ is the transition function of A. The resulting DFA has n states and this upper bound is met by the language $b^* a^{n-2}$ if $n \geq 4$, cf. [23, Lemmas 3, 4].
(b) We may assume that the DFA A for L is non-returning and has a non-final sink state. To get a non-returning NFA for L^+, omit this sink state and then add the transitions $(f, a, s \cdot a)$ for each final state f of A and each symbol a in Σ. Then the subset automaton corresponding to this NFA has at most $2^{n-2}+1$ reachable and pairwise distinguishable states. This gives the upper bound. Cmorik's witness for star in [9, Theorem 3] meets this upper bound; notice that his proof works for positive closure as well.
(c) We have $L \subseteq L^+$, and if L is right or left ideal, then $L^+ \subseteq L$. Therefore we have $L = L^+$. The unary all-sided ideal $a^{n-1}a^*$ meets the upper bound n.
(d) If L is prefix-closed, then $\varepsilon \in L$, so $L^+ = L^*$. Hence this case is covered by the result on star on prefix-closed languages from [8, Theorem 13].
(e) Similarly as in case (d), this case is covered by the result on star on suffix-closed languages from [4, Theorem 4(2)].
(f) By Theorem 7, we have $L^+ = \Gamma^*$ for some Γ with $\emptyset \subseteq \Gamma \subseteq \Sigma$. This gives the upper bound 2, which is met by the unary subword-closed language $\{\varepsilon\}$.

□

It follows from [5, Proposition 5] that the upper bound for positive closure on prefix-convex languages is $2^{n-2}+2^{n-3}$, and it is met by a language defined over a five-letter alphabet. Similarly, [28, Theorem 2] shows that the upper bound $2^{n-1}+2^{n-2}-1$ for positive closure in the general case of regular languages is met by a quaternary suffix-convex language. The results from the theorem above provide the lower bound n for positive closure on the classes of factor-, and subword-convex languages. The upper bounds in these classes remain open.

Table 1. Nondeterministic complexity of the k-th power and positive closure.

Class\Operation	L^k	$\|\Sigma\|$	L^+	$\|\Sigma\|$
prefix-, suffix-, factor-, subword-free	$k(n-1)+1$	1	n	1
right, left, two-sided, all-sided ideal	$k(n-1)+1$	1	n	1
prefix-, suffix-closed	kn	2	n	2
factor-closed	kn	2	1	1
subword-closed	kn	3	1	1
unary closed	$k(n-1)+1$		1	
prefix-, suffix-, factor-convex	kn	2	n	1
subword-convex	kn	3	n	1
unary convex	$k(n-1)+1$		n	
regular	kn	2 [10]	n	1 [13]
unary regular	$k(n-1)+1 \leq \cdot \leq kn$	[10]	n	[13]

Table 2. Deterministic complexity of the k-th power and positive closure. We have $(n-k)2^{(k-1)(n-k)} \leq \circ \leq n2^{(k-1)n}$.

Class\Operation	L^k	$\|\Sigma\|$	L^+	$\|\Sigma\|$
prefix-free	$k(n-2)+2$	1	n	2
suffix-free	?		$2^{n-2}+1$	2
factor-, subword-free	$k(n-2)+2$	1	n	2
unary free	$k(n-2)+2$		$n-1$	
right ideal	$n+(k-1)2^{n-2}$	2	n	1
left, two-sided, all-sided ideal	$k(n-1)+1$	1	n	1
prefix-closed	?		$2^{n-2}+1$	2
suffix-closed	?		n	2
factor-, subword-closed	$k(n-1)+1$	2	2	1
unary closed	$k(n-2)+2$		2	
regular	$\circ$	6 [10]	$2^{n-1}+2^{n-2}-1$	1 [31]
unary regular	$k(n-1)+1$	[26]	$(n-1)^2$	[31]

5 Conclusions

We investigated the nondeterministic state complexity of the k-th power and positive closure in the subclasses of convex languages. We considered the classes of prefix-, suffix-, factor-, and subword-free, -closed, and -convex languages, and the classes of right, left, two-sided, and all-sided ideals. We found the exact complexities of both operations in each of the above mentioned classes.

We also considered the deterministic state complexity of these operations in the classes of prefix-, suffix-, factor-, and subword-free and -closed languages, and the classes of right, left, two-sided, and all-sided ideals. For positive closure, we found the exact complexities on each of the classes, and for the k-th power, we only left open the cases of suffix-free and prefix- and suffix-closed languages.

Tables 1 and 2 provide an overview of our results and they also display the sizes of alphabet used to describe the witness languages. For describing the witness languages for the k-th power on subword-closed and subword-convex languages, we used a ternary alphabet. All the remaining witness languages are described over a binary or unary alphabet. Moreover, whenever a binary alphabet is used, it is always optimal in the sense that the corresponding upper bound cannot be met by any unary language.

References

1. Birget, J.: Intersection and union of regular languages and state complexity. Inf. Process. Lett. **43**(4), 185–190 (1992). https://doi.org/10.1016/0020-0190(92)90198-5
2. Brzozowski, J., Jirásková, G., Li, B., Smith, J.: Quotient complexity of bifix-, factor-, and subword-free regular languages. Acta Cybernet. **21**(4), 507–527 (2014). https://doi.org/10.14232/actacyb.21.4.2014.1
3. Brzozowski, J.A., Jirásková, G., Li, B.: Quotient complexity of ideal languages. Theor. Comput. Sci. **470**, 36–52 (2013). https://doi.org/10.1016/j.tcs.2012.10.055
4. Brzozowski, J.A., Jirásková, G., Zou, C.: Quotient complexity of closed languages. Theory Comput. Syst. **54**(2), 277–292 (2014). https://doi.org/10.1007/s00224-013-9515-7
5. Brzozowski, J.A., Sinnamon, C.: Complexity of left-ideal, suffix-closed and suffix-free regular languages. In: Drewes, F., Martín-Vide, C., Truthe, B. (eds.) LATA 2017. LNCS, vol. 10168, pp. 171–182. Springer, Cham (2017). https://doi.org/10.1007/978-3-319-53733-7_12
6. Čevorová, K.: Square on ideal, closed and free languages. In: Shallit and Okhotin [27], pp. 70–80. https://doi.org/10.1007/978-3-319-19225-3_6
7. Čevorová, K.: Square on closed languages. In: Bordihn, H., Freund, R., Nagy, B., Vaszil, G. (eds.) NCMA 2016. books@ocg.at, vol. 321, pp. 121–130. Österreichische Computer Gesellschaft (2016)
8. Čevorová, K., Jirásková, G., Mlynárčik, P., Palmovský, M., Šebej, J.: Operations on automata with all states final. In: Ésik, Z., Fülöp, Z. (eds.) Proceedings of 14th International Conference on Automata and Formal Languages, AFL 2014. EPTCS, vol. 151, pp. 201–215 (2014). https://doi.org/10.4204/EPTCS.151.14

9. Cmorik, R., Jirásková, G.: Basic operations on binary suffix-free languages. In: Kotásek, Z., Bouda, J., Černá, I., Sekanina, L., Vojnar, T., Antoš, D. (eds.) MEMICS 2011. LNCS, vol. 7119, pp. 94–102. Springer, Heidelberg (2012). https://doi.org/10.1007/978-3-642-25929-6_9
10. Domaratzki, M., Okhotin, A.: State complexity of power. Theor. Comput. Sci. **410**(24–25), 2377–2392 (2009). https://doi.org/10.1016/j.tcs.2009.02.025
11. Han, Y., Salomaa, K.: Nondeterministic state complexity for suffix-free regular languages. In: McQuillan and Pighizzini [24], pp. 189–196. https://doi.org/10.4204/EPTCS.31.21
12. Han, Y., Salomaa, K., Wood, D.: Nondeterministic state complexity of basic operations for prefix-free regular languages. Fund. Inform. **90**(1–2), 93–106 (2009). https://doi.org/10.3233/FI-2009-0008
13. Holzer, M., Kutrib, M.: Nondeterministic descriptional complexity of regular languages. Int. J. Found. Comput. Sci. **14**(6), 1087–1102 (2003). https://doi.org/10.1142/S0129054103002199
14. Hopcroft, J.E., Ullman, J.D.: Introduction to Automata Theory, Languages and Computation. Addison-Wesley, Reading (1979)
15. Hospodár, M., Jirásková, G., Mlynárčik, P.: Nondeterministic complexity of operations on closed and ideal languages. In: Han, Y.-S., Salomaa, K. (eds.) CIAA 2016. LNCS, vol. 9705, pp. 125–137. Springer, Cham (2016). https://doi.org/10.1007/978-3-319-40946-7_11
16. Hospodár, M., Jirásková, G., Mlynárčik, P.: Nondeterministic complexity of operations on free and convex languages. In: Carayol, A., Nicaud, C. (eds.) CIAA 2017. LNCS, vol. 10329, pp. 138–150. Springer, Cham (2017). https://doi.org/10.1007/978-3-319-60134-2_12
17. Hospodár, M., Jirásková, G., Mlynárčik, P.: A survey on fooling sets as effective tools for lower bounds on nondeterministic complexity. In: Böckenhauer, H.-J., Komm, D., Unger, W. (eds.) Adventures Between Lower Bounds and Higher Altitudes. LNCS, vol. 11011, pp. 17–32. Springer, Cham (2018). https://doi.org/10.1007/978-3-319-98355-4_2
18. Hospodár, M., Jirásková, G., Mlynárčik, P.: Nondeterministic complexity in subclasses of convex languages. Theor. Comput. Sci. (2019). https://doi.org/10.1016/j.tcs.2018.12.027
19. Jirásková, G.: State complexity of some operations on binary regular languages. Theor. Comput. Sci. **330**(2), 287–298 (2005). https://doi.org/10.1016/j.tcs.2004.04.011
20. Jirásková, G., Krausová, M.: Complexity in prefix-free regular languages. In: McQuillan and Pighizzini [27], pp. 197–204. https://doi.org/10.4204/EPTCS.31.22
21. Jirásková, G., Mlynárčik, P.: Complement on prefix-free, suffix-free, and non-returning NFA languages. In: Jürgensen, H., Karhumäki, J., Okhotin, A. (eds.) DCFS 2014. LNCS, vol. 8614, pp. 222–233. Springer, Cham (2014). https://doi.org/10.1007/978-3-319-09704-6_20
22. Jirásková, G., Olejár, P.: State complexity of intersection and union of suffix-free languages and descriptional complexity. In: Bordihn, H., Freund, R., Holzer, M., Kutrib, M., Otto, F. (eds.) NCMA 2009. books@ocg.at, vol. 256, pp. 151–166. Österreichische Computer Gesellschaft (2009)
23. Jirásková, G., Palmovský, M., Šebej, J.: Kleene closure on regular and prefix-free languages. In: Holzer, M., Kutrib, M. (eds.) CIAA 2014. LNCS, vol. 8587, pp. 226–237. Springer, Cham (2014). https://doi.org/10.1007/978-3-319-08846-4_17

24. McQuillan, I., Pighizzini, G. (eds.): DCFS 2010, EPTCS, vol. 31 (2010). https://doi.org/10.4204/EPTCS.31
25. Mlynárčik, P.: Complement on free and ideal languages. In: Shallit and Okhotin [27], pp. 185–196. https://doi.org/10.1007/978-3-319-19225-3_16
26. Rampersad, N.: The state complexity of L^2 and L^k. Inf. Process. Lett. **98**(6), 231–234 (2006). https://doi.org/10.1016/j.ipl.2005.06.011
27. Shallit, J., Okhotin, A. (eds.): DCFS 2015. LNCS, vol. 9118. Springer, Cham (2015). https://doi.org/10.1007/978-3-319-19225-3
28. Sinnamon, C.: Complexity of proper suffix-convex regular languages. In: Câmpeanu, C. (ed.) CIAA 2018. LNCS, vol. 10977, pp. 324–338. Springer, Cham (2018). https://doi.org/10.1007/978-3-319-94812-6_27
29. Sipser, M.: Introduction to the Theory of Computation. Cengage Learning, Boston (2012)
30. Yu, S.: Regular languages. In: Rozenberg, G., Salomaa, A. (eds.) Handbook of Formal Languages, vol. 1, pp. 41–110. Springer, Heidelberg (1997). https://doi.org/10.1007/978-3-642-59136-5_2
31. Yu, S., Zhuang, Q., Salomaa, K.: The state complexities of some basic operations on regular languages. Theor. Comput. Sci. **125**(2), 315–328 (1994). https://doi.org/10.1016/0304-3975(92)00011-F

Partitioning a Symmetric Rational Relation into Two Asymmetric Rational Relations

Stavros Konstantinidis[1(✉)], Mitja Mastnak[1], and Juraj Šebej[1,2]

[1] Saint Mary's University, Halifax, NS, Canada
s.konstantinidis@smu.ca, mmastnak@cs.smu.ca
[2] Institute of Computer Science, Faculty of Science, P. J. Šafárik University, Košice, Slovakia
juraj.sebej@gmail.com

Abstract. We consider the problem of partitioning effectively a given symmetric (and irreflexive) rational relation R into two asymmetric rational relations. This problem is motivated by a recent method of embedding an R-independent language into one that is maximal R-independent, where the method requires to use an asymmetric partition of R. We solve the problem when R is realized by a zero-avoiding transducer (with some bound k): if the absolute value of the input-output length discrepancy of a computation exceeds k then the length discrepancy of the computation cannot become zero. This class of relations properly contains the recognizable, the left synchronous, and the right synchronous relations. We leave the asymmetric partition problem open when R is not zero-avoiding. We also show examples of total word-orderings for which there is a relation R that cannot be partitioned into two asymmetric rational relations with respect to the given word-orderings.

Keywords: Asymmetric relations · Transducers · Synchronous relations · Word orderings

1 Introduction

The abstract already serves as the first paragraph of the introduction.

The structure of the paper is as follows. The next section contains basic concepts about relations, word orderings and transducers. Section 3 contains the mathematical statement of the rational asymmetric partition problem and its motivation. Section 4 presents the concept of a C-copy of a transducer $\boldsymbol{t}$, which is another transducer containing a copy c of the states of $\boldsymbol{t}$, for each $c \in C$. A C-copy of $\boldsymbol{t}$, for appropriate C, produces a transducer realizing one asymmetric part of the relation of $\boldsymbol{t}$. Section 5 deals with the simple case where the transducer is letter-to-letter (Proposition 10). Section 6 introduces zero avoiding transducers $\boldsymbol{t}$ with some bound $k \geq 0$ and shows a few basic properties: the minimum k is less than the number of states of $\boldsymbol{t}$ (Proposition 17); every left (or right)

M. Hospodár and G. Jirásková (Eds.): CIAA 2019, LNCS 11601, pp. 171–183, 2019.
https://doi.org/10.1007/978-3-030-23679-3_14

synchronous relation is realized by some zero-avoiding transducer with bound 0 (Proposition 19). Section 7 shows a construction, from a given input-altering transducer $\boldsymbol{s}$, that produces a certain C-copy $\alpha(\boldsymbol{s})$ of $\boldsymbol{s}$ realizing the set of all pairs in $\mathrm{R}(\boldsymbol{s})$ for which the input is greater than the output with respect to the radix total order of words (Theorem 24). This construction solves the rational asymmetric partition problem when the given relation is realized by a zero-avoiding transducer. Section 8 discusses a variation of the problem, where we have a certain fixed total word ordering $[>]$ and we want to know whether there is a rational symmetric S such that not both of $S \cap [>]$ and $S \cap [<]$ are rational (Proposition 26). This section also offers as an open problem the general rational asymmetric partition problem (that is when the given R is not zero-avoiding). The last section contains a few concluding remarks.

2 Basic Terminology and Notation

We assume the reader is familiar with basic concepts of formal languages: alphabet, words (or strings), empty word λ, language (see e.g., [4,6]). We shall use a totally ordered alphabet Σ; in fact for convenience we assume that $\Sigma = \{0, 1, \ldots, q-1\}$, for some integer $q > 0$. If a word w is of the form $w = uv$ then u is called a prefix and v is called a suffix of w. We shall use x/y to denote the pair of words x and y. A (binary word) relation R over Σ is a subset of $\Sigma^* \times \Sigma^*$, that is, $R \subseteq \Sigma^* \times \Sigma^*$. We shall use the infix notation xRy to mean that $x/y \in R$; then, $x\not{R}y$ means $x/y \notin R$.
The domain $\mathrm{dom}R$ of R is the set $\{x \mid x/y \in R\}$. The inverse R^{-1} of R is the relation $\{y/x \mid x/y \in R\}$.

Word Orderings. Let x, y, z be any words in Σ^*. A relation R is called irreflexive, if $x\not{R}x$; reflexive, if xRx for all $x \in \mathrm{dom}R$; symmetric, if xRy implies yRx; transitive, if "xRy and yRz" implies xRz. A relation A is called asymmetric, if xAy implies $y\not{A}x$. In this case, A must be irreflexive and we have that

$$A \cap A^{-1} = \emptyset \quad \text{and} \quad A \subseteq (\Sigma^* \times \Sigma^*) \setminus \{w/w : w \in \Sigma^*\}.$$

A total asymmetry is an asymmetric relation A such that either uAv or vAu, for all words u, v with $u \neq v$. We shall use the notation '$[>]$' for an arbitrary total asymmetry, as well as the notation '$[>_\alpha]$' for a specific total asymmetry where α is some identifying subscript. Then, we shall write $u > v$ to indicate that $u/v \in [>]$. Moreover, we shall write $[<]$ (and $[<_\alpha]$) for the inverse of $[>]$ (and $[<_\alpha]$). A total strict ordering $[<]$ is a total asymmetry that is also transitive. Examples of this are the radix '$[<_r]$' and the lexicographic '$[<_l]$' ordering. The lexicographic ordering is the standard dictionary order, for example, $112 <_l 12 <_l 3$. The radix ordering is the standard integer ordering when words are viewed as integers and no symbol of Σ is interpreted as zero: $3 <_r 12 <_r 112$. In both of these orderings, the empty word is the smallest one. □

A path P of a labelled (directed) graph $G = (V, E)$ is a string of consecutive edges, that is, $P \in E^*$ and is of the form

$$P = (q_0, \alpha_1, q_1)(q_1, \alpha_2, q_2) \cdots (q_{\ell-1}, \alpha_\ell, q_\ell),$$

for some integer $\ell \geq 0$, where each $q_i \in V$, each α_i is a label, and each $(q_{i-1}, \alpha_i, q_i) \in E$. The empty path is denoted by $\boldsymbol{\lambda}$. We shall use the following shorthand notation for the above path: $P = \langle q_{i-1}, \alpha_i, q_i \rangle_{i=1}^{\ell}$.

Transducers ([1,7,9]). A transducer is a quintuple[1] $\boldsymbol{t} = (Q, \Sigma, E, I, F)$ such that (Q, E) is a labelled graph with labels of the form x/y, for some $x, y \in \Sigma \cup \{\lambda\}$, and $I, F \subseteq Q$ with $I \neq \emptyset$. The set of vertices Q is also called the set of states of $\boldsymbol{t}$. The set of edges E is also called the set of transitions of $\boldsymbol{t}$. In a transition $e = (p, x/y, q)$ of $\boldsymbol{t}$, p is called the source state of e, and q is called the destination state of e. The sets I, F are called the initial and final states of $\boldsymbol{t}$, respectively. The label of a path $\langle q_{i-1}, x_i/y_i, q_i \rangle_{i=1}^{\ell}$ is the pair $x_1 \cdots x_\ell / y_1 \cdots y_\ell$. We write label($P$) to denote the label of a path P. In particular, label($\boldsymbol{\lambda}$) $= \lambda/\lambda$. A computation of $\boldsymbol{t}$ is a path P of $\boldsymbol{t}$ such that, either P is empty, or the first state of P is in I. We write Comput($\boldsymbol{t}$) to denote the set of all computations of $\boldsymbol{t}$. The computation P is called accepting if, either $P = \boldsymbol{\lambda}$ and $I \cap F \neq \emptyset$, or $P \neq \boldsymbol{\lambda}$ and the last state of P is in F. We write AccComput($\boldsymbol{t}$) to denote the set of accepting computations of $\boldsymbol{t}$. The relation realized by $\boldsymbol{t}$ is the set $\mathrm{R}(\boldsymbol{t}) = \{\,\mathrm{label}(P) \mid P \in \mathrm{AccComput}(\boldsymbol{t})\}$. If $\mathrm{R}(\boldsymbol{t})$ is irreflexive then $\boldsymbol{t}$ is called input-altering. If $\mathrm{R}(\boldsymbol{t}) \subseteq [>]$, for some total asymmetry $[>]$, then $\boldsymbol{t}$ is called input-decreasing (with respect to $[>]$). If $\boldsymbol{t}, \boldsymbol{s}$ are transducers then: $\boldsymbol{t}^{-1}$ denotes the inverse of $\boldsymbol{t}$ such that $\mathrm{R}(\boldsymbol{t}^{-1}) = \mathrm{R}(\boldsymbol{t})^{-1}$; $\boldsymbol{ts}$ denotes a transducer such that $\mathrm{R}(\boldsymbol{ts}) = \mathrm{R}(\boldsymbol{t})\mathrm{R}(\boldsymbol{s})$; $\boldsymbol{t} \vee \boldsymbol{s}$ denotes a transducer such that $\mathrm{R}(\boldsymbol{t} \vee \boldsymbol{s}) = \mathrm{R}(\boldsymbol{t}) \cup \mathrm{R}(\boldsymbol{s})$.

3 Statement and Motivation of the Main Problem

Let I be an irreflexive relation. An asymmetric partition of I is a partition $\{A, B\}$ of I such that A, B are asymmetric. If I is rational, then a rational asymmetric partition of I is an asymmetric partition $\{A, B\}$ of I such that A, B are rational.

Remark 1. If I is any irreflexive relation and $[>]$ is any total asymmetry then $\{I \cap [>], I \cap [<]\}$ is an asymmetric partition of I. As any asymmetric A is irreflexive, we also have that $\{A \cap [>], A \cap [<]\}$ is an asymmetric partition of A. If S is a symmetric and irreflexive relation and $\{A, B\}$ is an asymmetric partition of S then $B = A^{-1}$.

The Rational Asymmetric Partition Problem. Which symmetric-and-irreflexive rational relations have a rational asymmetric partition?

[1] In general, $\boldsymbol{t}$ has an input and an output alphabet, but here these are equal.

Remark 2. Any relation R that is not irreflexive cannot have an asymmetric partition; otherwise, R would contain a pair u/u, which cannot be an element of any asymmetric relation. We also note the following: If A is any rational asymmetric relation then $\{A, A^{-1}\}$ is a rational asymmetric partition of $A \cup A^{-1}$.

Motivation for the Above Problem. For a relation R and language L, we say that L is R-independent, [8,10], if "$uRv, u \in L, v \in L$" implies $u = v$. It is a fact that L is R-independent, if and only if it is $(R \cup R^{-1})$-independent—of course $(R \cup R^{-1})$ is *always* symmetric. The concept of R-independence provides tools for studying code-related properties such as prefix codes and error-detecting languages (according to R). In [5], for a given input-altering transducer $\boldsymbol{t}$ and regular language L that is $\mathrm{R}(\boldsymbol{t})$-independent, the authors provide a formula for embedding L into a maximal $\mathrm{R}(\boldsymbol{t})$-independent language, provided that $\boldsymbol{t}$ is input-decreasing with respect to $[>_r]$. Of course then, $\mathrm{R}(\boldsymbol{t})$ is asymmetric. Thus, to embed an S-independent language L into a maximal one, where S is symmetric, it is necessary to find a transducer $\boldsymbol{t}$ such that $S = \mathrm{R}(\boldsymbol{t}) \cup \mathrm{R}(\boldsymbol{t}^{-1})$ and $\mathrm{R}(\boldsymbol{t})$ is asymmetric.

4 Multicopies of Transducers

In this section we fix a finite nonempty set C, whose elements are called copy labels. Let S be any set and let $c \in C$. The copy c of S is the set $S^c = \{s^c \mid s \in S\}$.

Definition 3. *Let* $\boldsymbol{t} = (Q, \Sigma, T, I, F)$ *be a transducer. A* C*-copy of* $\boldsymbol{t}$ *is any transducer* $\boldsymbol{t}' = (Q', \Sigma, T', I', F')$ *satisfying the following conditions.*

1. $Q' = \cup_{c \in C} Q^c$, $I' \subseteq \cup_{c \in C} I^c$, $F' \subseteq \cup_{c \in C} F^c$.
2. $T' \subseteq \{(p^c, x/y, q^d) \mid c, d \in C, (p, x/y, q) \in T\}$. *If* $e' = (p^c, x/y, q^d) \in T'$ *then the edge* $(p, x/y, q)$ *of* $\boldsymbol{t}$ *is called the edge of* $\boldsymbol{t}$ *corresponding to* e' *and is denoted by* $\mathrm{corr}(e')$.

For each edge e *of* $\boldsymbol{t}$*, we define the set of edges of* $\boldsymbol{t}'$ *corresponding to* e *to be the set* $\mathrm{Corr}(e) = \{e' \mid e = \mathrm{corr}(e')\}$.

Example 4. The transducer $\alpha_0(\boldsymbol{s})$ in Fig. 1 is a C-copy of $\boldsymbol{s}$, where $C = \{\lambda, A, R\}$. It has three copies of the states of $\boldsymbol{s}$. We have that

$$\mathrm{Corr}(q_1, 0/1, q_2) = \{(q_1^\lambda, 0/1, q_2^R),\ (q_1^A, 0/1, q_2^A),\ (q_1^R, 0/1, q_2^R)\}.$$

Each edge $(p, x/y, q)$ of $\boldsymbol{s}$ has corresponding edges in $\alpha_0(\boldsymbol{s})$ of the form $(p^c, x/y, q^d)$ such that the source state p^c is in the copy c (initially, $c = \lambda$) and the destination state q^d is in the copy d, where possibly $d = c$. Edges of $\alpha_0(\boldsymbol{s})$ with source state in the copies A, R have a destination state in the same copy. On the other, an edge of $\alpha_0(\boldsymbol{s})$, with some label x/y, whose source state is in the copy λ has a destination state in the copy λ if $x = y$; in the copy A if $x >_r y$; and in the copy R if $x <_r y$. As $\alpha_0(\boldsymbol{s})$ has final states only in the copy A, it follows that for any $u/v \in \mathrm{R}(\alpha_0(\boldsymbol{s}))$ we have that $u >_r v$ and $u/v \in \mathrm{R}(\boldsymbol{s})$. This example is useful when solving the rational asymmetric partitioning problem for letter-to-letter transducers—see Sect. 5.

Remark 5. Let $\boldsymbol{t}$ be a transducer and let $\boldsymbol{t}'$ be a C-copy of $\boldsymbol{t}$. We note that (i) To define the edges of a C-copy of $\boldsymbol{t}$, it is sufficient to specify the sets $\mathrm{Corr}(e)$, for all edges e of $\boldsymbol{t}$. (ii) If $\boldsymbol{t}'$ has a state that is both initial and final then so does $\boldsymbol{t}$; thus, if $\boldsymbol{\lambda} \in \mathrm{AccComput}(\boldsymbol{t}')$ then $\boldsymbol{\lambda} \in \mathrm{AccComput}(\boldsymbol{t})$ and $\lambda/\lambda \in \mathrm{R}(\boldsymbol{t})$.

Definition 6. *Let $\boldsymbol{t}'$ be a C-copy of a transducer $\boldsymbol{t}$, and let $P' = \langle e_i' \rangle_{i=1}^{\ell} \in \mathrm{Path}(\boldsymbol{t}') - \{\boldsymbol{\lambda}\}$. For each edge e_i' of P', let $e_i = \mathrm{corr}(e_i')$. Then the string $\langle e_i \rangle_{i=1}^{\ell}$ is a path of $\boldsymbol{t}$ and is called the (unique) path of $\boldsymbol{t}$ corresponding to P' and is denoted by $\mathrm{corr}(P')$. Conversely, if $P = \langle e_i \rangle_{i=1}^{\ell}$ is a path of $\boldsymbol{t}$, then we define the set of paths of $\boldsymbol{t}'$ corresponding to P to be the set of all paths of $\boldsymbol{t}'$ of the form $\langle e_i' \rangle_{i=1}^{\ell}$, where each $e_i' \in \mathrm{Corr}(e_i)$; this set is denoted by $\mathrm{Corr}(P)$. We also define $\mathrm{corr}(\boldsymbol{\lambda}) = \boldsymbol{\lambda}$ and $\mathrm{Corr}(\boldsymbol{\lambda}) = \{\boldsymbol{\lambda}\}$.*

Lemma 7. *If $\boldsymbol{t}'$ is a C-copy of a transducer $\boldsymbol{t}$, then $\mathrm{R}(\boldsymbol{t}') \subseteq \mathrm{R}(\boldsymbol{t})$.*

5 Asymmetric Partition of Letter-to-Letter Transducers

A transducer $\boldsymbol{t}$ is called letter-to-letter, [7], if all its transition labels are of the form σ/τ, where $\sigma, \tau \in \Sigma$. Here we provide a solution to the asymmetric partition problem for letter-to-letter transducers in Proposition 10, which is based on Construction 8 below. We note that this construction is a special case of the more general construction for zero-avoiding transducers in Sect. 7, but we present it separately here as it is simpler than the general one.

Construction 8. *Let $\boldsymbol{s} = (Q, \Sigma, T, I, F)$ be a letter-to-letter transducer. Let $C = \{\lambda, A, R\}$. We construct a transducer $\alpha_0(\boldsymbol{s}) = (Q', \Sigma, T', I', F')$, which is a C-copy of $\boldsymbol{s}$, as follows. First, $Q' = Q^{\lambda} \cup Q^{A} \cup Q^{R}$, $I' = I^{\lambda}$ and $F' = F^{A}$. Then, T' is defined as follows.*

$$
\begin{aligned}
T' = &\{(p^c, \sigma/\tau, q^c) \mid (p, \sigma/\tau, q) \in T,\ c \in \{A, R\}\} \\
&\cup \{(p^{\lambda}, \sigma/\sigma, q^{\lambda}) \mid (p, \sigma/\sigma, q) \in T\} \\
&\cup \{(p^{\lambda}, \sigma/\tau, q^{A}) \mid (p, \sigma/\tau, q) \in T,\ \sigma >_r \tau\} \\
&\cup \{(p^{\lambda}, \sigma/\tau, q^{R}) \mid (p, \sigma/\tau, q) \in T,\ \sigma <_r \tau\}.
\end{aligned}
$$

Explanation. The transducer $\alpha_0(\boldsymbol{s})$ includes two exact copies of $\boldsymbol{s}$: one whose states are the A copies of Q, and one whose states are the R copies of Q; $\alpha_0(\boldsymbol{s})$ also includes a sub-copy of $\boldsymbol{s}$ which contains a λ copy of Q and only transitions with labels of the form σ/σ. Any computation P' of $\alpha_0(\boldsymbol{s})$ starts at an initial state i^{λ} and continues with states in the λ copy of Q as long as transition labels are of the form σ/σ. If a transition label is σ/τ with $\sigma >_r \tau$ then the computation P' continues in the A copy and never leaves that copy. As final states are only in the A copy, we have that P' is accepting if and only if $\mathrm{corr}(P')$ is accepting and $\mathrm{label}(P') = u/v$ such that u is of the form $x\sigma y_1$ and v of the form $x\tau y_2$ with

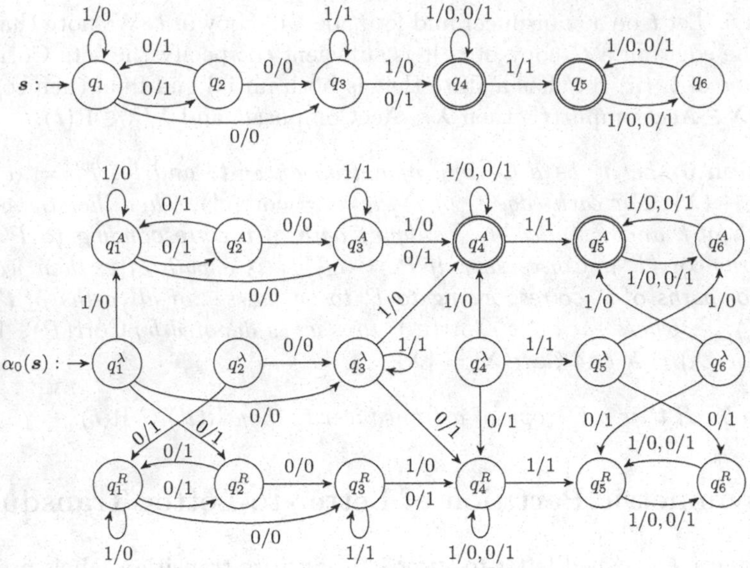

Fig. 1. Construction 8 applied to transducer $\boldsymbol{s}$ to get transducer $\alpha_0(\boldsymbol{s})$.

$\sigma >_r \tau$ and $|u| = |v|$. Note that, in the computation P', if a transition label is σ/τ with $\sigma <_r \tau$ and the current state is in the λ copy, then P' would continue in the R copy of $\alpha_0(\boldsymbol{s})$, which has no final states, so P' would not be accepting.

Remark 9. In fact the R copy of $\boldsymbol{s}$ is not necessary as it has no final states. It was included to make the construction a little more intuitive.

Using Lemma 7 and based on the above explanation, we have the following proposition—it is a special case of the main result in Sect. 7.

Proposition 10. *Let* $\boldsymbol{s}$ *be any input-altering letter-to-letter transducer. Let* $\boldsymbol{t}_1 = \alpha_0(\boldsymbol{s})$ *and* $\boldsymbol{t}_2 = \big(\alpha_0(\boldsymbol{s}^{-1})\big)^{-1}$. *Then* $\{\mathrm{R}(\boldsymbol{t}_1), \mathrm{R}(\boldsymbol{t}_2)\}$ *is a rational asymmetric partition of* $\mathrm{R}(\boldsymbol{s})$.

6 Discrepancies of Computations and Zero-Avoiding Transducers

Here we introduce the concept of a zero-avoiding transducer with some bound $k \in \mathbb{N}_0$, which relates to length discrepancies of the computations of the transducer. We show that the minimum bound k is less than the number of states of the transducer. We also show that the zero-avoiding relations contain properly all left and right synchronous relations. Thus, they also include all recognizable relations and all relations of bounded length discrepancy [7].

Definition 11. *Let $u, v \in \Sigma^*$, let $\mathbf{t}$ be a transducer and let $P = \langle q_{i-1}, x_i/y_i, q_i\rangle_{i=1}^{\ell} \in \mathrm{Path}(\mathbf{t})$. The* length discrepancy *of the pair u/v is the integer $d(u/v) = |u| - |v|$. The* length discrepancy *of P is the integer $d(P) = d(x_1x_2\cdots x_\ell/y_1y_2\cdots y_\ell)$. The* maximum absolute length discrepancy *of P is the integer*

$$d_{max}(P) = \max_{Q\in\mathrm{Prefix}(P)} \{|d(Q)|\}.$$

Remark 12. We have that $d(\lambda/\lambda) = 0$ and $d_{max}(\boldsymbol{\lambda}) = 0$. Moreover, if P_1P_2 is a path of $\mathbf{t}$, then $d(P_1P_2) = d(P_1) + d(P_2)$.

Definition 13. *A transducer $\mathbf{t}$ is called zero-avoiding, if there is an integer $k \geq 0$ such that the following condition is satisfied:*

$$\textit{for any } P \in \mathrm{Comput}(\mathbf{t}), \textit{ if } d_{max}(P) > k \textit{ then } d(P) \neq 0.$$

In this case, $\mathbf{t}$ is called zero-avoiding with bound *k. It is called zero-avoiding with* minimum bound *k, if it is zero-avoiding with bound k but not with bound $k-1$.*[2]

Remark 14. The fact that $\mathbf{t}$ is zero-avoiding does not imply that every trim transducer realizing $\mathrm{R}(\mathbf{t})$ is zero-avoiding. For example, $(0/\lambda + \lambda/0)^*$ can be realized by a zero-avoiding transducer with bound 0 as well as by a trim transducer that is not zero-avoiding[3]. In a zero-avoiding transducer with bound k, if a computation P has length discrepancy $>k$, or $<-k$, then any continuation of P cannot have zero as its length discrepancy.

Remark 15. Let $\mathbf{t} = (Q, \Sigma, T, I, F)$ be a transducer. For any path P of $\mathbf{t}$ there is a unique path P^{-1} of $\mathbf{t}^{-1}$ whose labels are the inverses of the labels in P. Thus, $d(P^{-1}) = -d(P)$ and $|d(P^{-1})| = |d(P)|$. This implies that if $\mathbf{t}$ is zero-avoiding with some bound k then also $\mathbf{t}^{-1}$ is zero-avoiding with bound k.

Remark 16. Let $\mathbf{s} = (Q, \Sigma, T, I, F)$ be a transducer and let $\mathbf{t} = (Q', \Sigma, T', I', F')$ be a C-copy of $\mathbf{s}$. Let P' be a computation of $\mathbf{t}$, and let $P = \mathrm{corr}(P')$; then P and P' have exactly the same sequence of labels in their transitions. Thus we have: (i) $d_{max}(P') = d_{max}(P)$; (ii) if $\mathbf{s}$ is zero-avoiding with some bound k then also $\mathbf{t}$ is zero-avoiding with the same bound k.

Proposition 17. *Let $\mathbf{t}$ be an n-state transducer, for some integer $n \geq 1$. If $\mathbf{t}$ is zero-avoiding with minimum bound k then $k < n$.*

Proposition 18. *Let $\mathbf{t}$ be an n-state transducer, for some integer $n \geq 1$. The following statements are equivalent: (i) $\mathbf{t}$ is not zero-avoiding. (ii) $\mathbf{t}$ has a computation P with $d_{max}(P) \geq n$ and $d(P) = 0$. (iii) $\mathbf{t}$ has a computation P of the form $P = BC_1AC_2D$ such that C_1, C_2 are cycles with $d(C_1)d(C_2) < 0$.*

---

[2] This is well-defined: if $\mathbf{t}$ is zero-avoiding with bound k then it is also zero-avoiding with bound k' for all $k' > k$.

[3] Further explanations of claims will be given in a journal version of this paper.

Relating Left (right) Synchronous and Zero-Avoiding Relations. A natural question arising is how zero-avoiding relations are related to the well-known left (or right) synchronous relations. A relation R is called left synchronous, [7], if it is a finite union of relations, each of the form $S(A \times \{\lambda\})$ or $S(\{\lambda\} \times A)$, where A is a regular language and S is realized by a letter-to-letter transducer. The concept of a right synchronous relation is symmetric: via finite unions of relations of the form $(A \times \{\lambda\})S$ or $(\{\lambda\} \times A)S$.

The proof of the below proposition uses the above definition of left synchronous relation as well as the equivalent definition in [2,3].

Proposition 19. *The classes of left synchronous relations and right synchronous relations are proper subsets of the class of zero-avoiding relations with bound 0.*

Zero-Avoiding Relations are Not Closed Under Intersection: One considers the intersection of the zero-avoiding relations $(0/0)^*(\lambda/1)^*$ and $(\lambda/0)^*$ $(0/1)^*$.

7 Asymmetric Partition of Zero-Avoiding Transducers

We present here a solution to the asymmetric partition problem for any relation realized by a zero-avoiding transducer $\boldsymbol{s}$ with some bound k (Construction 21 and Theorem 24). The required asymmetric relation is realized by a C-copy $\alpha(\boldsymbol{s})$ of $\boldsymbol{s}$, where C is shown in (1) further below. In fact $\mathrm{R}(\alpha(\boldsymbol{s})) = (\mathrm{R}(\boldsymbol{s}) \cap [>_r])$; thus, $u/v \in \mathrm{R}(\alpha(\boldsymbol{s}))$ implies $u >_r v$. The set of states of $\alpha(\boldsymbol{s})$ is $Q' = \cup_{c \in C} Q^c$. The reason why all these copies of Q are needed is to know at any point during a computation P' of $\alpha(\boldsymbol{s})$ whether $d_{max}(P')$ has exceeded k.

Meaning of States of $\alpha(\boldsymbol{s})$ in Construction 21. A state q^c of $\alpha(\boldsymbol{s})$ has the following meaning. Let $P' \in \mathrm{Comput}(\alpha(\boldsymbol{s}))$ ending with q^c and having some label $w_{\mathrm{in}}/w_{\mathrm{out}}$. Then, q^c specifies which one of the following mutually exclusive facts about P' holds.

- $q^c = q^\lambda$ means: $w_{\mathrm{in}} = w_{\mathrm{out}}$.
- $q^c = q^{+u}$ means: $w_{\mathrm{in}} = w_{\mathrm{out}} u$, for some word u with $1 \le |u| \le k$, so $w_{\mathrm{in}} >_r w_{\mathrm{out}}$.
- $q^c = q^{-u}$ means: $w_{\mathrm{out}} = w_{\mathrm{in}} u$, for some word u with $1 \le |u| \le k$, so $w_{\mathrm{in}} <_r w_{\mathrm{out}}$.
- $q^c = q^{A\ell}$ means: $w_{\mathrm{in}} = x\sigma y$, $w_{\mathrm{out}} = x\tau z$, $\sigma >_r \tau$, $\ell = |y| - |z| = d(P')$, and $-k \le \ell \le k$. Note that the A in $q^{A\ell}$ is a reminder of $\sigma >_r \tau$ and indicates that P' could be the prefix of an Accepting computation Q' having $d(Q') \ge 0$, in which case $w'_{\mathrm{in}} >_r w'_{\mathrm{out}}$ where $w'_{\mathrm{in}}/w'_{\mathrm{out}}$ is the label of Q'.

- $q^c = q^{R\ell}$ means: $w_{\text{in}} = x\sigma y$, $w_{\text{out}} = x\tau z$, $\sigma <_r \tau$, $\ell = |y| - |z| = d(P')$, and $-k \le \ell \le k$. Note that the R in $q^{R\ell}$ is a reminder of $\sigma <_r \tau$ and indicates that P' could be the prefix of a Rejecting computation Q' having $d(Q') \le 0$, in which case $w'_{\text{in}} <_r w'_{\text{out}}$ where $w'_{\text{in}}/w'_{\text{out}}$ is the label of Q'.
- $q^c = q^A$ means: $d_{max}(P') > k$ and $d(P') = |w_{\text{in}}| - |w_{\text{out}}| > 0$.
- $q^c = q^R$ means: $d_{max}(P') > k$ and $d(P') = |w_{\text{in}}| - |w_{\text{out}}| < 0$.

Final States in Construction 21. Based on the meaning of the states and the requirement that the label $w_{\text{in}}/w_{\text{out}}$ of an accepting computation P' of $\alpha(\boldsymbol{s})$ satisfies $w_{\text{in}} >_r w_{\text{out}}$, the final states of $\alpha(\boldsymbol{s})$ are shown in (2) further below. Let f be any final state of $\boldsymbol{s}$. State f^A of $\alpha(\boldsymbol{s})$ is final because, if P' ends in f^A, we have $d(P') > 0$, which implies $w_{\text{in}} >_r w_{\text{out}}$. On the other hand, state f^R is not final because any computation P' of $\alpha(\boldsymbol{s})$ ending in f^R has $d(P') < 0$, which implies $w_{\text{in}} <_r w_{\text{out}}$. State $f^{R\ell}$, with $\ell > 0$, is final because any computation P' of $\alpha(\boldsymbol{s})$ ending in $f^{R\ell}$ has $|w_{\text{in}}| - |w_{\text{out}}| = \ell > 0$, so $w_{\text{in}} >_r w_{\text{out}}$. On the other hand, state $f^{R\ell}$, with $\ell \le 0$, is not final because any computation P' of $\alpha(\boldsymbol{s})$ ending in $f^{R\ell}$ has $|w_{\text{in}}| - |w_{\text{out}}| = \ell \le 0$, and $w_{\text{in}} <_r w_{\text{out}}$. □

Example 20. The transducer $\alpha(\boldsymbol{s})$ consists of several modified copies of $\boldsymbol{s}$ (see Fig. 2a) such that, for any $P \in \text{Comput}(\boldsymbol{s})$ with label $w_{\text{in}}/w_{\text{out}}$ there is at least one corresponding computation of $\alpha(\boldsymbol{s})$ with the same label $w_{\text{in}}/w_{\text{out}}$ which goes through copies of the same states appearing in P. The initial states of $\alpha(\boldsymbol{s})$ are in the copy Q^λ, where any computation involving only states in Q^λ has equal input and output labels. For a transition $e = (p, 1/\lambda, q)$ of $\boldsymbol{s}$, $e' = (p^\lambda, 1/\lambda, q^{+1})$ is a transition of $\alpha(\boldsymbol{s})$ corresponding to e, where the transition e' starts at the copy Q^λ of Q and goes to the copy Q^{+1} of Q (see Fig. 2b). In a computation of $\alpha(\boldsymbol{s})$ that ends in the copy Q^{+1}, the input label is of the form $x1$ and the output label is of the form x. Then, Fig. 2c shows all possible transitions from state p^{+1} to other states of $\alpha(\boldsymbol{s})$, which could be in the same or different copies of Q. □

A λ/λ-free transducer is a transducer that has no label λ/λ. Using tools from automata theory, we have that every transducer realizes the same relation as one of a λ/λ-free transducer.

Construction 21. *Let $\boldsymbol{s} = (Q, \Sigma, T, I, F)$ be a λ/λ-free and zero-avoiding transducer with some bound k. The transducer $\alpha(\boldsymbol{s}) = (Q', \Sigma, T', I', F')$ is a C-copy of $\boldsymbol{s}$ as follows. The set C is*

$$\{\lambda, A, R\} \cup \{+u, -u \mid u \in \Sigma^*, 1 \le |u| \le k\} \cup \{A\ell, R\ell \mid \ell \in \mathbb{Z}, -k \le \ell \le k\} \quad (1)$$

We have $Q' = \cup_{c \in C} Q^c$, $I' = I^\lambda$,

$$F' = F^A \cup F^{A0} \cup \big(\cup_{1 \le |u| \le k} F^{+u} \big) \cup \big(\bigcup_{\ell=1}^{k} (F^{A\ell} \cup F^{R\ell}) \big) \quad (2)$$

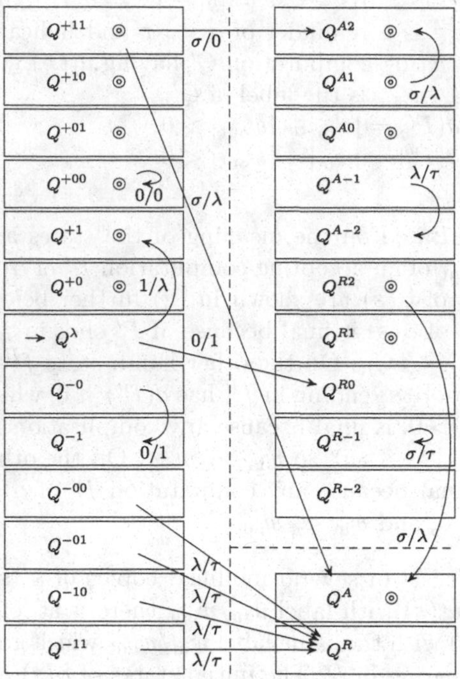

(a) Overview of copies of states of transducer $\boldsymbol{s}$ in transducer $\alpha(\boldsymbol{s})$. The figure also depicts some chosen transitions involving $\sigma, \tau \in \Sigma$. The symbol ◎ represents that the copy contains some final states; initial states are only in copy Q^{λ}.

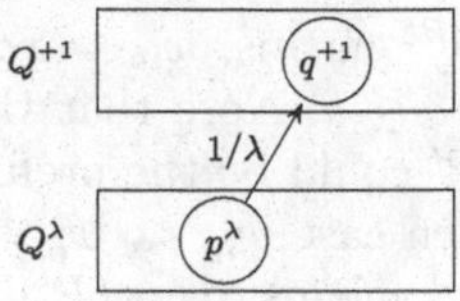

(b) If $(p, 1/\lambda, q)$ is a transition of $\boldsymbol{s}$ then $(p^{\lambda}, 1/\lambda, q^{+1})$ is a transition of $\alpha(\boldsymbol{s})$.

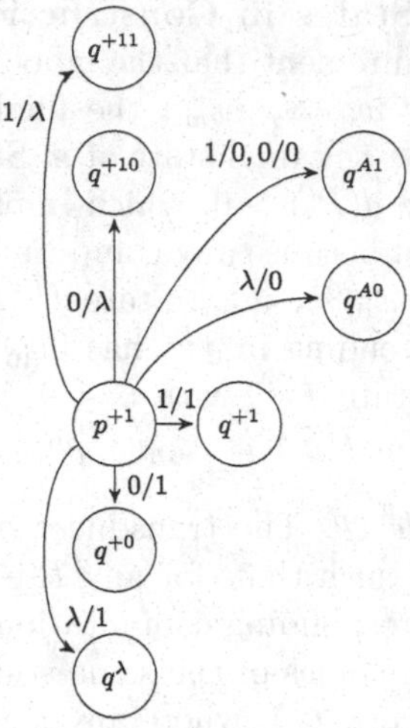

(c) Sketch of transitions in $\alpha(\boldsymbol{s})$, assuming that there are transitions with every possible label from state p to state q of the transducer $\boldsymbol{s}$.

Fig. 2. Sketch of a transducer $\alpha(\boldsymbol{s})$ which is the result of Construction 21 on some transducer $\boldsymbol{s}$. We use $\Sigma = \{0, 1\}$ and $k = 2$. Notice that 0 in Q^{+0} is the string 0 and 0 in Q^{A0} is the number zero (length discrepancy).

The set T' of transitions is defined next. More specifically, for each transition $(p, x/y, q) \in T$, with $x/y \in \{\sigma/\tau, \sigma/\lambda, \lambda/\tau \mid \sigma, \tau \in \Sigma\}$, we define the set $\mathrm{Corr}(p, x/y, q)$. *For each state $p^c \in Q'$ the transition $(p^c, x/y, q^d)$ is in* $\mathrm{Corr}(p, x/y, q)$, *where q^d depends on p^c and x/y as follows.*

If $p^c = p^{\lambda}$:
if $x/y = \sigma/\sigma$ then $q^d = q^{\lambda}$;
if $x/y = \sigma/\tau$ and $\sigma >_r \tau$ then $q^d = q^{A0}$;
if $x/y = \sigma/\tau$ and $\sigma <_r \tau$ then $q^d = q^{R0}$;
if $x/y = \sigma/\lambda$, then $q^d = q^{+\sigma}$ if $k > 0$, and $q^d = q^A$ if $k = 0$;
if $x/y = \lambda/\tau$, then $q^d = q^{-\tau}$ if $k > 0$, and $q^d = q^R$ if $k = 0$.

If $p^c = p^{+u}$:
if $x/y = \sigma/\lambda$ *and* $|u| < k$ *then* $q^d = q^{+u\sigma}$;
if $x/y = \sigma/\lambda$ *and* $|u| = k$ *then* $q^d = q^A$;
if $x/y = \lambda/\tau$ *and* $u[0] = \tau$ *then* $q^d = q^{u[1..]}$;
if $x/y = \lambda/\tau$ *and* $u[0] >_r \tau$ *then* $q^d = q^{A\ell}$ *where* $\ell = |u[1..]|$;
if $x/y = \lambda/\tau$ *and* $u[0] <_r \tau$ *then* $q^d = q^{R\ell}$ *where* $\ell = |u[1..]|$;
if $x/y = \sigma/\tau$ *and* $u[0] = \tau$ *then* $q^d = q^{+u[1..]\sigma}$;
if $x/y = \sigma/\tau$ *and* $u[0] >_r \tau$ *then* $q^d = q^{A\ell}$ *where* $\ell = |u|$;
if $x/y = \sigma/\tau$ *and* $u[0] <_r \tau$ *then* $q^d = q^{R\ell}$ *where* $\ell = |u|$.

If $p^c = p^{-u}$:
if $x/y = \sigma/\lambda$ *and* $u[0] = \sigma$ *then* $q^d = q^{-u[1..]}$;
if $x/y = \sigma/\lambda$ *and* $u[0] >_r \sigma$ *then* $q^d = q^{R\ell}$ *where* $\ell = |u[1..]|$;
if $x/y = \sigma/\lambda$ *and* $u[0] <_r \sigma$ *then* $q^d = q^{A\ell}$ *where* $\ell = |u[1..]|$;
if $x/y = \lambda/\tau$ *and* $|u| < k$ *then* $q^d = q^{-u\tau}$;
if $x/y = \lambda/\tau$ *and* $|u| = k$ *then* $q^d = q^R$;
if $x/y = \sigma/\tau$ *and* $u[0] = \sigma$ *then* $q^d = q^{-u[1..]\tau}$;
if $x/y = \sigma/\tau$ *and* $u[0] >_r \sigma$ *then* $q^d = q^{R\ell}$ *where* $\ell = |u|$;
if $x/y = \sigma/\tau$ *and* $u[0] <_r \sigma$ *then* $q^d = q^{A\ell}$ *where* $\ell = |u|$.

If $p^c = p^{X\ell}$ *with* $X \in \{A, R\}$:
if $x/y = \sigma/\lambda$ *and* $\ell < k$ *then* $q^d = q^{X(\ell+1)}$;
if $x/y = \sigma/\lambda$ *and* $\ell = k$ *then* $q^d = q^A$;
if $x/y = \lambda/\tau$ *and* $\ell > -k$ *then* $q^d = q^{X(\ell-1)}$;
if $x/y = \lambda/\tau$ *and* $\ell = -k$ *then* $q^d = q^R$;
if $x/y = \sigma/\tau$ *then* $q^d = q^{X\ell}$.

If $p^c \in \{p^A, p^R\}$: $q^d = q^c$. □

Remark 22. The transitions of $\alpha(\boldsymbol{s})$ have been defined so that the meaning of the states is preserved. Note that any transition of $\alpha(\boldsymbol{s})$ with source state p^A has a destination state of the form q^A. This is because both $\boldsymbol{s}$ and $\alpha(\boldsymbol{s})$ are zero-avoiding with bound k, so any computation P' of $\alpha(\boldsymbol{s})$ ending at p^A has $d_{max}(P') > k$ and $d(P') > 0$ and, moreover, any computation Q' of $\alpha(\boldsymbol{s})$ having P' as prefix will be such that $d_{max}(Q') > k$ and $d(Q') > 0$. For similar reasons, any transition of $\alpha(\boldsymbol{s})$ with source state p^R has a destination state of the form q^R.

Lemma 23. *Let* $\boldsymbol{s}$ *be a* λ/λ*-free and zero-avoiding transducer. The transducer* $\alpha(\boldsymbol{s})$ *in Construction 21 is such that* $\mathrm{R}(\alpha(\boldsymbol{s})) = \mathrm{R}(\boldsymbol{s}) \cap \{u/v : u >_r v\}$.

The below theorem solves effectively the rational asymmetric partition problem for every irreflexive relation realized by some zero-avoiding transducer.

Theorem 24. *Let* $\boldsymbol{s}$ *be any input-altering and zero-avoiding transducer with some bound* $k \geq 0$. *Let* $\boldsymbol{t}_1 = \alpha(\boldsymbol{s})$ *and let* $\boldsymbol{t}_2 = \left(\alpha(\boldsymbol{s}^{-1})\right)^{-1}$, *where* $\alpha(\boldsymbol{s})$ *is the transducer produced in Construction 21. Then,* $\{\mathrm{R}(\boldsymbol{t}_1), \mathrm{R}(\boldsymbol{t}_2)\}$ *is a rational asymmetric partition of* $\mathrm{R}(\boldsymbol{s})$.

Now we have the following consequence of Theorem 24 and Proposition 19.

Corollary 25. *Every left synchronous and every right synchronous irreflexive rational relation has a rational asymmetric partition.*

8 An Unsolved Case and a Variation of the Problem

Recall that Theorem 24 solves the rational asymmetric partition problem for any irreflexive relation realized by some zero-avoiding transducer. The main open question is the following.

Open Question. *Does there exist any rational irreflexive relation that has no rational asymmetric partition?* If this turns out to be difficult, what about adding a restriction to the rational irreflexive relation (being symmetric or other)?

We also offer a more specific open question. Consider the rational symmetric relation: $R = R_1 \cup R_1^{-1} \cup R_2 \cup R_2^{-1}$, where

$$R_1 = \{(0^a 1^i 0^j 1^b / 0^i 1^c 0^j 1^d) \mid a, b, c, d, i, j \in \mathbb{N}\} \quad \text{and}$$
$$R_2 = \{(0^a 1^i 0^j 1^b / 0^c 1^i 0^d 1^j) \mid a, b, c, d, i, j \in \mathbb{N}\}.$$

The more specific question is the following: *Does there exist a rational asymmetric relation A such that $A \cup A^{-1} = R$?*

We note the following facts about R: (i) $R_1 \cap R_2 = \{(0^a 1^i 0^j 1^b, 0^i 1^i 0^j 1^j) \mid a, b, i, j \in \mathbb{N}\}$ is not rational. (ii) Also non rational are: $R_1 \cap R_1^{-1}$, $R_1 \cap R_2^{-1}$, $R_2 \cap R_1^{-1}$, $R_1 \cap R_1^{-1}$, $R_1^{-1} \cap R_2^{-1}$, $R_1 \cap R_1^{-1}$. (iii) Also non-rational is the intersection $R_1 \cap R_1^{-1} \cap R_2 \cap R_2^{-1}$.

Lemma 23 implies that every zero-avoiding and irreflexive-and-symmetric rational relation S has a rational partition according to the order $[>_r]$; that is, $\{S \cap [>_r], S \cap [<_r]\}$ is a rational partition of S. A question that arises here is whether there are examples of irreflexive-and-symmetric rational S for which at least one of $S \cap [>], S \cap [<]$ is not rational, where $[>]$ is a fixed total asymmetry. The question would be answered if we find an asymmetric rational A such that at least one of $S \cap [>], S \cap [<]$ is not rational, where $S = A \cup A^{-1}$.

The Rational Non-partition Problem for a Fixed Asymmetry. Let $[>]$ be a fixed total asymmetry. Is there an asymmetric rational relation A such that at least one of $(A \cup A^{-1}) \cap [>]$ and $(A \cup A^{-1}) \cap [<]$ is not rational? If the answer is yes, then A is called a rational non-partition witness for $[>]$; else, A is called a rational partition witness for $[>]$.

Proposition 26. *There are asymmetric rational relations A, B such that (i) A is a rational non-partition witness for $[>_r]$ and a rational partition witness for $[>_l]$; (ii) B is a rational non-partition witness for both $[>_r]$ and $[>_l]$.*

9 Conclusions

Motivated by the embedding problem for rationally independent languages, we have introduced the rational asymmetric partition problem. Our aim was to find the largest class of rational relations that have a rational asymmetric partition. In doing so we introduced zero-avoiding transducers. These define a class of rational relations that properly contain the left and right synchronous relations and admit rational asymmetric partitions. Whether all rational relations admit such partitions remains open.

Acknowledgement. We thank Jacques Sakarovitch for looking at this open problem and offering the opinion that it indeed appears to be non trivial.

References

1. Berstel, J.: Transductions and Context-Free Languages. B.G. Teubner, Stuttgart (1979)
2. Carton, O.: Left and right synchronous relations. In: Diekert, V., Nowotka, D. (eds.) DLT 2009. LNCS, vol. 5583, pp. 170–182. Springer, Heidelberg (2009). https://doi.org/10.1007/978-3-642-02737-6_13
3. Choffrut, C.: Relations over words and logic: a chronology. Bull. Eur. Assoc. Theor. Comput. Sci. EATCS **89**, 159–163 (2006)
4. Hopcroft, J.E., Ullman, J.D.: Introduction to Automata Theory, Languages, and Computation. Addison-Wesley, Reading (1979)
5. Konstantinidis, S., Mastnak, M.: Embedding rationally independent languages into maximal ones. J. Autom. Lang. Comb. **21**, 311–338 (2016)
6. Rozenberg, G., Salomaa, A. (eds.): Handbook of Formal Languages, vol. 1. Springer, Heidelberg (1997). https://doi.org/10.1007/978-3-642-59136-5
7. Sakarovitch, J.: Elements of Automata Theory. Cambridge University Press, Cambridge (2009)
8. Shyr, H.J., Thierrin, G.: Codes and binary relations. In: Malliavin, M.P. (ed.) Séminaire d'Algèbre Paul Dubreil Paris 1975–1976 (29ème Année). LNM, vol. 586, pp. 180–188. Springer, Heidelberg (1977). https://doi.org/10.1007/BFb0087133
9. Yu, S.: Regular languages. In: Rozenberg, Salomaa [6], pp. 41–110. https://doi.org/10.1007/978-3-642-59136-5_2
10. Yu, S.S.: Languages and Codes. Tsang Hai Book Publishing, Taichung (2005)

Partial Derivatives of Regular Expressions over Alphabet-Invariant and User-Defined Labels

Stavros Konstantinidis[1(✉)], Nelma Moreira[2], João Pires[2], and Rogério Reis[2]

[1] Saint Mary's University, Halifax, NS, Canada
s.konstantinidis@smu.ca

[2] CMUP and DCC, Faculdade de Ciências da Universidade do Porto, Rua do Campo Alegre, 4169-007 Porto, Portugal
{nam,rvr}@dcc.fc.up.pt

Abstract. We are interested in regular expressions that represent word relations in an alphabet-invariant way—for example, the set of all word pairs u, v where v is a prefix of u independently of what the alphabet is. This is the second part of a recent paper on this topic which focused on labelled graphs (transducers and automata) with alphabet-invariant and user-defined labels. In this paper we study derivatives of regular expressions over labels (atomic objects) in some set B. These labels can be any strings as long as the strings represent subsets of a certain monoid. We show that one can define partial derivative labelled graphs of type B expressions, whose transition labels can be elements of another label set X as long as X and B refer to the same monoid. We also show how to use derivatives directly to decide whether a given word pair is in the relation of a regular expression over pairing specs. Set specs and pairing specs are useful label sets allowing one to express languages and relations over large alphabets in a natural and compact way.

Keywords: Alphabet-invariant expressions · Regular expressions · Partial derivatives · Algorithms · Monoids

1 Introduction

We are interested in regular expressions whose alphabet is not of fixed cardinality, or whose alphabet is even unknown. Consider the alphabet $\Gamma = \{0, 1, \ldots, n-1\}$, where n is variable, and the 2D regular expressions[1]

$$\big(0/0 + \cdots + (n-1)/(n-1)\big)^* \big(0/\mathbf{e} + \cdots + (n-1)/\mathbf{e}\big)^*, \quad (1)$$

$$\big(0/0 + \cdots + (n-1)/(n-1)\big)^* \ \big(\boldsymbol{r}_0 + \cdots + \boldsymbol{r}_{n-1}\big) \ \big(0/0 + \cdots + (n-1)/(n-1)\big)^* \quad (2)$$

[1] These are expressions for word relations.

Research supported by NSERC (Canada) and by FCT project UID/MAT/00144/2019 (Portugal).

M. Hospodár and G. Jirásková (Eds.): CIAA 2019, LNCS 11601, pp. 184–196, 2019.
https://doi.org/10.1007/978-3-030-23679-3_15

where $\mathbf{e}$ represents the empty string, and each $\boldsymbol{r}_i$ is the sum of all i/j with $j \neq i$ and $i, j \in \Gamma$. The first expression has $O(n)$ symbols and represents the prefix relation, that is, all word pairs (u, v) such that v is a prefix of u. The second regular expression has $O(n^2)$ symbols and represents all word pairs (u, v) such that the Hamming distance of u, v is 1. We want to be able to use special labels in expressions such as those in the expression below.

$$(\forall/{=})^* \ (\forall/\forall{\neq}) \ (\forall/{=})^*. \tag{3}$$

The label $(\forall/{=})$ represents the set $\{(a, a) \mid a \in \Gamma\}$ and the label $(\forall/\forall{\neq})$ represents the set $\{(a, a') \mid a, a' \in \Gamma, a \neq a'\}$ (these labels are called *pairing specs*). This expression has only a fixed number of symbols. Similarly, using these special labels, the expression (1) can be written as

$$(\forall/{=})^*(\forall/\mathbf{e})^*. \tag{4}$$

Note that the new regular expressions are *alphabet invariant* as they contain no symbol of the intended alphabet Γ.

The present paper is the continuation of the recent paper [10] on the topic of labelled graphs (e.g., automata, transducers) and regular expressions whose labels are strings such that each string represents a subset of a specific monoid. The intention is to define algorithms that *work directly* on regular expressions and graphs with special labels, without of course having to expand these labels to sets of monoid elements. Thus, for example, we would like to have an algorithm that computes whether a pair (u, v) of words is in the relation represented by either of the expressions (3) and (4). While the first paper [10] focused on labelled graphs, the present paper focuses on derivatives of regular expressions over any desirable set of labels B. An expression with special labels in this work can be considered to be a *syntactic version* of a regular expression over some monoid M in the sense of [16].

Paper Structure and Main Results. The next section discusses *alphabets* Γ of non-fixed size and provides a summary of concepts from [10]. In particular, a *label set* B is a nonempty set such that each $\beta \in B$ is simply a nonempty string that represents a subset $\mathcal{I}(\beta)$ of a monoid denoted by $\mathsf{mon}\, B$. Section 3 defines the set of partial derivatives $\mathsf{PD}(\boldsymbol{r})$ of any type B regular expression $\boldsymbol{r}$, where $\mathsf{mon}\, B$ is a graded monoid. As in [1], partial derivatives are defined via the concept of linear form $\mathsf{n}(\boldsymbol{r})$ of $\boldsymbol{r}$. Here we define partial derivatives $\partial_x(\boldsymbol{r})$ of $\boldsymbol{r}$ *with respect to* $x \in X$, where X is a second label set (which could be B) such that $\mathsf{mon}\, X = \mathsf{mon}\, B$. Theorem 1 says that the set $\mathsf{PD}(\boldsymbol{r})$ of partial derivatives of $\boldsymbol{r}$ is finite. Section 4 defines the type X graph $\hat{a}_{\mathrm{PD}}(\boldsymbol{r})$ corresponding to any given type B regular expression $\boldsymbol{r}$ and shows (Theorem 2) that $\hat{a}_{\mathrm{PD}}(\boldsymbol{r})$ and $\boldsymbol{r}$ have the same behaviour. We note that the states of $\hat{a}_{\mathrm{PD}}(\boldsymbol{r})$ are elements of $\mathsf{PD}(\boldsymbol{r})$ and the transitions of $\hat{a}_{\mathrm{PD}}(\boldsymbol{r})$ are elements of X. Section 5 uses derivatives to decide whether a given word pair is in the relation represented by a regular expression involving pairing specs, without constructing the associated transducer (Theorem 3).

2 Terminology and Summary of Concepts from [10]

The set of positive integers is denoted by $\mathbb{N}$. Then, $\mathbb{N}_0 = \mathbb{N} \cup \{0\}$. An *alphabet space* Ω is an infinite and totally ordered set whose elements are called *symbols*. We shall assume that Ω is fixed and contains the digits $0, 1, \ldots, 9$ and the letters $\mathtt{a}, \mathtt{b}, \ldots, \mathtt{z}$, which are ordered as usual, as well as the following *special symbols:* $\forall$, $\exists$, $\nexists$, $=$, $\neq$, $/$, $\mathbf{e}$, $\oplus$, $\oslash$.

As usual we use the term *string* or *word* to refer to any finite sequence of symbols. The *empty string* is denoted by ε. Let $g \in \Omega$ and w be a string. The expression $|w|_g$ denotes the number of occurrences of g in w, and the expression $\mathsf{alph}\, w$ denotes the set $\{g \in \Omega : |w|_g > 0\}$, that is, the set of symbols that occur in w. For example, $\mathsf{alph}(1122010) = \{0, 1, 2\}$.

An *alphabet* is any finite nonempty subset of Ω. In the following definitions we shall consider alphabets Σ, Δ as well as an alphabet Γ, called the alphabet of *reference*, and we assume that Γ *contains at least two symbols and no special symbols* and that Γ is not of fixed size (it is unbounded). Let Σ, Δ be alphabets. A (binary word) *relation* of type $[\Sigma, \Delta]$ is a subset R of $\Sigma^* \times \Delta^*$.

2.1 Set Specifications and Pairing Specifications

Set specs are intended to represent nonempty subsets of the alphabet Γ. These can be used as labels in automata-type objects (labelled graphs) and regular expressions defined in subsequent sections.

Definition 1. *A* set specification, *or* set spec *for short, is any string of one of the three forms* $\forall$, $\exists w$, $\nexists w$, *where* w *is any sorted nonempty string containing no repeated symbols and no special symbols. The set of set specs is denoted by* SSP.

Definition 2. *Let* Γ *be an alphabet of reference and let* F *be a set spec. We say that* F respects Γ, *if the following restrictions hold when* F *is of the form* $\exists w$ *or* $\nexists w$: "$w \in \Gamma^*$ *and* $0 < |w| < |\Gamma|$." *In this case, the* language $\mathcal{L}(F)$ *of* F (with respect *to* Γ) *is the subset of* Γ *defined as follows:* $\mathcal{L}(\forall) = \Gamma$, $\mathcal{L}(\exists w) = \mathsf{alph}\, w$, $\mathcal{L}(\nexists w) = \Gamma \setminus \mathsf{alph}\, w$. *The set of set specs that respect* Γ *is denoted as* $\mathrm{SSP}[\Gamma] = \{\alpha \in \mathrm{SSP} \mid \alpha \text{ respects } \Gamma\}$.

Now we define expressions for describing certain finite relations that are subsets of $\big((\Gamma \cup \{\varepsilon\}) \times (\Gamma \cup \{\varepsilon\})\big) \setminus \{(\varepsilon, \varepsilon)\}$.

Definition 3. *A* pairing specification, *or* pairing spec *for short, is a string of one the five forms* $\mathbf{e}/G, F/\mathbf{e}, F/G, F/{=}, F/G{\neq}$, *where* F, G *are set specs. The set of pairing specs is denoted by* PSP. *A pairing spec is called* alphabet invariant *if it contains no set spec of the form* $\exists w, \nexists w$. *The alphabet invariant pairing specs are* $\mathbf{e}/\forall, \forall/\mathbf{e}, \forall/\forall, \forall/{=}, \forall/\forall{\neq}$.

Definition 4. *Let* Γ *be an alphabet of reference and let* p *be a pairing spec. We say that* p respects Γ, *if any set spec occurring in* p *respects* Γ. *The set of* *pairing specs that respect Γ is denoted as* $\mathrm{PSP}[\Gamma] = \{\mathsf{p} \in \mathrm{PSP} : \mathsf{p}$ *respects* $\Gamma\}$. *The* relation $\mathcal{R}(\mathsf{p})$ *described by* p *(with respect to* Γ*) is the subset of* $\Gamma^* \times \Gamma^*$ *defined as follows.*

$\mathcal{R}(\mathbf{e}/G) = \{(\varepsilon, y) \mid y \in \mathcal{L}(G)\}$; $\mathcal{R}(F/\mathbf{e}) = \{(x, \varepsilon) \mid x \in \mathcal{L}(F)\}$;
$\mathcal{R}(F/G) = \{(x, y) \mid x \in \mathcal{L}(F), y \in \mathcal{L}(G)\}$; $\mathcal{R}(F/{=}) = \{(x, x) \mid x \in \mathcal{L}(F)\}$;
$\mathcal{R}(F/G{\neq}) = \{(x, y) \mid x \in \mathcal{L}(F), y \in \mathcal{L}(G), x \neq y\}$.

2.2 Label Sets and Their Monoid Behaviours

We shall use the notation ε_M for the *neutral element* of the monoid M. If S, S' are any two subsets of M then, as usual, we define $SS' = \{mm' \mid m \in S, m' \in S'\}$, $S^i = S^{i-1}S$ and $S^* = \cup_{i=0}^{\infty} S^i$, where $S^0 = \{\varepsilon_M\}$ and the monoid operation is denoted by simply concatenating elements. We shall only consider *finitely generated* monoids M where each $m \in M$ has a *canonical* (string) representation $\underline{m}$. Then, we write $\underline{M} = \{\underline{m} \mid m \in M\}$.

Example 1. We shall consider two standard monoids. (i) The free monoid Γ^* whose neutral element is ε. The canonical representation of a nonempty word w is w itself and that of ε is $\mathbf{e}$, that is, $\underline{\varepsilon} = \mathbf{e}$. (ii) The monoid $\Sigma^* \times \Delta^*$ (or $\Gamma^* \times \Gamma^*$) whose neutral element is $(\varepsilon, \varepsilon)$. The canonical representation of a word pair (u, v) is $\underline{u}/\underline{v}$. In particular, $\underline{(\varepsilon, \varepsilon)} = \mathbf{e}/\mathbf{e}$.

A *label set* B is a nonempty set of nonempty strings (over Ω). A *label behaviour* is a mapping $\mathcal{I} : B \to 2^M$, where M is a monoid. Thus, the behaviour $\mathcal{I}(\beta)$ is a subset of M. We shall consider label sets B with *fixed behaviours*, so we shall denote by $\mathsf{mon}\, B$ the *monoid of* B via its fixed behaviour.

We shall make the *convention* that for any label sets B_1, B_2 with fixed behaviours $\mathcal{I}_1, \mathcal{I}_2$, if $\mathsf{mon}\, B_1 = \mathsf{mon}\, B_2$ then $\mathcal{I}_1(\beta) = \mathcal{I}_2(\beta)$, for all $\beta \in B_1 \cap B_2$. With this convention we can simply use a single behaviour notation $\mathcal{I}$ for all label sets with the same behaviour monoid, that is, we shall use $\mathcal{I}$ for any B_1, B_2 with $\mathsf{mon}\, B_1 = \mathsf{mon}\, B_2$. This convention is applied in the example below: we use $\mathcal{L}$ for the behaviour of both the label sets Σ and $\mathrm{SSP}[\Gamma]$.

Example 2. We shall use the following label sets and their fixed label behaviours.

1. Σ with behaviour $\mathcal{L} : \Sigma \to 2^{\Sigma^*}$ such that $\mathcal{L}(g) = \{g\}$, for $g \in \Sigma$. Thus, $\mathsf{mon}\, \Sigma = \Sigma^*$.
2. $\mathrm{SSP}[\Gamma]$ with behaviour $\mathcal{L} : \mathrm{SSP}[\Gamma] \to 2^{\Gamma^*}$, as specified in Definition 2. Thus, $\mathsf{mon}\, \mathrm{SSP}[\Gamma] = \Gamma^*$.
3. $[\Sigma, \Delta] = \{x/y \mid x \in \Sigma \cup \{\mathbf{e}\}, y \in \Delta \cup \{\mathbf{e}\}\} \setminus \{\mathbf{e}/\mathbf{e}\}$ with behaviour $\mathcal{R}()$ such that $\mathcal{R}(x/\mathbf{e}) = \{(x, \varepsilon)\}$, $\mathcal{R}(\mathbf{e}/y) = \{(\varepsilon, y)\}$, $\mathcal{R}(x/y) = \{(x, y)\}$, for any $x \in \Sigma$ and $y \in \Delta$. Thus, $\mathsf{mon}[\Sigma, \Delta] = \Sigma^* \times \Delta^*$.
4. $\mathrm{PSP}[\Gamma]$ with behaviour $\mathcal{R} : \mathrm{PSP}[\Gamma] \to 2^{\Gamma^* \times \Gamma^*}$ as specified in Definition 4. Thus, $\mathsf{mon}\, \mathrm{PSP}[\Gamma] = \Gamma^* \times \Gamma^*$.
5. If B_1, B_2 are label sets with behaviours $\mathcal{I}_1, \mathcal{I}_2$, respectively, then $[B_1, B_2]$ is the label set $\{\beta_1/\beta_2 \mid \beta_1 \in B_1, \beta_2 \in B_2\}$ with behaviour and monoid such that $\mathcal{I}(\beta_1/\beta_2) = \mathcal{I}_1(\beta_1) \times \mathcal{I}_2(\beta_2)$ and $\mathsf{mon}[B_1, B_2] = \mathsf{mon}\, B_1 \times \mathsf{mon}\, B_2$.

For any monoid of interest M and $m \in M$, $\underline{M}$ is a label set such that $\mathsf{mon}\,\underline{M} = M$ and $\mathcal{I}(\underline{m}) = \{m\}$. Thus, $\mathcal{I}(\underline{\varepsilon_M}) = \{\varepsilon_M\}$. Also, as $\mathsf{mon}\,\mathrm{PSP}[\Gamma] = \mathsf{mon}\,\underline{\Gamma^* \times \Gamma^*} = \Gamma^* \times \Gamma^*$ and the behaviour of PSP is denoted by $\mathcal{R}$, we have $\mathcal{R}(\underline{(0,1)}) = \mathcal{R}(0/1) = \{(0,1)\} = \mathcal{R}(\exists 0/\exists 1)$.

2.3 Labelled Graphs, Automata, Transducers

Let B be a label set with behaviour $\mathcal{I}$. A ***type*** B ***graph*** is a quintuple $\hat{g} = (Q, B, \delta, I, F)$ such that Q is a nonempty set whose elements are called ***states***; $I \subseteq Q$ is the nonempty set of initial, or start states; $F \subseteq Q$ is the set of final states; δ is a set, called the set of ***edges*** or ***transitions***, consisting of triples (p, β, q) such that $p, q \in Q$ and $\beta \in B \cup \{\underline{\varepsilon_{\mathsf{mon}\,B}}\}$. The set of ***labels of*** $\hat{g}$ is the set $\mathrm{Labels}(\hat{g}) = \{\beta \mid (p, \beta, q) \in \delta\}$. We shall use the term ***labelled graph*** to mean a type B graph as defined above, for some label set B. The labelled graph is called ***finite*** if Q and δ are both finite. *In the sequel, a labelled graph will be assumed to be finite.* A ***path*** P of $\hat{g}$ is a sequence of consecutive transitions, that is, $P = \langle q_{i-1}, \beta_i, q_i \rangle_{i=1}^{\ell}$ such that each (q_{i-1}, β_i, q_i) is in δ. The path P is called ***accepting***, if $q_0 \in I$ and $q_\ell \in F$. If $\ell = 0$ then P is empty and it is an accepting path if $I \cap F \neq \emptyset$.

Definition 5. *Let* $\hat{g} = (Q, B, \delta, I, F)$ *be a labelled graph, for some label set* B *with behaviour* $\mathcal{I}$. *We define the* behaviour $\mathcal{I}(\hat{g})$ *of* $\hat{g}$ *as the set of all* $m \in \mathsf{mon}\,B$ *such that there is an accepting path* $\langle q_{i-1}, \beta_i, q_i \rangle_{i=1}^{\ell}$ *of* $\hat{g}$ *with* $m \in \mathcal{I}(\beta_1) \cdots \mathcal{I}(\beta_\ell)$. *The* expansion $\exp \hat{g}$ *of* $\hat{g}$ *is the labelled graph* $(Q, \underline{\mathsf{mon}\,B}, \delta_{\exp}, I, F)$ *such that* $\delta_{\exp} = \{(p, \underline{m}, q) \mid \exists\, (p, \beta, q) \in \delta : m \in \mathcal{I}(\beta)\}$.

Lemma 1. *For each labelled graph* $\hat{g}$, *we have that* $\mathcal{I}(\hat{g}) = \mathcal{I}(\exp \hat{g})$.

Example 3. Let Σ, Δ, Γ be alphabets. An ***automaton***, or ***ε-NFA***, is a labelled graph $\hat{a} = (Q, \Sigma, \delta, I, F)$. If $\mathrm{Labels}(\hat{a}) \subseteq \Sigma$ then $\hat{a}$ is called an NFA. The language $\mathcal{L}(\hat{a})$ is the behaviour of $\hat{a}$. An ***automaton with set specs*** is a labelled graph $\hat{b} = (Q, \mathrm{SSP}[\Gamma], \delta, I, F)$. The ***language*** $\mathcal{L}(\hat{b})$ is the behaviour of $\hat{b}$. A ***transducer (in standard form)*** is a labelled graph $\hat{t} = (Q, [\Sigma, \Delta], \delta, I, F)$. The ***relation*** $\mathcal{R}(\hat{t})$ realized by $\hat{t}$ is the behaviour of $\hat{t}$. A ***transducer with set specs*** is a labelled graph $\hat{s} = (Q, \mathrm{PSP}[\Gamma], \delta, I, F)$. The ***relation*** $\mathcal{R}(\hat{s})$ ***realized*** by $\hat{s}$ is the behaviour of $\hat{s}$.

2.4 Regular Expressions over Label Sets

We extend the definition of regular expressions to include set specs and pairing specs, respectively. We start off with a definition that would work with any label set (called set of atomic formulas in [16]).

Definition 6. *Let* B *be a label set with behaviour* $\mathcal{I}$ *such that no* $\beta \in B$ *contains the special symbol* $\oslash$. *The set* REG B *of* type B regular expressions *is the set of strings consisting of the 1-symbol string* $\oslash$ *and the strings in the set* Z *that is defined inductively as follows: (i)* $\underline{\varepsilon_{\mathsf{mon}\,B}}$ *is in* Z. *(ii) Every* $\beta \in B$ *is in* Z. *(iii)*

If $r, s \in Z$ then $(r+s), (rs), (r^*)$ are in Z. The behaviour $\mathcal{I}(r)$ *of a type B regular expression r is defined inductively as follows.*

- $\mathcal{I}(\oslash) = \emptyset$ *and* $\mathcal{I}(\varepsilon_{\mathsf{mon}\,B}) = \{\varepsilon_{\mathsf{mon}\,B}\}$*;*
- $\mathcal{I}(\beta)$ *is the subset of* $\mathsf{mon}\,B$ *already defined by the behaviour* $\mathcal{I}$ *on* B*;*
- $\mathcal{I}(r+s) = \mathcal{I}(r) \cup \mathcal{I}(s)$*;* $\mathcal{I}(rs) = \mathcal{I}(r)\mathcal{I}(s)$*;* $\mathcal{I}(r^*) = \mathcal{I}(r)^*$.

Example 4. Using Σ as a label set, we have that REGΣ is the set of ordinary regular expressions over Σ. For the label set $[\Sigma, \Delta]$, we have that REG$[\Sigma, \Delta]$ is the set of rational expressions over $\Sigma^* \times \Delta^*$ in the sense of [16]. The expressions (3) and (4) are examples of type PSP$[\Gamma]$ regular expressions.

3 Partial Derivatives of Type B Regular Expressions

Here we consider any label set B with some behaviour $\mathcal{I}$ such that no $\beta \in B$ contains the special symbol $\oslash$, and we define the partial derivatives of a type B regular expression r w.r.t. an element $x \in X$, where X is also a label set such that $\mathsf{mon}\,B = \mathsf{mon}\,X$. The intention is that further below (Sect. 4) one can define the labelled graph corresponding to r such that the states are partial derivatives of r (type B regular expressions) and the transition labels are in X.

Derivative based methods for the manipulation of regular expressions have been widely studied [1,3–5,7,11,12]. In recent years, partial derivative automata were defined and characterised for several kinds of expressions. Not only they are in general more succinct than other equivalent constructions but also for several operators they are easily defined (e.g. for intersection [2] or tuples [8]). The partial derivative automaton of an ordinary (type Σ) regular expression was introduced independently by Mirkin [12] and Antimirov [1]. Champarnaud and Ziadi [6] proved that the two formulations are equivalent. Lombardy and Sakarovitch [11] generalised these constructions to weighted regular expressions, and recently Demaille [8] defined derivative automata for multitape weighted regular expressions.

Without further mention, the operator $\mathcal{I}$ as well as the operators $\mathsf{n}, \mathsf{c}, \downarrow_2, \pi_i, \pi$ defined below are extended in a union-respecting way, i.e $\phi(S) = \cup_{s \in S}\phi(s)$ for any operator ϕ.

Our Assumptions About the Label Set B and the Monoid $\mathsf{mon}\,B$:

$$\forall \beta \in B : \mathcal{I}(\beta) \neq \emptyset \tag{5}$$

$$\forall \beta \in B : \mathcal{I}(\beta) \neq \{\varepsilon_{\mathsf{mon}\,B}\}. \tag{6}$$

Moreover we shall assume that $\mathsf{mon}\,B$ is a ***graded monoid***, [15, p. 383]. For our purposes, we only need the following implication of this assumption.

$$\forall m_1, m_2 \in \mathsf{mon}\,B : \; m_1 m_2 = \varepsilon_{\mathsf{mon}\,B} \longrightarrow m_1 = m_2 = \varepsilon_{\mathsf{mon}\,B}. \tag{7}$$

The *size* of an expression r is inductively defined as follows:

$\|\oslash\| = 0$, $\|\varepsilon_{\mathsf{mon}\,B}\| = 0$, $\|\beta\| = 1$

$\|\boldsymbol{r}+\boldsymbol{s}\| = \|\boldsymbol{r}\| + \|\boldsymbol{s}\|$, $\|\boldsymbol{rs}\| = \|\boldsymbol{r}\| + \|\boldsymbol{s}\|$, $\|\boldsymbol{r}^*\| = \|\boldsymbol{r}\|$.

We define the *constant part* $\mathsf{c} : \mathrm{REG}\, B \to \{\underline{\varepsilon_{\mathsf{mon}\,B}}, \oslash\}$ by $\mathsf{c}(\boldsymbol{r}) = \underline{\varepsilon_{\mathsf{mon}\,B}}$ if $\varepsilon_{\mathsf{mon}\,B} \in \mathcal{I}(\boldsymbol{r})$, and $\mathsf{c}(\boldsymbol{r}) = \oslash$ otherwise. For a set R of regular expressions, $\mathsf{c}(R) = \underline{\varepsilon_{\mathsf{mon}\,B}}$ if and only if there exists $\boldsymbol{r} \in R$ such that $\mathsf{c}(\boldsymbol{r}) = \underline{\varepsilon_{\mathsf{mon}\,B}}$.

The Second Label Set X. The linear form $\mathsf{n}(\boldsymbol{r})$ of a regular expression $\boldsymbol{r}$, defined below, is a set of pairs $(x, \boldsymbol{r}')$, in which case $\boldsymbol{r}'$ is a partial derivative of $\boldsymbol{r}$ *with respect to* $x \in X$. The label set X is such that $\mathsf{mon}\, X = \mathsf{mon}\, B$. When the following condition (8) is satisfied, the partial derivative graph of $\boldsymbol{r}$ can be defined (Sect. 4) and will have as states the partial derivatives of $\boldsymbol{r}$, including $\boldsymbol{r}$, and transitions $(\boldsymbol{r}_1, x, \boldsymbol{r}_2)$ when $(x, \boldsymbol{r}_2) \in \mathsf{n}(\boldsymbol{r}_1)$.

$$\forall \beta \in B : \mathcal{I}(\beta) = \mathcal{I}(\mathsf{c}(\beta)) \cup \mathcal{I}(\mathsf{n}(\beta)). \tag{8}$$

Some Notation. Let $\beta \in B$ and let $\boldsymbol{r}, \boldsymbol{r}', \boldsymbol{s}, \boldsymbol{s}', \boldsymbol{z} \in \mathrm{REG}\, B \setminus \{\oslash\}$ such that $\mathcal{I}(\boldsymbol{s}) \neq \{\varepsilon_{\mathsf{mon}\,B}\}$, $\mathcal{I}(\boldsymbol{s}') \neq \{\varepsilon_{\mathsf{mon}\,B}\}$, $\mathcal{I}(\boldsymbol{z}) = \{\varepsilon_{\mathsf{mon}\,B}\}$. The binary operation $\diamond$ between any two expressions in $\mathrm{REG}\, B \setminus \{\oslash\}$ is defined as follows: $\boldsymbol{r} \diamond \boldsymbol{z} = \boldsymbol{z} \diamond \boldsymbol{r} = \boldsymbol{r}$ and $\boldsymbol{s} \diamond \boldsymbol{s}' = \boldsymbol{ss}'$. For any $\tilde{S} \subseteq X \times (\mathrm{REG}\, B \setminus \{\oslash\})$, we define $\mathcal{I}(\tilde{S}) = \bigcup_{(x,\boldsymbol{s}) \in \tilde{S}} \mathcal{I}(x)\mathcal{I}(\boldsymbol{s})$ and

$$\oslash \tilde{S} = \emptyset, \ \tilde{S}\boldsymbol{s}' = \{ (x, \boldsymbol{s} \diamond \boldsymbol{s}') \mid (x, \boldsymbol{s}) \in \tilde{S} \}, \ \boldsymbol{s}'\tilde{S} = \{ (x, \boldsymbol{s}' \diamond \boldsymbol{s}) \mid (x, \boldsymbol{s}) \in \tilde{S} \}.$$

For any $R \subseteq \mathrm{REG}\, B \setminus \{\oslash\}$, we also define $\oslash R = \emptyset$, $R\boldsymbol{s}' = \{ \boldsymbol{s} \diamond \boldsymbol{s}' \mid \boldsymbol{s} \in R \}$, $\boldsymbol{s}'R = \{ \boldsymbol{s}' \diamond \boldsymbol{s} \mid \boldsymbol{s} \in R \}$.

Definition 7. *A* linear form *(of type (X, B)) of a regular expression is defined inductively as follows:*

$$\mathsf{n}(\oslash) = \emptyset, \quad \mathsf{n}(\underline{\varepsilon_{\mathsf{mon}\,B}}) = \emptyset,$$
$$\mathsf{n}(\beta) = \textit{a chosen finite nonempty subset of } X \times \{\underline{\varepsilon_{\mathsf{mon}\,B}}\},$$
$$\mathsf{n}(\boldsymbol{r} + \boldsymbol{r}') = \mathsf{n}(\boldsymbol{r}) \cup \mathsf{n}(\boldsymbol{r}'), \quad \mathsf{n}(\boldsymbol{rr}') = \mathsf{n}(\boldsymbol{r})\boldsymbol{r}' \cup \mathsf{c}(\boldsymbol{r})\, \mathsf{n}(\boldsymbol{r}'), \quad \mathsf{n}(\boldsymbol{r}^*) = \mathsf{n}(\boldsymbol{r})\boldsymbol{r}^*.$$

Example 5. The default linear form: $X = B$ and $\forall \beta \in B : \mathsf{n}(\beta) = \{(\beta, \underline{\varepsilon_{\mathsf{mon}\,B}})\}$. Trivially, this n satisfies condition (8). *The* expanding linear form: when

$$\mathcal{I}(\beta) \subseteq \Phi, \quad X = \underline{\Phi}, \quad \forall \beta \in B : \mathsf{n}(\beta) = \{(\underline{m}, \underline{\varepsilon_{\mathsf{mon}\,B}}) \mid m \in \mathcal{I}(\beta)\},$$

where Φ is a finite set of generators of $\mathsf{mon}\, B$. Again, the expanding linear form satisfies condition (8). For example, if $B = \mathrm{SSP}[\Gamma]$ then $\Phi = \Gamma$ and, for any set spec F, $\mathsf{n}(F) = \{(f, \mathbf{e}) \mid f \in \mathcal{L}(F)\}$. □

For any $x \in X$ and any $\boldsymbol{r} \in \mathrm{REG}\, B$, the *set of partial derivatives of* $\boldsymbol{r}$ *w.r.t.* x is $\partial_x(\boldsymbol{r}) = \{\boldsymbol{r}' \mid (x, \boldsymbol{r}') \in \mathsf{n}(\boldsymbol{r})\}$. For all $\boldsymbol{r}, \boldsymbol{r}' \in \mathrm{REG}\, B \setminus \{\oslash\}$ and $x \in X$, one can confirm that

$$\partial_x(\oslash) = \partial_x(\underline{\varepsilon_{\mathsf{mon}\,B}}) = \emptyset, \qquad \partial_x(\boldsymbol{r} + \boldsymbol{r}') = \partial_x(\boldsymbol{r}) \cup \partial_x(\boldsymbol{r}'),$$
$$\partial_x(\boldsymbol{rr}') = \partial_x(\boldsymbol{r})\boldsymbol{r}' \cup \mathsf{c}(\boldsymbol{r})\partial_x(\boldsymbol{r}'), \quad \partial_x(\boldsymbol{r}^*) = \partial_x(\boldsymbol{r})\boldsymbol{r}^*.$$

As in the case of ordinary derivatives, [1], the following result explains how the behaviour of the linear form of $\boldsymbol{r}$ relates to the behaviour of $\boldsymbol{r}$.

Lemma 2. *Let the linear form* n *satisfy condition* (8). *For all* $\boldsymbol{r} \in \mathrm{REG}\, B$, *we have* $\mathcal{I}(\boldsymbol{r}) = \mathcal{I}(c(\boldsymbol{r})) \cup \mathcal{I}(\mathsf{n}(\boldsymbol{r}))$.

Next we explain how to iterate $\mathsf{n}(\boldsymbol{r})$ to obtain the set of derivatives of the regular expression $\boldsymbol{r}$. We start with defining the operator

$$\pi_0(\boldsymbol{r}) = \downarrow_2(\mathsf{n}(\boldsymbol{r})),$$

where $\downarrow_2(s,t) = t$ is the standard second projection on pairs of objects. We can iteratively apply the operator π_0 on any expression $\boldsymbol{x} \in \pi_0(\boldsymbol{r})$. The set of all the resulting expressions is denoted by $\pi(\boldsymbol{r})$, and iteratively defined by

$$\pi_i(\boldsymbol{r}) = \pi_0(\pi_{i-1}(\boldsymbol{r})) \quad (i \in \mathbb{N}), \qquad \pi(\boldsymbol{r}) = \bigcup_{i\in\mathbb{N}_0} \pi_i(\boldsymbol{r}).$$

Let $\mathsf{PD}(\boldsymbol{r}) = \pi(\boldsymbol{r}) \cup \{\boldsymbol{r}\}$ be the *set of partial derivatives* of $\boldsymbol{r}$.

Example 6. Consider the case of the default linear form and the type PSP[Γ] regular expression $\boldsymbol{r} = (\forall/{=})^*(\forall/\mathsf{e})^*$. We have

$$\mathsf{n}((\forall/{=})^*) = \mathsf{n}(\forall/{=})(\forall/{=})^* = \{(\forall/{=}, \mathsf{e}/\mathsf{e})\}(\forall/{=})^* = \{(\forall/{=}, (\forall/{=})^*)\}$$
$$\mathsf{n}((\forall/\mathsf{e})^*) = \mathsf{n}(\forall/\mathsf{e})(\forall/\mathsf{e})^* = \{(\forall/\mathsf{e}, \mathsf{e}/\mathsf{e})\}(\forall/\mathsf{e})^* = \{(\forall/\mathsf{e}, (\forall/\mathsf{e})^*)\}.$$

As $(\varepsilon,\varepsilon) \in \mathcal{R}((\forall/{=})^*)$, we have $\mathsf{n}(\boldsymbol{r}) = \mathsf{n}((\forall/{=})^*)(\forall/\mathsf{e})^* \cup \mathsf{n}((\forall/\mathsf{e})^*) = \{(\forall/{=}, \boldsymbol{r}),\ (\forall/\mathsf{e}, (\forall/\mathsf{e})^*)\}$. Then, $\pi_0(\boldsymbol{r}) = \{\boldsymbol{r}, (\forall/\mathsf{e})^*\}$, $\pi_1(\boldsymbol{r}) = \pi_0(\boldsymbol{r}) \cup \pi_0((\forall/\mathsf{e})^*) = \pi_0(\boldsymbol{r})$, $\pi(\boldsymbol{r}) = \{\boldsymbol{r}, (\forall/\mathsf{e})^*\}$.

Example 7. Consider the type SSP[Γ] regular expression $\boldsymbol{r} = (\forall^*)(\exists\mathsf{b})$ and the case of the expanding linear form n such that $\mathsf{n}(F) = \{(f,\mathsf{e}) \mid f \in \mathcal{L}(F)\}$, for any set spec F, and $X = \Gamma = \{\mathsf{a}, \mathsf{b}, \ldots, \mathsf{z}\}$. We have

$$\mathsf{n}(\forall^*) = \mathsf{n}(\forall)(\forall^*) = (\Gamma \times \{\mathsf{e}\})(\forall^*) = \Gamma \times \{\forall^*\} \quad \text{and} \quad \mathsf{n}(\exists\mathsf{b}) = \{(\exists\mathsf{b}, \mathsf{e})\}.$$

Also, as $\varepsilon \in \mathcal{L}(\forall^*)$, we have $\mathsf{n}(\boldsymbol{r}) = \mathsf{n}(\forall^*)(\exists\mathsf{b}) \cup \mathsf{n}(\exists\mathsf{b}) = \Gamma \times \{\boldsymbol{r}\} \cup \{(\mathsf{b},\mathsf{e})\}$. Then, $\pi_0(\boldsymbol{r}) = \{\boldsymbol{r}, \mathsf{e}\}$, $\pi_1(\boldsymbol{r}) = \pi_0(\boldsymbol{r})$, $\pi(\boldsymbol{r}) = \pi_0(\boldsymbol{r})$, $\partial_{\mathsf{a}}(\boldsymbol{r}) = \{\boldsymbol{r}, \mathsf{e}\}$ and $\partial_{\mathsf{b}}(\boldsymbol{r}) = \{\boldsymbol{r}\}$.

Theorem 1. *Suppose that partial derivatives are defined based on some type* (X, B) *linear form. For all* $\boldsymbol{r} \in \mathrm{REG}\, B$, $|\pi(\boldsymbol{r})| \le \|\boldsymbol{r}\|$ *and* $|\mathsf{PD}(\boldsymbol{r})| \le \|\boldsymbol{r}\| + 1$.

4 The Partial Derivative Graph of a Regular Expression

Here we consider a label set B to be used for type B regular expressions $\boldsymbol{r}$ and a label set X that will be used to define the type X labelled graph $\hat{a}_{\mathrm{PD}}(\boldsymbol{r})$, such that $\mathsf{mon}\, B = \mathsf{mon}\, X$ and condition (8) is satisfied for all $\beta \in B$—recall that $\mathsf{n}(\beta) \subseteq X \times \{\varepsilon_{\mathsf{mon}\, B}\}$. The objective is to prove that the behaviour of $\hat{a}_{\mathrm{PD}}(\boldsymbol{r})$ is exactly $\mathcal{I}(\boldsymbol{r})$—see Theorem 2. This is analogous to the case of ordinary regular expressions [1,12]. Thus, to decide whether a given $m \in \mathsf{mon}\, B$ is in $\mathcal{I}(\boldsymbol{r})$, one computes $\hat{a}_{\mathrm{PD}}(\boldsymbol{r})$ and then tests whether $\hat{a}_{\mathrm{PD}}(\boldsymbol{r})$ accepts m. This test depends on the particular monoid $\mathsf{mon}\, B$ [10].

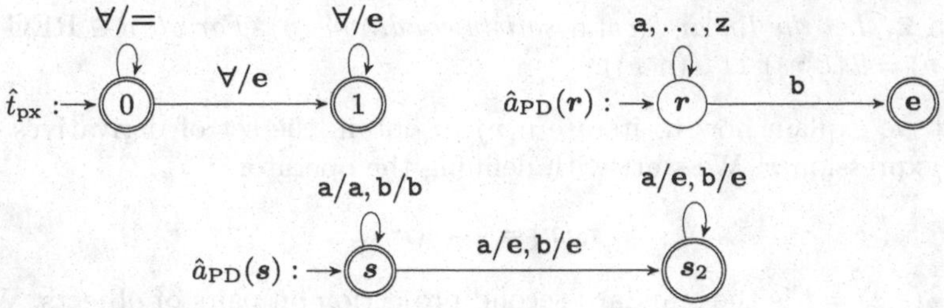

Fig. 1. The transducer $\hat{t}_{\mathrm{px}}$ is alphabet invariant and realizes all (u, v) such that v is a prefix of u. The automaton $\hat{a}_{\mathrm{PD}}(\boldsymbol{r})$ accepts all words in $\{\mathtt{a}, \mathtt{b}, \ldots, \mathtt{z}\}^*$ ending with b. The transducer $\hat{a}_{\mathrm{PD}}(\boldsymbol{s})$ realizes all (u, v) such that v is a prefix of u and $\Gamma = \{\mathtt{a}, \mathtt{b}\}$.

Definition 8. *The type X* partial derivative graph *of a type B regular expression $\boldsymbol{r}$ is the labelled graph* $\hat{a}_{\mathrm{PD}}(\boldsymbol{r}) = (\mathsf{PD}(\boldsymbol{r}), X, \delta_{\mathrm{PD}}, \{\boldsymbol{r}\}, \lambda(\boldsymbol{r}))$, *where* $\lambda(\boldsymbol{r}) = \{\, \boldsymbol{r}_1 \in \mathsf{PD}(\boldsymbol{r}) \mid \mathsf{c}(\boldsymbol{r}_1) = \underline{\varepsilon_{\mathsf{mon}\, B}} \,\}$ *and* $\delta_{\mathrm{PD}} = \{\, (\boldsymbol{r}_1, x, \boldsymbol{r}_2) \mid \boldsymbol{r}_1 \in \mathsf{PD}(\boldsymbol{r}) \wedge (x, \boldsymbol{r}_2) \in \mathsf{n}(\boldsymbol{r}_1) \,\}$.

Theorem 2. *Suppose that partial derivatives are defined based on some type (X, B) linear form. For any $\boldsymbol{r} \in \mathrm{REG}\, B$, we have that $\mathcal{I}(\hat{a}_{\mathrm{PD}}(\boldsymbol{r})) = \mathcal{I}(\boldsymbol{r})$.*

Example 8. Consider again the regular expression $\boldsymbol{r} = (\forall/{=})^*(\forall/\mathtt{e})^*$ over $\mathrm{PSP}[\Gamma]$ representing all word pairs (u, v) such that v is a prefix of u. We compute the partial derivative graph $\hat{a}_{\mathrm{PD}}(\boldsymbol{r})$ using the default linear form for $X = B = \mathrm{PSP}[\Gamma]$. In Example 6, we computed $\mathsf{n}(\boldsymbol{r}) = \{(\forall/{=}, \boldsymbol{r}), (\forall/\mathtt{e}, (\forall/\mathtt{e})^*)\}$ and $\pi(\boldsymbol{r}) = \{\boldsymbol{r}, (\forall/\mathtt{e})^*\}$. Using the linear forms $\mathsf{n}(\boldsymbol{r})$ and $\mathsf{n}((\forall/\mathtt{e})^*)$, we see that the partial derivative graph $\hat{a}_{\mathrm{PD}}(\boldsymbol{r})$ is exactly the transducer $\hat{t}_{\mathrm{px}}$ in Fig. 1.

Example 9. Consider again the type $\mathrm{SSP}[\Gamma]$ regular expression $\boldsymbol{r} = (\forall^*)(\exists \mathtt{b})$ of Example 7, representing all words ending with b. The partial derivative graph $\hat{a}_{\mathrm{PD}}(\boldsymbol{r})$ is the automaton in Fig. 1.

Corollary 1. *Consider the default linear form for $X = B = [\Sigma, \Delta]$. For any type $[\Sigma, \Delta]$ regular expression $\boldsymbol{r}$, the type $[\Sigma, \Delta]$ partial derivative graph $\hat{a}_{\mathrm{PD}}(\boldsymbol{r})$ is a transducer (in standard) form such that $\mathcal{R}(\boldsymbol{r}) = \mathcal{R}(\hat{a}_{\mathrm{PD}}(\boldsymbol{r}))$.*

Example 10. Let $\Sigma = \Delta = \{\mathtt{a}, \mathtt{b}\}$ and let n be the default linear form for $X = B = [\Sigma, \Delta]$. The type $[\Sigma, \Delta]$ expression $\boldsymbol{s} = (\mathtt{a}/\mathtt{a} + \mathtt{b}/\mathtt{b})^*(\mathtt{a}/\mathtt{e} + \mathtt{b}/\mathtt{e})^*$ represents all (u, v) such that v is a prefix of u. Let $\boldsymbol{s}_1 = (\mathtt{a}/\mathtt{a} + \mathtt{b}/\mathtt{b})^*$ and $\boldsymbol{s}_2 = (\mathtt{a}/\mathtt{e} + \mathtt{b}/\mathtt{e})^*$. Then, $\mathsf{n}(\boldsymbol{s}_1) = \{(\mathtt{a}/\mathtt{a}, \boldsymbol{r}_1), (\mathtt{b}/\mathtt{b}, \boldsymbol{r}_1)\}$, $\mathsf{n}(\boldsymbol{s}_2) = \{(\mathtt{a}/\mathtt{e}, \boldsymbol{s}_2), (\mathtt{b}/\mathtt{e}, \boldsymbol{s}_2)\}$, $\mathsf{n}(\boldsymbol{r}) = \{(\mathtt{a}/\mathtt{a}, \boldsymbol{r}), (\mathtt{b}/\mathtt{b}, \boldsymbol{r}), (\mathtt{a}/\mathtt{e}, \boldsymbol{s}_2), (\mathtt{b}/\mathtt{e}, \boldsymbol{s}_2)\}$. The graph $\hat{a}_{\mathrm{PD}}(\boldsymbol{s})$ is shown in Fig. 1.

5 2D Regular Expressions

By 2D regular expressions we mean type B regular expressions with $\mathsf{mon}\, B = \Sigma^* \times \Delta^*$ (or $\mathsf{mon}\, B = \Gamma^* \times \Gamma^*$). We want a direct algorithm to decide if (u, v)

belongs to $\mathcal{R}(\boldsymbol{r})$, without constructing the transducer $\hat{a}_{\mathrm{PD}}(\boldsymbol{r})$ and then testing whether $\hat{a}_{\mathrm{PD}}(\boldsymbol{r})$ accepts (u,v). To this end, we shall define partial derivatives $\partial_\psi(\beta)$, where $\psi \in X$, a little differently. Due to space limitation we shall deal only with the case of $X = \{F/\mathbf{e}, \mathbf{e}/F \mid F \in \mathrm{SSP}[\Gamma]\}$ and[1] $B = \mathrm{PSP}_{\neq\emptyset}[\Gamma]$. See [14] for the case of $X = \{x/\mathbf{e}, \mathbf{e}/y \mid x \in \Sigma, y \in \Delta\}$ and $B = [\Sigma, \Delta]$.

Consider the monoid $\Sigma^* \times \Delta^*$ with set of generators $\{(x,\varepsilon), (\varepsilon, y) \mid x \in \Sigma \wedge y \in \Delta\}$ and set of equations $\{\,(x,\varepsilon)(\varepsilon,y) \doteq (x,y), (\varepsilon,y)(x,\varepsilon) \doteq (x,y) \mid x \in \Sigma \wedge y \in \Delta\,\}$. The partial derivatives of this section are related to the quotient of relations $R \subseteq \Sigma^* \times \Delta^*$, by word pairs. But now one needs to take in account the above equations. For instance, for $x \in \Sigma$ and $y \in \Delta$, we have

$$(x,\varepsilon)^{-1}R = \{\,(\varepsilon,y)w \mid (x,y)w \in R\}, \qquad (\varepsilon,y)^{-1}R = \{\,(x,\varepsilon)w \mid (x,y)w \in R\}.$$

Quotients can be extended appropriately: For θ a pair as above and ω a concatenation of such pairs, $(\varepsilon,\varepsilon)^{-1}R_1 = R_1$, $(\omega\theta)^{-1}R_1 = \theta^{-1}(\omega^{-1}R_1)$. For $R_1 \subseteq (\Sigma^* \times \{\varepsilon\}) \cup (\{\varepsilon\} \times \Delta^*)$, we have $R_1{}^{-1}R_2 = \bigcup_{\theta \in R_1} \theta^{-1}R_2$.

The partial derivatives of any $\mathsf{p} \in \mathrm{PSP}_{\neq\emptyset}[\Gamma]$ are defined w.r.t. elements in $X = \{F/\mathbf{e}, \mathbf{e}/F \mid F \in \mathrm{SSP}[\Gamma]\}$ are as follows.

$$\begin{aligned}
&\partial_{\mathbf{e}/F}(G/\mathbf{e}) = \partial_{F/\mathbf{e}}(\mathbf{e}/G) = \emptyset,\\
&\partial_{\mathbf{e}/F}(\mathbf{e}/G) = \partial_{F/\mathbf{e}}(G/\mathbf{e}) = \{\mathbf{e}/\mathbf{e}\} \quad \text{if } \mathcal{L}(F) \cap \mathcal{L}(G) \neq \emptyset,\\
&\partial_{\mathbf{e}/F}(G/C) = \{G/\mathbf{e}\} \quad \text{if } \mathcal{L}(F) \cap \mathcal{L}(C) \neq \emptyset,\\
&\partial_{\mathbf{e}/F}(G/{=}) = \{(F \cap G)/\mathbf{e}\} \quad \text{if } \mathcal{L}(F) \cap \mathcal{L}(G) \neq \emptyset,\\
&\partial_{\mathbf{e}/F}(G/C{\neq}) = \begin{cases} \{(G \cap \nexists b)/\mathbf{e}\} & \text{if } \mathcal{L}(F \cap C) = \{b\} \wedge \mathcal{L}(G) \setminus \{b\} \neq \emptyset,\\ \{G/\mathbf{e}\} & \text{if } |\mathcal{L}(F \cap C)| \geq 2, \end{cases}\\
&\partial_{F/\mathbf{e}}(G/{=}) = \{\mathbf{e}/(F \cap G)\} \quad \text{if } \mathcal{L}(F) \cap \mathcal{L}(G) \neq \emptyset,\\
&\partial_{F/\mathbf{e}}(G/C{\neq}) = \begin{cases} \{\mathbf{e}/(C \cap \nexists b)\} & \text{if } \mathcal{L}(F \cap G) = \{b\} \wedge \mathcal{L}(C) \setminus \{b\} \neq \emptyset,\\ \{\mathbf{e}/C\} & \text{if } |\mathcal{L}(F \cap G)| \geq 2. \end{cases}
\end{aligned}$$

For each case above, if the conditions do not hold then the set of partial derivatives is $\emptyset$. Above we have used the operation $\cap$ between any two set specs, defined in [10] in a natural way, e.g., $\exists 035 \cap \exists 1358 = \exists 35$, $\nexists 035 \cap \exists 1358 = \exists 18$.

Partial derivatives $\partial_{F/\mathbf{e}}(\boldsymbol{r})$ and $\partial_{\mathbf{e}/F}(\boldsymbol{r})$ of any $\boldsymbol{r} \in \mathrm{REG\,PSP}_{\neq\emptyset}[\Gamma]$ are defined as in Sect. 3, except for the concatenation $\boldsymbol{rs}$. Let φ be either of $F/\mathbf{e}, \mathbf{e}/F$:

$$\partial_\varphi(\oslash) = \partial_\varphi(\mathbf{e}/\mathbf{e}) = \emptyset, \quad \partial_\varphi(\boldsymbol{r}+\boldsymbol{s}) = \partial_\varphi(\boldsymbol{r}) \cup \partial_\varphi(\boldsymbol{s}), \quad \partial_\varphi(\boldsymbol{r}^*) = \partial_\varphi(\boldsymbol{r})\boldsymbol{r}^*,$$
$$\partial_{F/\mathbf{e}}(\boldsymbol{rs}) = \partial_{F/\mathbf{e}}(\boldsymbol{r})\boldsymbol{s} \cup \mathsf{c}_{in}(\boldsymbol{r})\partial_{F/\mathbf{e}}(\boldsymbol{s}), \quad \partial_{\mathbf{e}/F}(\boldsymbol{rs}) = \partial_{\mathbf{e}/F}(\boldsymbol{r})\boldsymbol{s} \cup \mathsf{c}_{out}(\boldsymbol{r})\partial_{\mathbf{e}/F}(\boldsymbol{s});$$

where c_{in} is the ***constant-input part*** defined such that $\mathsf{c}_{in}(\mathbf{e}/\mathbf{e}) = \mathbf{e}/\mathbf{e}$, $\mathsf{c}_{in}(\mathbf{e}/F) = \mathbf{e}/F$, and $\mathsf{c}_{in}(\mathsf{p}) = \oslash$ for all other pairing specs p. Moreover for $F \in \mathrm{SSP}[\Gamma]$ and $\boldsymbol{r}, \boldsymbol{s} \in \mathrm{REG\,PSP}_{\neq\emptyset}[\Gamma]$,

---

[1] Because of condition (5), here we consider labels in $\mathrm{PSP}_{\neq\emptyset}[\Gamma]$, that is, only those labels $\mathsf{p} \in \mathrm{PSP}[\Gamma]$ for which $\mathcal{R}(\mathsf{p}) \neq \emptyset$.

$$\mathsf{c}_{in}(\boldsymbol{rs}) = \mathsf{c}_{in}(\boldsymbol{r})\,\mathsf{c}_{in}(\boldsymbol{s}), \quad \mathsf{c}_{in}(\oslash \boldsymbol{s}) = \mathsf{c}_{in}(\boldsymbol{r}\oslash) = \mathsf{c}_{in}(\oslash) = \oslash,$$
$$\mathsf{c}_{in}(\boldsymbol{r}+\boldsymbol{s}) = \mathsf{c}_{in}(\boldsymbol{r}) + \mathsf{c}_{in}(\boldsymbol{s}), \quad \mathsf{c}_{in}(\oslash + \boldsymbol{s}) = \mathsf{c}_{in}(\boldsymbol{s}), \quad \mathsf{c}_{in}(\boldsymbol{r}+\oslash) = \mathsf{c}_{in}(\boldsymbol{r}),$$
$$\mathsf{c}_{in}(\boldsymbol{r}^*) = (\mathsf{c}_{in}(\boldsymbol{r}))^*, \ \mathsf{c}_{in}(\oslash^*) = \mathsf{e}/\mathsf{e}.$$

The *constant-output part* is analogous except that $\mathsf{c}_{out}(F/\mathsf{e}) = F/\mathsf{e}$.

Lemma 3. *For all* $\boldsymbol{r} \in \text{REG}\,\text{PSP}_{\neq\emptyset}[\Gamma]$, *we have* $\mathcal{R}(\mathsf{c}_{in}(\boldsymbol{r})) = \mathcal{R}(\boldsymbol{r}) \downarrow \{\varepsilon\}$ *and* $\mathcal{R}(\mathsf{c}_{out}(\boldsymbol{r})) = \mathcal{R}(\boldsymbol{r}) \uparrow \{\varepsilon\}$. *Moreover* $\mathcal{R}(\mathsf{c}_{in}(\mathsf{c}_{out}(\boldsymbol{r}))) = \mathcal{R}(\mathsf{c}(\boldsymbol{r})) = \mathcal{R}(\mathsf{c}_{out}(\mathsf{c}_{in}(\boldsymbol{r})))$.

Theorem 3. *For all* (u,v) *with* $u = x_1 \cdots x_n$ *and* $v = y_1 \cdots y_m$, *we have that* $(u,v) \in \mathcal{R}(\boldsymbol{r})$ *if and only if* $\mathsf{c}(\partial_{\exists x_1/\mathsf{e},\ldots,\exists x_n/\mathsf{e},\,\mathsf{e}/\exists y_1,\ldots,\mathsf{e}/\exists y_m}(\boldsymbol{r})) = \mathsf{e}/\mathsf{e}$.

Remark 1. It can be shown that $\partial_{\exists x/\mathsf{e}}$ and $\partial_{\mathsf{e}/\exists y}$ commute on any $\boldsymbol{r}$; thus, we have that $\mathsf{c}(\partial_{\exists x_1/\mathsf{e},\ldots,\exists x_n/\mathsf{e},\,\mathsf{e}/\exists y_1,\ldots,\mathsf{e}/\exists y_m}(\boldsymbol{r})) = \mathsf{c}(\partial_{\exists x_1/\mathsf{e},\,\mathsf{e}/\exists y_1,\exists x_2/\mathsf{e},\mathsf{e}/\exists y_2,\ldots}(\boldsymbol{r}))$.

Example 11. Consider the word pair (aaba, aaaa) and the type $\text{PSP}_{\neq\emptyset}[\Gamma]$ regular expression $\boldsymbol{r} = (\forall/{=})^*(\forall/\forall{\neq})(\forall/{=})^*$. We confirm that $(\mathsf{aaba},\mathsf{aaaa}) \in \mathcal{R}(\boldsymbol{r})$ by showing that there is $\boldsymbol{r}_1 \in \partial_{\exists\mathsf{a}/\mathsf{e},\exists\mathsf{a}/\mathsf{e},\exists\mathsf{b}/\mathsf{e},\exists\mathsf{a}/\mathsf{e},\exists\mathsf{e}/\mathsf{a},\exists\mathsf{e}/\mathsf{a},\exists\mathsf{e}/\mathsf{a},\exists\mathsf{e}/\mathsf{a}}(\boldsymbol{r})$ such that $(\varepsilon,\varepsilon) \in \mathcal{R}(\boldsymbol{r}_1)$. Note that the only information about the alphabet is that it contains the letters a and b. We shall compute only the necessary derivatives that lead to such an $\boldsymbol{r}_1$.

First we have: $\partial_{\exists\mathsf{a}/\mathsf{e}}((\forall/{=})^*) = \{(\mathsf{e}/\exists\mathsf{a})(\forall/{=})^*\}$, $\partial_{\exists\mathsf{a}/\mathsf{e}}(\forall/\forall{\neq}) = \{\mathsf{e}/\nexists\mathsf{a}\}$,

$$\mathsf{c}_{in}((\forall/{=})^*) = \mathsf{e}/\mathsf{e}, \qquad \mathsf{c}_{in}(\forall/\forall{\neq}) = \oslash.$$

Let $\boldsymbol{r}_1 = (\forall/{=})^*$ and $\boldsymbol{r}_2 = (\forall/\forall{\neq})$. Then

$$\begin{aligned}
\partial_{\exists\mathsf{a}/\mathsf{e}}(\boldsymbol{r}) &= \partial_{\exists\mathsf{a}/\mathsf{e}}(\boldsymbol{r}_1)\boldsymbol{r}_2\boldsymbol{r}_1 \cup \mathsf{c}_{in}(\boldsymbol{r}_1)\partial_{\exists\mathsf{a}/\mathsf{e}}(\boldsymbol{r}_2\boldsymbol{r}_1)\\
&= \{(\mathsf{e}/\exists\mathsf{a})\boldsymbol{r}\} \cup \partial_{\exists\mathsf{a}/\mathsf{e}}(\boldsymbol{r}_2)\boldsymbol{r}_1 \cup \mathsf{c}_{in}(\boldsymbol{r}_2)\partial_{\exists\mathsf{a}/\mathsf{e}}(\boldsymbol{r}_1)\\
&= \{(\mathsf{e}/\exists\mathsf{a})\boldsymbol{r},\ (\mathsf{e}/\nexists\mathsf{a})\boldsymbol{r}_1\}.\\
\partial_{\exists\mathsf{a}/\mathsf{e}}((\mathsf{e}/\exists\mathsf{a})\boldsymbol{r}) &= (\mathsf{e}/\exists\mathsf{a})\partial_{\exists\mathsf{a}/\mathsf{e}}(\boldsymbol{r}) = \{(\mathsf{e}/\exists\mathsf{a})(\mathsf{e}/\exists\mathsf{a})\boldsymbol{r}\} \cup \cdots\\
\partial_{\exists\mathsf{b}/\mathsf{e}}((\mathsf{e}/\exists\mathsf{a})(\mathsf{e}/\exists\mathsf{a})\boldsymbol{r}) &= \{(\mathsf{e}/\exists\mathsf{a})(\mathsf{e}/\exists\mathsf{a})(\mathsf{e}/\nexists\mathsf{b})\boldsymbol{r}_1\} \cup \cdots\\
\partial_{\exists\mathsf{a}/\mathsf{e}}((\mathsf{e}/\exists\mathsf{a})(\mathsf{e}/\exists\mathsf{a})(\mathsf{e}/\nexists\mathsf{b})\boldsymbol{r}_1) &= \{(\mathsf{e}/\exists\mathsf{a})(\mathsf{e}/\exists\mathsf{a})(\mathsf{e}/\nexists\mathsf{b})(\mathsf{e}/\exists\mathsf{a})\boldsymbol{r}_1\} \cup \cdots\\
\partial_{\mathsf{e}/\exists\mathsf{a}}((\mathsf{e}/\exists\mathsf{a})(\mathsf{e}/\exists\mathsf{a})(\mathsf{e}/\nexists\mathsf{b})(\mathsf{e}/\exists\mathsf{a})\boldsymbol{r}_1) &= \{(\mathsf{e}/\exists\mathsf{a})(\mathsf{e}/\nexists\mathsf{b})(\mathsf{e}/\exists\mathsf{a})\boldsymbol{r}_1\} \cup \cdots\\
\partial_{\mathsf{e}/\exists\mathsf{a}}((\mathsf{e}/\exists\mathsf{a})(\mathsf{e}/\nexists\mathsf{b})(\mathsf{e}/\exists\mathsf{a})\boldsymbol{r}_1) &= \{(\mathsf{e}/\nexists\mathsf{b})(\mathsf{e}/\exists\mathsf{a})\boldsymbol{r}_1\} \cup \cdots\\
\partial_{\mathsf{e}/\exists\mathsf{a}}((\mathsf{e}/\nexists\mathsf{b})(\mathsf{e}/\exists\mathsf{a})\boldsymbol{r}_1) &= \{(\mathsf{e}/\exists\mathsf{a})\boldsymbol{r}_1\} \cup \cdots\\
\partial_{\mathsf{e}/\exists\mathsf{a}}((\mathsf{e}/\exists\mathsf{a})\boldsymbol{r}_1) &= \{\boldsymbol{r}_1\} \cup \cdots \qquad \text{Thus, } (\varepsilon,\varepsilon) \in \mathcal{R}(\boldsymbol{r}_1).
\end{aligned}$$

6 Concluding Remarks

Label sets can have any desired format as long as one provides their monoidal behaviour. Using the elements of a label set B we can build type B regular expressions, which can have a significantly reduced size when the alphabet of reference is large. At this broad level, we were able to obtain a few basic results on partial derivatives of these expressions. Already FAdo [9] includes implementations of partial derivative (PD) algorithms for ordinary (1D) regular expressions and of type $[\Sigma, \Delta]$ regular expressions. We are currently implementing PD algorithms for type SSP$[\Gamma]$ and PSP$[\Gamma]$ expressions.

A research direction is to investigate the efficiency of the two approaches to the regular expression $\boldsymbol{r}$ membership (word) problem: directly or via building $\hat{a}_{\mathrm{PD}}(\boldsymbol{r})$. Solving the regular expression membership problem directly for 2D expressions required a modified definition of partial derivatives (PDs). So another research direction is to find a good way to generalize the definition of linear form n such that $\mathsf{n}(\beta)$ is a finite nonempty subset of $X \times B \cup \{\varepsilon_{\underline{\mathsf{mon}\,B}}\}$ and $\mathsf{n}(\boldsymbol{rs})$ is defined appropriately to include both the original and the modified PDs.

Acknowledgement. We are grateful to the reviewers of CIAA 2019 for their constructive suggestions for improvement. We have applied most of these suggestions, and we plan to apply the remaining ones in the journal version where more pages are allowed. The idea of using special labels on automata to denote sets is also explored in [13] with different objectives.

References

1. Antimirov, V.M.: Partial derivatives of regular expressions and finite automaton constructions. Theoret. Comput. Sci. **155**(2), 291–319 (1996)
2. Bastos, R., Broda, S., Machiavelo, A., Moreira, N., Reis, R.: On the average complexity of partial derivative automata for semi-extended expressions. J. Autom. Lang. Comb. **22**(1–3), 5–28 (2017). https://doi.org/10.25596/jalc-2017-005
3. Broda, S., Machiavelo, A., Moreira, N., Reis, R.: On the average state complexity of partial derivative automata: an analytic combinatorics approach. Internat. J. Found. Comput. Sci. **22**(7), 1593–1606 (2011)
4. Brzozowski, J.: Derivatives of regular expressions. J. ACM **11**, 481–494 (1964)
5. Caron, P., Champarnaud, J.-M., Mignot, L.: Partial derivatives of an extended regular expression. In: Dediu, A.-H., Inenaga, S., Martín-Vide, C. (eds.) LATA 2011. LNCS, vol. 6638, pp. 179–191. Springer, Heidelberg (2011). https://doi.org/10.1007/978-3-642-21254-3_13
6. Champarnaud, J.M., Ziadi, D.: From Mirkin's prebases to Antimirov's word partial derivatives. Fund. Inform. **45**(3), 195–205 (2001)
7. Champarnaud, J.M., Ziadi, D.: Canonical derivatives, partial derivatives and finite automaton constructions. Theoret. Comput. Sci. **289**, 137–163 (2002). https://doi.org/10.1016/S0304-3975(01)00267-5
8. Demaille, A.: Derived-term automata of multitape expressions with composition. Sci. Ann. Comput. Sci. **27**(2), 137–176 (2017). https://doi.org/10.7561/SACS.2017.2.137
9. FAdo: Tools for formal languages manipulation. http://fado.dcc.fc.up.pt/. Accessed Mar 2019
10. Konstantinidis, S., Moreira, N., Reis, R., Young, J.: Regular expressions and transducers over alphabet-invariant and user-defined labels. CoRR abs/1805.01829 (2018). http://arxiv.org/abs/1805.01829
11. Lombardy, S., Sakarovitch, J.: Derivatives of rational expressions with multiplicity. Theoret. Comput. Sci. **332**(1–3), 141–177 (2005). https://doi.org/10.1016/j.tcs.2004.10.016

12. Mirkin, B.G.: An algorithm for constructing a base in a language of regular expressions. Eng. Cybern. **5**, 51–57 (1966)
13. Newton, J.: Representing and computing with types in dynamically typed languages. Ph.D. thesis, Sorbonne Université, Paris, France, November 2018
14. Pires, J.: Transducers and 2D regular expressions. Master's thesis, Departamento de Ciência de Computadores, Faculdade de Ciências da Universidade do Porto, Porto, Portugal (2018)
15. Sakarovitch, J.: Elements of Automata Theory. Cambridge University Press, Berlin (2009)
16. Sakarovitch, J.: Automata and rational expressions. CoRR abs/1502.03573 (2015). http://arxiv.org/abs/1502.03573

Input-Driven Multi-counter Automata

Martin Kutrib(✉), Andreas Malcher, and Matthias Wendlandt

Institut für Informatik, Universität Giessen,
Arndtstr. 2, 35392 Giessen, Germany
{kutrib,andreas.malcher,matthias.wendlandt}@informatik.uni-giessen.de

Abstract. The model of deterministic input-driven multi-counter automata is introduced and studied. On such devices, the input letters uniquely determine the operations on the underlying data structure that is consisting of multiple counters. We study the computational power of the resulting language families and compare them with known language families inside the Chomsky hierarchy. In addition, it is possible to prove a proper counter hierarchy depending on the alphabet size. This means that any input alphabet induces an upper bound which depends on the alphabet size only, such that $k+1$ counters are more powerful than k counters as long as k is less than this bound. The hierarchy interestingly collapses at the level of the bound. Furthermore, we investigate the closure properties of the language families. Finally, the undecidability of the emptiness problem is derived for input-driven two-counter automata.

1 Introduction

Multi-counter automata are finite state automata equipped with multiple counters which can be incremented, decremented, and tested for zero. It is well known that general one-way deterministic two-counter automata are computationally universal, that is, they can simulate Turing machines [17]. However, the latter simulation may need an unbounded amount of space. Hence, deterministic space-bounded as well as time-bounded multi-counter automata have been considered in [7] where, in particular, the case when the available time is restricted to real-time is studied. The authors establish in this case an infinite and strict counter hierarchy as well as positive and negative closure results. The generalization to multi-counter automata that may work nondeterministically as well as may use two-way motion on the input tape has been done in [8]. Since one-counter automata can be seen as a special case of pushdown automata, multi-counter automata may be considered a special case of multi-pushdown automata introduced in [6].

A recently introduced restriction to pushdown automata which turned out to provide nice closure properties and decidability questions is the requirement to work in an *input-driven* way. This means that input-driven pushdown automata are ordinary pushdown automata where the actions on the pushdown store are dictated by the input symbols. In particular, if an input symbol forces the machine to pop a symbol from the empty pushdown store, the computation

M. Hospodár and G. Jirásková (Eds.): CIAA 2019, LNCS 11601, pp. 197–208, 2019.
https://doi.org/10.1007/978-3-030-23679-3_16

continues with empty pushdown store. This variant of pushdown automata has originally been introduced in 1980 by Mehlhorn [16] and further investigations have been done in 1985 by von Braunmühl and Verbeek [5]. The results of both papers comprise the equivalence of nondeterministic and deterministic models and the proof that the membership problem is solvable in logarithmic space. The model has been revisited under the name of visibly pushdown automata in 2004 [1]. Complexity results on the model are summarized in the survey [18]. An input-driven variant of one-counter automata has been introduced in [2] and two recent papers [9,12] examine algebraic and logical aspects of input-driven counter automata. The above-mentioned generalization to multi-pushdown automata in terms of input-driven devices is described in [15] where several additional restrictions are put on the general model in order to obtain manageable models with positive closure properties and decidable questions. Finally, we mention that the computational power of input-driven automata using the storage medium of a stack and a queue, respectively, have been investigated in [3,13].

In this paper, we will introduce and investigate the model of input-driven multi-counter automata which are basically the input-driven variant of the real-time multi-counter automata discussed in [7]. It should be noted that this model is different from the model of "input-driven pushdown automata with counters" recently introduced by Ibarra [11]. This model is basically an input-driven pushdown automaton with additional reversal-bounded counters (see also [10]), where the input symbols govern the behavior on the pushdown store, but not necessarily on the counters. In contrast, our model has a counter update function which solely depends on the input alphabet. The paper is organized as follows. In the next section we introduce the necessary notations on multi-counter automata and their input-driven versions. In Sect. 3 we study the computational capacity of input-driven multi-counter automata and their relation to the language families of the Chomsky hierarchy. Then, a hierarchy on the number of counters is established that interestingly depends on the size of the input alphabet. This means that every alphabet size n determines a bound $f(n)$ such that k counters with $1 \leq k < f(n)$ are less powerful that $k+1$ counters, but any number of counters larger than $f(n)$ is as powerful as $f(n)$ counters. Sections 4 and 5 are devoted to investigating the closure properties of and decidability questions for input-driven multi-counter automata. The main result in the latter section is that already two input-driven counters are sufficient to obtain that all usually studied decidability questions are undecidable, whereas all but one of the questions is decidable for input-driven one-counter automata.

2 Preliminaries

Let Σ^* denote the set of all words over the finite alphabet Σ. The *empty word* is denoted by λ and the *reversal* of a word w by w^R. For the *length* of w we write $|w|$. We use $\subseteq$ for *inclusions* and $\subset$ for *strict inclusions*.

Let $k \geq 0$ be a natural number. A (one-way) deterministic k-counter automaton (DCA(k)) is a finite automaton having a single read-only input tape. In addition, it is equipped with k counters. At the outset of a computation the counter automaton is in the designated initial state, the counters are set to zero, and the head of the input tape scans the leftmost input symbol. Dependent on the current state, the currently scanned input symbol, and the information whether the counters are zero or not, the counter automaton changes its state, increases or decreases the counters or leaves the counters unchanged, and moves the input head one square to the right. The automata have no extra output tape but the states are partitioned into accepting and rejecting states.

A counter automaton is called *input-driven* if the input symbols currently read define the next action on the counters. To this end, we assume that each input symbol is associated with actions to be applied to the counters. Let Σ be the input alphabet. Then $\alpha\colon \Sigma \to \{-1,0,1\}^k$ gives these actions, where the ith component $\alpha(x)_i$ of $\alpha(x)$, for $1 \le i \le k$ and $x \in \Sigma$, is added to the current value of counter i. The subtraction is in natural numbers, that is, decreasing a counter value 0 gives counter value 0. This behavior is in line with the definition of input-driven pushdown automata that may pop from the empty pushdown store leaving the pushdown store empty. For any $x \ge 0$ we define the function $\mathrm{sg}(0) = \perp$ and $\mathrm{sg}(x) = +$ for $x \ge 1$.

An *input-driven counter automaton with* $k \ge 0$ *counters* (IDCA(k)) *is a system* $M = \langle Q, \Sigma, k, q_0, F, \alpha, \delta\rangle$, where Q is the finite set of *internal states*, Σ is the finite set of *input symbols*, $k \ge 0$ is the *number of counters*, $q_0 \in Q$ is the *initial state*, $F \subseteq Q$ is the set of *accepting states*, $\alpha\colon \Sigma \to \{-1,0,1\}^k$ is the *counter update function*, and $\delta\colon Q \times \Sigma \times \{+,\perp\}^k \to Q$ is the partial transition function that determines the successor state dependent on the current state, the current input symbol, and the current statuses of the counters (+ indicates a positive value and $\perp$ a zero).

A *configuration* of an IDCA(k) $M = \langle Q, \Sigma, k, q_0, F, \alpha, \delta\rangle$ is a $(k+2)$-tuple $(q, w, c_1, c_2, \ldots, c_k)$, where $q \in Q$ is the current state, $w \in \Sigma^*$ is the unread part of the input, and $c_i \ge 0$ is the current value of counter i, $1 \le i \le k$. The *initial configuration* for input w is set to $(q_0, w, 0, 0, \ldots, 0)$. During the course of its computation, M runs through a sequence of configurations. One step from a configuration to its successor configuration is denoted by $\vdash$. Let $q, q' \in Q$, $a \in \Sigma$, $w \in \Sigma^*$, and $c_i \ge 0$, $1 \le i \le k$. We set

$$(q, aw, c_1, c_2, \ldots, c_k) \vdash (q', w, c_1 + \alpha(a)_1, c_2 + \alpha(a)_2, \ldots, c_k + \alpha(a)_k)$$

if and only if $\delta(q, a, \mathrm{sg}(c_1), \mathrm{sg}(c_2), \ldots, \mathrm{sg}(c_k)) = q'$ (recall that the subtraction is in natural numbers). As usual, we define the reflexive and transitive closure of $\vdash$ by $\vdash^*$.

The language accepted by the IDCA(k) M is the set $L(M)$ of words for which there exists some computation beginning in the initial configuration and halting in a configuration in which the whole input is read and an accepting state is entered. Formally:

$$L(M) = \{\, w \in \Sigma^* \mid (q_0, w, 0, 0, \ldots, 0) \vdash^* (q, \lambda, c_1, c_2, \ldots, c_k) \text{ with } q \in F, c_i \ge 0 \text{ for } 1 \le i \le k \,\}.$$

So, an input-driven k-counter automaton is a realtime device since it cannot perform stationary moves. It halts within n steps on inputs of length n. For each counter C_i, the definitions imply the partition of the input alphabet into the sets $\Sigma_D^{(i)}$, $\Sigma_R^{(i)}$, and $\Sigma_N^{(i)}$ that control the actions increase or drive (D), decrease or reverse (R), and leave unchanged or neutral (N) of counter C_i. Such a partition is called a *signature*.

The family of all languages which can be accepted by some device X is denoted by $\mathscr{L}(\mathsf{X})$.

To clarify our notion we continue with an example.

Example 1. The language $L = \{abb\bar{a}^3\bar{b}\bar{b}a^5bb\bar{a}^7\bar{b}\bar{b}\cdots a^{4n+1}b \mid n \geq 0\}$ is non-semilinear and accepted by the IDCA(2) $M = \langle Q, \Sigma, 2, q_0, F, \alpha, \delta\rangle$ with state set $Q = \{q_0, q_1, q_2, q_3, q_4\}$, final states $F = \{q_2\}$, counter update function defined by $\alpha(a) = (-1, 1)$, $\alpha(b) = (0, 1)$, $\alpha(\bar{a}) = (1, -1)$, $\alpha(\bar{b}) = (1, 0)$, and transition function

1. $\delta(q_0, a, \bot, \bot) = q_1$
2. $\delta(q_1, b, \bot, +) = q_2$
3. $\delta(q_2, b, \bot, +) = q_3$
4. $\delta(q_3, \bar{a}, \bot, +) = q_3$
5. $\delta(q_3, \bar{a}, +, +) = q_3$
6. $\delta(q_3, \bar{b}, +, \bot) = q_4$
7. $\delta(q_4, \bar{b}, +, \bot) = q_1$
8. $\delta(q_1, a, +, \bot) = q_1$
9. $\delta(q_1, a, +, +) = q_1$

The IDCA(2) M uses its second counter to store the number of consecutive a's. The following two b's are used to increment the counter by two in order to match the number of $\bar{a}$'s in the following block. The comparison is made by decreasing the second counter on $\bar{a}$'s. Simultaneously, the first counter is increased to store the number of $\bar{a}$'s for the verification of the next block length. The addition of two is done while reading two symbols $\bar{b}$'s. Similarly the length of an $\bar{a}$ block is compared with the length of the following a block. These comparisons are done alternately.

The correct format of the input is checked in the states.

Finally, the total length of an accepted input is $(2n+2)^2 - 2$ and, thus, the language is not semilinear. ■

3 Computational Capacity

We start the investigation of the computational capacity of input-driven counter automata by considerations on unary languages. Example 1 shows that even two counters are sufficient to push the power of input-driven counter automata beyond the edge of semilinearity and, thus, context-freeness. However, to this end non-unary witness languages have to be used. In fact, for unary languages any number of counters does not help to accept a non-regular language.

Proposition 2. *Any unary language accepted by some IDCA is regular.*

Proof. Let $M = \langle Q, \{a\}, k, q_0, F, \alpha, \delta\rangle$ be an IDCA(k) accepting a unary language $L(M) \subseteq a^*$. If $k = 0$, then M is a finite automaton and the accepted language is regular. If $k > 0$, the signature of any counter C_i, $1 \leq i \leq k$, consists of one singleton and two empty sets. If $\Sigma_R^{(i)}$ or $\Sigma_N^{(i)}$ is non-empty then M will never increase counter C_i from its initial value zero. So, counter C_i is useless and can be omitted. If $\Sigma_D^{(i)}$ is non-empty then counter C_i is never decreased to zero once it has been increased to one. This fact can be remembered in the state such that counter C_i can be omitted in this case either. In this way all counters can be omitted and we end up in a finite automaton that accepts $L(M)$. □

Clearly, any regular language is accepted by some IDCA(0). So, for any $k \geq 0$ the family of unary languages accepted by IDCA(k) coincides with the family of regular languages. Moreover, any IDCA can be simulated by a deterministic linear bounded automaton in a straightforward way. This implies that the family of languages accepted by IDCA is included in the family of deterministic context-sensitive languages. The inclusion is even strict, since the (deterministic) (linear) context-free language $\{ a^n \$ a^n \mid n \geq 0 \}$ is not accepted by any IDCA.

Lemma 3. *Language $L = \{ a^n \$ a^n \mid n \geq 0 \}$ is not accepted by any IDCA.*

Proof. Contrarily assume that there is some IDCA(k) $M = \langle Q, \Sigma, k, q_0, F, \alpha, \delta \rangle$ that accepts L.

We give evidence that the counters cannot help. Let C_i, $1 \leq i \leq k$, be a counter. If $a \in \Sigma_R^{(i)}$ or $a \in \Sigma_N^{(i)}$ then M will increase counter C_i at most once on reading the \$. This fact can be remembered in the state and counter C_i can be omitted.

If $a \in \Sigma_D^{(i)}$ and $n \geq 2$ then counter C_i is never decreased to zero once two a's have been read from the input. This fact can be remembered in the state as well such that counter C_i can be omitted in this case either.

In this way all counters can be omitted and we end up in a finite automaton that accepts L. This is a contradiction since L is not regular. □

The next corollary summarizes the relationships with the linguistic families of the Chomsky hierarchy.

Corollary 4. *Let $k \geq 1$ be an integer. Then the family of regular languages is strictly included in $\mathscr{L}$(IDCA(k)) which, in turn, is strictly included in the family of deterministic context-sensitive languages.*

For $k \geq 2$, the family $\mathscr{L}$(IDCA(k)) is incomparable with the family of (deterministic) (linear) context-free languages.

Next, we turn to examine the power of the number of counters.

Lemma 5. *Let Σ be an m-symbol alphabet and $k = 3^m - 2^{m+1} + 1$. Then any IDCA($k + i$), $i \geq 1$, can be simulated by an IDCA(k).*

Proof. Let $i \geq 1$ and $M = \langle Q, \Sigma, k + i, q_0, F, \alpha, \delta \rangle$ be an IDCA($k + i$).

The proof of Proposition 2 revealed that a counter whose signature does not associate an increase *and* a decrease operation with some alphabet symbol can safely be omitted. So, any useful signature has non-empty sets Σ_R and Σ_D. There are 3^m different signatures of Σ. From these, 2^m signatures have an empty set Σ_R. Another 2^m signatures have an empty set Σ_D. Moreover, there is exactly one signature with both sets Σ_R and Σ_D empty. Therefore, there are at most $3^m - 2^{m+1} + 1$ different useful signatures.

Clearly, if two counters of M have the same signature, one of them can be omitted. The same is true for a counter with a useless signature. We conclude that at least i counters can be removed from M without affecting the language accepted. □

In particular, Lemma 5 shows that any counter hierarchy for IDCA necessarily collapses at a level that is solely determined by the alphabet size. Next, we turn to show that, in fact, these hierarchies exist.

Theorem 6. *Let $m \geq 2$ be an integer. For $1 < k \leq 3^m - 2^{m+1} + 1$, the family of languages accepted by IDCA($k-1$) over an alphabet of size m is strictly included in the family of languages accepted by IDCA(k) over an alphabet of size m.*

Proof. Let $\Sigma = \{a_1, a_2, \ldots, a_m\}$ be some alphabet of size $m \geq 2$. The proof of Lemma 5 showed that there are $k_{max} = 3^m - 2^{m+1} + 1$ different useful signatures $S_i = (\Sigma_D^{(i)}, \Sigma_R^{(i)}, \Sigma_N^{(i)})$, $1 \leq i \leq k_{max}$. For each signature S_i language $L_i \subseteq \Sigma^*$ is defined as

$$L_i = \{\, w_1 w_2 w_3 \mid w_1 \in (\Sigma_D^{(i)})^+, w_2 \in (\Sigma_N^{(i)})^*, w_3 \in (\Sigma_R^{(i)})^+, |w_3| = |w_1| + 1 \,\}.$$

First, we show that, for any subset $I = \{i_1, i_2, \ldots, i_k\} \subseteq \{1, 2, \ldots, k_{max}\}$, language $L_I = \bigcup_{i \in I} (L_i)^+$ is accepted by some IDCA(k) M. To this end, the counter update function α of M associates signature S_{i_j} with counter C_j, for $i_j \in I$. In this way, when starting with counter value zero, for any input factor $w_1 w_2 w_3$ from L_{i_j}, counter C_j is incremented to $|w_1|$ while M processes the prefix w_1 of the factor. On w_2 the value of counter C_j is unchanged. Since $|w_3| = |w_1| + 1$, counter C_j is decremented to value zero for the first time when only one input symbol of the factor is left. The next transition of M on counter value zero drives M into an accepting state while the value of counter C_j remains zero. Therefore, M accepts if the input has been processed entirely. Otherwise it repeats the process for the next input factor from L_{i_j}. Moreover, since $\left((\Sigma_D^{(i_j)})^+ (\Sigma_N^{(i_j)})^* (\Sigma_R^{(i_j)})^+\right)^+$ is regular, M can determine in its states whether the input has the format of all words in $(L_{i_j})^+$. Since M has as many counters as languages are joined to L_I, an input can be accepted if and only if it belongs to L_I.

Second, we show that, for any subset $I = \{i_1, i_2, \ldots, i_k\} \subseteq \{1, 2, \ldots, k_{max}\}$, language L_I is not accepted by any IDCA($k-1$). In contrast to the assertion assume that there is some subset $I = \{i_1, i_2, \ldots, i_k\}$ and some IDCA($k-1$) $M = \langle Q, \Sigma, k-1, q_0, F, \alpha, \delta \rangle$ that accepts L_I. Since L_I is the union of k languages which in turn are defined by k signatures, but M has only $k-1$ counters, there is at least one of the joined languages, say $(L_j)^+$, whose underlying signature $S_j = (\Sigma_D^{(j)}, \Sigma_R^{(j)}, \Sigma_N^{(j)})$ does not appear as the signature of any of the counters.

In order to obtain a contradiction, we next turn to construct an input word $\varphi \in (L_j)^+$ that fools all counters of M simultaneously. To this end, let

$$\Sigma_D^{(j)} = \{x_1, x_2, \ldots, x_p\}, \Sigma_N^{(j)} = \{y_1, y_2, \ldots, y_q\}, \text{ and } \Sigma_R^{(j)} = \{z_1, z_2, \ldots, z_r\}.$$

The word φ is the concatenation of r words $u_1, u_2, \ldots, u_r$ from L_j that are as follows. Let $c > r+2$ be a fixed constant. Then

$$u_i = (x_1 x_2 \cdots x_p)^c z_i^{c \cdot p+1}, \text{ for } 1 \leq i \leq r-1.$$

So, the length of u_i is $2 \cdot c \cdot p + 1$. Now we set $c_r = (r-1)(2 \cdot c \cdot p+1) + p + |Q|$ and $s = (p+1) \cdot c_r$, and define

$$u_r = (x_1 x_2 \cdots x_p)^{c_r} y_1^{2 \cdot s} y_2^{2^2 \cdot s} \cdots y_q^{2^q \cdot s} z_r^{c_r \cdot p+1}.$$

Next we determine how the counters of M evolve on input $\varphi = u_1 u_2 \cdots u_r$ that belongs to $L(M)$. To this end, we distinguish three cases dependent on the signatures of the counters.

Case 1. Let $\Sigma_N^{(j)} \not\subseteq \Sigma_N^{(i)}$ for some counter C_i.

To determine how counter C_i evolves on input φ we consider the greatest index ℓ from $\{1, 2, \ldots, q\}$ such that $y_\ell \notin \Sigma_N^{(i)}$.

The length of the prefix of φ up to but not including the factor $y_\ell^{2^\ell \cdot s}$ from u_r is $(r-1)(2 \cdot c \cdot p+1) + c_r \cdot p + 2 \cdot s + 2^2 \cdot s + \cdots + 2^{\ell-1} \cdot s < s + 2 \cdot s + 2^2 \cdot s + \cdots + 2^{\ell-1} \cdot s = (2^\ell - 1) \cdot s$. Therefore, after processing the prefix, the value of counter C_i is at most $(2^\ell - 1) \cdot s$.

If $y_\ell \in \Sigma_R^{(i)}$ then the value of counter C_i is decremented to zero after processing the following factor $y_\ell^{2^\ell \cdot s}$. Furthermore, since ℓ has been chosen to be the greatest index, the value of counter C_i remains zero until the first symbol z_r appears in the input. Dependent on whether z_r belongs to $\Sigma_D^{(i)}$ or $\Sigma_N^{(i)} \cup \Sigma_R^{(i)}$ the value of counter C_i increases on the remaining input suffix $z_r^{c_r \cdot p+1}$ or remains zero. In both cases the status of counter C_i does not change on the last $c_r \cdot p$ input symbols.

If $y_\ell \in \Sigma_D^{(i)}$ then the value of counter C_i is at least $2^\ell \cdot s$ after processing the following factor $y_\ell^{2^\ell \cdot s}$. Furthermore, since ℓ has been chosen to be the greatest index, the value of counter C_i does not change until the first symbol z_r appears in the input. Moreover, since $c_r \cdot p + 1 < 2^\ell \cdot s$ the status of counter C_i does not change on the last $c_r \cdot p$ input symbols.

Case 2. Let $\Sigma_N^{(j)} \subseteq \Sigma_N^{(i)}$ and $\Sigma_D^{(j)} \not\subseteq \Sigma_D^{(i)}$ for some counter C_i.

The length of the prefix $u_1 u_2 \cdots u_{r-1}$ of φ is $(r-1)(2 \cdot c \cdot p+1)$. Therefore, after processing the prefix, the value of counter C_i is at most $(r-1)(2 \cdot c \cdot p+1)$. Since there is at least one symbol from $\{x_1, x_2, \ldots, x_p\}$ that does not belong to $\Sigma_D^{(i)}$, the value of counter C_i increases by at most $c_r \cdot (p-1)$ on processing the following factor $(x_1 x_2 \cdots x_p)^{c_r}$. This gives a counter value of at most $(r-1)(2 \cdot c \cdot p+1) + c_r \cdot (p-1) = c_r - p - |Q| + c_r \cdot p - c_r = c_r \cdot p - p - |Q|$.

Dependent on whether z_r belongs to $\Sigma_D^{(i)} \cup \Sigma_N^{(i)}$ or $\Sigma_R^{(i)}$ the value of counter C_i increases or remains unchanged, or decreases by $c_r \cdot p+1$ on the remaining input suffix $z_r^{c_r \cdot p+1}$. In the former case, clearly, the status of counter C_i does not change on the last $c_r \cdot p$ input symbols. In the latter case the counter is decreased to zero after processing at most $c_r \cdot p - p - |Q|$ input symbols z_r. So, the status of counter C_i does not change on the last $p + |Q| + 1$ input symbols.

Case 3. Let $\Sigma_N^{(j)} \subseteq \Sigma_N^{(i)}$ and $\Sigma_D^{(j)} \subseteq \Sigma_D^{(i)}$ for some counter C_i.

In this case we know that at least one of the inclusions is strict and obtain $\Sigma_R^{(i)} \subset \Sigma_R^{(j)}$. Let ℓ be the greatest index from $\{1, 2, \ldots, r\}$ such that $z_\ell \notin \Sigma_R^{(i)}$.

Since counter C_i increases on all input factors $x_1 x_2 \cdots x_p$ by p, after processing the prefix $(x_1 x_2 \cdots x_p)^c$ of u_ℓ if $\ell < r$ or $(x_1 x_2 \cdots x_p)^{c_r}$ of u_r if $\ell = r$, the counter value is at least $c \cdot p$ in the former and at least $c_r \cdot p$ in the latter case. Since $z_\ell \notin \Sigma_R^{(i)}$, the value does not decrease on suffix $z_\ell^{c \cdot p+1}$ of u_ℓ if $\ell < r$ or $z_\ell^{c_r \cdot p+1}$ of u_r if $\ell = r$.

If $\ell = r$ this implies immediately that the status of counter C_i does not change on the last $c_r \cdot p$ input symbols.

If $\ell < r$, the value of counter C_i is at least $c \cdot p$ after processing factor u_ℓ of φ. The value increases by $c \cdot p$ and subsequently possibly decreases by $c \cdot p+1$ on each of the remaining $r - \ell - 1$ factors $u_{\ell+1}, u_{\ell+2}, \ldots, u_{r-\ell-1}$. Finally, on the prefix $(x_1 x_2 \cdots x_p)^{c_r}$ of u_r it increases by $c_r \cdot p$. At that time its value is at least $c \cdot p - (r - \ell - 1) + c_r \cdot p$. Recall that $p, r \geq 1$ since S_j is useful. Since $\Sigma_N^{(j)} \subseteq \Sigma_N^{(i)}$, it decreases by at most $c_r \cdot p+1$ on the remaining input suffix. By $c \cdot p - (r - \ell - 1) + c_r \cdot p > c \cdot p - r + c_r \cdot p > (r+2) \cdot p - r + c_r \cdot p > 2 + c_r \cdot p$ we conclude that counter C_i is not decremented to zero on the suffix and, thus, the status of counter C_i does not change on the last $c_r \cdot p$ input symbols. This concludes Case 3.

Cases 1 to 3 show that the status of all counters of M at least do not change on the last $p + |Q| \geq 1 + |Q|$ input symbols. Since these input symbols are all the same, that is, they are z_r, automaton M enters some state at least twice when processing this suffix. Let z_r^n with $1 \leq n \leq |Q|$ drive M from some state q to state q when processing this suffix. Define φ' to be the word φ with n symbols z_r chopped off. Since φ is accepted we conclude that φ' is accepted as well. However, φ' does not belong to $(L_j)^+$.

Since $L(M) = L_I$, it remains to be shown that φ' does not belong to any of the languages $(L_i)^+$ with $i \in I = \{i_1, i_2, \ldots, i_k\}$ and $i \neq j$.

Assume there is such an i such that $\varphi' \in (L_i)^+$. We consider the structure of all words in $(L_i)^+$. It follows that $x_1 \in \Sigma_D^{(i)}$ and $z_r \in \Sigma_R^{(i)}$.

Case 1. Let there be some $x_t \in \{x_2, x_3, \ldots, x_p\}$ that does not belong to $\Sigma_D^{(i)}$. Since the symbol after x_p is $x_1 \in \Sigma_D^{(i)}$ this implies that a prefix of $x_1 x_2 \cdots x_p$ belongs to $(L_i)^+$. If this prefix is proper, the prefix $(x_1 x_2 \cdots x_p)^2$ of φ' shows that φ' cannot belong to $(L_i)^+$. Therefore, the prefix is not proper and we conclude that the word $x_1 x_2 \cdots x_p$ itself belongs to $(L_i)^+$. However, in this case the prefix $(x_1 x_2 \cdots x_p)^c z_1^{c \cdot p+1} x_1 x_2 \cdots x_p$ of φ' implies that φ' is in a wrong format if $z_1 \in \Sigma_N^{(i)}$ and cannot belong to $(L_i)^+$ if $z_1 \in \Sigma_D^{(i)} \cup \Sigma_R^{(i)}$.

Case 2. We have $\Sigma_D^{(i)} \supseteq \Sigma_D^{(j)}$. Since all symbols $z \in \{z_1, z_2, \ldots, z_{r-1}\}$ have predecessor symbol $x_p \in \Sigma_D^{(i)}$ and successor symbol $x_1 \in \Sigma_D^{(i)}$ in φ', they must belong either to $\Sigma_R^{(i)}$ or to $\Sigma_D^{(i)}$.

If there is some $1 \leq t < r-1$ such that $z_t \in \Sigma_D^{(i)}$ and $z_{t+1} \in \Sigma_R^{(i)}$ then the number $c \cdot p+1$ of symbols z_{t+1} does not match one plus the number of symbols from $\Sigma_D^{(i)}$ appearing directly before the z_{t+1}. So, φ' does not belong to $(L_i)^+$ in this case. We conclude that if there is some $z_t \in \Sigma_D^{(i)}$, for $1 \leq t \leq r-1$, then all $z \in \{z_t, z_{t+1}, \ldots, z_{r-1}\}$ belong to $\Sigma_D^{(i)}$. Since in the suffix u_r of φ' there are less than $c_r \cdot p + 1$ symbols $z_r \in \Sigma_R^{(i)}$ but $c_r \cdot p$ symbols from $\Sigma_D^{(i)}$, at least one of the symbols from $\{y_1, y_2, \ldots, y_q\}$ must belong to $\Sigma_R^{(i)}$ in order to make φ' belong to $(L_i)^+$. Since any y from $\{y_1, y_2, \ldots, y_q\}$ appears more frequently than the length of its prefix from φ', the word φ' does not belong to $(L_i)^+$ in this case as well. So, we have $\{z_1, z_2, \ldots, z_{r-1}\} \subseteq \Sigma_R^{(i)}$.

Case 3. We have $\Sigma_D^{(i)} \supseteq \Sigma_D^{(j)}$ and $\Sigma_R^{(i)} \supseteq \Sigma_R^{(j)}$. So, the prefix $u_1 u_2 \cdots u_{r-1}$ of φ' belongs to $(L_i)^+$. Now, if there is some $y_t \in \{y_1, y_2, \ldots, y_q\}$ that does not belong to $\Sigma_N^{(i)}$ then a straightforward calculation shows that the suffix $(x_1 x_2 \cdots x_p)^{c_r} y_1^{2 \cdot s} y_2^{2^2 \cdot s} \cdots y_q^{2^q \cdot s} z_r^{c_r \cdot p+1-n}$ does not belong to $(L_i)^+$. So, φ' does not belong to $(L_i)^+$ either. This concludes Case 3.

Cases 1 to 3 show that in any case φ' does not belong to $(L_i)^+$. The contradiction implies that φ' does not belong to L_I which in turn is a contradiction to the assumption that L_I is accepted by M. □

4 Closure Properties

Here we are interested in the closure properties of the language families accepted by input-driven counter automata. However, the results for ordinary k-counter automata are complemented by deriving closure under complementation which, in turn, yields non-closure under intersection. The results are summarized in Table 1.

Table 1. Closure properties of the language families discussed. Symbols $\cup_c$, $\cap_c$, and $\cdot_c$ denote union, intersection, and concatenation with compatible signatures. Such operations are not defined for non-input-driven devices and are marked with '—'.

	$\overline{}$	$\cup$	$\cap$	$\cup_c$	$\cap_c$	$\cdot$	$\cdot_c$	$*$	$h_{l.p.}$	REV
REG	yes	yes	yes	—	—	yes	—	yes	yes	yes
$\mathscr{L}$(IDCA(k))	yes	no	no	yes	yes	no	no	no	no	no
$\mathscr{L}$(IDCA)	yes	yes	yes	yes	yes	no	no	no	no	no
$\mathscr{L}$(DCA(k))	yes	no	no	—	—	no	—	no	no	no
$\mathscr{L}$(DCA)	yes	yes	yes	—	—	no	—	no	no	no

We say that two signatures $\Sigma = \Sigma_D \cup \Sigma_R \cup \Sigma_N$ and $\hat{\Sigma} = \hat{\Sigma}_D \cup \hat{\Sigma}_R \cup \hat{\Sigma}_N$ are *compatible* if the symbols shared by both alphabets have the same effect on the counters. That is, if $\bigcup_{j\in\{D,R,N\}}(\Sigma_j \setminus \hat{\Sigma}_j) \cap \hat{\Sigma}$ and $\bigcup_{j\in\{D,R,N\}}(\hat{\Sigma}_j \setminus \Sigma_j) \cap \Sigma$ are empty. Two input-driven counter automata M and M' have compatible signatures, if for any counter of M there is a counter of M' with compatible signature, and vice versa.

Since the devices under consideration are deterministic and are working in realtime, the closure of the accepted language families under complementation can be derived.

Proposition 7. *Let $k \geq 0$. The families of languages accepted by DCA(k), IDCA(k), and IDCA are closed under complementation.*

The property of working input-driven suggests to consider closure properties for the cases where the languages are accepted by devices having compatible signatures.

Proposition 8. *Let $k \geq 0$. The family of languages accepted by IDCA(k) is closed under union and intersection with compatible signatures.*

If we drop the restriction of compatible signatures then multi-counter automata accept language families that are still closed under union and intersection.

Proposition 9. *The family of languages accepted by IDCA is closed under union and intersection.*

We conclude the investigation of closures under Boolean operations by stressing that the restriction to compatible signatures is a serious one. If we drop that restriction for a fixed number of counters, the positive closure property gets lost.

Proposition 10. *Let $k \geq 1$. The family of languages accepted by IDCA(k) is neither closed under union nor under intersection.*

We conclude the section with the investigation of the closure properties under the operations concatenation, iteration, reversal, and length-preserving homomorphism. We use $\{a^m b^n \mid 0 \leq n \leq m\}$, which may leave an unbounded amount of garbage in the counters, as basic witness language to show the non-closures.

Proposition 11. *Let $k \geq 1$. The families of languages accepted by IDCA(k) and IDCA are not closed under concatenation with compatible signatures, iteration, reversal, and length-preserving homomorphism.*

5 Decidability Problems

In this section we turn to explore the decidability problems of emptiness, finiteness, universality, inclusion, equivalence, and regularity for IDCA(k) with $k \geq 0$

counters. Since IDCA(0) are deterministic finite automata, all decidability questions mentioned are decidable. If $k = 1$, we obtain one-counter machines which are special cases of deterministic pushdown automata. Since emptiness, finiteness, universality, equivalence, and regularity is decidable for such automata, we obtain these decidability results for IDCA(1) as well. Finally, the decidability of inclusion for IDCA(1) with compatible signatures is shown in [14]. However, it is shown in [14] as well that the inclusion problem for IDCA(1) becomes undecidable if the signatures are not necessarily compatible.

The complexity of the equivalence problem for DCA(1) is known to be NL-complete [4]. So, it is in NL for IDCA(1) as well. Moreover, since the emptiness problem for deterministic finite automata is already NL-hard, and the emptiness problem easily reduces to the equivalence problem, the latter is NL-complete for IDCA(1).

The inclusion problem for deterministic input-driven pushdown automata with compatible signatures is P-complete [18]. From the NL-hardness of the equivalence problem for IDCA(1) the NL-hardness of the inclusion problem follows. The constructions for the closure under complementation and intersection together with the fact that the emptiness problem for IDCA(1) is in NL yields an NL algorithm for the inclusion problem for IDCA(1). So, the inclusion problem for IDCA(1) is NL-complete.

Now, we consider the case of IDCA with at least two counters. It turns out that in this case undecidability results can be obtained, since it is possible to utilize the undecidability of the halting problem for two-counter machines shown by Minsky [17].

Theorem 12. *Let $k \geq 2$ and M be an IDCA(k). Then it is undecidable whether or not $L(M)$ is empty as well as whether or not $L(M)$ is finite.*

The closure under complementation relates the questions of emptiness and universality, whereas inclusion and equivalence questions can be reduced to universality questions.

Corollary 13. *Let $k \geq 2$ and M be an IDCA(k) over some input alphabet Σ. Then it is undecidable whether or not $L(M) = \Sigma^*$.*

Proof. Due to Proposition 7 it is possible for an IDCA(2) M to construct an IDCA(2) M' accepting the complement $\overline{L(M)}$. Hence, the question of whether $L(M) = \Sigma^*$ is equivalent to $L(M') = \overline{L(M)} = \emptyset$. Since the latter question is undecidable due to Theorem 12 we obtain the claim of the theorem. □

Corollary 14. *Let $k \geq 2$ and M and M' be two IDCA(k) with compatible signatures. Then it is neither decidable whether or not $L(M) \subseteq L(M')$ nor whether or not $L(M) = L(M')$.*

Finally, we obtain that the regularity problem is undecidable as well.

Theorem 15. *Let $k \geq 2$ and M be an IDCA(k). Then it is undecidable whether or not M accepts a regular language.*

The undecidability results obtained obviously hold also for the stronger variants of IDCA as well as for the corresponding non-input-driven counter machines.

References

1. Alur, R., Madhusudan, P.: Visibly pushdown languages. In: Babai, L. (ed.) STOC 2004, pp. 202–211. ACM (2004). https://doi.org/10.1145/1007352.1007390
2. Bárány, V., Löding, C., Serre, O.: Regularity problems for visibly pushdown languages. In: Durand, B., Thomas, W. (eds.) STACS 2006. LNCS, vol. 3884, pp. 420–431. Springer, Heidelberg (2006). https://doi.org/10.1007/11672142_34
3. Bensch, S., Holzer, M., Kutrib, M., Malcher, A.: Input-driven stack automata. In: Baeten, J.C.M., Ball, T., de Boer, F.S. (eds.) TCS 2012. LNCS, vol. 7604, pp. 28–42. Springer, Heidelberg (2012). https://doi.org/10.1007/978-3-642-33475-7_3
4. Böhm, S., Göller, S., Jančar, P.: Equivalence of deterministic one-counter automata is NL-complete. In: Boneh, D., Roughgarden, T., Feigenbaum, J. (eds.) STOC 2013, pp. 131–140. ACM (2013). https://doi.org/10.1145/2488608.2488626
5. von Braunmühl, B., Verbeek, R.: Input-driven languages are recognized in $\log n$ space. In: Topics in the Theory of Computation, Mathematics Studies, vol. 102, pp. 1–19, North-Holland (1985). https://doi.org/10.1007/3-540-12689-9_92
6. Breveglieri, L., Cherubini, A., Citrini, C., Crespi-Reghizzi, S.: Multi-push-down languages and grammars. Int. J. Found. Comput. Sci. **7**, 253–292 (1996). https://doi.org/10.1142/S0129054196000191
7. Fischer, P.C., Meyer, A.R., Rosenberg, A.L.: Counter machines and counter languages. Math. Syst. Theory **2**, 265–283 (1968). https://doi.org/10.1007/BF01694011
8. Greibach, S.A.: Remarks on blind and partially blind one-way multicounter machines. Theor. Comput. Sci. **7**, 311–324 (1978). https://doi.org/10.1016/0304-3975(78)90020-8
9. Hahn, M., Krebs, A., Lange, K.-J., Ludwig, M.: Visibly counter languages and the structure of NC^1. In: Italiano, G.F., Pighizzini, G., Sannella, D.T. (eds.) MFCS 2015. LNCS, vol. 9235, pp. 384–394. Springer, Heidelberg (2015). https://doi.org/10.1007/978-3-662-48054-0_32
10. Ibarra, O.H.: Reversal-bounded multicounter machines and their decision problems. J. ACM **25**, 116–133 (1978). https://doi.org/10.1145/322047.322058
11. Ibarra, O.H.: Visibly pushdown automata and transducers with counters. Fund. Inform. **148**, 291–308 (2016). https://doi.org/10.3233/FI-2016-1436
12. Krebs, A., Lange, K., Ludwig, M.: Visibly counter languages and constant depth circuits. In: Mayr, E.W., Ollinger, N. (eds.) STACS 2015. LIPIcs, vol. 30, pp. 594–607 (2015). https://doi.org/10.4230/LIPIcs.STACS.2015.594
13. Kutrib, M., Malcher, A., Mereghetti, C., Palano, B., Wendlandt, M.: Deterministic input-driven queue automata: finite turns, decidability, and closure properties. Theor. Comput. Sci. **578**, 58–71 (2015)
14. Kutrib, M., Malcher, A., Wendlandt, M.: Tinput-driven pushdown, counter, and stack automata. Fund. Inform. **155**, 59–88 (2017). https://doi.org/10.3233/FI-2017-1576
15. La Torre, S., Napoli, M., Parlato, G.: Scope-bounded pushdown languages. Int. J. Found. Comput. Sci. **27**, 215–234 (2016)
16. Mehlhorn, K.: Pebbling mountain ranges and its application to DCFL-recognition. In: de Bakker, J., van Leeuwen, J. (eds.) ICALP 1980. LNCS, vol. 85, pp. 422–435. Springer, Heidelberg (1980). https://doi.org/10.1007/3-540-10003-2_89
17. Minsky, M.L.: Recursive unsolvability of Post's problem of "tag" and other topics in theory of Turing machines. Ann. Math. **74**, 437–455 (1961). 2nd S
18. Okhotin, A., Salomaa, K.: Complexity of input-driven pushdown automata. SIGACT News **45**, 47–67 (2014). https://doi.org/10.1145/2636805.2636821

Two-Dimensional Pattern Matching Against Basic Picture Languages

František Mráz[1], Daniel Průša[2(✉)], and Michael Wehar[3]

[1] Faculty of Mathematics and Physics, Charles University, Prague, Czech Republic
frantisek.mraz@mff.cuni.cz

[2] Faculty of Electrical Engineering, Czech Technical University, Prague, Czech Republic
daniel.prusa@fel.cvut.cz

[3] Temple University, Philadelphia, PA, USA
michael.wehar@temple.edu

Abstract. Given a two-dimensional array of symbols and a picture language over a finite alphabet, we study the problem of finding rectangular subarrays of the array that belong to the picture language. We formulate four particular problems – finding maximum, minimum, any or all match(es) – and describe algorithms solving them for basic classes of picture languages, including local picture languages and picture languages accepted by deterministic on-line tessellation automata or deterministic four-way finite automata. We also prove that the matching problems cannot be solved for the class of local picture languages in linear time unless the problem of triangle finding is solvable in quadratic time. This shows there is a fundamental difference in the pattern matching complexity regarding the one-dimensional and two-dimensional setting.

Keywords: Two-dimensional pattern matching · Picture languages · Local picture languages · Two-dimensional finite-state automata

1 Introduction

The string pattern matching for a text is an intensively studied and well understood task. The problem of searching for a matching substring described by a set of strings or a regular expression has very efficient implementations and a wide applicability [2]. The problem extends to higher dimensions. In this extended setting, the situation is clear if we search for a fixed pattern – several algorithms have been proposed to solve this task, considering either exact or approximate matching [4,11]. An algorithm solving the two-dimensional (2D) matching against a finite set of equally sized patterns has been described in [20]. In addition, results involving equally sized patterns generated by an extension

D. Průša—Supported by the Czech Science Foundation grant 19-09967S.

M. Hospodár and G. Jirásková (Eds.): CIAA 2019, LNCS 11601, pp. 209–221, 2019.
https://doi.org/10.1007/978-3-030-23679-3_17

of the regular matrix grammar [18] have recently been presented [8]. On the other hand, the research of the problem of finding rectangular subpictures of arbitrary sizes that belong to a picture language, specified by a two-dimensional recognizing system, is limited. Few simple two-dimensional matching problems of this type are popular enough to be given in algorithms courses or as programming interview questions (e.g., in a binary matrix, find a maximum subrectangle filled/surrounded by ones [13]), however, a more systematic study is missing.

We aim to fill this gap and address the 2D matching against a picture language without considering any size restrictions on matches. We define four problems, varying in the required output. We show how these problems can be solved for local picture languages [7] and two incomparable classes of picture languages presented as possible generalizations of the regular languages, namely the classes of picture languages accepted by the deterministic four-way automaton (4DFA) [5] and deterministic on-line tessellation automaton (2DOTA) [9], which is closely related to the class of deterministic recognizable languages (DREC) [3]. These models allow the design of 2D pattern matching algorithms faster than a brute force solution. However, unlike in the one-dimensional setting, they are not linear with respect to the area of input pictures. We derive a conditional lower bound which prevents us from designing linear-time matching algorithms even in the case of the very basic local picture languages.

The paper is structured as follows. Section 2 recalls notations from the theory of picture languages. Section 3 defines four variants of the matching problem and demonstrates by examples that solving the problems is of practical importance even in the case of patterns specified by simple picture languages. The complexity of the tasks is studied for local picture languages in Sect. 4 – an upper bound is established, a conditional non-linear lower bound is derived, and a subclass with linear-time complexity is identified. Results on matching against picture languages accepted by 4DFA and 2DOTA are reported in Sect. 5. The paper concludes with Sect. 6, which discusses achieved results and open problems.

2 Preliminaries

We use the common notation and terms on picture languages [7]. A *picture* P over a finite alphabet Σ is a 2D array of symbols from Σ. If P has m rows and n columns, it is of size $m \times n$ and of area mn. Rows of P are indexed from 1 to m, columns of P are indexed from 1 to n. In graphical visualizations, position $(1, 1)$ is associated with the top-left corner. The symbol in the i-th row and j-th column of P is referred by $P(i, j)$. For integers $1 \le i \le k \le m$ and $1 \le j \le \ell \le n$, $P(i, j : k, \ell)$ denotes the non-empty *subpicture* of P of size $(k-i+1) \times (\ell-j+1)$ whose top-left and bottom-right corner is in P at coordinate (i, j) and (k, ℓ), respectively. For $a \in \Sigma$, $|P|_a$ is the number of occurrences of symbol a in P. The empty picture of size 0×0 is denoted by Λ. The set of all pictures over Σ of size $m \times n$ is denoted by $\Sigma^{m,n}$ and the set of all non-empty pictures over Σ is $\Sigma^{+,+} = \bigcup_{i=1}^{\infty} \bigcup_{j=1}^{\infty} \Sigma^{i,j}$. For $j \ge 1$, we also write $\Sigma^{+,j} = \bigcup_{i=1}^{\infty} \Sigma^{i,j}$ and $\Sigma^{j,+} = \bigcup_{i=1}^{\infty} \Sigma^{j,i}$. A *picture language* is a subset of $\Sigma^{*,*} = \Sigma^{+,+} \cup \{\Lambda\}$.

Let # be the background symbol not contained in any considered alphabet. For a picture $P \in \Sigma^{m,n}$, we define its *boundary picture* $\hat{P}$ over $\Sigma \cup \{\#\}$ of size $(m+2) \times (n+2)$, which fulfils $\hat{P}(2, 2 : m+1, n+1) = P$ and $\hat{P}(i,j) = \#$ iff $i \in \{1, m+2\}$ or $j \in \{1, n+2\}$. We also define *partial* border pictures, namely $\hat{P}^{\mathrm{t,b}}$, $\hat{P}^{\mathrm{l,t,b}}$ and $\hat{P}^{\mathrm{r,t,b}}$, where the rows and columns of #'s are located only at the borders prescribed by the super scripts (l, r, t and b stands for the left, right, top and bottom border, respectively). See Fig. 1 for examples. For $k, \ell \in \mathbb{N}$, let $B_{k,\ell}(P)$ denote the set of all subpictures of P which are of size $k \times \ell$. For a set of pictures L, define $B_{k,\ell}(L) = \bigcup_{P \in L} B_{k,\ell}(P)$. A *tile* is a square picture of size 2×2. A picture language $L \subseteq \Sigma^{*,*}$ is called a *local* picture language if there is a finite set of tiles Θ over $\Sigma \cup \{\#\}$ such that $L = \{ P \in \Sigma^{*,*} \mid B_{2,2}(\hat{P}) \subseteq \Theta \}$, that is, $P \in L$ iff all tiles that are subpictures of $\hat{P}$ belong to Θ. This fact is expressed as $L = L(\Theta)$. The family of local picture languages is denoted as LOC.

#	#	#	#	#	#	#
#	1	0	0	0	0	#
#	1	1	1	0	0	#
#	0	0	1	0	1	#
#	#	#	#	#	#	#

(a)

#	#	#	#	#
1	0	0	0	0
1	1	1	0	0
0	0	1	0	1
#	#	#	#	#

(b)

#	#	#	#	#	#
1	0	0	0	0	#
1	1	1	0	0	#
0	0	1	0	1	#
#	#	#	#	#	#

(c)

Fig. 1. For a picture P over $\{0, 1\}$ of size 3×5, there is its (a) boundary picture $\hat{P}$, (b) partial boundary picture $\hat{P}^{\mathrm{t,b}}$ and (c) partial boundary picture $\hat{P}^{\mathrm{r,t,b}}$.

The deterministic four-way finite automaton (4DFA) [5] is a generalization of the two-way finite automaton. It is a bounded automaton whose head moves in four directions, represented by the set of head movements $\{\mathrm{U, D, L, R}\}$ where the elements stand for up, down, left and right, respectively. Formally, it is a tuple $\mathcal{A} = (Q, \Sigma, \delta, q_0, F)$ where Q is a finite set of states, Σ is an input alphabet, $\delta : Q \times (\Sigma \cup \{\#\}) \to Q \times \{\mathrm{U, D, L, R}\}$ is a transition function, $q_0 \in Q$ is the initial state and $F \subseteq Q$ is a set of accepting states. A picture $P \in \Sigma^{*,*}$ is accepted by $\mathcal{A}$ if starting at the top-left corner of P in the initial state q_0, the automaton $\mathcal{A}$ reaches an accepting state from F while not leaving $\hat{P}$.

The deterministic two-dimensional on-line tessellation automaton (2DOTA) [9] is a restricted 2D cellular automaton. Formally, it is a tuple $\mathcal{A} = (Q, \Sigma, \delta, F)$, where Q is a finite set of states, Σ is an input alphabet, $\delta : (Q \cup \{\#\}) \times \Sigma \times (Q \cup \{\#\}) \to Q$ is a transition function and $F \subseteq Q$ is a set of accepting states. For an input picture $P \in \Sigma^{m,n}$, we define $P^{\mathcal{A}} \in Q^{m,n}$ by the recurrent formula: $P^{\mathcal{A}}(i,j) = \delta(q_L, P(i,j), q_U)$ where

$$q_L = \begin{cases} \#, & \text{if } j = 1; \\ P^{\mathcal{A}}(i, j-1), & \text{otherwise,} \end{cases} \quad \text{and} \quad q_U = \begin{cases} \#, & \text{if } i = 1; \\ P^{\mathcal{A}}(i-1, j), & \text{otherwise.} \end{cases}$$

$P^{\mathcal{A}}$ represents final states of the cells. $\mathcal{A}$ accepts P if $P^{\mathcal{A}}(m,n) \in F$.

3 Background

3.1 Examples of Two-Dimensional Pattern Matching

2D patterns emerge in many domains like spreadsheets, timetables, discrete maps, board games, crosswords or other puzzles. Useful queries over such data can be specified by means of basic picture languages as demonstrated in Fig. 2 where the first two tasks involve matching against local picture languages and the third task involves matching against a picture language in $L(\text{2DOTA}) \cap L(\text{4DFA})$.

	Java	C++	Ruby	Pearl
Miller	X		X	x
Smith		x	x	
Taylor	X		X	

(a)

	1	2	3	4	5	6
Miller	X	X	X		x	
Smith			x	x	x	
Taylor	x	X	X	X		

(b)

(c)

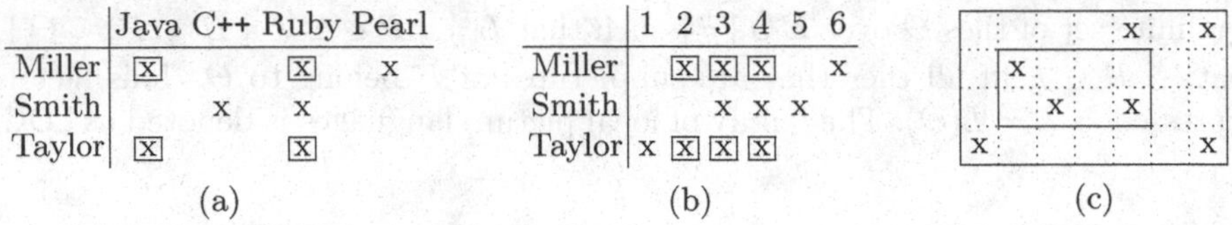

Fig. 2. Examples of (binary) 2D pattern matching tasks and their solutions. (a) In a table listing employees programming skills, find two employees who know the same two programming languages. (b) In a lab occupancy timetable, find a pair of employees that share the lab for the maximum number of consecutive time slots. (c) In a grid map with resources, find a smallest rectangular area covering at least 3 resources.

3.2 Task Formulations

Let L be a picture language over Σ. For $P \in \Sigma^{*,*}$, let $M(P, L) = \{(i, j : k, \ell) \mid P(i, j : k, \ell) \in L\}$ be the set of rectangular areas in P whose content equals a picture from L. We define the following two-dimensional pattern matching tasks.

1. Problem $\mathcal{M}_{\text{MAX}}(L)$: Given an input $P \in \Sigma^{*,*}$, output some $R \in M(P, L)$ with the maximum area. Return NO if $M(P, L)$ is empty.
2. Problem $\mathcal{M}_{\text{MIN}}(L)$: Given an input $P \in \Sigma^{*,*}$, output some $R \in M(P, L)$ with the minimum area. Return NO if $M(P, L)$ is empty.
3. Problem $\mathcal{M}_{\text{ANY}}(L)$: Given an input $P \in \Sigma^{*,*}$, output any $R \in M(P, L)$. Return NO if $M(P, L)$ is empty.
4. Problem $\mathcal{M}_{\text{ALL}}(L)$: Given an input $P \in \Sigma^{*,*}$, output the set $\{(k, \ell) \mid \exists i, j : (i, j : k, \ell) \in M(P, L)\}$, i.e., list the bottom-right corners of all matches.

Our goal is to study time complexity of the stated matching problems for picture languages from families LOC, $L(\text{2DOTA})$ and $L(\text{4DFA})$. For such picture languages, the membership problem is decidable in time linear in the area of input pictures, hence the brute force approach to the pattern matching yields a trivial cubic upper bound (given an input $P \in \Sigma^{m,n}$, each of $\Theta(m^2 n^2)$ subpictures in P is checked for a match in $O(mn)$ time). We will study existence of more efficient algorithms. On the other hand, it is not promising to consider more powerful (but non-deterministic) families such as REC [7], for which the membership problem is NP-complete, and this hardness is inherited by the matching tasks.

3.3 One-Dimensional Pattern Matching

We show that all the matching problems defined in the previous section can be solved in linear time for regular (string) languages and string inputs.

Theorem 1. *Let L be a regular (string) language. Problems $\mathcal{M}_{\text{MAX}}(L)$, $\mathcal{M}_{\text{MIN}}(L)$, $\mathcal{M}_{\text{ANY}}(L)$ and $\mathcal{M}_{\text{ALL}}(L)$ can be solved in time linear in the length of the input string.*

Proof. Let $\mathcal{A} = (Q, \Sigma, \delta, q_0, F)$ be a deterministic finite automaton accepting the language $L = L(\mathcal{A}) \subseteq \Sigma^*$, where Q is a finite set of states, Σ is a finite alphabet, $q_0 \in Q$ is the initial state, $F \subseteq Q$ is a set of accepting states and $\delta : Q \times \Sigma \to Q$ is the transition function of $\mathcal{A}$, which extends to $\delta : Q \times \Sigma^* \to Q$ in the standard way. We will sketch an algorithm solving $\mathcal{M}_{\text{MAX}}(L)$, i.e., which for a given string $w = a_1 \cdots a_n$, with $a_1, \ldots, a_n \in \Sigma$, returns either NO if no non-empty subword of w belongs to L or a pair of integers (i_s, i_e) such that

$$a_{i_s} a_{i_s+1} \cdots a_{i_e} \in L \quad \text{and} \quad i_e - i_s = \max_{1 \le s \le e \le n} \{e - s \mid a_s a_{s+1} \cdots a_e \in L\},$$

that is, $a_{i_s} a_{i_s+1} \cdots a_{i_e}$ is a subword of w of maximal length belonging to L.

The algorithm will compute a sequence of arrays $A_0, \ldots, A_n$ indexed by Q such that for $t = 0, \ldots, n$ either $A_t(q) = +\infty$ when there is no suffix u of $a_1 \cdots a_t$ such that $\delta(q_0, u) = q$ or $P_t(q) = i \in \mathbb{N}$ and $u = a_i \cdots a_t$ is the longest suffix of $a_1 \cdots a_t$ such that $\delta(q_0, u) = q$. Note that we adopt $a_i \cdots a_t = \lambda$ whenever $i > t$.

For $t = 0$, we put $A_0(q_0) = 1$ and $A_0(q) = +\infty$, for all $q \in Q \setminus \{q_0\}$. From A_t, the array A_{t+1} can be obtained in the following way. For all states $q \in Q$, set $A_{t+1}(q)$ to $+\infty$ if $\delta(p, a_t) \neq q$, for all $p \in Q$, otherwise set $A_{t+1}(q)$ to $\min\{A_t(p) \mid \delta(p, a_t) = q\}$. Additionally, if $A_{t+1}(q_0) = +\infty$, replace $+\infty$ by $t + 2$.

Then, the maximal length of a subword of $a_1 \cdots a_n$ which belongs to L can be extracted as $\max\{t - A_t(q) \mid q \in F,\ t = 1, \ldots, n\}$. It is also easy to extract the starting and ending position of such a subword.

The time complexity of the above algorithm is $O(n \cdot |Q|) = O(n)$. The algorithm is easily adaptable to solve the other matching problems, too. □

4 Matching Against Local Picture Languages

4.1 General Algorithm

The following lemma gives an equivalent characterization of pictures belonging to a given picture language. Its purpose is to simplify the proof of Theorem 2.

Lemma 1. *Let Θ be a finite set of tiles over $\Sigma \cup \{\#\}$ and*

$$L_{\text{S}} = \{P \in \Sigma^{+,1} \mid P \in L(\Theta)\}, \qquad L_{\text{L}} = \{P \in \Sigma^{+,2} \mid B_{2,2}(\hat{P}^{\text{l,t,b}}) \subseteq \Theta\},$$
$$L_{\text{R}} = \{P \in \Sigma^{+,2} \mid B_{2,2}(\hat{P}^{\text{r,t,b}}) \subseteq \Theta\}, \qquad L_{\text{I}} = \{P \in \Sigma^{+,3} \mid B_{2,2}(\hat{P}^{\text{t,b}}) \subseteq \Theta\}.$$

A non-empty picture $P \in \Sigma^{m,n}$ is in $L(\Theta)$ if and only if either $P \in L_{\text{S}}$ or $n \ge 2$, $P(1, 1 : m, 2) \in L_{\text{L}}$, $P(1, n-1 : m, n) \in L_{\text{R}}$, and, for all $i = 1, \ldots, n-2$, $P(1, i : m, i+2) \in L_{\text{I}}$.

Proof. The validity of the lemma is obvious in the case of one-column pictures. In the case a picture $P \in \Sigma^{m,n}$ with more columns, the validity follows from the observation that each 2×2 subpicture of $\hat{P}$ is contained in $\hat{P}^{\mathrm{l,t,b}}(1,1:m+2,3)$, $\hat{P}^{\mathrm{r,t,b}}(1,n:m+2,n+2)$, or in $\hat{P}^{\mathrm{t,b}}(1,i:m+2,i+2)$ for some $i \in \{1,\ldots,n\}$. Since the allowed tiles in pictures from L_{L}, L_{R} and L_{I} coincide with Θ, the lemma statement has been proved. □

Theorem 2. *Let Θ be a finite set of tiles over $\Sigma \cup \{\#\}$ and $L = L(\Theta)$. There are algorithms solving problems $\mathcal{M}_{\mathrm{MAX}}(L)$, $\mathcal{M}_{\mathrm{MIN}}(L)$, $\mathcal{M}_{\mathrm{ANY}}(L)$ and $\mathcal{M}_{\mathrm{ALL}}(L)$ in time $O(mn\min\{m,n\})$ for pictures of size $m \times n$.*

Proof. Let $P \in \Sigma^{m,n}$ be an input. Assume, w.l.o.g., $m \leq n$. We give an algorithm solving $\mathcal{M}_{\mathrm{MAX}}(L)$, which is easily modifiable to solve the other problems.

The algorithm processes all rows of P. For a row r, it detects maximum matching subpictures of P that have their bottom row located in r. There are two phases. The first phase assigns to each cell of P at coordinates (i,j), $i \leq r$, a subset of the four-marker set {S, L, R, I}, based on the following criteria:

- A cell is marked as *single* (S) iff $P(i,j:r,j) \in L_{\mathrm{S}}$,
- a cell is marked as *left* (L) iff $j < n$ and $P(i,j:r,j+1) \in L_{\mathrm{L}}$,
- a cell is marked as *right* (R) iff $j > 1$ and $P(i,j-1:r,j) \in L_{\mathrm{R}}$, and
- a cell is marked as *inner* (I) iff $1 < j < n$ and $P(i,j-1:r,j+1) \in L_{\mathrm{I}}$.

To compute the markers, it suffices to use a finite-state device equipped by a scanning window of size 3×3. This device processes each column of P. For a column j, it starts at cell (r,j) and moves up to cell $(1,j)$.

Within the second phase, the algorithm iterates through rows $i = 1,\ldots,r$. In the i-th row, it searches for a longest continuous subsequence of markers described by the regular expression S+LI*R. By Theorem 1, this is done in time $O(n)$. If such a longest subsequence starts at cell (i,j) and ends at cell (i,k), then $P_{i,r} = P(i,j:r,k)$ is a matching subpicture of maximum area for a given i and r. The result is then $P_{i,r}$ with maximum area when considered all $1 \leq i \leq r \leq m$.

For each row r, both phases are done in time $O(mn)$, hence the algorithm finishes in time $O(m^2 n)$. □

4.2 Nonlinear Conditional Lower Bound

Background: Triangle Finding is a classical algorithmic problem that is solvable in polynomial time. Formally, the problem can be stated as follows. Given an undirected graph $G = (V,E)$, do there exist vertices a, b, $c \in V$ such that $\{a,b\}$, $\{b,c\}$, $\{c,a\} \in E$?

There is an efficient reduction from Triangle Finding to Boolean Matrix Multiplication (see [10]) meaning that Triangle Finding can be solved in time $O(n^{\omega})$ where $n = |V|$ and $\omega < 2.373$ denotes the matrix multiplication constant [21]. However, it is currently unknown if Triangle Finding can be solved in time $O(n^2)$.

Efficient reductions known as fine-grained reductions (see [22]) have been introduced to provide conditional lower bounds. In particular, the existence of a fine-grained reduction from Triangle Finding to a problem X establishes a conditional lower bound such that X cannot be solved more efficiently unless Triangle Finding can be solved more efficiently.

Conditional lower bounds based on Triangle Finding are known for several classical problems in formal language theory such as Context-Free Grammar Parsing [1,12], NFA Length Acceptance [15], and Two DFA Intersection Non-Emptiness [14].

Local Picture Language: We show that there is a local picture language L over a ternary alphabet such that $\mathcal{M}_{\text{ANY}}(L)$ cannot be solved in time $O(mn)$ unless there is an algorithm solving Triangle Finding in time $O(n^2)$. This result suggests that matching against simple picture languages is a fundamentally harder task than matching against string regular languages (see Theorem 1).

Let L_{corn2} be a picture language over $\Sigma = \{0, 1, 2\}$ such that L_{corn2} contains a picture $P \in \Sigma^{*,*}$ if and only if P has at least two rows and two columns, the top-right corner of P contains symbol 2 and the other corners contain symbol 1. This picture language is local. It is yielded by the set of tile templates

$$\begin{matrix}\#\#\\ \#1\end{matrix},\ \begin{matrix}\#1\\ \#\#\end{matrix},\ \begin{matrix}1\#\\ \#\#\end{matrix},\ \begin{matrix}\#\#\\ 2\#\end{matrix},\ \begin{matrix}\#\#\\ XY\end{matrix},\ \begin{matrix}\#X\\ \#Y\end{matrix},\ \begin{matrix}XY\\ \#\#\end{matrix},\ \begin{matrix}X\#\\ Y\#\end{matrix},\ \begin{matrix}XY\\ ZT\end{matrix}$$

where X, Y, Z, T are symbols of Σ.

Theorem 3. *$\mathcal{M}_{\text{ANY}}(L_{\text{corn2}})$ cannot be solved in time $O(mn)$ unless Triangle Finding can be solved in time $O(n^2)$.*

Proof. We give a fine-grained reduction from Triangle Finding to $\mathcal{M}_{\text{ANY}}(L_{\text{corn2}})$.

Let a graph $G = (V, E)$ be given. Let the set of vertices be $V = \{v_i \mid i \in \{1, \dots, n\}\}$. We construct a picture $P \in \{0, 1, 2\}^{n,n}$ such that G contains a triangle if and only if P has a subpicture which is in L_{corn2}.

Define P such that for all i and j, $P(i, j) = 2$ if $i = j$, $P(i, j) = 1$ if $i \neq j$ and $\{v_i, v_j\} \in E$, and $P(i, j) = 0$ otherwise. Since 2's are only present along the diagonal of the picture, we have that there is a subpicture within P where the upper right corner is 2 and the other corners are 1 if and only if there are numbers i, j, and k with $i < j < k$ such that $P(j, j) = 2$, $P(j, i) = 1$, $P(k, i) = 1$, and $P(k, j) = 1$. For this subpicture, $P(j, j)$ is upper right corner, $P(j, i)$ is upper left corner, $P(k, i)$ is lower left corner, and $P(k, j)$ is lower right corner.

Let numbers i, j, and k such that $i < j < k$ be given. We have that $P(j, j) = 2$, and $P(j, i) = P(k, i) = P(k, j) = 1$ iff $\{v_i, v_j\} \in E$, $\{v_j, v_k\} \in E$, and $\{v_k, v_i\} \in E$ by the definition of P. Therefore, there exist i, j, and k with $i < j < k$ such that $P(j, j) = 2$, $P(j, i) = P(k, i) = P(k, j) = 1$ iff there exist i, j, and k with $i < j < k$ such that $\{v_i, v_j\} \in E$, $\{v_j, v_k\} \in E$, and $\{v_k, v_i\} \in E$. It follows that G contains a triangle iff $\mathcal{M}_{\text{ANY}}(L_{\text{corn2}})$ has a solution for P.

Since P can be efficiently constructed in time $O(n^2)$, we have a fine-grained reduction from Triangle Finding to $\mathcal{M}_{\text{ANY}}(L_{\text{corn2}})$. Therefore, if we could solve

$\mathcal{M}_{\mathrm{ANY}}(L_{\mathrm{corn2}})$ in $O(n^2)$ time for n by n pictures, then we would be able to solve Triangle Finding in $O(n^2)$ time for graphs with at most n vertices. □

Remark 1. Let $h : \{0,1,2\} \to \{0,1\}$ be a homomorphism such that $h(0) = 00$, $h(1) = 11$, and $h(2) = 10$. The picture language $h(L_{\mathrm{corn2}})$ still encodes Triangle Finding. It is no longer a local picture language, however, it is accepted by a 2DOTA and a 4DFA, hence the conditional non-linear lower bound extends to L(2DOTA) and L(4DFA) over binary alphabets. It is an open problem if there is a binary local picture language that can be used to encode Triangle Finding.

4.3 Matching in Linear Time

In this section we present two types of linear time matching algorithms for selected local picture languages: (1) The binary local picture language $L_{\mathrm{corn}} = \pi(L_{\mathrm{corn2}})$ where $\pi : \{0,1,2\} \to \{0,1\}$ is a projection such that $\pi(0) = 0$ and $\pi(1) = \pi(2) = 1$. (2) A subclass of local picture languages called *border-unaware local picture languages.*

Lemma 2. *$\mathcal{M}_{\mathrm{ANY}}(L_{\mathrm{corn}})$ is solvable in time $O(mn)$ for pictures of size $m \times n$.*

Proof. It is shown in [19] that every m by n Boolean matrix M is in one to one correspondence with a bipartite graph $G = (V_1 \cup V_2, E)$ with disjoint sets of vertices V_1 and V_2, such that $|V_1| = m$ and $|V_2| = n$, corresponding to the rows and columns of M, respectively. There is an edge $(i,j) \in E$ if and only if $M(i,j) = 1$. Further, it is shown that M has a 2 by 2 (scattered) submatrix of 1's if and only if G has a $K_{2,2}$ subgraph (i.e. a four cycle).

Detecting if a graph contains a four cycle is solvable in time quadratic in the number of vertices [17,23]. A slight improvement can be made for bipartite graphs to time $O(mn)$. Therefore, $\mathcal{M}_{\mathrm{ANY}}(L_{\mathrm{corn}})$ is solvable in time $O(mn)$. □

Definition 1 (Border-unaware local picture language). A local picture language $L = L(\Theta)$ over Σ is called *border-unaware* if it holds

$$L \setminus (\{\Lambda\} \cup \Sigma^{1,+} \cup \Sigma^{+,1}) = \{P \in \Sigma^{*,*} \mid B_{2,2}(P) \neq \emptyset \wedge B_{2,2}(P) \subseteq (\Theta \cap \Sigma^{2,2})\}.$$

We define the class of border-unaware picture languages (bu-LOC) which is a proper subclass of LOC[1]. One of the simplest non-empty picture languages over $\Sigma = \{0,1\}$ in bu-LOC is $L_{\mathrm{uni}} = \{P \mid P \in \{1\}^{+,+}\}$, consisting of all non-empty (uniform) pictures of 1's. The problem $\mathcal{M}_{\mathrm{MAX}}(L_{\mathrm{uni}})$ is known as a search for a largest uniform rectangular area in a 0-1 matrix. It can be solved in time linear in the matrix area using the algorithm finding a largest rectangular area in a histogram [13]. We will utilize this fact in the proof of Theorem 4.

Let a histogram of n values be represented as a one-dimensional array H of length n where each $H(i) \in \mathbb{N}$ is the height of the histogram bar at position $i \in \{1,\ldots,n\}$. For $1 \le k \le \ell \le n$, let $R_{k,\ell} = (\ell - k + 1)\min\{H(i) \mid k \le i \le \ell\}$ denote the largest area of a rectangle that is covered by the bars from k to ℓ.

[1] E.g. the local picture languages L_{corn} and L_{corn2} are not in bu-LOC.

Lemma 3 **([13, Chapter 2]).** *Given a histogram H with n bars, there is an algorithm running in time $O(n)$ that finds positions $k \leq \ell$ such that $R_{k,\ell} \geq R_{i,j}$ for all $1 \leq i \leq j \leq n$.*

Theorem 4. *Let $L \in$ bu-LOC. The problems $\mathcal{M}_{\mathrm{MAX}}(L)$, $\mathcal{M}_{\mathrm{MIN}}(L)$, $\mathcal{M}_{\mathrm{ANY}}(L)$ and $\mathcal{M}_{\mathrm{ALL}}(L)$ are solvable in time $O(mn)$ for each input of size $m \times n$.*

Proof. Let $L = L(\Theta) \in$ bu-LOC where $\Theta \subseteq (\Sigma \cup \{\#\})^{2,2}$. Let $P \in \Sigma^{m,n}$ be an input picture.

To find one-row and one-column matching subpictures in P, each row/column of P is processed independently in time linear in its length (see Theorem 1).

To find matching subpictures of sizes $k \times \ell$, $k, \ell \geq 2$, the task becomes trivial for $\mathcal{M}_{\mathrm{MIN}}(L)$, $\mathcal{M}_{\mathrm{ANY}}(L)$ and $\mathcal{M}_{\mathrm{ALL}}(L)$ since it suffices to locate subpictures of P of size 2×2 that belong to $\Theta \cap \Sigma^{2,2}$.

To solve $\mathcal{M}_{\mathrm{MAX}}(L)$, the dynamic programming technique is used to compute matrix M of size $(m-1) \times (n-1)$ where

$$M(i,j) = \max\{k \mid (k=0) \vee (2 \leq k \leq i \wedge P(i-k+1, j : i, j+1) \in L)\}.$$

The matrix is obtained in time $O(mn)$. Finally, the algorithm from Lemma 3 is applied to each row of M to return a largest subpicture of P which is in L. □

5 Matching Against Picture Languages Accepted by 2DOTA and 4DFA

Theorem 5. *Let L be a picture language accepted by a 2DOTA. There are algorithms solving problems $\mathcal{M}_{\mathrm{MAX}}(L)$, $\mathcal{M}_{\mathrm{MIN}}(L)$, $\mathcal{M}_{\mathrm{ANY}}(L)$ and $\mathcal{M}_{\mathrm{ALL}}(L)$ in time $O(m^2n^2)$ for pictures of size $m \times n$.*

Proof. Let $L = L(\mathcal{A})$ for some 2DOTA $\mathcal{A}$ and let P be a picture of size $m \times n$ in which we search for subpictures from L. To solve all four matching problems, run $\mathcal{A}$ over each subpicture $P(s,t : m,n)$ where $1 \leq s \leq m$ and $1 \leq t \leq n$. If $P^{\mathcal{A}}(s,t : m,n)(k,\ell)$ is an accepting state for some $1 \leq k \leq m-s+1$, $1 \leq \ell \leq n-t+1$, then $P(s,t : s+k-1, t+\ell-1)$ is in L. Since there are $\Theta(mn)$ subpictures $P(s,t : m,n)$ and each of them is processed by $\mathcal{A}$ in $O(mn)$ time, all the matching problems are solved in $O(m^2n^2)$ time. □

Theorem 6. *Let L be a picture language accepted by a 4DFA. There are algorithms solving problems $\mathcal{M}_{\mathrm{MAX}}(L)$, $\mathcal{M}_{\mathrm{MIN}}(L)$, $\mathcal{M}_{\mathrm{ANY}}(L)$ and $\mathcal{M}_{\mathrm{ALL}}(L)$ in time $O(m^2n^2 \min\{m,n\})$ for pictures of size $m \times n$.*

Proof. Let $L = L(\mathcal{A})$ where $\mathcal{A} = (Q, \Sigma, \delta, q_0, F)$ is a 4DFA. Assume that whenever $\mathcal{A}$ enters a border cell storing #, then it returns back to the closest cell of the input picture in the next computation step.

Let $P \in \Sigma^{m,n}$. Assume, w.l.o.g., $n \leq m$. Given a coordinate (s,t) in P and $\ell \in \mathbb{N}$ such that $t \leq \ell \leq n$, there is a procedure finding in $O((m-s+1)(\ell-t+1)) = O(mn)$ time those $k \in \{s, \ldots, m\}$ for which $P(s,t : k, \ell) \in L$. This implies that all the matching problems can be solved in $O(m^2n^3)$ time.

The procedure is as follows: Iterate through rows $s, \ldots, m$. For a processed row r, let $P_r = P(s, t : r, \ell)$. Compute a mapping $\delta_r : \{1, \ldots, \ell - t + 1\} \times Q \rightarrow (\{1, \ldots, \ell - t + 1\} \times Q) \cup \{\text{acc}, \text{rej}, \text{down}\}$ with values based on the computation of $\mathcal{A}$ over $\hat{P}_r$. Let $\mathcal{A}$ be in a state q and let its head scan the j-th cell of the bottom row of P_r, storing $a \in \Sigma$. Distinguish three situations: (1) The transition specified by $\delta(q, a)$ moves the head of $\mathcal{A}$ down to the bottom border of $\hat{P}_r$. We define $\delta_r(j, q) = \text{down}$. (2) The transition specified by $\delta(q, a)$ does not move the head of $\mathcal{A}$ down and the successive computation of $\mathcal{A}$ visits the bottom row of P_r again. Let this happen for the first time in a j'-th cell of the bottom row of P_r, when $\mathcal{A}$ is in a state q'. We define $\delta_r(j, q) = (j', q')$. (3) The transition specified by $\delta(q, a)$ moves the head of $\mathcal{A}$ up and the successive computation of $\mathcal{A}$ never returns back to the bottom row of P_r. The automaton $\mathcal{A}$ either accepts (we define $\delta_r(j, q) = \text{acc}$) or rejects by entering a rejecting state or a cycle (we define $\delta_r(j, q) = \text{rej}$).

The initial mapping δ_s for picture P_s of size $1 \times (\ell - t + 1)$ is easily computed in time $O(\ell - t)$. Assuming δ_r is computed for some r, we show how to compute δ_{r+1} in time $O(\ell - t)$, based on another mapping $\sigma_r : \{1, \ldots, \ell - t + 1\} \times Q \rightarrow (\{1, \ldots, \ell - t + 1\} \times Q) \cup \{\text{acc}, \text{rej}\}$ defined as follows: (1) Assume the computation of $\mathcal{A}$ which started in a state q with the head scanning the j-th cell of the bottom row of P_r never enters the bottom row of $\hat{P}_r$. If $\mathcal{A}$ accepts, we define $\sigma_r(j, q) = \text{acc}$, if it does not accept, we define $\sigma_r(j, q) = \text{rej}$. (2) Assume the computation of $\mathcal{A}$ enters the bottom row of $\hat{P}_r$ for the first time within a j'-th column of P_r, in a state q'. We define $\sigma_r(j, q) = (j', q')$.

To derive values of δ_{r+1}, assume $\mathcal{A}$ in a state q scans the j-th cell of the bottom row of P_{r+1} containing $a \in \Sigma$. If $\delta(q, a) = (p, \text{U})$, then $\delta_{r+1}(j, q) = \sigma_r(j, p)$. If $\delta(q, a) = (p, \text{D})$, then $\delta_{r+1}(j, q) = \text{down}$. If $\delta(q, a) = (p, \text{L})$ then $\delta_{r+1}(j, q)$ equals $(j - 1, p)$ for $j > 1$ and $(\delta(p, \#), j)$ for $j = 1$. The case $\delta(q, a) = (p, \text{R})$ is handled analogously.

To compute σ_r, use an auxiliary 2D Boolean array B indexed by elements of $\{1, \ldots, \ell - t + 1\} \times Q$, with all cells initially set to $false$. Moreover, use a stack $\mathcal{S}$. Execute the following procedure.

```
for each (j, q) ∈ {1, ..., ℓ − t + 1} × Q do
    while σ_r(j, q) not defined do
        S.push(j, q);
        if B(j, q) = false then
            B(j, q) := true;
            if δ_r(j, q) ∈ {acc, rej} then
                σ_r(j, q) := δ_r(j, q);
            else if δ_r(j, q) = down then
                (p, d) := δ(q, P_r(r − s + 1, j)); σ_r(j, q) := (j, p);
            else
                (j, q) := δ_r(j, q);
        else // a cycle detected
            σ_r(j, q) := rej;
    while S not empty do
        (i, p) := S.pop; σ_r(i, p) := σ_r(j, q);
```

Each pair (j, q) is accessed $O(1)$ times, hence the procedure runs in time $O(|Q|(\ell - t + 1)) = O(\ell - t)$.

Finally, we describe how the algorithm checks whether $P_r \in L(\mathcal{A})$ for $r = s, \ldots, m$. Let C_r be the configuration in which $\mathcal{A}$ reaches the bottom row of P_r from the initial configuration for the first time (note that C_s is the initial configuration and C_r need not exist for $r > s$). Given C_r and σ_r, there is a procedure (similar to one iteration of the pseudocode main while loop) running in time $O(\ell - t)$ that decides whether $P_r \in L(\mathcal{A})$ and computes C_{r+1}. □

6 Conclusions

We have studied four matching problems for 2D inputs and patterns defined by picture languages. We have demonstrated that even patterns definable via basic picture languages are of practical importance and involve non-trivial matching algorithms, which are unlikely to work in linear time even in the case of LOC family. The upper bounds on the time complexity of the matching problems established for the considered families of picture languages are summarized bellow.

bu-LOC	LOC	L(2DOTA), DREC	L(4DFA)
$O(mn)$	$O(mn\min\{m, n\})$	$O(m^2n^2)$	$O(m^2n^2\min\{m, n\})$

Note that DREC is the closure of L(2DOTA) under rotation, hence it shares the time complexity with L(2DOTA).

One can ask what matching algorithms can be found for families of picture languages defined by more powerful deterministic finite-state systems such as the deterministic one-marker four-way automaton [5], Sudoku-determinism [6], or deterministic sgraffito automaton [16]. However, since the upper bound established for L(4DFA) is close to the trivial cubic upper bound, we cannot propose very efficient algorithms for the more powerful families without improving the matching algorithm for L(4DFA). It is thus an important open problem to determine how tight the upper bound is for L(4DFA).

References

1. Abboud, A., Backurs, A., Williams, V.V.: If the current clique algorithms are optimal, so is Valiant's parser. In: Guruswami, V. (ed.) FOCS 2015, pp. 98–117. IEEE Computer Society (2015). https://doi.org/10.1109/FOCS.2015.16
2. Aho, A.V.: Algorithms for finding patterns in strings. In: van Leeuwen, J. (ed.) Algorithms and Complexity, Handbook of Theoretical Computer Science, vol. A, pp. 255–300. The MIT Press, Cambridge (1990)

3. Anselmo, M., Giammarresi, D., Madonia, M.: From determinism to non-determinism in recognizable two-dimensional languages. In: Harju, T., Karhumäki, J., Lepistö, A. (eds.) DLT 2007. LNCS, vol. 4588, pp. 36–47. Springer, Heidelberg (2007). https://doi.org/10.1007/978-3-540-73208-2_7
4. Baeza-Yates, R., Régnier, M.: Fast two-dimensional pattern matching. Inf. Process. Lett. **45**(1), 51–57 (1993). https://doi.org/10.1016/0020-0190(93)90250-D
5. Blum, M., Hewitt, C.: Automata on a 2-dimensional tape. In: SWAT 1967, pp. 155–160. IEEE Computer Society (1967). https://doi.org/10.1109/FOCS.1967.6
6. Borchert, B., Reinhardt, K.: Deterministically and sudoku-deterministically recognizable picture languages. In: Loos, R., Fazekas, S., Martín-Vide, C. (eds.) LATA 2007, pp. 175–186. Report 35/07, Tarragona (2007)
7. Giammarresi, D., Restivo, A.: Two-dimensional languages. In: Rozenberg, G., Salomaa, A. (eds.) Handbook of Formal Languages, pp. 215–267. Springer, Heidelberg (1997). https://doi.org/10.1007/978-3-642-59126-6_4
8. Han, Y.-S., Průša, D.: Template-based pattern matching in two-dimensional arrays. In: Brimkov, V.E., Barneva, R.P. (eds.) IWCIA 2017. LNCS, vol. 10256, pp. 79–92. Springer, Cham (2017). https://doi.org/10.1007/978-3-319-59108-7_7
9. Inoue, K., Nakamura, A.: Some properties of two-dimensional on-line tessellation acceptors. Inf. Sci. **13**(2), 95–121 (1977). https://doi.org/10.1016/0020-0255(77)90023-8
10. Itai, A., Rodeh, M.: Finding a minimum circuit in a graph. In: Hopcroft, J.E., Friedman, E.P., Harrison, M.A. (eds.) STOC 1977, pp. 1–10. ACM (1977). https://doi.org/10.1145/800105.803390
11. Karp, R.M., Rabin, M.O.: Efficient randomized pattern-matching algorithms. IBM J. Res. Dev. **31**(2), 249–260 (1987). https://doi.org/10.1147/rd.312.0249
12. Lee, L.: Fast context-free grammar parsing requires fast Boolean matrix multiplication. J. ACM **49**(1), 1–15 (2002). https://doi.org/10.1145/505241.505242
13. Morgan, C.: Programming from Specifications. Prentice Hall International Series in Computer Science, 2nd edn. Prentice Hall, Upper Saddle River (1994)
14. de Oliveira Oliveira, M., Wehar, M.: Intersection non-emptiness and hardness within polynomial time. In: Hoshi, M., Seki, S. (eds.) DLT 2018. LNCS, vol. 11088, pp. 282–290. Springer, Cham (2018). https://doi.org/10.1007/978-3-319-98654-8_23
15. Potechin, A., Shallit, J.: Lengths of words accepted by nondeterministic finite automata. CoRR abs/1802.04708 (2018). http://arxiv.org/abs/1802.04708
16. Průša, D., Mráz, F., Otto, F.: Two-dimensional Sgraffito automata. RAIRO Theor. Inf. Appl. **48**, 505–539 (2014). https://doi.org/10.1051/ita/2014023
17. Richards, D., Liestman, A.L.: Finding cycles of a given length. In: Alspach, B., Godsil, C. (eds.) Annals of Discrete Mathematics (27): Cycles in Graphs, North-Holland Mathematics Studies, vol. 115, pp. 249–255, North-Holland (1985)
18. Siromoney, G., Siromoney, R., Krithivasan, K.: Abstract families of matrices and picture languages. Comput. Graph. Image Process. **1**(3), 284–307 (1972)
19. Sun, X., Nobel, A.B.: On the size and recovery of submatrices of ones in a random binary matrix. J. Mach. Learn. Res. **9**(Nov), 2431–2453 (2008)
20. Toda, M., Inoue, K., Takanami, I.: Two-dimensional pattern matching by two-dimensional on-line tessellation acceptors. Theor. Comput. Sci. **24**, 179–194 (1983). https://doi.org/10.1016/0304-3975(83)90048-8
21. Williams, V.V.: Multiplying matrices faster than Coppersmith-Winograd. In: STOC 2012, pp. 887–898. ACM, New York (2012). https://doi.org/10.1145/2213977.2214056

22. Williams, V.V.: Hardness of easy problems: basing hardness on popular conjectures such as the strong exponential time hypothesis (invited talk). In: Husfeldt, T., Kanj, I.A. (eds.) IPEC 2015. LIPIcs, vol. 43, pp. 17–29. Schloss Dagstuhl - Leibniz-Zentrum fuer Informatik (2015). https://doi.org/10.4230/LIPIcs.IPEC.2015.17
23. Yuster, R., Zwick, U.: Finding even cycles even faster. SIAM J. Discrete Math. **10**(2), 209–222 (1997). https://doi.org/10.1137/S0895480194274133

Decision Problems for Restricted Variants of Two-Dimensional Automata

Taylor J. Smith(✉) and Kai Salomaa(✉)

School of Computing, Queen's University, Kingston, ON K7L 2N8, Canada
{tsmith,ksalomaa}@cs.queensu.ca

Abstract. A two-dimensional finite automaton has a read-only input head that moves in four directions on a finite array of cells labelled by symbols of the input alphabet. A three-way two-dimensional automaton is prohibited from making upward moves, while a two-way two-dimensional automaton can only move downward and rightward.

We show that the language emptiness problem for unary three-way nondeterministic two-dimensional automata is NP-complete, and is in P for general-alphabet two-way nondeterministic two-dimensional automata. We show that the language equivalence problem for two-way deterministic two-dimensional automata is decidable. This is the first known positive decidability result for the equivalence problem on two-dimensional automata over a general alphabet. We show that there exists a unary three-way deterministic two-dimensional automaton with a nonregular column projection, and we show that the row projection of a unary three-way nondeterministic two-dimensional automaton is always regular.

Keywords: Decision problem · Language emptiness · Language equivalence · Three-way automata · Two-dimensional automata · Two-way automata

1 Introduction

A two-dimensional automaton is a generalization of a one-dimensional finite automaton that operates on two-dimensional input words; that is, on arrays or matrices of symbols from an alphabet Σ. The two-dimensional automaton model was originally introduced by Blum and Hewitt [2].

In the one-dimensional case, we may consider either one-way or two-way automaton models. The one-way model is the classical definition of a finite automaton, while the two-way model allows the input head of the automaton to move both leftward and rightward within the input word. It is well-known that both one-way and two-way automata recognize the regular languages.

Smith and Salomaa were supported by Natural Sciences and Engineering Research Council of Canada Grant OGP0147224.

M. Hospodár and G. Jirásková (Eds.): CIAA 2019, LNCS 11601, pp. 222–234, 2019.
https://doi.org/10.1007/978-3-030-23679-3_18

Table 1. Decidability results for two-dimensional automaton models. Decidable problems are marked with ✓, undecidable problems are marked with ✗, and unknown results are marked with a ? symbol. New decidability results presented in this paper are circled. Decision problems for which we provide a complexity bound are indicated by ✓*. Decision problems for which we provide a complexity bound for the unary case are indicated by ✓†.

	2DFA-4W	2NFA-4W	2DFA-3W	2NFA-3W	2DFA-2W	2NFA-2W
Membership	✓	✓	✓	✓	✓	✓
Emptiness	✗	✗	✓	✓†	✓*	✓*
Universality	✗	✗	✓	✗	✓	✗[a]
Equivalence	✗	✗	?	✗	(✓)	✗[a]

[a] Following the submission of this paper, the authors proved that the equivalence and universality problems for two-way nondeterministic two-dimensional automata are undecidable. These results will be added to an expanded version of this paper.

The input head of a two-dimensional automaton can move in four directions, where the direction is specified by the transition function. In this paper, we focus on restricted variants of the two-dimensional automaton model. Such restrictions arise from limiting the movement of the input head of the automaton. If we prevent the input head from moving upward, then we obtain a three-way two-dimensional automaton. If we further prevent the input head from moving leftward, then we obtain a two-way two-dimensional automaton. The three-way two-dimensional automaton model was introduced by Rosenfeld [15]. The two-way two-dimensional automaton model was introduced by Dong and Jin [3], but a similar model was used by Anselmo et al. in an earlier paper [1].

The emptiness problem for four-way two-dimensional automata is undecidable [17], while the same problem is known to be decidable for three-way deterministic two-dimensional automata [8,13]. Decision problems for two-way two-dimensional automata have not been considered much in the literature. Since a two-way two-dimensional automaton moves only right and down, it cannot visit any symbol of the input word more than once. However, the equivalence problem for two-way two-dimensional automata is, perhaps, not as simple as one might expect, because the automata tested for equivalence can visit the input word using a very different strategy and the computations may partially overlap.

Our results are as follows. Using an old result by Galil [4], we show that deciding emptiness of unary three-way nondeterministic two-dimensional automata is NP-complete, while emptiness of two-way nondeterministic two-dimensional automata over general alphabets can be decided in polynomial time. As the main result, we show that equivalence of two-way deterministic two-dimensional automata over general alphabets is decidable. We also consider row and column projection languages of two-way and three-way two-dimensional automata.

Table 1 lists a selection of known decidability results for various two-dimensional automaton models. Note that almost no problems are decidable for four-way two-dimensional automata since neither the emptiness nor universality problems are decidable for that model. More details about the two-dimensional automaton model and associated problems can be found in survey articles by Inoue and Takanami [9] and Kari and Salo [11], as well as in a recent survey by the first author [16].

2 Preliminaries

A two-dimensional word consists of a finite array, or rectangle, of cells labelled by a symbol from a finite alphabet. The cells around the two-dimensional word are labelled by a special boundary marker #. We denote the number of rows (resp., columns) of a two-dimensional word W by $|W|_{\mathrm{R}}$ (resp., $|W|_{\mathrm{C}}$).

We begin by defining the deterministic two-dimensional automaton model, also known as a four-way deterministic two-dimensional automaton. A two-dimensional automaton has a finite state control and is capable of moving its input head in four directions within a two-dimensional input word: up, down, left, and right (denoted U, D, L, and R, respectively). The squares around the input word are labelled by the boundary symbol # and, by remembering the direction of the last move, the input head can move back into the word from the boundary. We assume that the machine accepts by entering a designated accept state q_{accept}, and the machine halts and accepts when it enters q_{accept}. Other equivalent definitions are possible and the precise mode of acceptance is not important unless one considers questions like state complexity. Without loss of generality, we can assume that the input head begins its computation in the upper-left corner of the input word.

Definition 1 (Deterministic Two-Dimensional Automaton). *A deterministic two-dimensional finite automaton (2DFA-4W) is a tuple* $(Q, \Sigma, \delta, q_0, q_{\mathrm{accept}})$*, where* Q *is a finite set of states,* Σ *is the input alphabet (with* $\# \notin \Sigma$ *acting as a boundary symbol),* $\delta : (Q \setminus \{q_{\mathrm{accept}}\}) \times (\Sigma \cup \{\#\}) \to Q \times \{U, D, L, R\}$ *is the partial transition function, and* $q_0, q_{\mathrm{accept}} \in Q$ *are the initial and accepting states, respectively.*

We can modify a two-dimensional automaton to be nondeterministic (2NFA-4W) in the usual way by changing the transition function to map to the power set $2^{Q \times \{U,D,L,R\}}$.

By restricting the movement of the input head, we obtain the aforementioned restricted variants of the two-dimensional automaton model.

Definition 2 (Three-Way Two-Dimensional Automaton). *A three-way two-dimensional automaton (2DFA-3W/2NFA-3W) is a tuple* $(Q, \Sigma, \delta, q_0, q_{\mathrm{accept}})$ *as in Definition 1, where the transition function* δ *is restricted to use only the directions* $\{D, L, R\}$.

Definition 3 (Two-Way Two-Dimensional Automaton). *A two-way two-dimensional automaton (2DFA-2W/2NFA-2W) is a tuple* $(Q, \Sigma, \delta, q_0, q_{\mathrm{accept}})$ *as in Definition 1, where the transition function* δ *is restricted to use only the directions* $\{D, R\}$.

Both the two-way and three-way automaton variants can be either deterministic or nondeterministic, depending on their transition function δ. The power of the two-way two-dimensional automaton model was discussed and compared to related automaton models by Dong and Jin [3]. The fact that upward and leftward movements are prohibited means that the input head can never return to a row if it moves down or to a column if it moves right. Thus, the two-way two-dimensional automaton is a "read-once" automaton, in the sense that it cannot visit any symbol twice.

A two-way deterministic two-dimensional automaton cannot visit all symbols of an input word that has at least two rows and two columns. The same applies to a given computation of a two-way nondeterministic two-dimensional automaton; however, different computations of a nondeterministic automaton have the ability to visit all squares. In fact, it is known that a two-way nondeterministic two-dimensional automaton cannot be simulated by a three-way deterministic two-dimensional automaton.

Proposition 1 (Dong and Jin [3], Kari and Salo [11]). *The recognition power of the two-way nondeterministic two-dimensional automaton model and the three-way deterministic two-dimensional automaton model are incomparable.*

3 Language Emptiness

The language emptiness problem for three-way two-dimensional automata is decidable [8,13]. Using a result by Galil [4], we show that deciding emptiness of unary three-way two-dimensional automata is NP-complete. Galil [4] has shown that deciding emptiness of two-way one-dimensional automata is in NP. Note that decidability of emptiness is not obvious because the tight bound for converting a unary two-way deterministic one-dimensional automaton to a one-way nondeterministic one-dimensional automaton is superpolynomial [14].

Theorem 1. *The emptiness problem for unary three-way nondeterministic two-dimensional automata is* NP*-complete.*

Proof. Let $\mathcal{A}$ be a unary three-way nondeterministic two-dimensional automaton with n states. We restrict the input head of $\mathcal{A}$ to operate only on the first row of the input word by replacing all downward moves with "stay-in-place" moves. Call the resulting two-way one-dimensional automaton $\mathcal{A}'$. By doubling the number of states of $\mathcal{A}'$, we can eliminate "stay-in-place" moves.

Now, $L(\mathcal{A}) \neq \emptyset$ if and only if $L(\mathcal{A}') \neq \emptyset$. Emptiness of unary two-way one-dimensional automata can be decided in NP [4]. Furthermore, a unary two-way one-dimensional automaton is a special case of a unary three-way two-dimensional automaton, and it is known that emptiness for the former class is NP-hard [4]. □

In the general alphabet case, the emptiness problem for two-way deterministic one-dimensional automata is PSPACE-hard [6], and it follows that the same applies to deterministic three-way two-dimensional automata. Emptiness of deterministic and nondeterministic three-way two-dimensional automata is decidable [13]; however, the known decision algorithm does not operate in polynomial space. The question of whether emptiness of deterministic or nondeterministic three-way two-dimensional automata over general alphabets is in PSPACE remains open.

3.1 Two-Way Two-Dimensional Automata

The emptiness problem for two-way nondeterministic two-dimensional automata is known to be decidable, and the proof of decidability also acts as a trivial proof that the problem is in NP: simply have the automaton guess an accepting computation. It turns out that the problem can be solved in deterministic polynomial time.

Theorem 2. *The emptiness problem for two-way nondeterministic two-dimensional automata is in* P.

Proof. We can check language emptiness of a two-way nondeterministic two-dimensional automaton $\mathcal{A}$ via the following procedure:

1. Beginning in the initial state of $\mathcal{A}$, q_0, compute the set of states reachable from q_0. Denote this set by $Q_{\text{reachable}}$.
2. If q_{accept} appears in $Q_{\text{reachable}}$, halt. Otherwise, continue.
3. For each $q \in Q_{\text{reachable}}$, repeat as long as new states get added to $Q_{\text{reachable}}$:
   (a) Compute the set of states reachable from q. Denote this set by $Q'_{\text{reachable}}$.
   (b) If q_{accept} appears in $Q'_{\text{reachable}}$, halt. Otherwise, continue.
   (c) Add all states in $Q'_{\text{reachable}}$ to $Q_{\text{reachable}}$ if they do not already occur in that set.
4. Halt.

If the procedure reaches step 4, then q_{accept} was not encountered up to that point and, therefore, the language of $\mathcal{A}$ is empty. Otherwise, the procedure encountered q_{accept}, so there exists a sequence of alphabet symbols on which the input head of $\mathcal{A}$ can transition from q_0 to q_{accept}.

At each stage of the procedure, the set of reachable states is computed by considering all possible transitions on all alphabet symbols from the current state. Since $\mathcal{A}$ is a two-way two-dimensional automaton, the input head of $\mathcal{A}$ cannot visit the same cell of the input word more than once, which means that at each step both downward and rightward moves on each alphabet symbol are possible. If $\mathcal{A}$ has n states, then step 3 is repeated at most n times, which means that the algorithm terminates in polynomial time. □

4 Language Equivalence

Language equivalence is known to be undecidable for four-way deterministic two-dimensional automata [2], as well as for three-way nondeterministic two-dimensional automata [8]. The equivalence problem for two-way two-dimensional automata can be expected to be decidable, but turns out to be perhaps not as straightforward as one might initially assume.

To obtain the main result of this section, we use a technical lemma (Lemma 1) roughly based on the following idea. Suppose that we have a pair of two-way deterministic two-dimensional automata $\mathcal{A}$ and $\mathcal{B}$, where $\mathcal{A}$ has an accepting computation $C_{\mathcal{A}}$ and $\mathcal{B}$ has a rejecting computation $C_{\mathcal{B}}$ on some sufficiently large input word W. Intuitively speaking, our lemma uses a pumping property to reduce the dimension of W by finding repeated states in $C_{\mathcal{A}}$ and $C_{\mathcal{B}}$. To do this, we have to be careful to avoid cases where reducing the size of the input word would force the computations to overlap (in parts where they did not originally overlap) because in such a situation there would be, in general, no guarantee that the underlying symbols in the overlapping parts match.

Lemma 1. *Let $\mathcal{A}$ and $\mathcal{B}$ be two-way deterministic two-dimensional automata with m and n states, respectively. Denote $z = m \cdot n \cdot |\Sigma|^2 + 1$ and $f(z) = z^2 \cdot (z^2+z-1)$. If $L(\mathcal{A}) - L(\mathcal{B}) \neq \emptyset$, then $L(\mathcal{A}) - L(\mathcal{B})$ contains a two-dimensional word with at most $f(z)$ rows and $f(z)$ columns.*

Proof. Consider a two-dimensional word $W \in L(\mathcal{A}) - L(\mathcal{B})$ and suppose that $|W|_{\mathrm{C}} > f(z)$. Let $C_{\mathcal{A}}$ (resp., $C_{\mathcal{B}}$) denote an accepting computation of $\mathcal{A}$ (resp., a rejecting computation of $\mathcal{B}$) on W. Without loss of generality, we can assume that $C_{\mathcal{A}}$ accepts (resp., $C_{\mathcal{B}}$ rejects) when entering a cell containing the border marker; that is, each computation reads through all columns or all rows of the input word. If the original automata are allowed to accept/reject inside the input word, then they can be easily modified to equivalent automata that accept/reject only at border markers. (Note that a two-way two-dimensional automaton cannot enter an infinite loop.)

We show that $L(\mathcal{A}) - L(\mathcal{B})$ either (i) contains a word with strictly fewer than $|W|_{\mathrm{C}}$ columns and no more than $|W|_{\mathrm{R}}$ rows, or (ii) contains a word with no more than $|W|_{\mathrm{C}}$ columns and strictly fewer than $|W|_{\mathrm{R}}$ rows.

If $C_{\mathcal{A}}$ and $C_{\mathcal{B}}$ share at least z positions in W, then two of these shared positions must have been reached via the same states of $\mathcal{A}$ and $\mathcal{B}$ on the same alphabet symbol. These shared positions can be identified and removed to produce a word in $L(\mathcal{A}) - L(\mathcal{B})$ of strictly smaller dimension. (See Fig. 1a.)

Otherwise, $C_{\mathcal{A}}$ and $C_{\mathcal{B}}$ share fewer than z positions in W. Then, there exists some subword Z in W consisting of $z \cdot (z^2 + z - 1)$ consecutive complete columns of W where $C_{\mathcal{A}}$ and $C_{\mathcal{B}}$ do not intersect.

If $C_{\mathcal{A}}$ and $C_{\mathcal{B}}$ do not enter the subword Z, then we can reduce the dimension of W without affecting either of the computations $C_{\mathcal{A}}$ and $C_{\mathcal{B}}$, and a similar reduction is easy to do if only one of $C_{\mathcal{A}}$ and $C_{\mathcal{B}}$ enters the subword Z.

If $C_{\mathcal{A}}$ and $C_{\mathcal{B}}$ enter the subword Z, then without loss of generality, assume that within the subword Z, $C_{\mathcal{A}}$ is above $C_{\mathcal{B}}$ and $C_{\mathcal{A}}$ continues to the last row of Z. It is possible for $C_{\mathcal{B}}$ to finish earlier if it rejects at the bottom border of W. If neither $C_{\mathcal{A}}$ nor $C_{\mathcal{B}}$ visit all columns of Z, then we can directly reduce the number of columns of W.

If $C_{\mathcal{A}}$ contains a vertical drop of at least z steps within Z, or if $C_{\mathcal{A}}$ finishes at least z positions higher than $C_{\mathcal{B}}$ within Z—which can occur only when Z consists of the last columns of W—then the number of rows of W can be strictly reduced without affecting either of the computations $C_{\mathcal{A}}$ and $C_{\mathcal{B}}$. If such a scenario occurs in the jth column of W, then $C_{\mathcal{A}}$ contains two cells (i_1, j) and (i_2, j) where $i_1 < i_2$ and where the cells are reached by the same states on the same alphabet symbol, and both states and symbol are matched by $C_{\mathcal{B}}$ on rows i_1 and i_2. Thus, we can reduce the number of rows of W by $i_2 - i_1$. (See Fig. 1b.) This involves moving the remainder of the computation $C_{\mathcal{B}}$ to the left and adding new cells in the input word to guarantee that the input word is a rectangle. Note that moving the remainder of $C_{\mathcal{B}}$ to the left cannot force it to overlap with $C_{\mathcal{A}}$.

Now, we know that $C_{\mathcal{A}}$ is above $C_{\mathcal{B}}$ within Z and the vertical distance between the two computations by the end is at most z. Denote by $\max_Z$ the maximal vertical difference of $C_{\mathcal{A}}$ and $C_{\mathcal{B}}$ at any fixed column in Z. We consider two cases:

1. Suppose $\max_Z \geq z^2 + z$. Suppose that the leftmost value of maximal vertical difference occurs at column k within Z. Since, at the end, the vertical difference of $C_{\mathcal{A}}$ and $C_{\mathcal{B}}$ is at most z, and since $C_{\mathcal{A}}$ cannot contain a vertical drop of more than z steps, then there must exist z "designated" columns between k and the last column of Z where the vertical difference between $C_{\mathcal{A}}$ and $C_{\mathcal{B}}$ either monotonically decreases or stays the same. (See Fig. 1c.)
   At two of these "designated" columns, say k_1 and k_2, the states of $C_{\mathcal{A}}$ and $C_{\mathcal{B}}$ and the corresponding alphabet symbols coincide, and we can continue the computation $C_{\mathcal{A}}$ (resp., $C_{\mathcal{B}}$) from column k_1 in the same way as from column k_2.
   Note that this transformation is not possible when the vertical distance in the "designated" columns is not monotonically decreasing, since if we move $C_{\mathcal{A}}$ and $C_{\mathcal{B}}$ so that the computations continue from column k_1 in the same way as from column k_2, the computations could be forced to overlap and we can no longer guarantee a matching of alphabet symbols. (See Fig. 1d.)
2. Suppose $\max_Z \leq z^2 + z - 1$. Then Z consists of $z \cdot (z^2 + z - 1)$ columns, so there must exist z columns where the vertical difference between $C_{\mathcal{A}}$ and $C_{\mathcal{B}}$ is the same. The choice of z implies that, in two of these columns, the states of $C_{\mathcal{A}}$ and $C_{\mathcal{B}}$ and the corresponding alphabet symbols coincide. Thus, we can strictly reduce the number of columns of W without affecting either of the computations $C_{\mathcal{A}}$ and $C_{\mathcal{B}}$.

Altogether, the previous cases establish a method for reducing the number of columns of W when $|W|_{\mathrm{C}} > f(z)$. The method for reducing the number of rows of W when $|W|_{\mathrm{R}} > f(z)$ is completely analogous. □

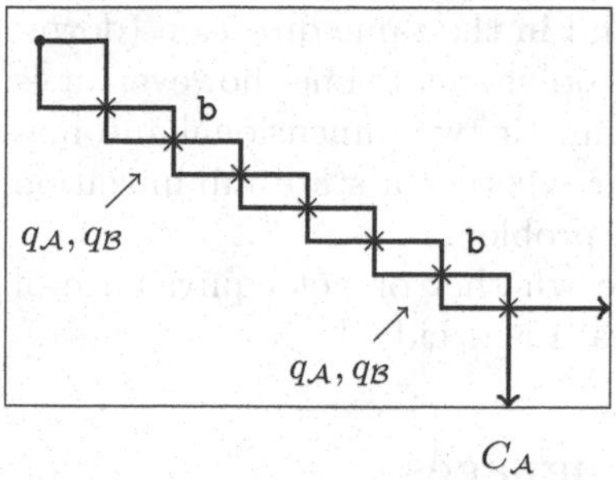

(a) Removing shared computations

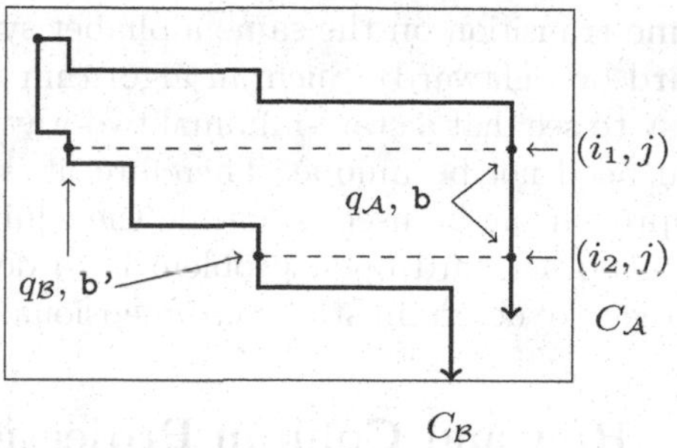

(b) Removing rows within vertical drop

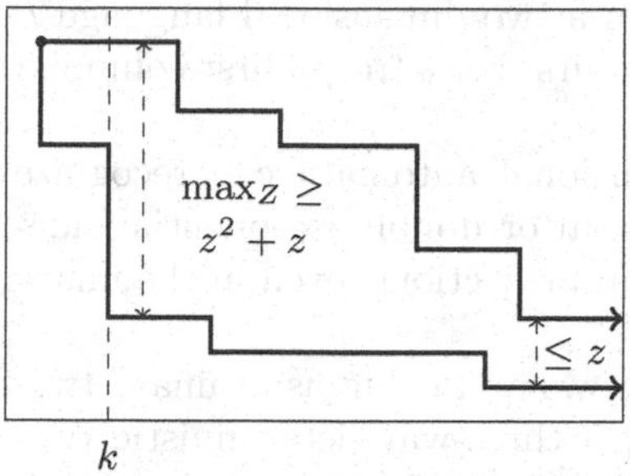

(c) Removing columns after row removal

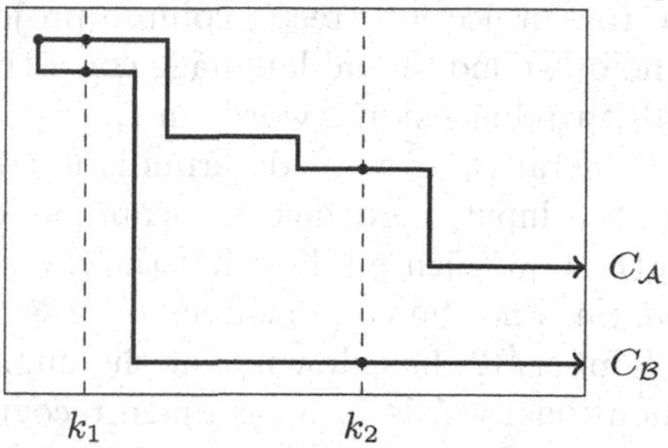

(d) Situation with non-removable columns

Fig. 1. Illustrations depicting various scenarios in Lemma 1.

Lemma 1 gives a brute-force algorithm to decide equivalence for two-way deterministic two-dimensional automata by checking all input words up to a given dimension, and the algorithm depends only on the two automata in question. As a consequence of the existence of such an algorithm, we obtain the following result.

Theorem 3. *The equivalence problem for two-way deterministic two-dimensional automata over a general alphabet is decidable.*

Lemma 1 also decides the inclusion problem and it follows that inclusion of two-way deterministic two-dimensional automata is decidable.

However, the brute-force algorithm given by Lemma 1 is extremely inefficient. The question of whether there exists a more efficient decidability procedure remains open.

Note that a two-way deterministic two-dimensional automaton cannot visit a symbol in the input word more than once, so we can reduce the number of states of such an automaton in a manner analogous to reducing states in a one-way deterministic one-dimensional automaton: mark pairs of states (q_i, q_j) as distinguishable if one of q_i and q_j is final and the other is not, then iteratively mark pairs of states as distinguishable if both states reach a previously-marked pair on some transition on the same alphabet symbol and in the same direction (downward or rightward). Such an algorithm runs in polynomial time; however, it is easy to see that a state-minimal two-way deterministic two-dimensional automaton need not be unique. Therefore, it is unclear whether a state minimization approach can be used to decide the equivalence problem.

Another hard open problem is to determine whether or not equivalence of three-way deterministic two-dimensional automata is decidable.

5 Row and Column Projection Languages

The row projection (resp., column projection) of a two-dimensional language L is the one-dimensional language consisting of the first rows (resp., first columns) of all two-dimensional words in L.

General (four-way) deterministic two-dimensional automata can recognize that the input word has, for example, exponential or doubly-exponential side-length [10], which implies that the row or column projections, even in the unary case, need not be context-free.

Kinber [12] has shown that the numbers of rows and columns of unary two-dimensional words in a language recognized by a three-way deterministic two-dimensional automaton are connected by certain bilinear forms.

Here, we consider the row and column projection languages of unary languages recognized by three-way two-dimensional automata, and we get differing regularity results for the row and column projection languages, respectively.

Theorem 4. *Given a unary three-way nondeterministic two-dimensional automaton $\mathcal{A}$, the row projection language of $L(\mathcal{A})$ is regular.*

Proof. The same argument as in the proof of Theorem 1 applies here. Construct a two-way nondeterministic one-dimensional automaton $\mathcal{B}$ to simulate the computation of $\mathcal{A}$ and replace downward moves with "stay-in-place" moves. □

For the column projection operation, however, we are not guaranteed to have regularity even with unary three-way deterministic two-dimensional automata. As a counterexample, we use the following unary language:

$$L_{\text{composite}} = \{a^m \mid m > 1 \text{ and } m \text{ is not prime}\}.$$

Clearly, $L_{\text{composite}}$ is nonregular since its complement is nonregular. The nonregularity of $L_{\text{composite}}$ plays a key role in the following lemma.

Lemma 2. *There exists a unary three-way deterministic two-dimensional automaton $\mathcal{C}$ such that the column projection language of $L(\mathcal{C})$ is equal to $L_{composite}$.*

Proof. We construct the automaton $\mathcal{C}$ as follows. Given an input word of dimension $m \times n$, $\mathcal{C}$ first verifies that $m > 1$; that is, that the input word has more than one row. Then, moving in a diagonal manner from the upper-left symbol of the input word, the input head of $\mathcal{C}$ travels rightward and downward until it reaches the boundary symbol of row n. From there, the input head moves back onto the word, then travels leftward and downward until it reaches the boundary symbol of row $2n$.

The automaton $\mathcal{C}$ accepts the input word if, after making at least two sweeps across the input word, the input head reaches the lower-left or lower-right corner of the input word after completing its current sweep.

The input head of $\mathcal{C}$ is able to detect when it has reached the lower-left or lower-right corner of the input word in the following way:

- If the input head reads # following a leftward move, make a downward move followed by a rightward move and check that both symbols read are #. If so, accept. Otherwise, if the second symbol read is not #, continue.
- If the input head reads # following a rightward move, make a downward move followed by a leftward move and check that both symbols read are #. If so, accept. Otherwise, if the second symbol read is not #, continue.
- If the input head reads # following a downward move, reject.

Following this construction, we see that $L(\mathcal{C})$ consists of words of dimension $m \times n$ where $m > 1$ and m is a multiple of n, and the column projection language of $L(\mathcal{C})$ consists of all strings of length at least 2 that do not have prime length; that is, $L_{\text{composite}}$. The computation of $\mathcal{C}$ is completely deterministic. □

Using Lemma 2, we obtain the main result pertaining to column projection languages.

Theorem 5. *Given a unary three-way deterministic two-dimensional automaton $\mathcal{A}$, the column projection language of $L(\mathcal{A})$ is not always regular.*

Remark 1. In a classical work, Greibach used the language $L_{\text{composite}}$ to show that one-way nondeterministic checking stack automata can recognize nonregular unary languages [5].

Ibarra et al. [7] introduced the notion of an accepting run of a two-way automaton. An accepting run is, roughly speaking, a sequence of states that the automaton enters during the course of some accepting computation. They showed that the set of accepting runs of a two-way automaton can be nonregular.

The proof of Lemma 2 provides an example where the set of accepting runs of a unary two-way nondeterministic automaton is not regular. Using the automaton $\mathcal{C}$ from Lemma 2, simulate the computation of $\mathcal{C}$ with a two-way one-dimensional automaton $\mathcal{B}$ as in Theorem 4. Then, the set of accepting runs of $\mathcal{B}$ will not be regular because the number of "stay-in-place" moves is guaranteed to be a composite number. Note that, although $\mathcal{C}$ is deterministic, the simulating two-way one-dimensional automaton $\mathcal{B}$ will be nondeterministic because it has to guess when $\mathcal{C}$ has reached the last row and when the computation should accept.

5.1 Two-Way Two-Dimensional Automata over General Alphabets

As opposed to the three-way case, we can establish regularity results for both the row projection and column projection languages of two-way nondeterministic two-dimensional automata. Furthermore, we no longer require that the automaton has a unary alphabet.

Theorem 6. *Given a two-way nondeterministic two-dimensional automaton $\mathcal{A}$, the row projection language of $L(\mathcal{A})$ is regular.*

Proof. Let $\mathcal{A}$ be a two-way nondeterministic two-dimensional automaton. Construct a one-way nondeterministic one-dimensional automaton $\mathcal{B}$ (with "stay-in-place" moves) to recognize the row projection language of $L(\mathcal{A})$ as follows:

1. Use $\mathcal{B}$ to nondeterministically simulate rightward moves of $\mathcal{A}$.
2. Simulate state changes of $\mathcal{A}$ after a downward move via a "stay-in-place" move, and nondeterministically guess the alphabet character that $\mathcal{A}$ reads on the next row.
3. After $\mathcal{A}$ makes the first downward move, begin simulating rightward moves of $\mathcal{A}$ by moving right but nondeterministically selecting an alphabet character for the simulated transition of $\mathcal{A}$. After this point, $\mathcal{B}$ ignores its own input.

Note that, after $\mathcal{A}$ makes a downward move, it can never return to the previous row. Therefore, we do not care about the remaining contents of the previous row.

From here, $\mathcal{B}$ must count the number of rightward moves it simulates and check that there exists an accepting computation of $\mathcal{A}$ where the number of rightward moves and the length of the remaining input to $\mathcal{B}$ are equal.

Since the row projection language of $\mathcal{A}$ is recognized by a nondeterministic one-dimensional automaton, it is regular. □

As opposed to the three-way case, the handling of rows and columns for two-way two-dimensional automata is symmetric: a row or column is read one way and cannot be returned to after a downward or rightward move, respectively. Using a completely analogous construction as in the proof of Theorem 6, we obtain a similar result for column projection languages.

Theorem 7. *Given a two-way nondeterministic two-dimensional automaton $\mathcal{A}$, the column projection language of $L(\mathcal{A})$ is regular.*

6 Conclusion

In this paper, we considered decision problems for three-way and two-way two-dimensional automata. We showed that the language emptiness problem is NP-complete for unary three-way nondeterministic two-dimensional automata and in P for two-way nondeterministic two-dimensional automata over a general alphabet. We also proved that the language equivalence problem is decidable for two-way deterministic two-dimensional automata. Lastly, we investigated the row projection and column projection operations and found that the resulting languages are regular for two-way nondeterministic two-dimensional automata over a general alphabet. In the three-way case, only the row projection of a unary two-dimensional language is regular.

As mentioned throughout this paper, some open problems remain in this area of study. For three-way two-dimensional automata, it is unknown whether the general-alphabet emptiness problem belongs to PSPACE. A positive result would imply that the problem is PSPACE-complete. For two-way two-dimensional automata, it could be interesting to investigate whether an efficient algorithm exists to decide the equivalence problem in the deterministic case (possibly by using a state minimization approach). Table 1 in Sect. 1 lists a selection of decidability questions for various two-dimensional automaton models that remain unresolved, and for most problems listed as decidable in Table 1, exact complexity bounds have not yet been determined.

References

1. Anselmo, M., Giammarresi, D., Madonia, M.: New operations and regular expressions for two-dimensional languages over one-letter alphabet. Theor. Comput. Sci. **340**(2), 408–431 (2005). https://doi.org/10.1016/j.tcs.2005.03.031
2. Blum, M., Hewitt, C.: Automata on a 2-dimensional tape. In: Miller, R.E. (ed.) SWAT 1967, pp. 155–160 (1967). https://doi.org/10.1109/FOCS.1967.6
3. Dong, J., Jin, W.: Comparison of two-way two-dimensional finite automata and three-way two-dimensional finite automata. In: Yang, X. (ed.) CSSS 2012, pp. 1904–1906 (2012). https://doi.org/10.1109/CSSS.2012.474
4. Galil, Z.: Hierarchies of complete problems. Acta Inf. **6**(1), 77–88 (1976). https://doi.org/10.1007/BF00263744
5. Greibach, S.: Checking automata and one-way stack languages. J. Comput. Syst. Sci. **3**(2), 196–217 (1969). https://doi.org/10.1016/S0022-0000(69)80012-7
6. Hunt III, H.B.: On the time and tape complexity of languages I. In: Aho, A.V. (ed.) STOC 1973, pp. 10–19 (1973). https://doi.org/10.1145/800125.804030
7. Ibarra, O.H., Dang, Z., Li, Q.: Accepting runs in a two-way finite automation. Inf. Comput. **260**, 1–8 (2018). https://doi.org/10.1016/j.ic.2018.03.002
8. Inoue, K., Takanami, I.: A note on decision problems for three-way two-dimensional finite automata. Inf. Process. Lett. **10**(4–5), 245–248 (1980). https://doi.org/10.1016/0020-0190(80)90151-9
9. Inoue, K., Takanami, I.: A survey of two-dimensional automata theory. Inf. Sci. **55**(1–3), 99–121 (1991). https://doi.org/10.1016/0020-0255(91)90008-I
10. Kari, J., Moore, C.: Rectangles and squares recognized by two-dimensional automata. In: Karhumäki, J., Maurer, H., Păun, G., Rozenberg, G. (eds.) Theory Is Forever. LNCS, vol. 3113, pp. 134–144. Springer, Heidelberg (2004). https://doi.org/10.1007/978-3-540-27812-2_13
11. Kari, J., Salo, V.: A survey on picture-walking automata. In: Kuich, W., Rahonis, G. (eds.) Algebraic Foundations in Computer Science. LNCS, vol. 7020, pp. 183–213. Springer, Heidelberg (2011). https://doi.org/10.1007/978-3-642-24897-9_9
12. Kinber, E.B.: Three-way automata on rectangular tapes over a one-letter alphabet. Inform. Sci. **35**, 61–77 (1985). https://doi.org/10.1016/0020-0255(85)90041_6

13. Petersen, H.: Some results concerning two-dimensional Turing machines and finite automata. In: Reichel, H. (ed.) FCT 1995. LNCS, vol. 965, pp. 374–382. Springer, Heidelberg (1995). https://doi.org/10.1007/3-540-60249-6_69
14. Pighizzini, G.: Two-way finite automata: old and recent results. Fund. Inf. **126**(2–3), 225–246 (2013). https://doi.org/10.3233/FI-2013-879
15. Rosenfeld, A.: Picture Languages: Formal Models for Picture Recognition. Computer Science and Applied Mathematics. Academic Press, New York (1979)
16. Smith, T.J.: Two-dimensional automata. Technical report 2019–637, Queen's University, Kingston (2019)
17. Taniguchi, K., Kasami, T.: Some decision problems for two-dimensional nonwriting automata. Trans. Inst. Electron. Comm. Engrs. Jpn. **54–C**(7), 578–585 (1971)

Streaming Ranked-Tree-to-String Transducers

Yuta Takahashi[1(✉)], Kazuyuki Asada[2], and Keisuke Nakano[2]

[1] The University of Electro-Communications, Chofu, Japan
takahashi@ipl.cs.uec.ac.jp
[2] Tohoku University, Sendai, Japan
{asada,ksk}@riec.tohoku.ac.jp

Abstract. *Streaming tree transducers with single-use restriction* ($\mathrm{STT}_{\mathrm{sur}}$s) were introduced by Alur and D'Antoni as an analyzable, executable, and expressive model for transforming unranked ordered trees in a single pass. The equivalence problem of $\mathrm{STT}_{\mathrm{sur}}$s is decidable because their class is as expressive as the class of MSO-definable tree transformations. In this paper, we present *streaming ranked-tree-to-string transducers* (SRTSTs), based on $\mathrm{STT}_{\mathrm{sur}}$s: SRTSTs are released from the single-use restriction while their input and output are restricted to ranked trees and strings, respectively. We show that the expressiveness of SRTSTs coincides with that of *deterministic top-down tree transducers with regular look-ahead* ($\mathrm{yDT}^{\mathrm{R}}$s), whose equivalence problem is known to be decidable. Our proof is done by constructing equivalent transducers in both directions.

Keywords: Ranked trees · Streaming transducers · Expressiveness · Equivalence

1 Introduction

[1]*Streaming tree transducers with single-use restriction* ($\mathrm{STT}_{\mathrm{sur}}$s) were introduced in [1] which can characterize MSO-definable tree transformations in a single path. An $\mathrm{STT}_{\mathrm{sur}}$ defines a function over unranked ordered trees (and forests), which are encoded as *nested words*. A nested word is a string over symbols tagged with *open/close* brackets. An $\mathrm{STT}_{\mathrm{sur}}$ reads an input nested word from left to right in a single path. Here each state is equipped with *a visibly pushdown stack* and a finite number of *variables* that store output chunks. An $\mathrm{STT}_{\mathrm{sur}}$ updates variables and a stack that stores *stack symbols* along with updated values of variables.

Intuitively, the single-use restriction is a restriction that variables are updated in a manner that ensures that each value of a variable contributes *at most once* to the eventual output without duplication (see [1] for the definition). Due to this restriction, the class of $\mathrm{STT}_{\mathrm{sur}}$s equals that of MSO-definable tree transducers.

[1] The full version (with full proofs) is found in: http://www.riec.tohoku.ac.jp/~asada/.

M. Hospodár and G. Jirásková (Eds.): CIAA 2019, LNCS 11601, pp. 235–247, 2019.
https://doi.org/10.1007/978-3-030-23679-3_19

The equivalence problem of transducers is an important topic in formal language theory. One of the remarkable results is that the equivalence of MSO-definable tree transducers is decidable [7]. Furthermore, in [1] the decidability of the equivalence problem for $\mathrm{STT_{sur}}$s was proved without using the result for MSO-definable transducers, with better complexity.

In this paper, we propose *streaming ranked-tree-to-string transducers* (SRTSTs) as a model of transformations from ranked trees to strings. The definition of SRTSTs is based on that of $\mathrm{STT_{sur}}$s but released from the single-use restriction. In addition, the input and output of SRTSTs are restricted to ranked trees and strings, respectively, while those of $\mathrm{STT_{sur}}$s are both unranked trees. SRTSTs with single-use restriction ($\mathrm{SRTST_{sur}}$s) (which are nothing but $\mathrm{STST_{sur}}$s [1] whose input is restricted to ranked trees) have the same expressive power as MSO-definable ranked-tree-to-string transducers (see the full version); and SRTSTs are more expressive than $\mathrm{SRTST_{sur}}$s. Streaming transducers without single-use restriction were not studied in [1].[2]

Deterministic top-down tree-to-string transducers with regular look-ahead ($\mathrm{yDT^R}$s) [4] are a classical model for structural-recursive tree-to-string transformation. A $\mathrm{yDT^R}$ defines a transformation from ranked trees to strings by mutually recursive functions with regular look-ahead. The equivalence of $\mathrm{yDT^R}$shad been a long-standing open problem [5], that was recently solved by Seidl et al. [11,12]. For a subclass of $\mathrm{yDT^R}$, the notion of *finite copying* for top-down tree transducers was introduced in [8]. Intuitively, a $\mathrm{yDT^R}$ is finite copying ($\mathrm{yDT^R_{fc}}$), if each subtree of an input is copied at most a bounded number of times. The expressiveness of $\mathrm{yDT^R_{fc}}$s coincides with that of MSO-definable tree-to-string transducers [6], thereby $\mathrm{yDT^R_{fc}}$ and $\mathrm{SRTST_{sur}}$ are equi-expressive.

In this paper, we characterize the class of SRTSTs in terms of $\mathrm{yDT^R}$s. Our contributions are:

(i) SRTSTs and $\mathrm{yDT^R}$s are equi-expressive,
(ii) bottom-up SRTSTs and SRTSTs are equi-expressive, and
(iii) the equivalence problem for SRTSTs is decidable.

Our main contribution is (i). In Sect. 4, we show how to construct equivalent transducers for each direction. In the direction from $\mathrm{yDT^R}$s to SRTSTs,used we construct the equivalent SRTST to be bottom-up one for every given $\mathrm{yDT^R}$, which shows (ii). As an immediate corollary, (iii) is derived from (i) and the decidability of the equivalence problem for $\mathrm{yDT^R}$s [12].

Related Work. There is a subclass of $\mathrm{yDT^R}$s besides $\mathrm{yDT^R_{fc}}$s, called $\mathrm{yDT_{seq}}$s, which are restricted to non-copying and order-preserving on input variables occurring in right-hand sides of rules. $\mathrm{yDT_{seq}}$s are equi-expressive to *deterministic nested word-to-word transducers* [13], which is a subclass of $\mathrm{SRTST_{sur}}$s hence their equivalence problem is known to be decidable.

[2] In the current paper, notions with (resp. without) single-use restriction are written by words with (resp. without) the subscript $_{\mathrm{sur}}$ such as $\mathrm{STT_{sur}}$ (resp. STT). In [1], $\mathrm{STT_{sur}}$ and $\mathrm{STST_{sur}}$ are written just as STT and STST, respectively.

As for streaming string-to-string transducers rather than tree-to-string ones, *copyless streaming string transducers* (SST_{cl}s) have been introduced in [2]. The expressiveness of SST_{cl}s coincides with that of MSO-definable string transducers. *Copyful streaming string transducers* (SST_{cf}s) that are released from the copyless restriction are studied in [9]. It is shown that SST_{cf}s and HDT0L systems are equi-expressive.

Macro forest transducers that are richer than yDT^{R}s have been translated into streaming transducers to obtain efficient XML stream processors [10]. The streaming model is rather informal and its expressiveness has not been studied.

2 Preliminaries

For $n \in \mathbb{N}$, The Construction of we write $[n]$ for the set $\{1, \ldots, n\}$; in particular, $[0] = \emptyset$. We use boldface letters such as $\boldsymbol{t}$ to denote tuples. For a k-tuple $\boldsymbol{t}$, we write $|\boldsymbol{t}|$ for the length k of $\boldsymbol{t}$. For a set A and $k \in \mathbb{N}$, A^k denotes the set of all k-tuples of elements of A, and $A^{(\leq k)} \triangleq \bigcup_{i=0}^{k} A^i$. For $\boldsymbol{t} = (a_1, \ldots, a_k) \in A^k$ and $a \in A$, we denote by $\boldsymbol{t} \parallel a$ the $(k+1)$-tuple $(a_1, \ldots, a_k, a)$. We write ε for the empty string, and $\text{Dom}(f)$ for the domain of definition of a partial function f.

A *ranked alphabet* is a pair of a finite set Σ and a function $\text{rank}_\Sigma : \Sigma \to \mathbb{N}$; the value $\text{rank}_\Sigma(\sigma)$ of a symbol σ is called the *rank* of σ. We define $\Sigma^{(n)} \triangleq \{\sigma \in \Sigma \mid \text{rank}_\Sigma(\sigma) = n\}$, and write σ also as $\sigma^{(n)}$ when $\sigma \in \Sigma^{(n)}$. The set of (*ranked*) *trees over* Σ, denoted by $\mathcal{T}_\Sigma$, is the smallest set T such that if $\sigma \in \Sigma^{(n)}$ and $t_1, \ldots, t_n \in T$ then $\sigma(t_1, \ldots, t_n) \in T$. We use an English letter (mainly e) as a metavariable ranging over rank-0 letters, i.e., leaves; a tree of the form $e()$ is written as e.

An *alphabet* is just a finite set. Let Σ be an alphabet. A *tagged alphabet* $\hat{\Sigma}$ consists of the *call symbols* $\langle\sigma$, and the *return symbols* $\sigma\rangle$, for all $\sigma \in \Sigma$. A *nested word* over Σ is a finite sequence over $\hat{\Sigma}$. We simply write $\langle e\rangle$ for a nested word of the form $\langle e\ e\rangle$. A nested word w is called *well-matched* if all the left and right angle brackets occurring in w are well-bracketed; and w is called *well-labeled* if each matched pair of call and return symbols is labeled with the same symbol in Σ. Any well-labeled nested word is well-matched. For example, $\langle\mathtt{a}\ \mathtt{b}\rangle\ \langle\mathtt{a}\ \mathtt{b}\rangle$ is well-matched but not well-labeled; $\langle\mathtt{a}\ \mathtt{a}\rangle\ \langle\mathtt{b}\ \langle\mathtt{a}\ \mathtt{a}\rangle\ \mathtt{b}\rangle$ is well-labeled; and $\langle\mathtt{a}\ \mathtt{a}\rangle\ \langle\mathtt{b}\ \langle\mathtt{b}$ is not well-matched.

Let Σ be a ranked alphabet. A mapping from ranked trees to nested words $\lfloor - \rfloor : \mathcal{T}_\Sigma \to \hat{\Sigma}^*$ is defined by $\lfloor t \rfloor = \langle\sigma\ \lfloor t_1 \rfloor \cdots \lfloor t_n \rfloor\ \sigma\rangle$ for $t = \sigma(t_1, \ldots, t_n) \in \mathcal{T}_\Sigma$. The set of *ranked nested words*, denoted by $\lfloor \mathcal{T}_\Sigma \rfloor$, is defined by $\{\lfloor t \rfloor \mid t \in \mathcal{T}_\Sigma\}$. Ranked nested words respect ranks but well-labeled nested words do not necessarily (furthermore, well-labeled nested words can express not just unranked trees but even forests). For example, for $\sigma^{(2)} \in \Sigma$, $\langle\sigma\ \sigma\rangle$ is well-labeled, but is not a ranked nested word as $\sigma()$ is not a ranked tree. Note that $\lfloor - \rfloor$ is injective, and $\lfloor \mathcal{T}_\Sigma \rfloor$ is isomorphic to $\mathcal{T}_\Sigma$; we write the converse function from ranked nested words to ranked trees as $\lceil - \rceil : \lfloor \mathcal{T}_\Sigma \rfloor \to \mathcal{T}_\Sigma$. In this paper, we are interested in ranked nested words rather than well-labeled nested words.

Definition 1. A *non-deterministic finite state bottom-up tree automaton* (*NBTA*) is a tuple (Π, Σ, θ) where: (i) Π is a finite set of *states*, (ii) Σ is a ranked alphabet of *input symbols*, and (iii) $\theta : \bigcup_{n\in\mathbb{N}}(\Sigma^{(n)} \times \Pi^n) \to 2^{\Pi}$ is a function called a *transition function.*

Let $A = (\Pi, \Sigma, \theta)$ be an NBTA. We extend θ to $\hat{\theta} : \mathcal{T}_\Sigma \to 2^{\Pi}$ by induction: $\hat{\theta}(\sigma(t_1, \dots, t_n)) \triangleq \bigcup_{\pi_1\in\hat{\theta}(t_1),\dots,\pi_n\in\hat{\theta}(t_n)} \theta(\sigma, (\pi_1, \dots, \pi_n))$. We say that a state $\pi \in \Pi$ *accepts* a tree $t \in \mathcal{T}_\Sigma$ if $\pi \in \hat{\theta}(t)$. We denote by $\mathcal{L}_A(\pi)$ the set of trees accepted by π; we simply write $\mathcal{L}(\pi)$ for $\mathcal{L}_A(\pi)$ when A is clear from the context. We assume that $\mathcal{L}_A(\pi) \neq \emptyset$ for all $\pi \in \Pi$. An NBTA A is called a *deterministic finite state bottom-up tree automaton* (DBTA) if $\theta(\sigma, (\pi_1, \dots, \pi_n))$ has exactly one element for every $\sigma \in \Sigma^{(n)}$ and $\pi_1, \dots, \pi_n \in \Pi$. For a DBTA, we write $\theta(\sigma, (\pi_1, \dots, \pi_n))$ for its unique element. DBTAs and NBTAs recognize the same class of tree languages known as *regular tree languages* [3]. We denote by *REG* the set of all regular tree languages. *REG* is closed under union, intersection, and complementation.

3 Transducers

We here define the two main notions to be compared: $\mathrm{yDT^R}$ and SRTST.

3.1 Deterministic Top-Down Tree-to-String Transducers with Regular Look-Ahead

A deterministic top-down tree-to-string transducer with regular look-ahead ($\mathrm{yDT^R}$ for short) works on ranked trees.

First we prepare the range of the right hand sides of transition rules of $\mathrm{yDT^R}$s. We fix a set of input variables $X = \{x_1, x_2, \dots\}$ and define $X_n \triangleq \{x_1, \dots, x_n\}$ for $n \in \mathbb{N}$. Also, for a set Q and $n \in \mathbb{N}$, we define $Q(X_n) \triangleq \{q(x_i) \mid q \in Q, i \leq n\}$ where $q(x_i) \triangleq (q, x_i)$. For a finite set Q (of *states*), an alphabet Δ, and $n \in \mathbb{N}$, we define the set $\mathit{Rhs}_{Q,\Delta}(X_n)$ of *expressions* by $\tau ::= \varepsilon \mid a\tau \mid q(x_i)\tau$ where $a \in \Delta$ and $q(x_i) \in Q(X_n)$. The following definition of $\mathrm{yDT^R}$ is taken from [12], except that we adopt the style in [4] for regular look-ahead (i.e., we consider directly regular tree languages rather than states of an NBTA).

Definition 2 ($\mathrm{yDT^R}$). A *deterministic top-down tree-to-string transducer with regular look-ahead* ($\mathrm{yDT^R}$) is a tuple $(Q, \Sigma, \Delta, \mathit{Init}, R)$ satisfying the following conditions:

- Q is a finite set of *states.*
- Σ is a ranked alphabet of *input symbols.*
- Δ is an alphabet of *output symbols.*
- $\mathit{Init} \subseteq \mathit{Rhs}_{Q,\Delta}(X_1) \times (\mathit{REG} \setminus \{\emptyset\})$ is a finite set of *initial sequences*, and must satisfy that, for any two distinct initial sequences (τ, L) and (τ', L') in *Init*, $L \cap L' = \emptyset$. For $L \in \mathit{REG} \setminus \{\emptyset\}$, τ such that $(\tau, L) \in \mathit{Init}$ is unique (if it exists), and is denoted by $\mathit{Init}(L)$.

- $R \subseteq \bigcup_{n \in \mathbb{N}} (Q \times \Sigma^{(n)} \times Rhs_{Q,\Delta}(X_n) \times (REG \setminus \{\emptyset\})^n)$ is a finite set of *rules*, and must satisfy that, for any two distinct rules $(q, \sigma, \tau, (L_1, \dots, L_n))$ and $(q, \sigma, \tau', (L'_1, \dots, L'_n))$ in R, $L_i \cap L'_i = \emptyset$ for some $i \in [n]$. A rule $(q, \sigma, \tau, (L_1, \dots, L_n))$ is written as

$$q(\sigma(x_1, \dots, x_n)) \to \tau \qquad \langle L_1, \dots, L_n \rangle .$$

Here τ is uniquely determined (if it exists) from $(q, \sigma, (L_1, \dots, L_n))$; hence we call this rule a $(q, \sigma, (L_1, \dots, L_n))$-*rule*, and denote τ by $\mathrm{rhs}(q, \sigma, (L_1, \dots, L_n))$. We write $q(e) \to \tau$ for $q(e()) \to \tau\ \langle\rangle$ when $\mathrm{rank}_\Sigma(e) = 0$.

We define the semantics of a yDT^{R}, which transforms a tree in a top-down manner. Let $M = (Q, \Sigma, \Delta, Init, R)$ be a yDT^{R}, and we define a partial function $[\![M]\!] : \mathcal{T}_\Sigma \rightharpoonup \Delta^*$.

First, we define auxiliary partial functions $[\![q]\!]_M : \mathcal{T}_\Sigma \rightharpoonup \Delta^*$ (for $q \in Q$) and $[\![\tau]\!]_M : \mathcal{T}_\Sigma^n \rightharpoonup \Delta^*$ (for $n \in \mathbb{N}$ and $\tau \in Rhs_{Q,\Delta}(X_n)$), by simultaneous induction on input trees. Let $t = \sigma(t_1, \dots, t_n) \in \mathcal{T}_\Sigma$ and $q \in Q$. If there exist $L_1, \dots, L_n$ and a $(q, \sigma, (L_1, \dots, L_n))$-rule in R such that $t_i \in L_i$ for all $i \in [n]$, then $[\![q]\!]_{M(t)}$ is defined as

$$[\![q]\!]_M(\sigma(t_1, \dots, t_n)) \triangleq [\![\mathrm{rhs}(q, \sigma, (L_1, \dots, L_n))]\!]_M(t_1, \dots, t_n)$$

(if the r.h.s. is defined), and $[\![q]\!]_{M(t)}$ is not defined otherwise. Here note that, due to the condition on R, the tuple $(L_1, \dots, L_n)$ above is unique if exists. For $n \in \mathbb{N}$ and $\tau \in Rhs_{Q,\Delta}(X_n)$, $[\![\tau]\!]_M(t_1, \dots, t_n)$ is defined as follows:

$$\begin{aligned} [\![\varepsilon]\!]_M(t_1, \dots, t_n) &\triangleq \varepsilon \\ [\![a\tau']\!]_M(t_1, \dots, t_n) &\triangleq a\,[\![\tau']\!]_M(t_1, \dots, t_n) \\ [\![q'(x_i)\tau']\!]_M(t_1, \dots, t_n) &\triangleq [\![q']\!]_M(t_i)\,[\![\tau']\!]_M(t_1, \dots, t_n) . \end{aligned}$$

Now let us define $[\![M]\!] : \mathcal{T}_\Sigma \rightharpoonup \Delta^*$. For $t \in \mathcal{T}_\Sigma$, if there exists a pair $(\tau, L) \in$ *Init* such that $t \in L$ and if $[\![\tau]\!]_M(t)$ is defined, then we define $[\![M]\!](t) \triangleq [\![\tau]\!]_M(t)$; and $[\![M]\!](t)$ is not defined otherwise. Again, note that such a pair (τ, L) is unique. We denote by $\mathrm{Dom}(M)$ the domain of $[\![M]\!]$.

In the above definition, regular look-ahead is realized by regular tree languages directly. As a finite representation for expressing regular tree languages, we use an NBTA or a DBTA, switching the two styles conveniently. (Recall that the two notions recognize the same class of languages, *REG*.) We call an automaton used for regular look-ahead a *regular look-ahead automaton*. Given a regular look-ahead automaton, we use states of the automaton instead of regular tree languages when we refer to initial sequences or rules (e.g., we write $\mathrm{rhs}(q, \sigma, (\pi_1, \dots, \pi_n))$ for $\mathrm{rhs}(q, \sigma, (\mathcal{L}(\pi_1), \dots, \mathcal{L}(\pi_n)))$).

The equivalence problem for yDT^{R} is known to be decidable.

Theorem 3 (Corollary 8.1 in [12]). *Given two* yDT^{R}s M_1, M_2, *it is decidable whether* $[\![M_1]\!] = [\![M_2]\!]$.

3.2 Streaming Ranked-Tree-to-String Transducers

A streaming ranked-tree-to-string transducer (SRTST for short) works on ranked nested words. We first prepare some auxiliary definitions.

For a finite set Γ (of *variables*) and an alphabet Δ, the set $E(\Gamma, \Delta)$ of *expressions over* Γ *and* Δ is defined by the following grammar: $E ::= \varepsilon \mid aE \mid \gamma E$ where $a \in \Delta$ and $\gamma \in \Gamma$. Note that $E(\emptyset, \Delta) = \Delta^*$.

Let Γ and Γ' be finite sets and Δ be an alphabet. We call a mapping $\rho : \Gamma \to E(\Gamma', \Delta)$ an *assignment*, and denote ρ by $[\gamma_1 := e_1, \ldots, \gamma_n := e_n]$ where $\Gamma = \{\gamma_1, \ldots, \gamma_n\}$ and $e_i = \rho(\gamma_i)$; in this notation, $\gamma_i := e_i$ may be omitted if $e_i = \gamma_i$. An assignment ρ is naturally extended to $\rho : E(\Gamma, \Delta) \to E(\Gamma', \Delta)$: for $e \in E(\Gamma, \Delta)$, $\rho(e)$ is the expression over Γ' and Δ obtained by replacing all occurrences of every variable γ in e with $\rho(\gamma)$. We denote $\rho(e)$ by $e\rho$. The set of all assignments over Γ, Γ' and Δ is denoted by $\mathcal{A}(\Gamma, \Gamma', \Delta)$. An element of $\mathcal{A}(\Gamma, \emptyset, \Delta)$ (i.e., a function $\Gamma \to \Delta^*$) is called an *evaluation function*, and a returned value of an evaluation function is called a *variable value*.

Given two assignments $\rho_1 : \Gamma_1 \to E(\Gamma_1', \Delta)$ and $\rho_2 : \Gamma_2 \to E(\Gamma_2', \Delta)$, the assignment $\rho_1\rho_2 : \Gamma_1 \to E((\Gamma_1' \setminus \Gamma_2) \cup \Gamma_2', \Delta)$ is defined (as usual) as follows. For $\gamma \in \Gamma_1$, $(\rho_1\rho_2)(\gamma)$ is an expression in $E((\Gamma_1' \setminus \Gamma_2) \cup \Gamma_2', \Delta)$ obtained by replacing all occurrences of variable $\gamma_1' \in \Gamma_1' \cap \Gamma_2$ in $\rho_1(\gamma) \in E(\Gamma_1', \Delta)$ with $\rho_2(\gamma_1') \in E(\Gamma_2', \Delta)$, and keeping all occurrences of other variable $\gamma_1' \in \Gamma_1' \setminus \Gamma_2$ in $\rho_1(\gamma) \in E(\Gamma_1', \Delta)$. Given two assignments $\rho_1 : \Gamma_1 \to E(\Gamma, \Delta)$ and $\rho_2 : \Gamma_2 \to E(\Gamma, \Delta)$ where Γ_1 and Γ_2 are disjoint, the assignment $\rho_1 \uplus \rho_2 : \Gamma_1 \uplus \Gamma_2 \to E(\Gamma, \Delta)$ is defined by

$$\rho_1 \uplus \rho_2 \triangleq [\gamma_1 := \rho_1(\gamma_1), \ldots, \gamma_n := \rho_1(\gamma_n), \gamma_1' := \rho_2(\gamma_1'), \ldots, \gamma_m' := \rho_2(\gamma_m')]$$

where $\Gamma_1 = \{\gamma_1, \ldots, \gamma_n\}$ and $\Gamma_2 = \{\gamma_1', \ldots, \gamma_m'\}$.

We introduce the notion of an SRTST based on the definition of $\mathrm{STT_{sur}}$ in [1]. The difference is as follows: an $\mathrm{STT_{sur}}$ is restricted by *single-use restriction* (sur for short), while an SRTST is not restricted; the input and output of an $\mathrm{STT_{sur}}$ are well-matched nested words, while the input and output of an SRTST are ranked nested words and strings, respectively.

Definition 4. A *streaming ranked-tree-to-string transducer* (SRTST for short) is a tuple $(S, \Sigma, \Delta, P, s_0, \Gamma, F, \delta_c, \delta_r, \rho_c, \rho_r)$ where:

- S is a finite set of *states*,
- Σ is a ranked alphabet of *input symbols*,
- Δ is an alphabet of *output symbols*,
- P is a finite set of *stack symbols*,
- $s_0 \in S$ is an *initial state*,
- Γ is a finite set of *variables*,
- $F : S \rightharpoonup E(\Gamma, \Delta)$ is a partial function called an *output function*,
- $\delta_c : S \times \Sigma \to S \times P$ is a *call state-transition function*,
- $\delta_r : S \times P \times \Sigma \to S$ is a *return state-transition function*,
- $\rho_c : S \times \Sigma \to \mathcal{A}(\Gamma, \Gamma, \Delta)$ is a *call variable-update function*,
- $\rho_r : S \times P \times \Sigma \to \mathcal{A}(\Gamma, \Gamma \uplus \overline{\Gamma}, \Delta)$ is a *return variable-update function* where $\overline{\Gamma}$ is a "copy" of Γ, i.e., $\overline{\Gamma} \triangleq \{\overline{\gamma} \mid \gamma \in \Gamma\}$ and each $\overline{\gamma}$ is a fresh symbol.

We define the semantics of an SRTST, which transforms a tree (a ranked nested word) in a top-down and bottom-up way. Let $T = (S, \Sigma, \Delta, P, s_0, \Gamma, F, \delta_c, \delta_r, \rho_c, \rho_r)$ be an SRTST. We define the set of *configurations* of T, denoted by Ψ, as $\Psi := S \times (P \times \mathcal{A}(\Gamma, \emptyset, \Delta))^* \times \mathcal{A}(\Gamma, \emptyset, \Delta)$. For a configuration $(s, \Lambda, \alpha) \in \Psi$, Λ is called the *stack*, and α is called the *current evaluation function.* Let $\alpha_\varepsilon^\Gamma \triangleq [\gamma := \varepsilon]_{\gamma \in \Gamma}$, which is called the *emptyword evaluation function*; we often omit the superscript Γ of $\alpha_\varepsilon^\Gamma$. We call $(s_0, \varepsilon, \alpha_\varepsilon^\Gamma)$ the *initial configuration.* We define the *transition function* $\delta : \Psi \times \hat{\Sigma} \rightharpoonup \Psi$ *over configurations* as follows:

Call transitions. For $\sigma \in \Sigma$, $\delta\big((s, \Lambda, \alpha), \langle\sigma\big) \triangleq \big(s', (p, \alpha')\Lambda, \alpha_\varepsilon^\Gamma\big)$ where:
- $(s', p) \triangleq \delta_c(s, \sigma)$: we invoke the state-transition function δ_c, which reads $\langle\sigma$ in the state s,
- $\alpha' \triangleq \rho_c(s, \sigma)\alpha$: we push (p, α') on the stack Λ (rather than setting α' as the current evaluation function); α' is almost $\rho_c(s, \sigma)$ but each variable γ in $\rho_c(s, \sigma)$ is substituted for $\alpha(\gamma)$ (and $\alpha(\gamma)$ is discarded if γ does not occur in $\rho_c(s, \sigma)$),
- we reset the current evaluation function α to the emptyword evaluation function $\alpha_\varepsilon^\Gamma$.

Return transitions. For $\sigma \in \Sigma$, $\delta\big((s, (p, \beta)\Lambda, \alpha), \sigma\rangle\big) \triangleq \big(s', \Lambda, \alpha'\big)$ where:
- $s' \triangleq \delta_r(s, p, \sigma)$: we invoke the state-transition function δ_r, which read $\sigma\rangle$ in the state s with the stack symbol p on the stack,
- we pop (p, β) from the stack,
- $\alpha' \triangleq \rho_r(s, p, \sigma)(\alpha \uplus \overline{\beta})$ where $\overline{\beta}$ is the "copy" of β: i.e., $\overline{\beta} \triangleq [\overline{\gamma} := \beta(\gamma)]_{\gamma \in \Gamma}$: we replace α with α', which is almost $\rho_r(s, p, \sigma)$ but each variable γ in $\rho_r(s, p, \sigma)$ is substituted for $\alpha(\gamma)$ and each variable $\overline{\gamma}$ in $\rho_r(s, p, \sigma)$ is substituted for $\beta(\gamma)$ (and $\alpha(\gamma)/\beta(\gamma)$ is discarded if $\gamma/\overline{\gamma}$ does not occur in $\rho_c(s, \sigma)$).

Now we define the meaning $[\![T]\!] : \lfloor \mathcal{T}_\Sigma \rfloor \rightharpoonup \Delta^*$. First, the transition function $\delta : \Psi \times \hat{\Sigma} \rightharpoonup \Psi$ naturally extends to $\delta^* : \Psi \times \hat{\Sigma}^* \rightharpoonup \Psi$ by iterating δ. For a nested word $w \in \hat{\Sigma}^*$, we denote by $c \overset{w}{\Rightarrow}_T c'$ if $\delta^*(c, w) = c'$; we omit the subscript T if it is clear from the context. Note that for any configuration c and any well-matched nested word w, $\delta^*(c, w)$ is always defined. For a ranked nested word $w \in \lfloor \mathcal{T}_\Sigma \rfloor$, if $(s_0, \varepsilon, \alpha_\varepsilon^\Gamma) \overset{w}{\Rightarrow} (s, \varepsilon, \alpha)$ and if $F(s)$ is defined then $[\![T]\!](w) \triangleq F(s)\alpha$; otherwise $[\![T]\!](w)$ is undefined. We denote by $\mathrm{Dom}(T)$ the domain of $[\![T]\!]$.

Example 5. We give an SRTST T: let $S \triangleq \{s_?, s_\mathtt{a}, s_\mathtt{b}\}$; $\Sigma \triangleq \{\mathtt{f}^{(2)}, \mathtt{a}^{(0)}, \mathtt{b}^{(0)}\}$; $\Delta \triangleq \{\mathtt{a}, \mathtt{b}\}$; $P \triangleq \{p_?, p_\mathtt{a}, p_\mathtt{b}\}$; $s_0 \triangleq s_?$; $\Gamma \triangleq \{\gamma\}$; $F(s) \triangleq \gamma$ for every $s \in S$; $\delta_c(s_d, \sigma) \triangleq (s_?, p_d)$ for every $\sigma \in \Sigma$ and $d \in \{\mathtt{a}, \mathtt{b}, ?\}$; δ_r is defined by

$$\delta_r(s, p_d, \sigma) \triangleq s_d, \quad \delta_r(s_d, p_?, \sigma) \triangleq s_d, \quad \delta_r(s_?, p_?, \mathtt{f}) \triangleq s_?, \quad \delta_r(s_?, p_?, d) \triangleq s_d,$$

for every $s \in S$, $\sigma \in \Sigma$, $d \in \{\mathtt{a}, \mathtt{b}\}$; ρ_c is defined by

$$\rho_c(s, \mathtt{f}) \triangleq [\gamma := \gamma], \quad \rho_c(s_?, d) \triangleq [\gamma := d], \quad \rho_c(s_\mathtt{a}, d) \triangleq [\gamma := \gamma d], \quad \rho_c(s_\mathtt{b}, d) \triangleq [\gamma := d\gamma],$$

$$
\begin{aligned}
& (s_?, \lfloor\!\lfloor\rfloor\!\rfloor, \alpha_\varepsilon) \\
\xRightarrow{\langle \mathtt{f}}\ & (s_?, \lfloor\!\lfloor(p_?, \alpha_\varepsilon)\rfloor\!\rfloor, \alpha_\varepsilon) \\
\xRightarrow{\langle \mathtt{f}}\ & (s_?, \lfloor\!\lfloor(p_?, \alpha_\varepsilon)(p_?, \alpha_\varepsilon)\rfloor\!\rfloor, \alpha_\varepsilon) \\
\xRightarrow{\langle \mathtt{b}}\ & (s_?, \lfloor\!\lfloor(p_?, [\gamma{:=}\mathtt{b}])(p_?, \alpha_\varepsilon)(p_?, \alpha_\varepsilon)\rfloor\!\rfloor, \alpha_\varepsilon) \\
\xRightarrow{\mathtt{b}\rangle}\ & (s_\mathtt{b}, \lfloor\!\lfloor(p_?, \alpha_\varepsilon)(p_?, \alpha_\varepsilon)\rfloor\!\rfloor, [\gamma{:=}\mathtt{b}]) \\
\xRightarrow{\langle \mathtt{a}}\ & (s_?, \lfloor\!\lfloor(p_\mathtt{b}, [\gamma{:=}\mathtt{ab}])(p_?, \alpha_\varepsilon)(p_?, \alpha_\varepsilon)\rfloor\!\rfloor, \alpha_\varepsilon) \\
\xRightarrow{\mathtt{a}\rangle}\ & (s_\mathtt{b}, \lfloor\!\lfloor(p_?, \alpha_\varepsilon)(p_?, \alpha_\varepsilon)\rfloor\!\rfloor, [\gamma{:=}\mathtt{ab}]) \\
\xRightarrow{\mathtt{f}\rangle}\ & (s_\mathtt{b}, \lfloor\!\lfloor(p_?, \alpha_\varepsilon)\rfloor\!\rfloor, [\gamma{:=}\mathtt{ab}]) \\
\xRightarrow{\langle \mathtt{f}}\ & (s_?, \lfloor\!\lfloor(p_\mathtt{b}, [\gamma{:=}\mathtt{ab}])(p_?, \alpha_\varepsilon)\rfloor\!\rfloor, \alpha_\varepsilon) \\
\xRightarrow{\langle \mathtt{a}}\ & (s_?, \lfloor\!\lfloor(p_?, [\gamma{:=}\mathtt{a}])(p_\mathtt{b}, [\gamma{:=}\mathtt{ab}])(p_?, \alpha_\varepsilon)\rfloor\!\rfloor, \alpha_\varepsilon) \\
\xRightarrow{\mathtt{a}\rangle}\ & (s_\mathtt{a}, \lfloor\!\lfloor(p_\mathtt{b}, [\gamma{:=}\mathtt{ab}])(p_?, \alpha_\varepsilon)\rfloor\!\rfloor, [\gamma{:=}\mathtt{a}]) \\
\xRightarrow{\langle \mathtt{b}}\ & (s_?, \lfloor\!\lfloor(p_\mathtt{a}, [\gamma{:=}\mathtt{ab}])(p_\mathtt{b}, [\gamma{:=}\mathtt{ab}])(p_?, \alpha_\varepsilon)\rfloor\!\rfloor, \alpha_\varepsilon) \\
\xRightarrow{\mathtt{b}\rangle}\ & (s_\mathtt{a}, \lfloor\!\lfloor(p_\mathtt{b}, [\gamma{:=}\mathtt{ab}])(p_?, \alpha_\varepsilon)\rfloor\!\rfloor, [\gamma{:=}\mathtt{ab}]) \\
\xRightarrow{\mathtt{f}\rangle}\ & (s_\mathtt{b}, \lfloor\!\lfloor(p_?, \alpha_\varepsilon)\rfloor\!\rfloor, [\gamma{:=}\mathtt{abab}]) \\
\xRightarrow{\mathtt{f}\rangle}\ & (s_\mathtt{b}, \lfloor\!\lfloor\rfloor\!\rfloor, [\gamma{:=}\mathtt{abab}])
\end{aligned}
$$

Fig. 1. Transitions for $\lfloor \mathtt{f(f(b,a),f(a,b))} \rfloor$.

for every $s \in S$ and $d \in \{\mathtt{a}, \mathtt{b}\}$; and ρ_r is defined by

$$
\rho_r(s, p_?, \mathtt{f}) \triangleq [\gamma := \gamma], \quad \rho_r(s, p_\mathtt{a}, \mathtt{f}) \triangleq [\gamma := \overline{\gamma}\gamma], \quad \rho_r(s, p, \mathtt{a}) \triangleq [\gamma := \overline{\gamma}],
$$
$$
\rho_r(s, p_\mathtt{b}, \mathtt{f}) \triangleq [\gamma := \gamma\overline{\gamma}], \quad \rho_r(s, p, \mathtt{b}) \triangleq [\gamma := \overline{\gamma}],
$$

for every $s \in S$ and $p \in P$. Given $t \in \mathcal{T}_\Sigma$, $[\![T]\!](\lfloor t \rfloor)$ recursively swaps the two subtrees of the root if the leftmost leaf is b, and skip the swapping otherwise; and then produces the leaves as the output. For instance, $[\![T]\!]$ transforms $\lfloor \mathtt{f(f(b,a),f(a,b))} \rfloor$ as in Fig. 1, where for clarity we denote stacks with $\lfloor\!\lfloor - \rfloor\!\rfloor$.

4 SRTST and yDT$^\mathrm{R}$ Are Equi-Expressive

We show the equi-expressiveness between SRTSTs and yDT$^\mathrm{R}$s, by giving effective constructions in the both directions. Then (only) the construction of a yDT$^\mathrm{R}$ from an SRTST is used to show the decidability of the equivalence of SRTST. The both constructions are basically *component-wise*: the regular look-ahead automaton of a yDT$^\mathrm{R}$ M corresponds to the state-transition functions δ_c, δ_r of an SRTST T; rules of M correspond to the variable-update functions ρ_c, ρ_r of T; and *Init* of M corresponds to F of T.

4.1 The Construction of SRTST from yDT$^\mathrm{R}$

We construct a *bottom-up* SRTST T from a yDT$^\mathrm{R}$ M; an SRTST T is *bottom-up* [1] if $\delta_c(s, \sigma) = (s_0, p)$ for some p and $\rho_c(s, p, \sigma) = [\gamma := \gamma]_{\gamma \in \Gamma}$ for every s, p and σ, (i.e., if in any call transition T always resets the state s to the initial state and never change the evaluation function α being pushed on the stack). The construction in the next lemma is inspired by the proof of the decidability of the equivalence of yDT$^\mathrm{R}$s given in [11, Sections 3 and 4].

Lemma 6. *For any* yDT$^\mathrm{R}$ M*, there exists a bottom-up* SRTST T *such that* $\mathrm{Dom}(T) = \lfloor \mathrm{Dom}(M) \rfloor$ *and* $[\![T]\!](\lfloor t \rfloor) = [\![M]\!](t)$ *for all* $t \in \mathrm{Dom}(M)$.

Proof. Let $M = (Q, \Sigma, \Delta, Init, R)$ be a $\mathrm{yDT^R}$ and we assume that its regular look-ahead is given by DBTA $A = (\Sigma, \Pi, \theta)$. Further, w.l.o.g., we can assume that M satisfies the following conditions: (i) for any tree $\sigma(t_1, \dots, t_n)$ and $q \in Q$, $\sigma(t_1, \dots, t_n) \in \mathrm{Dom}([\![q]\!]_M)$ iff there exists a $(q, \sigma, (L_1, \dots, L_n))$-rule in R such that $t_i \in L_i$ for every $i \in [n]$; and (ii) $\mathrm{Dom}(M) = \bigcup_{(\tau,\pi)\in Init} \mathcal{L}(\pi)$.

We define an equivalent SRTST $T = (S, \Sigma, \Delta, P, s_0, \Gamma, F, \delta_c, \delta_r, \rho_c, \rho_r)$ as follows. (For its behavior, see also the explanation after the lemma.)

Let $m = \max(\{1\} \cup \{\mathrm{rank}_\Sigma(\sigma) \mid \sigma \in \Sigma\})$, $S = P = \Pi^{(\le m)}$, and $s_0 = ()$. We define $\Gamma = Q(X_m)$, so that $E(\Gamma, \Delta) = Rhs_{Q,\Delta}(X_m)$. We define the output (partial) function $F : S \rightharpoonup E(\Gamma, \Delta)$ as $F((\pi)) = Init(\mathcal{L}(\pi)) \in Rhs_{Q,\Delta}(X_1)$.

The call state-transition function $\delta_c : S \times \Sigma \to S \times P$ is defined by $\delta_c(\boldsymbol{\pi}, \sigma) = (s_0, \boldsymbol{\pi})$. The return state-transition function $\delta_r : S \times P \times \Sigma \to S$ is defined by $\delta_r(\boldsymbol{\pi}, \boldsymbol{\pi}', \sigma) = \boldsymbol{\pi}' \| \theta(\sigma, \boldsymbol{\pi})$ for $\boldsymbol{\pi}, \boldsymbol{\pi}' \in \Pi^{(\le m)}$ and $\sigma \in \Sigma$ such that $|\boldsymbol{\pi}| = \mathrm{rank}_\Sigma(\sigma)$ and $|\boldsymbol{\pi}'| \ne m$, and by $\delta_r(\boldsymbol{\pi}, \boldsymbol{\pi}', \sigma) = s_0$ for the other case of arguments $\boldsymbol{\pi}, \boldsymbol{\pi}', \sigma$.

The call variable-update function $\rho_c : S \times \Sigma \to \mathcal{A}(\Gamma, \Gamma, \Delta)$ is defined by $\rho_c(\boldsymbol{\pi}, \sigma) = [\gamma := \gamma]_{\gamma\in\Gamma}$. The return variable-update function $\rho_r : S \times P \times \Sigma \to \mathcal{A}(\Gamma, \Gamma \uplus \overline{\Gamma}, \Delta)$ is defined by

$$\begin{aligned}\rho_r(\boldsymbol{\pi}, \boldsymbol{\pi}', \sigma) = \quad & \left[q(x_k) := \overline{q(x_k)}\right]_{q\in Q,\, k\le|\boldsymbol{\pi}'|} \\ & \uplus \left[q(x_{|\boldsymbol{\pi}'|+1}) := \underline{\mathrm{rhs}}(q, \sigma, \boldsymbol{\pi})\right]_{q\in Q} \\ & \uplus \left[q(x_k) := \varepsilon\right]_{q\in Q,\, |\boldsymbol{\pi}'|+1<k\le m}\end{aligned}$$

for $\boldsymbol{\pi}, \boldsymbol{\pi}' \in \Pi^{(\le m)}$ and $\sigma \in \Sigma$ such that $|\boldsymbol{\pi}| = \mathrm{rank}_\Sigma(\sigma)$ and $|\boldsymbol{\pi}'| \ne m$, and by $\rho_r(\boldsymbol{\pi}, \boldsymbol{\pi}', \sigma) = \alpha_\varepsilon$ for the other case of arguments $\boldsymbol{\pi}, \boldsymbol{\pi}', \sigma$. Above, the function $\underline{\mathrm{rhs}} : \bigcup_{n\in\mathbb{N}}(Q \times \Sigma^{(n)} \times \Pi^n) \to E(\Gamma, \Delta)$ is defined by

$$\underline{\mathrm{rhs}}(q, \sigma, \boldsymbol{\pi}) = \begin{cases} \mathrm{rhs}(q, \sigma, \boldsymbol{\pi}), & \text{if } (q, \sigma, \boldsymbol{\pi})\text{-rule is defined;} \\ \varepsilon, & \text{otherwise,} \end{cases}$$

where $\mathrm{rhs}(q, \sigma, \boldsymbol{\pi}) \in Rhs_{Q,\Delta}(X_n) \subseteq E(\Gamma, \Delta)$. Above, ε in the definitions of ρ_r and $\underline{\mathrm{rhs}}$ are not used in the actual computation. We control "definedness" by the determinism of the DBTA A and the above assumptions (i) and (ii) for M. □

The construction of T is designed to behave for each input symbol as follows. Let $\sigma'(t'_1, \dots, t'_{n'})$ be a subtree of an input tree, and $t'_i = \sigma(t_1, \dots, t_n)$.

Call symbol $\langle\sigma$ **:** By the definitions of δ_c and ρ_c above, in general a call transition is $(\boldsymbol{\pi}', \Lambda, \beta) \overset{\langle\sigma}{\Longrightarrow} ((), (\boldsymbol{\pi}', \beta)\Lambda, \alpha_\varepsilon)$. Suppose that T starts the computation of $t'_i = \sigma(t_1, \dots, t_n)$. The computation so far for $t'_1, \dots, t'_{i-1}$ is recorded in $\boldsymbol{\pi}'$ and β and the further earlier computation is recorded in Λ. Then the call transition by $\langle\sigma$ saves the record $(\boldsymbol{\pi}', \beta)$ to the stack.

Return symbol $\sigma\rangle$ **:** A return transition is basically of the following form: $(\boldsymbol{\pi}, (\boldsymbol{\pi}', \beta)\Lambda, \alpha) \overset{\sigma\rangle}{\Longrightarrow} (\boldsymbol{\pi}' \,\|\, \theta(\sigma, \boldsymbol{\pi}), \Lambda, \alpha')$. Suppose that T is finishing the computation of some child tree $t'_i = \sigma(t_1, \dots, t_n)$.

The state-transition function δ_r simulates the DBTA A as follows. In the transition $\delta_r(\boldsymbol{\pi}, \boldsymbol{\pi}', \sigma) = \boldsymbol{\pi}' \mid\mid \theta(\sigma, \boldsymbol{\pi})$, $\boldsymbol{\pi} = (\pi_1, \ldots, \pi_n)$ is a tuple of A-states and $\pi_1, \ldots, \pi_n$ accept $t_1, \ldots, t_n$, respectively. Hence $\theta(\sigma, \boldsymbol{\pi})$ is an A-state which accepts $t_i' = \sigma(t_1, \ldots, t_n)$. Likewise, $\boldsymbol{\pi}'$ is a tuple of A-states which accept $t_1', \ldots, t_{i-1}'$, respectively. In this way, δ_r plays the role of regular look-ahead, and each component of a state $\boldsymbol{\pi}$ of T (and of a stack symbol $\boldsymbol{\pi}'$ on a stack) represents a regular language of the look-ahead.
According to the definitions of the semantics of an SRTST and of ρ_r,

$$\begin{aligned}\alpha' = \rho_r(\boldsymbol{\pi}, \boldsymbol{\pi}', \sigma)(\alpha \uplus \overline{\beta}) = \quad & [q(x_k) := \beta(q(x_k))]_{q \in Q,\, k \le |\boldsymbol{\pi}'|} \\ & \uplus\, [q(x_{|\boldsymbol{\pi}'|+1}) := \underline{\mathrm{rhs}}(q, \sigma, \boldsymbol{\pi})\alpha]_{q \in Q} \\ & \uplus\, [q(x_k) := \varepsilon]_{q \in Q,\, |\boldsymbol{\pi}'|+1 < k \le m} \,.\end{aligned}$$

Here, variable values of α are the result of computation of $t_1, \ldots, t_n$ by M (i.e., by every $q \in Q$), and hence $\underline{\mathrm{rhs}}(q, \sigma, \boldsymbol{\pi})\alpha$ is the result of computation of $t_i' = \sigma(t_1, \ldots, t_n)$ by q; note that $q(x_{|\boldsymbol{\pi}'|+1}) = q(x_i)$. Likewise, β is the result of computation of $t_1', \ldots, t_{i-1}'$ by M. In this way, T computes as M does, and the result is recorded in the current evaluation function α of a configuration (and evaluation function β on a stack).
Note that in our construction the finiteness of the width of trees is used for the finiteness of sets S, P, and Γ, in both δ_r and ρ_r.

4.2 The Construction of $\mathrm{yDT^R}$ from SRTST

For an SRTST T, $s_0, \ldots, s_n \in S$, and nested words $w_1 \ldots, w_n$, we write $s_0 \stackrel{w_1}{\Longrightarrow} s_1 \stackrel{w_2}{\Longrightarrow} \cdots \stackrel{w_n}{\Longrightarrow} s_n$ if $(s_0, \Lambda_0, \alpha_0) \stackrel{w_1}{\Longrightarrow} (s_1, \Lambda_1, \alpha_1) \cdots \stackrel{w_n}{\Longrightarrow} (s_n, \Lambda_n, \alpha_n)$ for some Λ_i and α_i ($i = 0, \ldots, n$). We write $s \stackrel{\langle\sigma}{\Longrightarrow}_p s'$ if $\delta_c(s, \sigma) = (s', p)$, and $s \stackrel{\sigma\rangle}{\Longrightarrow}_p s'$ if $\delta_r(s, p, \sigma) = s'$.

Lemma 7. *For any* SRTST T, *there exists a* $\mathrm{yDT^R}$ M *such that* $\mathrm{Dom}(M) = \lceil \mathrm{Dom}(T) \rceil$ *and* $[\![M]\!](\lceil w \rceil) = [\![T]\!](w)$ *for all* $w \in \mathrm{Dom}(T)$.

Proof. Let $T = (S, \Sigma, \Delta, P, s_0, \Gamma, F, \delta_c, \delta_r, \rho_c, \rho_r)$ be an SRTST. We define a $\mathrm{yDT^R}$ $M = (Q, \Sigma, \Delta, \mathit{Init}, R)$ with a regular look-ahead NBTA $A = (\Sigma, \Pi, \theta)$.
First we define a predicate vst (stands for *valid state transition*): for given $((s_{n+1}^c, \sigma, s_{n+1}), (s_1, \sigma_1, s_1^r), \ldots, (s_n, \sigma_n, s_n^r)) \in \bigcup_{n \in \mathbb{N}} (S \times \Sigma^{(n)} \times S) \times (S \times \Sigma \times S)^n$,

$$\mathrm{vst}((s_{n+1}^c, \sigma^{(n)}, s_{n+1}), (s_1, \sigma_1, s_1^r), \ldots, (s_n, \sigma_n, s_n^r)) \;\text{ if}$$

$$\begin{aligned} s_{n+1}^c \stackrel{\langle\sigma}{\Longrightarrow}_p s_1 \stackrel{\langle\sigma_1}{\Longrightarrow}_{p_1} s_1', \quad s_1^r \stackrel{\sigma_1\rangle}{\Longrightarrow}_{p_1} s_2 \stackrel{\langle\sigma_2}{\Longrightarrow}_{p_2} s_2', \quad s_2^r \stackrel{\sigma_2\rangle}{\Longrightarrow}_{p_2} s_3 \cdots \\ \cdots s_n \stackrel{\langle\sigma_n}{\Longrightarrow}_{p_n} s_n', \quad s_n^r \stackrel{\sigma_n\rangle}{\Longrightarrow}_{p_n} s_{n+1} \end{aligned} \tag{1}$$

where $s_i' \in S$ and $p, p_i \in P$ are given by the call-transitions in (1). Note that $\mathrm{vst}((s_1^c, \sigma^{(0)}, s_1))$ iff $s_1^c \stackrel{\langle\sigma}{\Longrightarrow}_p s_1$, when $n = 0$. Eq. (1) holds if we have

$$\begin{aligned} s_{n+1}^c \stackrel{\langle\sigma}{\Longrightarrow} s_1 \stackrel{\langle\sigma_1}{\Longrightarrow} s_1' \stackrel{w_1}{\Longrightarrow} s_1^r \stackrel{\sigma_1\rangle}{\Longrightarrow} s_2 \stackrel{\langle\sigma_2}{\Longrightarrow} s_2' \stackrel{w_2}{\Longrightarrow} s_2^r \stackrel{\sigma_2\rangle}{\Longrightarrow} s_3 \cdots \\ \cdots s_n \stackrel{\langle\sigma_n}{\Longrightarrow} s_n' \stackrel{w_n}{\Longrightarrow} s_n^r \stackrel{\sigma_n\rangle}{\Longrightarrow} s_{n+1} \end{aligned} \tag{2}$$

for some well-matched w_i. Conversely, to obtain (2) we need the condition vst recursively for the parts $s_i \xRightarrow{\langle\sigma_i} s_i' \xRightarrow{w_i} s_i^r$, which leads to the next definition. Note that (1) and (2) extend with $\xRightarrow{\sigma\rangle}_p s'$ and $\xRightarrow{\sigma\rangle} s'$ for some unique s', respectively.

States of NBTA. Let $\Pi_0 \triangleq \emptyset$, and for $i > 0$,

$$\begin{aligned}\Pi_i \;\triangleq\; \Pi_{i-1} \cup \{(s^c, \sigma^{(n)}, s^r) \in S \times \Sigma \times S \mid n \in \mathbb{N} \wedge \\ \exists(\pi_1,\dots,\pi_n) \in (\Pi_{i-1})^n.\ \mathrm{vst}((s^c,\sigma,s^r),\pi_1,\dots,\pi_n)\}.\end{aligned}$$

Thus we have defined a chain: $\Pi_0 \subseteq \Pi_1 \subseteq \Pi_2 \subseteq \cdots \subseteq S \times \Sigma \times S$, and we define the set of states as $\Pi \triangleq \bigcup_i \Pi_i \subseteq S \times \Sigma \times S$, which is finite. Then, $(s^c_{n+1}, \sigma^{(n)}, s_{n+1}) \in \Pi$ iff the T-transition (2) exists.

Transition function of NBTA. The transition function $\theta : \bigcup_{n\in\mathbb{N}}(\Sigma^{(n)} \times \Pi^n) \to 2^{\Pi}$ is defined by

$$\theta(\sigma^{(n)}, (\pi_1,\dots,\pi_n)) \triangleq \big\{(s^c,\sigma,s^r) \in S\times\Sigma\times S \;\big|\; \mathrm{vst}((s^c,\sigma,s^r),\pi_1,\dots,\pi_n)\big\}.$$

This ensures that a tree $\sigma(t_1,\dots,t_n) \in \mathcal{T}_\Sigma$ is accepted by an A-state (s^c,σ,s^r) iff a transition $s^c \xRightarrow{\langle\sigma\ \lfloor t_1\rfloor\cdots\lfloor t_n\rfloor} s^r \xRightarrow{\sigma\rangle} s'$ exists; any $t \in \mathcal{T}_\Sigma$ is accepted by at least one state of A (though $F(s')$ is not necessarily defined).

Rules. We define $Q = S \times S \times \Gamma$. For every $(s^c,\sigma,s^r) \in \Pi$, $\gamma \in \Gamma$, and $\pi_1,\dots,\pi_n \in \Pi$ such that $(s^c,\sigma,s^r) \in \theta(\sigma,(\pi_1,\dots,\pi_n))$, the following rule is added in R:

$$(s^c, s^r, \gamma)(\sigma(x_1,\dots,x_n)) \to \mathcal{W}(\pi_1,\dots,\pi_n)(\gamma) \qquad \langle\pi_1,\dots,\pi_n\rangle$$

where $\mathcal{W} : \Pi^n \to \mathcal{A}(\Gamma, Q(X_n), \Delta)$ is defined from ρ_c and ρ_r as follows, and note that $\mathcal{W}(\pi_1,\dots,\pi_n)(\gamma) \in E(Q(X_n),\Delta) = \mathit{Rhs}_{Q,\Delta}(X_n)$.

W.l.o.g., we assume that $Q(X_n) \cap (\Gamma \uplus \overline{\Gamma}) = \emptyset$. For $\pi_i = (s_i^c, \sigma_i, s_i^r)$ $(i \in [n])$, let $\delta_c(s_i^c,\sigma_i) = (s_i, p_i)$. Then

$$\mathcal{W}(\pi_1,\dots,\pi_n) \triangleq \beta_n^r\big(\eta_n \uplus (\beta_n^c\big(\cdots\big(\beta_1^r(\eta_1 \uplus (\beta_1^c\alpha_\varepsilon^\Gamma))\big)\cdots\big))\big) \qquad (3)$$

$$\begin{aligned}
\text{where: } \alpha_\varepsilon^\Gamma &= [\gamma := \varepsilon]_{\gamma\in\Gamma} && \in \mathcal{A}(\Gamma, Q(X_n), \Delta)\\
\beta_i^c &\triangleq \overline{\rho_c(s_i^c,\sigma_i)} && \in \mathcal{A}(\overline{\Gamma}, \Gamma, \Delta)\\
\eta_i &\triangleq [\gamma := (s_i^c, s_i^r, \gamma)(x_i)]_{\gamma\in\Gamma} && \in \mathcal{A}(\Gamma, Q(X_n), \Delta)\\
\beta_i^r &\triangleq \rho_r(s_i^r, p_i, \sigma_i) && \in \mathcal{A}(\Gamma, \Gamma \uplus \overline{\Gamma}, \Delta).
\end{aligned}$$

The intuition for the above rule is as follows. Recall that the computation of T is top-down and bottom up, by call and return transitions, respectively. Also recall that state-transition functions δ_c and δ_r are already simulated by regular look-ahead, resulting $\pi_i = (s_i^c, \sigma_i, s_i^r)$ $(i \in [n])$. In (3), β_1^c (with $\alpha_\varepsilon^\Gamma$) corresponds to the call transition by the root σ_1 of the leftmost subtree x_1:

$$(s_1^c,\ \Lambda,\ \alpha_\varepsilon^\Gamma) \ \xRightarrow{\langle\sigma_1}\ (s_1',\ (p_1, \rho_c(s_1^c,\sigma_1)\alpha_\varepsilon^\Gamma)\Lambda,\ \alpha_\varepsilon^\Gamma)$$

where s_1' and Λ are some state and stack, and the current evaluation function before this transition is $\alpha_\varepsilon^\Gamma$ because the configuration is just after the call transition for the parent σ. Then, η_1 is the recursive computation by T of the subtree x_1. And then $\beta_1^r(\eta_1 \uplus (\beta_1^c \alpha_\varepsilon^\Gamma))$ corresponds to the return transition

$$(s_1^r,\ (p_1, \rho_c(s_1^c, \sigma_1)\alpha_\varepsilon^\Gamma)\Lambda,\ \eta_1) \ \overset{\sigma_1\rangle}{\Longrightarrow}\ (s_2^c,\ \Lambda,\ \beta_1^r(\eta_1 \uplus (\beta_1^c \alpha_\varepsilon^\Gamma)))$$

where note that $\overline{\rho_c(s_1^c, \sigma_1)\alpha_\varepsilon^\Gamma} = \overline{\rho_c(s_1^c, \sigma_1)}\alpha_\varepsilon^\Gamma = \beta_1^c \alpha_\varepsilon^\Gamma$. Repeating this also for the remaining sibling subtrees $x_2, \ldots, x_n$, we obtain (3).

Initial sequences. Finally, we define *Init* in a similar way to R:

$$\mathit{Init} = \bigcup_{\sigma \in \Sigma} \Big\{ \big(F(s')\beta_{s^r,p,\sigma}^r(\eta_{s^r} \uplus (\beta_\sigma^c \alpha_\varepsilon^\Gamma)),\ (s_0, \sigma, s^r) \big) \ \Big| \ (s_0, \sigma, s^r) \in \Pi,\quad s_0 \overset{\langle\sigma}{\Longrightarrow}_p s_1,\quad s^r \overset{\sigma\rangle}{\Longrightarrow}_p s' \in \mathrm{Dom}(F) \Big\}$$

where: (i) s_0 is the initial state of T, and s_1, s', and p are given by the transitions, (ii) $\beta_\sigma^c \triangleq \overline{\rho_c(s_0, \sigma)}$, (iii) $\eta_{s^r} \triangleq [\gamma := (s_0, s^r, \gamma)(x_1)]_{\gamma \in \Gamma}$, and (iv) $\beta_{s^r,p,\sigma}^r \triangleq \rho_r(s^r, p, \sigma)$.

The intuition is as follows. Let $t = \sigma(t_1, \ldots, t_n)$ be an input tree, and

$$(s_0, \varepsilon, \alpha_\varepsilon^\Gamma) \overset{\langle\sigma}{\Longrightarrow} (s_1, (p, \rho_c(s_0, \sigma)\alpha_\varepsilon^\Gamma), \alpha_\varepsilon^\Gamma) \overset{\lfloor t_1 \rfloor}{\Longrightarrow} \cdots$$
$$\cdots \overset{\lfloor t_n \rfloor}{\Longrightarrow} (\tilde{s}^r, (p, \rho_c(s_0, \sigma)\alpha_\varepsilon^\Gamma), \tilde{\eta}) \overset{\sigma\rangle}{\Longrightarrow} (\tilde{s}', \varepsilon, \rho_r(\tilde{s}^r, p, \sigma)(\tilde{\eta} \uplus (\beta_\sigma^c \alpha_\varepsilon^\Gamma)))$$

be the transition for $\lfloor t \rfloor$. Now t, $\tilde{s}^r$, $\tilde{\eta}$, $\tilde{s}'$, and $\rho_r(\tilde{s}^r, p, \sigma)$ respectively correspond to x_1, s^r, η_{s^r}, s', and $\beta_{s^r,p,\sigma}^r = \rho_r(s^r, p, \sigma)$ in the above definition. Here η_{s^r} involves $[\![(s_0, s^r, \gamma)]\!]_M(t)$, which is computed as in **Rules** above. □

4.3 Expressiveness and Decidability of Equivalence

Combining Lemmas 6 and 7, we can conclude:

Theorem 8. SRTSTs *and* $\mathrm{yDT^R}$s *are equi-expressive.*

Theorem 9. *For all* SRTST T*, there exists a bottom-up* SRTST T' *such that* $[\![T]\!] = [\![T']\!]$. *Thus,* SRTSTs *and bottom-up* SRTSTs *are equi-expressive.*

The $\mathrm{STT_{sur}}$-version of Theorem 9 is given in [1, Theorem 3.7], where, though, it was shown directly. As an immediate consequence of Lemma 7 and Theorem 3, we have:

Theorem 10. *Given* SRTSTs T_1 *and* T_2*, it is decidable whether* $[\![T_1]\!] = [\![T_2]\!]$.

Concluding Remark. By dropping the condition of sur from $\mathrm{STT_{sur}}$, we obtain the notion of an STT. We hope that our method can be applied to a similar result to Theorem 8, modified from SRTST to a similar model to STT whose input and output are ranked trees. If we further consider STT, whose input and output are *unranked* trees, it is not clear what model we should compare STT with, to solve the open problem of the decidability of the equivalence for STTs.

Acknowledgments. We thank anonymous referees for useful comments. This work was supported by JSPS KAKENHI Grant Numbers JP17K00007, JP17H06099, JP18H04093, and JP18K11156.

References

1. Alur, R., D'Antoni, L.: Streaming tree transducers. J. ACM **64**(5), 31:1–31:55 (2017)
2. Alur, R., Černý, P.: Streaming transducers for algorithmic verification of single-pass list-processing programs. In: POPL 2011, pp. 599–610. ACM (2011)
3. Comon, H., Dauchet, M., Gilleron, R., Löding, C., Jacquemard, F., Lugiez, D., Tison, S., Tommasi, M.: Tree Automata Techniques and Applications (2007)
4. Engelfriet, J.: Top-down tree transducers with regular look-ahead. Math. Syst. Theory **10**(1), 289–303 (1976)
5. Engelfriet, J.: Some open questions and recent results on tree transducers and tree languages. In: Formal Language Theory, pp. 241–286. Academic Press (1980)
6. Engelfriet, J., Maneth, S.: Macro tree transducers, attribute grammars, and MSO definable tree translations. Inform. Comput. **154**(1), 34–91 (1999)
7. Engelfriet, J., Maneth, S.: The equivalence problem for deterministic MSO tree transducers is decidable. Inform. Process. Lett. **100**(5), 206–212 (2006)
8. Engelfriet, J., Rozenberg, G., Slutzki, G.: Tree transducers, L systems, and two-way machines. J. Comput. Syst. Sci. **20**(2), 150–202 (1980)
9. Filiot, E., Reynier, P.A.: Copyful streaming string transducers. In: Hague, M., Potapov, I. (eds.) Reachability Problems. LNCS, vol. 10506, pp. 75–86. Springer, Cham (2017). https://doi.org/10.1007/978-3-319-67089-8_6
10. Nakano, K., Mu, S.-C.: A pushdown machine for recursive XML processing. In: Kobayashi, N. (ed.) APLAS 2006. LNCS, vol. 4279, pp. 340–356. Springer, Heidelberg (2006). https://doi.org/10.1007/11924661_21
11. Seidl, H., Maneth, S., Kemper, G.: Equivalence of deterministic top-down tree-to-string transducers is decidable. In: FOCS 2015, pp. 943–962. IEEE (2015)
12. Seidl, H., Maneth, S., Kemper, G.: Equivalence of deterministic top-down tree-to-string transducers is decidable. J. ACM **65**(4), 21:1–21:30 (2018)
13. Staworko, S., Laurence, G., Lemay, A., Niehren, J.: Equivalence of deterministic nested word to word transducers. In: FCT 2009. LNCS, vol. 5699, pp. 310–322. Springer, Heidelberg (2009). https://doi.org/10.1007/978-3-642-03409-1_28

Author Index

Printed in the United States
By Bookmasters